Intervention Strategies to Follow Informal Reading Inventory Assessment

---

SO WHAT DO I DO NOW?

JoAnne Schudt Caldwell

Cardinal Stritch University

Lauren Leslie

Marquette University

PEARSON

Boston • New York • San Francisco
Mexico City • Montreal • Toronto • London • Madrid • Munich • Paris
Hong Kong • Singapore • Tokyo • Cape Town • Sydney

Executive Editor: *Aurora Martínez Ramos*
Series Editorial Assistant: *Kara Kikel*
Executive Marketing Manager: *Krista Clark*
Production Coordinator: *Mary Beth Finch*
Editorial Production Service: *Omegatype Typography, Inc.*
Composition Buyer: *Linda Cox*
Manufacturing Manager: *Megan Cochran*
Electronic Composition: *Omegatype Typography, Inc.*
Cover Administrator: *Linda Knowles*

For related titles and support materials, visit our online catalog at www.pearsonhighered.com.

Between the time website information is gathered and then published, it is not unusual for some sites to have closed. Also, the transcription of URLs can result in typographical errors. The publisher would appreciate notification where these errors occur so that they may be corrected in subsequent editions.

Library of Congress Cataloging-in-Publication Data

Caldwell, JoAnne (JoAnne Schudt)
   Intervention strategies to follow informal reading inventory
assessment : so what do I do now? / JoAnne Schudt Caldwell, Lauren
Leslie.—2nd ed.
           p.   cm.
   Includes bibliographical references and index.
   ISBN-13: 978-0-205-60855-3 (pbk.)
   ISBN-10: 0-205-60855-8 (pbk.)
  1. Reading—Remedial teaching.   2. Reading—Ability testing.   I.
Leslie, Lauren.   II. Title.
   LB1050.5.C27   2009
   372.43—dc22

                                             2008017395

Text Credit: Quotes from *Brown Bear, Brown Bear, What Do You See?* by Bill Martin Jr appear on pp. 69–70. Text copyright © 1967 by Holt, Rinehart, and Winston, renewed 1995 by Bill Martin Jr, copyright © by the Estate of Bill Martin Jr.   Reprinted by permission of Henry Holt and Company, LLC.

Printed in the United States of America

10 9 8 7 6   12 11

Allyn & Bacon
is an imprint of

www.pearsonhighered.com

ISBN 13: 978-0-205-60855-3
ISBN 10: 0-205-60855-8

Contents

CHAPTER FOUR

Phonological Awareness   45

CHAPTER FIVE

Word Identification Instruction: Phonics and More   63

CHAPTER SIX

Word Identification Instruction: Fluency   95

CHAPTER SEVEN

Prior Knowledge and Concept Development   115

CHAPTER EIGHT

Vocabulary Learning   127

CHAPTER NINE

Comprehension Instruction: Retelling Narrative Text   151

CHAPTER TEN

Comprehension Instruction: Expository Retelling   165

CHAPTER ELEVEN

Comprehension Instruction: Answering Questions   193

CHAPTER TWELVE

Comprehension Instruction: General Interactive Strategies   209

CHAPTER THIRTEEN

Pulling It All Together: Designing the Intervention Structure   231

Since the first edition of this book, a large proportion of students are still not learning to read well. The most recent NAEP results (2007) indicated that 67 percent of fourth graders and 66 percent of eighth graders are not reading proficiently. Yet in these days of implementation of NCLB, teachers continue to look for more effective ways to teach reading, and administrators try to avoid having their schools cited for noncompliance with adequate yearly progress expectations. The pressure for assessment is real and yet we believe that it must help teachers guide instruction if it is to be valid for their use. If it is only a dipstick measure of how students are generally performing, then other instruments are needed to provide teachers with more detailed information.

It is those "other instruments" that we consider. This book, like the first edition, is written specifically to connect the results obtained from an informal reading inventory (IRI), and more specifically the *Qualitative Reading Inventory* (Leslie & Caldwell, 2006), to effective instructional practices that improve student learning. Many of the practices that we recommend can be implemented in whole classrooms, whereas others are done best in small intervention groups. The *QRI* can provide the user with a wealth of information from which to plan instruction. For example, Valencia and Buly (2004) documented six profiles of reading problems in students who fell below the proficient level on the Washington state test given in fourth grade. These profiles illustrate that teaching students who struggle in reading is not a one-size-fits-all proposition. As an example, they found students with high oral reading accuracy scores on the *QRI* whose rate of reading was very slow. Other students were accurate and fast in oral reading, but low in comprehension. Only when teachers understand the variety of areas in which struggling readers have difficulty and understand the implications for instruction can we begin to prevent or remediate reading difficulties.

Since the publication of the first edition of this book, other books on assessment and instruction have been published, but none of them takes the results of a particular kind of test and shows the relationship between the student profiles and recommended instructional practices. In this second edition of this book, in addition to updating sections of the original book, we address three new areas of rising importance in the United States.

1. Do the instructional practices that we recommend apply to English language learners (ELLs)? ELL research and views of how English learners should be taught is complex and sometimes contradictory. The Report of the National Literacy Panel on Language-Minority Children and Youth (August & Shanahan, 2006) concluded that, as with native speakers of English, word awareness, letter knowledge, and phonemic awareness are predictors of word identification and reading fluency among the ELLs studied. Therefore, it appears that the basic processes of learning to read are similar across languages, but we cannot conclude that teaching ELLs to read English should be the same as teaching native speakers of English to read. Just because the processes are similar doesn't mean that the same instructional techniques should be used. One major consideration is the relationship between the students' native language and English. That is, is the native language alphabetical? Do the students know how to read in their native language? Experience in learning to read in one language seems to transfer to a new language. In addition, consider the cognitive and linguistic information that the reader has acquired that the nonreader has not. In addition to these factors, there are sociocultural factors that relate to how reading is used in the culture and the context in which students are used to learning. In Chapters 3 through 12 we have added research and practical suggestions on teaching ELLs to read, and we indicate how the suggestions fit with what we have recommended for native speakers of English.

2. Do the instructional practices that we recommend apply to adolescent learners who are struggling overall in reading or in their content areas? Similarly to how we addressed ELLs, we have examined how adolescents with reading problems should be taught. The publication of a synthesis of research on effective instruction for struggling adolescent readers (Deshler, Palincsar, Biancarosa, & Nair, 2007) provided many good references for us to investigate. In Chapters 3 through 12, we examine whether each chapter's intervention structures, research on literacy development, and teaching applications apply to adolescents as well. Specific programs designed for adolescents are also presented. As one might expect, the applications were much easier to make in some areas (e.g., vocabulary) than in others (e.g., phonemic awareness).

3. Do the instructional practices presented and appropriate assessments of them fit within the guidelines of Response to Intervention, a series of interventions designed to catch struggling readers early to address their weaknesses and prevent their qualification for special education? Each chapter also addresses how the Response to Intervention system applies to the chapter topic.

In Chapter 1, we begin with a brief perspective on past and present assessment and intervention practices and suggest that certain general principles should drive all intervention. We also address the major issues in the field—for example, the implications of No Child Left Behind and the Individuals with Disabilities Education Act (2004), which authorized use of Response to Intervention measures to identify children with learning disabilities. We also consider the conflicting recommendations for instruction of English language learners and adolescent learners.

We examine the informal reading inventory in Chapter 2 and show what can be learned from the administration of this instrument. This involves general information such as reading level and an indication of the severity of the reading problem but also includes more specific information regarding a student's performance.

In Chapter 3, we examine the structure of research-based interventions and suggest that a consistent and balanced structure based on the specific needs of the students should be designed. We include a matrix that summarizes the structures of the various interventions and have added new programs to this list.

In Chapter 4, we explain the importance of phonological awareness as a basis for reading. For students unable to successfully read preprimer text on an informal reading inventory, we must examine their level of phonological awareness. Chapter 4 suggests practical ways to assess and develop these abilities.

In Chapters 5 and 6, we address word identification decoding and fluency. In each chapter, we explain the role of the informal reading inventory in assessing word pronunciation and fluency. Then we delineate a variety of instructional activities for improving both components.

In Chapter 7, we discuss the role of prior knowledge in interpreting informal reading inventory results. This chapter also contains suggestions for developing prior knowledge in the classroom or intervention session.

Chapter 8 focuses on the importance of word learning to comprehension and suggests motivating and effective activities for incorporating word study into the intervention session.

Chapters 9 and 10 address retelling. Most informal reading inventories assess retelling in some way, but if retelling is sparse or confused, what should a teacher do? These chapters offer ideas for preparing students to structure their retelling in a logical and complete way based on text structure and knowledge of the topic.

Chapter 11 focuses on answering questions. All informal reading inventories determine reading level through asking questions. But are all questions equal? And if a student is not successful in finding answers, what can a teacher do about this? We present research and instructional techniques for improving students' abilities to answer questions.

Chapter 12 describes some general interactive strategies for developing comprehension, such as using think-alouds and discussion cards to enhance a student's engagement with text.

Drawing on the information from preceding chapters, Chapter 13 presents various in-class and pullout models for structuring different intervention sessions and concludes with a suggested generic lesson plan format that functions as a review of the contents of this book.

Acknowledgments

We would like to thank the following reviewers for their comments on this book: Yvonne Bouknight, Glen Ridge Public Schools; Diana Carr, Elgin Junior High School; Nancy Daniels, Helman Elementary School; and Donna Schweitzer, Forwood Elementary School. We would also like to thank Aurora Martínez Ramos at Allyn and Bacon.

References

August, D. L., & Shanahan, T. (2006). *Developing literacy in second language learners: Report of the national literacy panel on language-minority children and youth.* Mahwah, NJ: Erlbaum.

Deshler, D. D., Palincsar, A., Biancarosa, G., & Nair, M. (2007). *Informed choices for struggling adolescent readers: A research based guide to instructional programs and practices.* Newark, DE: International Reading Association.

Leslie, L., & Caldwell, J. (2006). *Qualitative Reading Inventory-4.* Boston: Allyn and Bacon.

Valencia, S. W., & Buly, M. R. (2004). Behind test scores: What struggling readers really need. *The Reading Teacher, 57,* 520–531.

An Overview of Reading Instruction for Struggling Readers

Reading Instruction—Past Perspectives

Watching a child learn to read is a wonderful, almost magical occurrence. We know the many and varied experiences that are available to readers, and we rejoice in the child's growing expertise and movement into the exhilarating world of print. But how do we react to the child who struggles with reading and turns away from literacy experiences because of frustration and a sense of failure? We feel worried, sometimes confused, often discouraged, and perhaps even resentful that our best efforts do not seem to help. We search frantically for a single instructional strategy or program that will turn things around and make it possible for our struggling reader to move confidently into the world of literacy. Educators have always been concerned about children who find learning to read difficult, and they have approached the problem from various perspectives. Our summary of these perspectives is based on a variety of sources that are listed as references at the end of this chapter.

In the past, we used the term *remediation* to describe the process of assessing and instructing struggling readers. The term suggested that we were identifying and applying a remedy to an already existing condition, in much the same way a physician would. Our model of literacy assessment and instruction paralleled a medical model (Johnston & Allington, 1991). We believed that different categories of reading problems (*diseases*) required different forms of instruction (*medications*). The term *diagnosis* was favored over the term *assessment*. We assumed that diagnosis would isolate the specific nature of the problem and that this would, in turn, point to specific instructional techniques.

Our medical model dictated certain categories of reading difficulties, just as there are certain categories of illnesses. Basically, this model focused on identifying deficits as opposed to strengths. Children labeled "learning disabled" were thought to require different instructional methods than those for "garden-variety" poor readers, who were not labeled as learning disabled because of a lower IQ (Johnston & Allington, 1991; Stanovich, 2000; Walmsley & Allington, 1995). Different educators assumed the responsibility for these separate categories and were trained differently in our colleges and universities. Special educators taught children with learning disabilities, and remedial reading teachers worked with children who were not placed in that category. Both groups employed different assessment tools and instructional techniques.

Despite the different perspectives of special educators and reading educators, both believed that each reader presented an individual mix of strengths and needs. As a result, instruction for one child was thought to be different from that for another. Educators developed long lists of reading skills, often referred to as scope and sequence charts. These included comprehensive listings of all of the separate consonant and vowel sounds believed to be necessary for learning to read. Similarly, the charts divided comprehension into many different components, such as drawing inferences, making judgments, and arriving at conclusions. Unfortunately, scope and sequence charts were unrealistic. First, it was impossible for educators to keep track of all the skills, known or unknown, of one reader, let alone several. Second, learning does not progress in such a stepwise and final fashion. Often a child recognized a consonant sound in one word or on one day and completely missed it in another word or on another day. Because we thought that comprehension skills were separate entities, educators struggled with differentiating among an inference, a judgment, and a conclusion, and between identifying main ideas and creating summaries. The scope and sequence model was impossibly unwieldy and difficult to put into effective practice. More important, it was not a realistic portrayal of the complex nature of the reading process as a vibrant and interactive whole.

The primary form of instruction for struggling readers was a pullout model (Allington, 1980; Johnston & Allington, 1991; Walmsley & Allington, 2007). Children with learning disabilities and children who were generally poor readers received remedial and supportive instruction apart from their regular classroom. There was generally a great disconnection between the content of the remedial services and classroom activities. Often students learned strategies in the pullout program that they were unable to apply in the regular classroom, where they encountered materials well above their reading levels. Unfortunately, many pullout programs focused on skill and drill activities and offered little opportunity for reading in a meaningful fashion. There was a definite stigma attached to leaving the classroom to receive supportive instruction. Peers tended to perceive those attending pullout sessions as being different or dumb, and this contributed to a lack of self-esteem.

The federal government funded much pullout instruction as part of Title I or Chapter I. These programs were originally developed to offer support to students who were economically disadvantaged, and there were great expectations for their effectiveness. Unfortunately, these expectations were not realized. It gradually became apparent that remedial programs past second grade were not effective and that poor readers in first grade still tended to be poor readers in third grade (Johnston & Allington, 1991; Juel, 1988; Juel, Griffith, & Gough, 1986; Walmsley & Allington, 2007).

Reading Instruction—Present Perspectives

Although we still place students in categories such as learning disabled, the literature is beginning to question whether readers with learning disabilities and other poor readers actually present different profiles and require different instructional interventions. Large-scale studies have failed to differentiate between the reading profiles of children with learning disabilities and poor readers who are not so labeled, and there is a growing awareness that there are no special and unique instructional techniques for specific categories of readers (Johnston & Allington, 1991; Mathes, Denton, Fletcher, Anthony, Francis, & Schatschneider, 2005; Stanovich, 2000; Walmsley & Allington, 2007).

In the past we attempted to "cure" an existing problem, and we often waited in vain for children to catch up. In some cases, children did not even qualify for special help until they were two years behind their peers. Now we are beginning to realize that reading difficulties can be prevented, and the term *reading intervention* has replaced *reading remediation.*

A growing number of studies suggest that early and intensive instruction can prevent reading difficulties for a large majority of children. In addition, we are learning that reorganizing instruction for struggling readers with a balanced focus on reading for meaning can result in impressive gains. At the end of this chapter, we list a variety of references for the interventions discussed in the following paragraphs.

Many interventions involve one-to-one tutoring of first graders using a pullout mode. Reading Recovery provides daily 30-minute tutoring for first graders who are in the lowest 20 percent of their class. Early Steps, which is quite similar to Reading Recovery, also provides daily 30-minute tutoring and uses some of the same instructional activities. However, it directs more explicit attention to letter–sound matching. Reading Rescue provides one-to-one tutoring for language minority first graders that covers all five components recommended by the National Reading Panel (2000): phonemic awareness, phonics, fluency, vocabulary, and comprehension. In the Book Buddies program, community volunteers tutor at-risk first graders for 45 minutes twice a week. Success for All, a total school reform program, employs daily individual tutoring for children of various ages who need extra support; the 20-minute tutoring session is closely coordinated with classroom instruction.

Some successful interventions focus on small groups. The Boulder Project uses instructional activities similar to those in Reading Recovery and Early Steps for groups of three. Project Success is an intervention program targeted for small groups of students in grades 3 and above.

In the past, pullout programs were the primary delivery vehicles of instruction for struggling readers. Despite their success, there is a growing awareness that classroom reading programs should be designed to accommodate the struggling reader. This allows for two things. First, children who do not qualify for pullout services will be helped. Second, those who are serviced in pullout models will receive additional and effective support in their classrooms. Several models have restructured the format and delivery system of the traditional classroom. The Winston-Salem Project, often referred to as the Four Block Model, was designed to eliminate ability grouping in first grade, but it was also successful in preventing reading failure. The Fluency Oriented Reading Program focused on improving student achievement in second grade by modifying instruction to develop fluency.

Structuring classrooms to accommodate struggling readers is in accord with the movement toward inclusion, whereby students with disabilities are taught in the least restrictive environment, their own classroom. Initial fears that inclusion would harm students are unfounded. Successful inclusion uses strategies that are effective for all students, such as an activity-based and integrated curriculum, flexible grouping patterns, performance-based assessments, parental involvement, and effective integration of support systems.

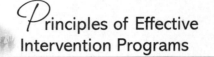

Principles of Effective Intervention Programs

At this point, it is probably a good idea to clearly define what we mean by an intervention. An intervention is instruction that is specifically designed based on the findings of an informal reading inventory or some other method of assessing reading proficiency. The intervention may occur in or out of the classroom setting, but the defining characteristic is a structure or series of activities based on the individual needs of a student. An intervention thus differs from a classroom lesson plan that may be based on principles of effective instruction but is not specifically targeted to the needs of an individual student.

What have we learned from successful literacy interventions and from classrooms that address the needs of all readers? Examining their similarities allows us to identify principles of effective reading interventions. Table 1.1 summarizes those elements.

The first principle is a strong emphasis on reading and writing for meaning. In short, students read and comprehend connected text as opposed to filling out worksheets and playing games. Provide access to materials that cover a wide range of interests and difficulty levels. Have students read for authentic purposes, to enjoy and to learn. Allow them the opportunity to informally discuss their reading and share their responses with peers.

The second principle requires that students learn and practice the strategies of successful readers and writers. They need to understand that the only purpose for reading is to make meaning and that reading can be an intensely rewarding experience. Struggling readers must acquire strategies for comprehending and remembering what they read, for identifying and spelling words, and for monitoring their own performance. Choose good strategies to model and help students to practice them in interesting and engaging text.

The third principle of effective intervention instruction is the provision of materials that students can handle successfully—text that is at their instructional and independent reading levels. Students should also read selections that they find interesting and personally meaningful. In the past, much time was wasted searching for the right skill sheet or the most effective practice booklet. We should have been spending our time helping struggling readers find reasons to read and choosing materials they found appealing. Reading instruction does not always have to include school-like text. Students can read directions for playing a computer game or read magazine excerpts about favorite stars or sports heroes. They can read song lyrics, comic books, and baseball cards. In short, they can read whatever is meaningful to them.

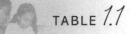

TABLE *1.1*   Components of Successful Interventions

Emphasize reading and writing for meaning.

Teach students the strategies that good readers and writers use.

Find text that students can read successfully.

Provide a consistent lesson structure.

Provide time for word study.

Focus on fluency development.

Keep the size of the group as small as possible.

The fourth principle involves the structure of the lesson. Each successful intervention has a clearly defined and consistent lesson structure. The teacher and students engage in the same category of activities each day, usually in the same sequence. Individualization occurs within this set structure. We will expand on this in Chapter 3.

The fifth principle emphasizes some form of word study. The ability to accurately identify words and assign meaning to the pronunciations is a requirement for comprehension. If we cannot read the words, we cannot comprehend, and, as one young fellow confided to us, comprehension is the "good stuff." However, comprehension is similar to the birthday present locked in a closet until the appointed day. We need a key to open the door, and saying words is the key to the treasure called comprehension. Word study can take many forms. In the successful interventions described previously, students manipulated magnetic letters and sorted picture or word cards. They transformed words by changing letters, and they built words from letter tiles. Word study does not have to be the dull phonics lessons popular so many years ago. Words are exciting, and we can transmit that excitement to our students.

The sixth principle requires a focus on fluency and helping students develop automatic and expressive word recognition through various forms of repeated reading. We often take fluency for granted. Think about all the things you do that are relatively automatic, such as driving, vacuuming, or weeding. Because you are fluent in these activities, you can think of something else at the same time. In the same way, readers need to be fluent in word identification so they can think about comprehension.

The seventh and final principle states that one-to-one tutoring is a very effective form of instruction. With the exception of the classroom programs, all intervention programs provided either one-to-one or very small group instruction. Admittedly, this is often extremely difficult to implement, but whenever possible, structure your groups to be as small as possible.

Current Issues

Designing and implementing successful intervention programs has taken on increased importance given the existence of two government-mandated initiatives: the No Child Left Behind Act of 2002 (NCLB) and the reauthorization of the Individuals with Disabilities Education Act of 2004 (IDEA), which identified Response to Intervention (RTI) as an approved means to identify a learning disability. In addition, the changing demographics of our schools in which English language learners represent the fastest-growing group lend urgency to the need for successful intervention (Vardell, Hadaway, & Young, 2006). As mentioned previously, many interventions have focused on the young child in an attempt to prevent, rather than "cure," a reading deficiency. However, despite the success of many early literacy programs, there are still a growing number of preadolescents and adolescents who struggle with literacy in our middle and high schools (NAEP, 2005, 2007).

No Child Left Behind (NCLB)

The No Child Left Behind Act was signed into law in 2002. The law mandates statewide testing in reading and math every year in grades 3 through 8 and at least once in grades 10 through 12. Science assessments must be in place by 2007–2008. States are required to compile a yearly report card with scores broken out according to economic background, race, ethnicity, English proficiency, and disability. Basically, NCLB uses standardized achievement scores as a way of identifying schools that are doing well and those that are not.

At the heart of NCLB is the concept of adequate yearly progress (AYP). Although individual states are allowed to define what they mean by adequate yearly progress, their definition must be approved by the Department of Education. AYP involves defining "separate measurable annual objectives for continuous and substantial improvement" for economically disadvantaged students, for those with disabilities and limited English proficiency, and for students from major racial and ethnic groups (Norlin, 2005, p. 1). Whichever formula a state decides to adopt, AYI is defined as growth indicated by standardized achievement scores.

According to NCLB, schools must demonstrate forward progress each year for all students and 100 percent proficiency must be reached by 2013–2014. If a school does not meet the state-constructed guidelines for AYP, the school will then be classified as needing improvement, which requires the creation of a two-year improvement plan. School status must be communicated to parents, who then have the option to withdraw their children. If no improvement is evident after year two, the district or state will take corrective action. This could involve replacement of school staff, implementation of new curricula, extension of the school day, and/or reorganization of school structure.

It is obvious that a school or district's success in meeting adequate yearly progress depends on students who are effective readers. If there are large percentages of struggling readers in a school or district, there is a strong likelihood that NCLB scores will be inadequate. Schools and districts that use various test-taking initiatives aimed at increasing test scores may find them effective for students who possess adequate literacy skills. However, they probably do not have a measurable effect on those who struggle with any one of the five components of literacy: phonemic awareness, phonics, fluency, vocabulary, and comprehension. For these students, something more is needed—the design and implementation of effective intervention strategies.

Response to Intervention (RTI)

In the past, a learning disability was identified by a discrepancy between student intelligence measured by an individually administered intelligence test and the student's level of functioning in academic areas such as reading, writing, and mathematics. That is, a student possessing average intelligence who performed below the level of peers was labeled as learning disabled. The reauthorized Individual with Disabilities Education Act (IDEA) changed this in 2004 by giving schools and districts the option of identifying students as learning disabled based on their response to instruction. In other words, "when a student's response is dramatically inferior to that of his peers, the student may be determined to have a learning disability" (Bender & Shores, 2007, p. 7). Funding is closely tied to the identification of learning disabilities inasmuch as schools receive federal money to provide instruction for children with special needs.

RTI is often conceptualized as embodying three tiers. The first is classroom instruction. The teacher implements screening measures to identify students achieving well below the level of their peers. These students then move into the second tier of instruction involving additional assessments to identify specifics of the problem and provision of small-group instruction to address student needs. Such instruction is usually offered two to three times a week in addition to regular classroom instruction and can be delivered by the classroom teacher, the reading specialist, the special education teacher, or a subject matter expert (McCook, 2006). The teacher systematically monitors student progress over time. A student who still fails to respond adequately moves into the third tier of instruction, which is usually individualized in format. At this point, a learning disability is generally identified.

RTI emphasizes "the role of data for decision-making" (Brown-Chidsey & Steege, 2005, p. 18). Student progress is monitored using "short, quick and easy-to-administer probes" (McCook, 2006, p. 14). Classroom screening establishes a baseline for scores; comparing performances of individual students to that baseline determines progress or lack of it. What forms do the short-and-quick assessments take? Currently, the most popular RTI assessment is oral reading fluency, the number of words read correctly in one or two minutes. Other RTI probes are the number of sounds and letters recognized and number of words correctly spelled within one to three minutes (Wright, 2007). Comprehension assessment generally takes two forms. The student orally reads a passage for one minute and then retells it. Retelling is scored as the number of words offered within a one-minute time frame. A second form of assessment is a three-minute cloze or maze task in which the student reads a passage with words deleted and supplies the words or selects them from three or four choices.

At the present time, the RTI assessment and intervention model primarily centers on early reading performance (Bender & Shores, 2007; Wright, 2007; McCook, 2006; Brown-Chidsey & Steege, 2005) and involves sound-based/phonological measures and reading fluency. These are highly predictive of future reading performance. However, Gersten and Dimino (2006) state that while such assessments are not inaccurate, they are incomplete and "only one part of the picture" (p. 104). Other measures also predict future reading performance such as oral language proficiency, expressive vocabulary, and passage recall. However, these do not necessarily lend themselves to short, quick, and easy-to-administer RTI probes.

RTI, as presently conceptualized, is primarily focused in the early elementary grades, but there is certainly a chance that the initiative will extend into the upper elementary, middle, and secondary levels, especially given the large numbers of students above grade 4 who struggle with reading. RTI is basically quite new and it remains to be seen how various schools and districts will interpret and implement the federal guidelines, which are fairly general. As always, the devil is in the details and there is a major caveat attached to RTI, which relies on the quality of instruction that children are exposed to in the regular classroom as well as in tiers 2 and 3. The government states that practitioners must "use scientifically-based research to guide their decisions about which interventions to implement" (U.S. Department of Education, 2003, p. 3). To put it another way, a lack of response to ineffective or unproven instruction cannot be used to identify the presence of a learning disability.

What does the government mean by scientifically-based research? Research that investigates program or strategy effectiveness must employ an experimental design that uses randomized controlled trials. That is, researchers must test program or strategy effectiveness by comparing a treatment group and a control group, with subjects assigned randomly to each group. Such research should also involve two or more typical school settings as opposed to research conducted in a university location or a site that does not approximate the average classroom context. In the absence of such conditions, research on program or strategy effectiveness should at least involve comparison group studies in which the groups are closely matched in academic achievement and demographics, as well as other characteristics such as length of study time and methods of data collection. Such studies are called "quasi-experimental." The government does not recognize pre–post studies in which students are pretested, exposed to an instructional method, and then posttested as providing evidence of effectiveness (U.S. Department of Education, 2003).

Limiting support of program or practice effectiveness to experimental or quasi-experimental studies may represent a somewhat limited view. Other forms of research can indicate the effectiveness of a specific intervention format or strategy. Pressley, Duke, and Boling (2004) recognize the usefulness of observational and correlational data and caution that many important research questions cannot be appropriately examined through experimental paradigms. In a position paper entitled *What Is Evidence-Based Reading Instruction?* the International Reading Association (2002) recognizes the value of qualitative studies focused on small groups or individuals, pointing out that a single study cannot determine the effectiveness of a program or practice; rather, converging evidence from numerous studies is needed.

In the last few years, many programs have claimed to be "research-based" without describing the supporting research. It is important to clarify that a research base, whether experimental, quasi-experimental, or qualitative in nature, can refer to an entire program or to components within a program. For example, Reading Recovery and Reading Rescue are total intervention programs that have been carefully validated by the type of research supported by the government. Other programs have not been researched as a whole but contain elements or practices that have. For example, a program may contain well-researched strategies for developing fluency or fostering comprehension. Educators have two basic options with regard to intervention. They can design their own, or they can purchase published intervention programs that claim to be research-based; in the busy world of schools, few educators have the time to carefully examine the validity of a publisher's claim.

With regard to RTI and research-based instructional practices, this book offers guidelines for designing intervention programs, for selecting intervention strategies, and for working with published programs by describing intervention practices that have a basis in research and a track record of effectiveness. It also provides a list of books and articles that address this topic.

English Language Learners (ELLs)

Approximately one-fifth of school-age children speak a first language other than English (Lenters, 2004/2005). While the total school population in the US grew by 6 percent between 1970 and 1999, the ELL population increased by 138 percent (Harper & deJong, 2004). The number of ELLs has doubled in the last ten years with a current count of approximately 5 million. This increase is accompanied by a growing shortage of teachers qualified to provide appropriate instruction (Hawkins, 2004). Addressing the literacy needs of ELLs is an issue of critical importance.

There is an ongoing debate about how best to foster English literacy in ELL students (Slavin & Cheung, 2005). Should instruction focus on English only (often referred to as English immersion) or should it take a bilingual format? There are two general forms of bilingual instruction. In one, students learn to read in their native language in the primary grades and transition to English between grades 2 and 4. A second format involves teaching both languages but at different times of the day.

Research seems to favor a bilingual approach and reading in the familiar language "may serve as a bridge to success in English as phonemic awareness, decoding, sound blending and general comprehension strategies clearly transfer among languages that use phonetic orthographies" (Slavin & Cheung, 2005, p. 274).

However, for many districts, bilingual instruction is not a possibility given the difficulty of finding qualified bilingual teachers. As a result, many districts assign ELL students to the English as a Second Language (ESL) teacher in a pullout program that focuses on developing basic English with minimal attention to literacy (Mohr, 2004). Another concern often arises when ELL students show proficiency in conversational English and are released from any additional support. Facility in conversation is not sufficient to deal successfully with the academic English of school textbooks and classroom discourse (Rea & Mercuri, 2006).

The literacy education of ELL students is no longer the province of special personnel. ELLs are present in our mainstream classrooms in ever-growing numbers. They are not a homogeneous group. They have different language backgrounds. Some can read in their native language; others cannot. Their command of English varies and they represent different levels of exposure to English, different educational histories, and different socio-economic levels. They will probably need additional intervention in order to develop to their full potential, and such intervention may have to be designed and implemented by the classroom teacher. Throughout this book, we will offer instructional strategies for developing the literacy of English language learners. These will include strategies that involve ELLs in activities with English-dominant students as well as strategies that can be used in an intervention setting.

Adolescent Readers

More than 8 million students in grades 4 through 12 are struggling readers (Fisher & Ivey, 2006). According to the National Assessment of Educational Progress (2007, 2005) only 31 percent of eighth graders and 35 percent of twelfth graders scored at or above a proficient level. Struggling adolescent readers exhibit a wide range of difficulties (Biancarosa, 2005).

While some still have difficulties with decoding multisyllabic words, many more have problems with comprehension (Santa, 2006).

In the past, the typical approach for dealing with struggling older readers has been "skill and drill." Based on the assumption that students lacked basic skills, intervention generally involved certain common elements (Johannessen, 2004). Students worked as a whole class or group. Instruction focused on short pencil-and-paper activities at a level of difficulty that guaranteed student success. Extensive practice and immediate feedback were frequent components. Students generally succeeded in the intervention, but there was minimal transfer to their regular classroom. When the intervention ended, students were still not able to comprehend their content area textbooks and assigned class materials.

Fisher and Ivey (2007) describe three categories of present adolescent literacy interventions. The "fix it" model identifies the student's greatest area of weakness and attempts to fix it. A second model focuses on a uniform sequence of intervention strategies delivered to all students. A third model is based on the five components of the National Reading Panel (2000). There is also an unfortunate tendency to believe that what works with younger readers will also work with older ones. That is, if phonemic awareness and phonics instruction helps primary readers, they should be equally effective for older students who probably lack these basic skills. Unfortunately, such instruction is no more effective than the skill-and-drill model. It does not help older students read better, nor does it make them want to read more (Ivey & Baker, 2004). Older students, even those reading at a primary level, have some basic understanding of letter–sound relationships and continuing an emphasis on basic sounds will not help them read their complex content area texts.

An alternative to skill and drill and phonics is instruction that facilitates comprehension and learning from text. Fisher and Ivey (2006) suggest several principles in developing interventions for adolescents. First, the school provides students "with significant opportunities for wide reading" as well as "access to a substantial number of readable, interesting books that focus on the content they are studying." In addition, students have "the opportunity to 'just read' books of their own choosing" (p. 181). Second, content teachers are actively involved in developing strategic reading skills in their students and use what Fisher and Ivey call "content literacy approaches to ensure that their students are engaged in meaningful curriculum" (p. 181). Intervention programs designed to complement such schoolwide initiatives should emphasize the critical role of the teacher, focus on comprehension, use engaging materials, be driven by relevant assessments, and include opportunities for authentic reading and writing.

Effective intervention instruction for adolescents involves explicit instruction in comprehension strategies that incorporates teacher modeling and active student engagement. It provides older struggling readers with "ongoing explanations and discussions about the process of reading and how to make sense of what they read" (Ivey & Baker, 2004, p. 37). Biancarosa (2005) stresses the importance of direct and explicit comprehension instruction, use of informational and content area texts, formation of collaborative learning teams, and promotion of self-directed learning. Santa (2006) delineates four principles for working with struggling adolescent readers: establishing a positive classroom community, implementing a consistent and explicit classroom structure, incorporating direct strategy instruction and teacher modeling, and promoting a metacognitive frame of mind. Throughout this book, we will highlight or comment on strategies that are particularly applicable for adolescent struggling readers.

Summary

In the past, we concentrated on a very individualized approach to instruction for struggling readers. Educators designed different lessons for each child based on scope and sequence charts and what were believed to be unique patterns of strengths and needs. Now we recognize a more important focus, that of providing a balanced approach to intervention and engaging all struggling readers in the actual reading process. We acknowledge the crucial importance of helping struggling readers to understand that reading is more than saying words. We recognize the need to teach them the strategies that good readers use to understand and remember text. The educator has become a model and a facilitator, not a distributor of worksheets and a manager of activities. Now educators recognize that there are certain common instructional strategies that benefit all children no matter how they may be categorized or who may be responsible for their instruction.

REFERENCES AND RECOMMENDED READINGS

Readings on Past and Present Perspectives

Aaron, P. G. (1997). The demise of the discrepancy formula. *Review of Educational Research, 67,* 461–502.

Allington, R. L. (1980). Teaching reading in compensatory classes: A descriptive summary. *The Reading Teacher, 34,* 178–183.

Allington, R. L. (1993). Michael doesn't go down the hall anymore (literacy for all children). *The Reading Teacher, 46,* 602–604.

Allington, R. L. (1994). What's special about special programs for children who find learning to read difficult? *Journal of Reading, 26,* 95–115.

Allington, R. L., & McGill-Franzen, A. (1989). School response to reading failure: Instruction for Chapter I and special education students in grades 2, 4, and 8. *Elementary School Journal, 89,* 529–543.

Bean, R. M., Cooley, W., Eichelberger, R. T., Lazar, M., & Zigmond, N. (1991). In-class or pull-out: Effects of setting on the remedial reading program. *Journal of Reading Behavior, 23,* 445–464.

Ganske, K., Monroe, J. K., & Strickland, D. S. (2003). Questions teachers ask about struggling readers and writers. *The Reading Teacher, 57,* 118–128.

Johnston, P., & Allington, R. (1991). Remediation. In R. Barr, M. L. Kamil, P. Mosenthal, & P. D. Pearson (Eds.), *Handbook of Reading Research* (Vol. 2, pp. 984–1012). New York: Longman.

Juel, C. (1988). Learning to read and write: A longitudinal study of fifty-four children from first through fourth grades. *Journal of Educational Psychology, 80,* 437–447.

Juel, C., Griffith, P. L., & Gough, P. B. (1986). Acquisition of literacy: A longitudinal study of children in first and second grade. *Journal of Educational Psychology, 78,* 243–255.

Klenk, L., & Kirby, M. W. (2000). Re-mediating reading difficulties: Appraising the past, reconciling the present, constructing the future. In M. L. Kamil, P. B. Mosenthal, P. D. Pearson, & R. Barr (Eds.), *Handbook of reading research* (Vol. III, pp. 667–690). Mahwah, NJ: Erlbaum.

Mathes, P. G., Denton, C. A., Fletcher, J. M., Anthony, J. L., Francis, D. J., & Schatschneider, C. (2005). The effects of theoretically different instruction and student characteristics on the skills of struggling readers. *Reading Research Quarterly, 40,* 148–182.

National Reading Panel. (2000). *Report of the National Reading Panel: Teaching children to read: An evidence-based assessment of scientific-based literature on reading and its implications for reading instruction.* Washington, DC: National Institute of Child Health and Human Development.

Pikulski, J. J. (1994). Preventing reading failure: A review of five effective programs. *The Reading Teacher, 48,* 30–39.

Snow, C. E., Burns, M. S., & Griffin, P. (1998). *Preventing reading difficulties in young children.* Washington, DC: National Academy Press.

Spear-Swerling, L., & Sternberg, R. J. (1996). *Off track: When poor readers become "learning disabled."* Boulder, CO: Westview Press.

Stanovich, K. E. (2000). *Progress in understanding reading: Scientific foundations and new frontiers.* New York: The Guilford Press.

Walmsley, S., & Allington, R. L. (2007). Redefining and reforming instructional support programs for at-risk readers. In R. Allington & S. Walmsley (Eds.), *No quick fix, The RTI edition: Rethinking literacy programs in America's elementary schools* (pp. 19–44). Newark, DE: International Reading Association.

Readings on Successful Interventions

Reading Recovery

Clay, M. M. (1993). *Reading Recovery: A guidebook for teachers in training.* Portsmouth, NH: Heinemann.

Lyons, C. A., & Beaver, J. (2007). Reducing retention and learning disability placement through Reading Recovery: An educationally sound cost-effective choice. In R. L. Allington & S. A. Walmsley (Eds.), *No quick fix, The RTI editon: Rethinking literacy in America's elementary schools* (pp. 116–136). New York: Teachers College Press.

Pinnell, G. S. (1989). Reading Recovery: Helping at-risk children learn to read. *The Elementary School Journal, 90,* 161–183.

Pinnell, G. S., Deford, D. E., & Lyons, C. A. (1988). *Reading recovery: Early intervention for at-risk first graders.* Arlington, VA: Educational Research Service.

Pinnell, G. S., Lyons, C. A., Deford, D. E., Bryk, A. S., & Seltzer, M. (1994). Comparing instructional models for the literacy education of high-risk first graders. *Reading Research Quarterly, 29,* 9–30.

Reading Rescue

Ehri, L. C., Dreyer, L. G., Flugman, B., & Gross, A. (2007). Reading Rescue: An effective tutoring intervention model for language-minority students who are struggling readers in first grade. *American Educational Research Journal, 44,* 414–448.

Early Steps

Morris, D., Shaw, B., & Perney, J. (1990). Helping low readers in grades 2 and 3: An after school volunteer tutoring program. *Elementary School Journal, 91,* 133–150.

Santa, C. M., Ford, A., Mickley, A., & Parker, D. (1997). *Reading intervention for primary students: First steps.* Paper presented at International Reading Association Convention, Atlanta, GA.

Santa, C. M., & Hoien, T. (1999). An assessment of Early Steps: A program for early intervention. *Reading Research Quarterly, 34,* 54–79.

Book Buddies

Invernizzi, M., Juel, C., & Rosemary, C. A. (1996/1997). A community volunteer tutorial that works. *The Reading Teacher, 50,* 304–311.

Invernizzi, M., Rosemary, C. A., Juel, C., & Richards, H. C. (1997). At-risk readers and community volunteers: A three year perspective. *Journal of the Scientific Studies of Reading, 3,* 277–300.

Success for All

Borman, G. D., Slavin, R. E., Cheung, A. C. K., Chamberlain, A. M., Madden, N. A., & Chambers, B. (2007). Final reading outcomes of the national randomized field trial of Success for All. *American Educational Research Journal, 44,* 701–731.

Slavin, R. E., Madden, N. A., Karweit, N. L., Dolan, L., & Wasik, B. A. (1992). *Success for All: A relentless approach to prevention and early intervention in elementary schools.* Arlington, VA: Educational Research Service.

Slavin, R. E., Madden, N. A., Karweit, N. L., Dolan, L., & Wasik, B. A. (1994). Success for all: Getting reading right the first time. In E. H. Hiebert & B. Taylor (Eds.), *Getting reading right from the start: Effective early literacy interventions* (pp. 125–148). Boston: Allyn & Bacon.

Slavin, R. E., Madden, N. A., Karweit, N. L., Livermon, B. J., & Dolan, L. (1990). Success for All: First year outcomes of a comprehensive plan for reforming urban education. *American Educational Research Journal, 27,* 255–278.

Boulder Project

Hiebert, E. F., Colt, J. M., Catto, S. L., & Gury, E. C. (1992). Reading and writing of first-grade students in a restructured Chapter I program. *American Educational Research Journal, 29,* 545–572.

Hiebert, E. H. (1994). A small-group literacy intervention with Chapter I students. In E. H. Hiebert & B. Taylor (Eds.), *Getting reading right from the start: Effective early literacy interventions* (pp. 85–106). Boston: Allyn & Bacon.

Early Intervention in Reading

Taylor, B. M., Frye, B. J., Short, R., & Shearer, B. (1992). Classroom teachers prevent reading failure among low-achieving first-grade students. *The Reading Teacher, 45,* 592–597.

Taylor, B. M., Strait, J., & Medo, M. A. (1994). Early intervention is reading: Supplemental instruction for groups of low-achieving students provided by first grade teachers. In E. H. Hiebert & B. M. Taylor (Eds.), *Getting reading right from the start: Effective early literacy interventions.* Boston: Allyn & Bacon.

Taylor, B., Short, R., Shearer, B., & Frye, B. (2007). First grade teachers provide early reading intervention in the classroom. In R. Allington & S. Walmsley (Eds.), *No quick fix, The RTI edition: Rethinking literacy programs in America's elementary schools* (pp. 159–176). Newark, DE: International Reading Association.

Project Success

Cooper, J. D. (1997). *Project success: Literacy intervention for grades 3–6.* Paper presented at International Reading Association Convention, Atlanta, GA.

Readings on Classroom Structures

Four Block

Cunningham, P. M., Hall, D. P., & Defee, M. (1991). Non-ability-grouped, multilevel instruction: A year in a first grade classroom. *The Reading Teacher, 44,* 566–571.

Cunningham, P. M., Hall, D. P., & Defee, M. (1998). Nonability-grouped, multilevel instruction: Eight years later. *The Reading Teacher, 51,* 652–654.

Hall, D. P., Prevatte, C., & Cunningham, P. M. (2007). Eliminating ability grouping and reducing failure in the primary grades. In R. Allington & S. Walmsley (Eds.), *No quick fix, The RTI edition: Rethinking literacy programs in America's elementary schools* (pp. 137–159). New York: Teachers College Press.

Fluency Oriented Reading Instruction

Kuhn, M. R., Schwanenflugel, P. J., Morris, R. D., Morrow, L. M., Woo, D. G., Meisinger, E. B., Sevcik, R. A., Bradley, B. A., & Stahl, S. A. (2006). Teaching children to become fluent and automatic readers. *Journal of Literacy Research, 38,* 357–388.

Stahl, S. A., & Heubach, K. (1993). *Changing reading instruction in second grade: A fluency oriented program.* University of Georgia: National Reading Research Center.

Stahl, S. A., & Heubach, K. M. (2005). Fluency-oriented reading instruction. *Journal of literacy research, 31,* 25–60.

Readings on Principles of Successful Interventions

Alvermann, D. E. (2001). Reading adolescents' reading identities: Looking back to see ahead. *Journal of Adolescent and Adult Literacy, 44,* 676–690.

Duffy-Hester, A. M. (1999). Teaching struggling readers in elementary school classrooms: A review of classroom reading programs and principles for instruction. *The Reading Teacher, 52,* 480–495.

Fischer, C. (1999/2000). An effective (and affordable) intervention model for at-risk high school readers. *Journal of Adolescent and Adult Literacy, 43,* 326–335.

Forsyth, S., & Roller, C. (1997/1998). Helping children become independent readers. *The Reading Teacher, 51,* 346–348.

Hettinger, H. R., & Knapp, N. F. (2001). Lessons from J. P.: Supporting underachieving readers in the elementary classroom. *The Reading Teacher, 55,* 26–28.

Ivey, G. (1999). Reflections on teaching struggling middle school readers. *Journal of Adolescent and Adult Literacy, 42,* 372–381.

Leslie, L., & Allen, L. (1999). Factors that predict success in an early literacy intervention project. *Reading Research Quarterly, 34,* 404–425.

McCray, A. D. (2001). Middle school students with reading disabilities. *The Reading Teacher, 55,* 298–300.

Richek, M. A., Caldwell, J. S., Jennings, J. H., & Lerner, J. W. (2006). *Reading problems: Assessment and teaching strategies.* Boston: Allyn & Bacon.

Sanacore, J. (1996). Ingredients for successful inclusion. *Journal of Adolescent and Adult Literacy, 40,* 222–226.

Wasik, B. A., & Slavin, R. E. (1993). Preventing early reading failure with one-to-one tutoring: A review of five programs. *Reading Research Quarterly, 23,* 108–122.

Readings on No Child Left Behind

Afflerbach, P. (2004). *National reading conference policy brief: High stakes testing and reading assessment.* Oak Creek, WI: National Reading Conference.

International Reading Association (IRA). (1999). High-stakes assessment in reading: A position statement of the IRA. *The Reading Teacher, 53,* 257–263.

Kohn, A. (2000). Burnt at the high stakes. *Journal of Teacher Education, 51,* 315–327.

Kohn, A. (2001). Fighting the test: A practical guide to rescuing our schools. *Phi Delta Kappan, 82*(5), 349–357.

Norlin, J. W. (2005). *NCLB and AYP: Consequences of failure.* Horsham, PA: LRP Publications:

Popham, W. J. (2001). *The truth about testing: An educator's call to action.* Alexandria, VA: Association for Supervision and Curriculum Development.

Stewart, M. T. (2004). Early literacy in the climate of NCLB. *The Reading Teacher, 57,* 732–743.

U.S. Department of Education (2005a). Testing: Frequently asked questions. Retrieved October 3, 2007, from www.ed.gov/print/nclb/accountability/ayp/testing-faq.html

U.S. Department of Education (2005b). Testing for results. Retrieved October 3, 2007, from www.ed.gov/print/nclb/accountability/ayp/testingforresults.html

Readings on Response to Intervention

Bender, W. N., & Shores, C. (2007). *Response to intervention: A practical guide for every teacher.* Thousand Oaks, CA: Corwin Press.

Brown-Chidsey, R., & Steege, M. W. (2005). *Response to intervention: Principles and strategies for effective practice.* New York: The Guilford Press.

Daugherty-Stahl, K. A. (2004). Proof, practice and promise: Comprehension strategy instructions in the primary grades. *The Reading Teacher, 57,* 598–607.

Fuchs, D., & Fuchs, L. S. (2006). Introduction to Response to Intervention: What, why and how valid is it? *Reading Research Quarterly, 41,* 93–99.

Gersten, R., & Dimino, J. A. (2006). RTI (Response to Intervention): Rethinking special education for students with reading difficulties (yet again). *Reading Research Quarterly, 41,* 99–108.

Individuals With Disabilities Education Improvement Act (IDEA). (2004). Federal Register 71, pp. 46539–46845. Retrieved October 3, 2007, from www.ed.gov/policy/speced/guid/idea2004.html

International Reading Association. (2002). Examining evidence. *Reading Today, 20*(1) (August/September), pp. 1, 4.

McCook, J. E. (2006). *The RTI guide: Developing and implementing a model in your schools.* Horsham, PA: LRP Publications.

McKenna, M. C., & Walpole, S. (2005). How well does assessment inform our reading instruction? *The Reading Teacher, 59,* 84–86.

Pressley, M., Duke, N. K., & Boling, E. C. (2004). The educational science and scientifically based instruction we need: Lessons from reading research and policymaking. *Harvard Education Review, 74,* 30–62. Retrieved May 4, 2006, from http://0-proquest.umi.com.topcat.switchlineinc.org

U.S. Department of Education. (2003). *Identifying and implementing educational practices supported by rigorous evidence: A user friendly guide.* Retrieved December 19, 2003, from www.ed.gov/print/rschstate/research/pubs/rigorousevid/guide.html

Wright, J. (2007). *RTI toolkit: A practical guide for schools.* Port Chester, NY: Dude Publishing.

Readings on English Language Learners

Ernst-Slavit, G., Moore, M., & Maloney, C. (2002). Changing lives: Teaching English and literature to ESL students. *Journal of Adolescent and Adult Literacy, 46,* 116–129.

Farrell, T. (2006). *Succeeding with English language learners: A guide for beginning teachers.* Thousand Oaks, CA: Corwin Press.

Harper, C., & deJong, E. (2004). Misconceptions about teaching English-language learners. *Journal of Adolescent and Adult Literacy, 48,* 152–162.

Hawkins, M. R. (2004). Researching English language and literacy development in schools. *Educational Researcher, 33,* 14–25.

Lenters, K. (2004/2005). No half measures: Reading instruction for young second language learners. *The Reading Teacher, 58,* 328–336.

Mohr, K. A. J. (2004). English as an accelerated language: A call to action for reading teachers. *The Reading Teacher, 58,* 18–26.

Opitz, M. F., & Harding-DeKim, J. L. (2007). Understanding and teaching English language learners. *The Reading Teacher, 60,* 590–593.

Rea, D. M., & Mercuri, S. P. (2006). *Research-based strategies for English language learners.* Portsmouth, NH: Heinemann.

Slavin, R. E., & Cheung, A. (2004). How do English language learners learn to read? *Educational Leadership, 61,* 52–57.

Slavin, R. E., & Cheung, A. (2005). A synthesis of research on the language of reading instruction for English Language Learners. *Review of Educational Research, 75,* 247–281.

Vardell, S. M., Hadaway, N. L., & Young, T. A. (2006). Matching books and readers: Selecting literature for English learners. *The Reading Teacher, 59,* 734–741.

Readings on Instruction for Adolescent Learners

Ambe, E. B. (2007). Inviting reluctant adolescent readers into the literacy club: Some comprehension strategies to tutor individuals or small groups of reluctant readers. *Journal of Adolescent and Adult Literacy, 50,* 632–639.

Biancarosa, G. (2005). After third grade. *Educational Leadership, 62,* 16–22.

Fisher, D., & Ivey, G. (2006). Evaluating the interventions for struggling adolescent readers. *Journal of Adolescent and Adult Literacy, 50,* 180–189.

Fisher, D., & Ivey, G. (2007). Evaluating interventions for struggling middle school readers. Paper presented at the annual meeting of the National Reading Conference, Austin, TX.

Ivey, G., & Baker, M. I. (2004). Phonics instruction for older students? Just say no. *Educational Leadership, 61,* 35–39.

Johannessen, L. R. (2004). Helping "struggling" readers achieve success. *Journal of Adolescent and Adult Literacy, 47,* 638–647.

National Assessment of Education Progress. (2005). Retrieved April 10, 2007, from http://nationsreportcard.gov/reading_math_grade12_2005/s0201.asp

National Assessment of Education Progress. (2007). Retrieved April 10, 2007, from http://ncas.ed.gov/nationsreportcard/pdf/main2007/2007496_3/pdf

Santa, C. M. (2006). A vision for adolescent literacy: Ours or theirs? *Journal of Adolescent and Adult Literacy, 49,* 468–478.

2

Patterns of Reading Difficulty

General Patterns

The informal reading inventory (IRI) has a long and proud tradition in helping educators identify the strengths and needs of struggling readers. Educators observe how accurately and fluently students identify words when reading orally or silently. Using informal reading inventory guidelines, educators determine a student's independent, instructional, or frustration reading levels and decide if the student is reading below his or her chronological grade level. They listen to the student's retelling, ask different types of questions, and use responses as indicators of comprehension. Educators obtain much information from an informal reading inventory, and this information must be distilled into a plan for effective instruction. What an educator learns about a student from an informal reading inventory should translate into objectives for the intervention that will follow.

Admittedly, there are numerous other instruments for assessing reading. There are standardized measures of word identification and comprehension, tests of early literacy skills, developmental spelling inventories (Bear, Invernizzi, Templeton, & Johnston, 2004), and observational checklists, to name just a few. We agree that they offer valuable insights into a student's performance, but examining them is not the purpose of this book. We have chosen to focus specifically on the informal reading inventory. First, it is an instrument that has proven itself over time. Second, it offers multiple perspectives on a student's performance. Third, its format closely parallels the format of authentic reading as students read passages, retell what they have read, and answer questions.

Reading is an extremely complex process, and the information obtained from an informal reading inventory can be similarly complex. You may have data from a variety of sources on a variety of levels: word lists, passage reading, and miscue analysis. For each passage, you may have access to a prior knowledge score, a word identification score, an estimation of reading rate, a measure of retelling, and a comprehension score based on answers to questions. Where should you focus your attention? What patterns of performance offer guidelines for effective instruction?

Each reader represents an individual pattern of strengths and needs; however, we can identify general patterns as a beginning point for instruction. Reading difficulties tend to fall into three areas. Some readers are challenged by word identification. They may not understand that letters represent sounds in a systematic way; they may experience difficulty in recognizing consistent patterns within this system. Other readers may be able to accurately decode but do so at a very slow and effortful rate. Still others may do well with short words but falter when faced with the multisyllabic words so often found in upper-level text. Lack of efficient word identification can seriously interfere with comprehension.

A second pattern involves readers who are challenged by fluency; that is, they do not have a large store of automatically recognized sight words. They may be relatively accurate decoders, but they often apply decoding strategies to words that they should know without overtly matching letters and sounds. They may experience difficulty with irregular words, or words that do not fit letter–sound patterns. As a result, they read slowly and, because they are primarily concerned with accurately identifying words, their comprehension often falters.

Readers who are primarily challenged by comprehension represent a third pattern of reading difficulties. They may be able to fluently identify words, but they lack workable strategies for comprehending and remembering what they read. They may lack a strong vocabulary base and be unable to assign meanings to a wide array of spoken words. These readers often do not understand that reading is a highly interactive process; they expect comprehension to just happen as a result of saying the words.

We suggest that these three general patterns provide the focus for planning balanced intervention instruction. In every lesson, some attention should be paid to word study, fluency development or maintenance, and comprehension, even though one area may be stressed more than the others. In the past, we tended to emphasize a student's weakness to the exclusion of other elements of reading. For example, it was quite common for a struggling reader to receive instruction only in phonics and to never actually read a book. As a result, many students equated the reading process with saying words as opposed to making meaning.

Once instruction begins, the educator soon becomes acquainted with the specific strengths and needs of each student and makes necessary adjustments. In a way, it is much like tending a garden. All plants need certain things in common: soil, water, sun, and fertilizer. Within these requirements, each plant has different needs. Some grow well in sandy soil, and others do not; some thrive in dry soil, and others need constant moisture; some do well in bright sunlight, and others prefer shade. In planning a garden, the wise gardener understands the importance of soil, water, sun, and fertilizer, but also provides for the different needs of each plant. In reading intervention, the educator understands the importance of a balanced approach to instruction that focuses on word recognition, fluency, and comprehension and includes all as part of the intervention framework.

The intervention programs discussed in Chapter 1 focused on all three components. Students were taught to pronounce words, but they also read and reread motivating text. They may have sorted words and pictures according to sound patterns, but they also talked and wrote about what they read. They may have worked with word cards or letter and sound drills, but they also were exposed to reading as an activity for making meaning. We encourage you to provide a well-rounded and balanced sequence of activities that foster reading as an activity to be valued and, within this framework, to provide individualized instruction for each reader.

The informal reading inventory can offer suggestions for the framework of the intervention instruction. A student who shows strength in word identification but experiences difficulties in comprehension needs a greater focus on reading for meaning. A student who has little understanding of letter–sound relationships may need a structure with a strong emphasis on letter and sound identification or strategies for decoding words. A student who displays a slow and deliberate reading rate may need more activities that focus on developing fluency.

Information from an informal reading inventory can also suggest the type of activities to include when reading for meaning, engaging in word study, or developing fluency. For example, a student whose miscues always begin with the same letters or sounds as in the original word may need activities that focus on vowel sounds or vowel patterns. A student who does well when answering questions but whose retelling is disorganized and sparse may profit from attention to text structure.

Information gleaned from an informal reading inventory can also offer valuable suggestions for choosing the most appropriate materials for the instructional session. The informal reading inventory identifies the student's reading level, which is important to know for selecting materials that he or she can read successfully. Results of an informal reading inventory can also suggest the type of text that should be emphasized. Students who are challenged by word identification need selections on familiar topics. A student who primarily experiences difficulty when reading expository text needs a focus on exposition.

Although a student's performance on the informal reading inventory can indicate how to balance activities in word identification, fluency, and comprehension, it can also offer ideas about the format and timing of the intervention to follow. For example, will the format be a pullout model or an in-class model? Often, the resources of the school or district dictate the format. Similarly, school or district resources may determine the timing of the intervention—how long and how often it occurs. However, results of the informal reading inventory can offer suggestions. An older student reading at a very low level might require a more individualized approach in a pullout format conducted over a long period of time. A student who is only slightly behind his or her peers might do quite well as a member of a small in-class support group.

It is not the purpose of this chapter to instruct the reader on how to administer and score an informal reading inventory. All informal reading inventories come with detailed instructions. We assume that you are already familiar with the informal reading inventory process or you would not have purchased this book. Perhaps you use an IRI or are in the process of learning how to do so. In this chapter, we intend to focus on general areas of information that can be identified from an informal inventory and used to describe a student's performance. However, we intend to go further in this book and show you how to use what you learn to inform the content and structure of the intervention.

Defining a Student's Reading Level

How do you begin to make sense of all the information from an informal reading inventory? You many have only one or two IRI passages to use; you may have several. Where do you begin? The first piece of information that you should identify is the student's instructional reading level—that is, the level at which *both* word identification and comprehension fall within the instructional or independent ranges. Often after reading a passage, a student will exhibit an instructional level for word identification and a frustration level for comprehension or vice versa. That is not a true instructional level. Move down until you have the level at which both are within either the instructional or the independent range (Leslie & Caldwell, 2006). Choosing an instructional reading level based only on word identification or comprehension can seriously inflate a reading level and camouflage an area of need.

Begin by examining passages that represent the student's best performance. This gives a more realistic and fair picture of the reader's strengths and needs. After all, if we are being evaluated on our performance, don't we want it to be under circumstances that allow us the best chance of demonstrating our ability? For most readers, this occurs in narrative text on familiar topics.

But what if there is no instructional reading level? What if the student reaches the frustration level in preprimer text? We could certainly call the student a nonreader, one who is unable to recognize words at the lowest level. However, we should delve a little further and estimate the student's listening level. In other words, what level of text can the student understand when it is read to him or her? If word recognition is not a concern, what level of comprehension can the student attain? Estimating a student's listening level allows us to determine if the student is challenged by word recognition, basic comprehension, or both. A student who exhibits a frustration level in preprimer text but has a listening comprehension level of first grade is much different from one who cannot recognize words or comprehend preprimer text.

Reading Level: An Indicator of Problem Severity

We suggest that your first piece of information, and perhaps the most important, is the student's instructional reading level compared to his or her chronological grade level. Knowing this allows you to estimate the severity of the problem. In other words, how extensive is the gap between the student's reading level as determined by the informal reading inventory and his or her grade placement?

The severity of the reading problem is signaled by the gap between what the student can read and what the student should read given his or her grade level. According to Spache (1981), if a first, second, or third grader is a year or more behind, the problem is severe; if a fourth, fifth, or sixth grader is two or more years behind, the problem is severe; for students in seventh grade and above, a severe problem means three or more years behind. It is important that educators have some idea of the severity of the problem. More severe problems indicate a more extensive program of intervention and may require individual instruction over a longer period of time. Knowing the severity of the problem also allows you to offer parents a realistic picture of future progress. For example, Morris, Ervin, and Conrad (1996) describe the successful progress of a sixth grader reading at the second-grade level who progressed to a fourth-grade level but only after 78 hours of tutoring over a two-year period. English language learners often show a gap between their listening level and their reading level. They may possess skills in conversational English but be unable to recognize printed English words. It is important to differentiate between the two. While instruction in reading should begin at an instructional reading level, the level of materials for teacher read-alouds may be higher.

Reading Level: An Indicator of Word Identification Proficiency

Knowing the student's instructional reading level also suggests a focus for instruction in word identification. Although it is important to provide a balanced assortment of activities that center on reading for meaning, word study, and fluency development, the emphasis you place on each of these can be determined from the student's reading level. In order to understand this, it is important to have a sense of how readers learn to identify words.

Readers move through different stages of word learning on their journey to proficient reading (Ehri, 1991; Gough & Juel, 1991; Spear-Swerling & Sternberg, 1996). The first stage of reading words is called the *logographic stage,* at which children identify words much as they identify pictures. They use visual cues as opposed to matching letters and sounds. For example, they can identify the word *stop* but only if enclosed in the familiar red sign. They can identify *McDonald's* but only in the presence of the familiar golden arches. They may correctly identify *monkey* because it has a tail on the end (*y*) just like the animal. However, when they meet *turkey* or *funny,* they call them *monkey* also because of the distinctive tail. Logographic readers generally have not mastered letter names and sounds, and that is why they do not use these as aids to word identification. Logographic readers are not true readers; we might call them prereaders. They may or may not understand that the black squiggles on the page stand for meaning, but they do not understand that letters represent sounds in a meaningful and systematic way. As a result, they cannot independently read preprimer text and their miscues often involve wild guesses that bear little resemblance to the original word.

The next stage of word learning is the *alphabetic stage.* A child's first awareness of the alphabet is called the stage of phonetic cue recoding (Ehri, 1991). Students begin to associate some of the letters they see with the sounds they hear. Ehri differentiates between the logographic stage and the phonetic cue recoding stage in this way: The logographic reader will see *yellow* and remember it because of "two sticks" in the middle; the phonetic cue recoding reader will associate the two *l*s with the sound of the letter and use this to remember the word. In this stage, readers begin to match letters and sounds, but in an incomplete way. They often focus on the beginnings and ends of words and therefore confuse words such as *boat, boot,* and *beat.* Their decoding of unfamiliar words is inaccurate because they use only partial letter and sound cues and they rely heavily on pictures and context to help them pronounce words and understand what they read. They read connected text very slowly, often in a laborious word-by-word manner. Readers at the preprimer, primer, and first-grade levels are often in this stage. They have a small store of known words that they have learned through some partial sound associations, and when they meet unknown words they attempt to utilize letter sounds. Readers in this stage often "pass" on a word; that is, because they know that letters make specific sounds and because they do not know the letters and sounds in a particular word, they do not even attempt pronunciation.

As readers move further into the alphabetic stage, they begin to use a variety of sound and spelling patterns to recognize words but they are not automatic in doing so. Spear-Swerling and Sternberg (1996) call this the stage of *controlled word recognition.* Students become less dependent on pictures and are more able to pronounce words in word lists or on word cards. However, word pronunciation is still a labor-intensive process and reading is often slow and effortful as indicated by a very slow reading rate. Students reading at a second-grade level often fall into the stage of controlled word recognition.

At some time, word pronunciation becomes almost effortless. Students recognize common familiar words automatically without sounding out, and they are able to decode unfamiliar words accurately and rapidly. They begin to recognize and employ letter patterns as pronunciation clues. For example, the reader who knows *lamp* uses knowledge of consonant sounds and the vowel pattern *amp* to pronounce *stamp, cramp,* and *damp.* It is at this point, according to Gough and Juel (1991), that word pronunciation becomes almost effortless. The reading rate of students in this stage begins to increase and, because readers are paying less attention to decoding, their oral reading becomes more expressive. This is the stage of *automatic word recognition,* a typical stage for some second graders and for normally achieving third graders. Gradually, as students read more difficult and complex text, they begin to acquire strategies for pronouncing longer words such as *lysogenic* and *revolution.*

These stages of word learning are not discrete. A reader in one stage does not identify all words in the same manner. The stage simply indicates the strategy that the reader primarily uses. For example, a reader may decode the majority of unfamiliar words (controlled word recognition), have a store of automatically recognized sight words (automatic word recognition), and still rely on visual cues for other words (logographic). What do you do when you meet an unfamiliar word? Although you are a proficient adult reader functioning primarily in the stage of automatic word recognition, you probably revert to letter–sound matching and sound it out. Even though the stages are not discrete, they provide a useful point of reference for noting patterns in struggling readers and pointing out instructional strategies for moving the student to the next stage.

When efficient word identification is in place, students can turn their attention to strategies for more advanced comprehension such as identifying important information, identifying word meanings from the context of the passage, synthesizing information, and removing comprehension roadblocks. Spear-Swirling and Sternberg (1996) call this stage *strategic reading*.

If we use these stages as a rough estimate of the strategies used by students at different reading levels, we can note the following general patterns in word identification.

Below Preprimer Instructional Level

Students at this level may exhibit very different understandings of the reading process. Some may not recognize any purpose for reading; others may lack basic print concepts (Clay, 1993) and may not know how to hold a book upright and turn the pages in a sequential fashion. Many students at this level are logographic readers who do not understand that letters stand for sounds and that words represent meaning. These prereaders may not know the letter names or the sounds they represent, or that several and different sounds make up a word (*phonemic awareness*). The student may not understand that we read from left to right and that words are defined by the spaces between them. Because few informal reading inventories contain tasks that assess these components, it is important that the focus of intervention be to determine exactly what the student does or does not know and to provide experiences to move him or her to the next stage of word identification.

Instructional Level in Preprimer, Primer, and First-Grade Texts

The student has entered the alphabetic stage and is attempting to match letters and sounds but is not successful in doing so. Word study for students at these levels should focus on letter and sound patterns and strategies for applying them to unfamiliar words. A miscue analysis can help you to determine if intervention should begin with a focus on consonant patterns or on vowel patterns. Instruction should also focus on developing fluency. Students need to develop a store of automatically recognized words. They can then use the letter patterns in these words to decode unfamiliar words. In addition, students need to automatically identify irregular words that do not follow a predictable pattern, such as *the, was, who,* and *thought.*

Instructional Level in Second-Grade Text

The student is beginning to use letter and sound patterns with more efficiency but is probably still working hard to decode unfamiliar words. Intervention should focus on helping the child move to greater automaticity through continued work with letter and sound patterns and through a fluency emphasis on developing an extensive sight vocabulary.

Instructional Level in Third-Grade Text

The student has achieved some control over matching letters and sounds and probably has a relatively large sight vocabulary. However, he or she needs to become more automatic in recognizing familiar words and in decoding unfamiliar ones. Because words tend to get longer and more complex in third-grade text and above, intervention should focus on strategies for pronouncing longer words. At this level, it is also important to move the child to effective and fluent silent reading.

Instructional Level in Fourth-Grade Text and Above

The student has an understanding of the letter and sound system of our language and is using this effectively for the most part. However, students whose reading levels are beyond third grade often need additional help in managing long words and understanding how prefixes, suffixes, and roots help both pronunciation and meaning.

Reading Level: An Indicator of Comprehension Proficiency

Comprehension does not develop in stages as word identification does; however, knowing the student's instructional reading level can suggest a focus for instruction. In order to understand this, it is important to realize how text varies at the different levels. In informal reading inventories, text levels are generally determined by readability formulas that basically measure word and sentence length—more difficult text has longer sentences, longer words, and more infrequent or unfamiliar words. But there are other differences that can affect comprehension. Selections written at the preprimer through third-grade levels are generally about familiar topics such as class trips, pets, friends, and games. The text at these levels also contains many pictures. Even expository text, often regarded as text that teaches, normally focuses on familiar topics such as seasons, food, and animals. The student already knows something about the content of these selections, and that makes them easier to comprehend. However, as we move into text at a fourth-grade level and above, more unfamiliar topics appear, such as narratives about unknown people in unfamiliar situations and expository selections about relatively new topics such as lasers and star life cycles. For all of us, topic familiarity affects our comprehension: We do better when we read about known topics. This is why it is important to determine a student's instructional level in familiar text, which represents a student's best performance. Many informal reading inventories have prereading measures to determine the student's familiarity with the topic and content of the selection. You often see a pattern in which a reader seems relatively familiar with a topic yet demonstrates poor comprehension. This student needs to use what she or he knows about the topic as an active aid to comprehension. Most readers beyond a third-grade level need instruction in comprehending and remembering unfamiliar text.

We can measure comprehension in several ways, and a student may perform differently in each. The number of questions that a student can answer successfully is the determinant of instructional level. There are two ways to evaluate this ability: One is to ask the student to answer questions without looking back in the text; the other is to allow the reader to look back to locate missing answers and correct erroneous ones. Both suggest possible patterns for intervention. Allowing a student to look back distinguishes between memory and understanding. If the student cannot answer a question, is it because he or she did not understand while reading or because he or she understood but forgot? If the student can locate that answer during the look-back procedure, you can assume that understanding is in place and forgetting is the culprit.

A student who cannot answer questions or improve performance when allowed to look back has a more serious comprehension problem than the one who can successfully engage in the look-back strategy. We strongly suggest that an instructional level for comprehension should represent a combination of questions answered with and without lookbacks. Unfortunately, not all informal reading inventories offer this option. The use of look-backs represents the student's best performance and is more like what good readers do when they read. Think about reading a newspaper editorial. If someone asks you a specific question about its contents, don't you often look back to verify the answer you intend to give or even perhaps in order to find it? If your student cannot effectively use the look-back strategy, you need to focus on this in your intervention.

If students cannot answer questions, you may want to determine if there is any pattern to the types of questions. Most informal reading inventories offer different question types. Does the student primarily miss factual, literal, or explicit questions? Do most errors occur in inferential or implicit questions? A pattern could suggest a focus for intervention. Chapter 11 focuses on the structure of questions and different strategies for helping students answer them successfully.

Some informal reading inventories assess retelling as well. We suggest that a student's retelling offers different information from answers to questions, and both are important. A retelling suggests the extent and structure of a student's memory. That is, does the student remember in a complete and coherent fashion, or is the retelling confused, incomplete, and inaccurate? If the student is unable to retell in a relatively complete and coherent manner, intervention may need to focus on elements of text structure that the reader can use as a framework for retelling. We will discuss activities for developing the skill of retelling in Chapters 9 and 10.

Is there a difference between the student's instructional level in narrative text as opposed to expository text? Often narrative performance is higher. If the student is above a third-grade level and expository text comprehension is problematic, he or she may need intervention that focuses on exposition. Even if the student did not read any expository selections, you may well consider focusing on expository text during the intervention sessions. There is a heavy focus on narrative text in elementary school, and even proficient readers are often ill equipped to deal successfully with expository selections. In Chapter 9, we focus on narrative text. Chapter 10 is devoted to expository text.

Designing the Intervention Focus

It is very easy to get bogged down with all the information that you may have at your command from an informal reading inventory. In order to design an effective intervention, you need to focus on broad patterns of reading performance. First, consider the severity of the problem. How extensive is the gap between the student's actual reading level and his or her chronological grade level? What does this tell you about the format, timing, and structure of the intervention session?

What is the student's approximate stage of word identification? Is she or he a logographic reader or a reader just entering the alphabetic stage? Perhaps your student is most comfortable in the controlled reading stage or the stage of automatic word recognition. Identifying these broad patterns points to the focus of your intervention. Your intervention will, of course, offer a balanced array of activities emphasizing reading for meaning, word study, and fluency development, but within this balance you will emphasize the area or areas that best fit the pattern exhibited by the student.

What about patterns of comprehension? Is there a difference between a student's ability to answer questions and his or her ability to retell? Does the student effectively use prior knowledge to comprehend? Is the student equally comfortable in narrative and expository text, or do the results on the informal reading inventory suggest that one receives greater focus?

Table 2.1 offers some general guidelines regarding patterns of reading performance and how these suggest different emphases in a balanced program of intervention. Future chapters will develop this in more detail.

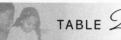 TABLE *2.1*   Patterns for Intervention Focus

Student Reading Level	Word Study	Fluency Development	Reading for Meaning
Below preprimer	XX Letter names; letter sounds	X Beginning sight vocabulary	XX Concepts about print; familiar text
Preprimer through first grade	XX Letter–sound patterns; decoding strategies	XX Basic sight vocabulary	X Familiar text
Second grade	XX Letter–sound patterns; decoding strategies	XX Sight vocabulary extension	X Familiar text
Third grade	X Multisyllabic words	XX Sight vocabulary; transition to silent reading	XX Use of prior knowledge; retelling strategies; question-answering strategies; general comprehension strategies; beginning focus on unfamiliar text and exposition
Fourth grade and above	X Multisyllabic words; prefixes, suffixes, roots	X Increase and/or maintain silent reading rate	XX Use of prior knowledge; retelling strategies; question-answering strategies; general comprehension and study strategies; focus on unfamiliar text and exposition

Key: XX suggests a strong intervention focus

 # Summary

This chapter addresses general patterns of reading performance that can be revealed by an informal reading inventory. Perhaps the most important information is identification of a student's reading level. This allows you to compare the student's instructional reading and chronological grade levels, which in turn suggest how severe the reading problem may be. We recommend that the instructional level be defined as the level at which both word recognition and comprehension fall within the instructional or independent range.

The student's level of word identification suggests which stage of word learning best describes his or her decoding strategies: logographic, alphabetic, controlled word recognition, or automatic word recognition. The student's comprehension level is determined by his or her ability to answer questions after reading a passage. We strongly suggest that, after answering questions, students be allowed to look back in the text to correct errors or locate missing information. A more realistic reading level is determined from a combination of questions answered with and without look-backs. Comprehension level should always be evaluated in terms of a student's prior knowledge and the structure of the text, that is, narrative as opposed to expository.

REFERENCES AND RECOMMENDED READINGS

Bear, D. R., Invernizzi, M., Templeton, S., & Johnston, F. (2004). *Words their way: Word study for phonics, vocabulary, and spelling instruction.* Upper Saddle River, NJ: Prentice-Hall.

Clay, M. M. (1993). *An observation survey of early literacy achievement.* Portsmouth, NH: Heinemann.

Ehri, L. C. (1991). Development of the ability to read words. In R. Barr, M. L. Kamil, P. Mosenthal, and P. D. Pearson (Eds.), *Handbook of reading research* (Vol. II, pp. 383–417). New York: Longman.

Gough, P. B., & Juel, C. (1991). The first stages of word recognition. In L. Rieben and C. A. Perfetti (Eds.), *Learning to read: Basic research and its implications* (pp. 47–56). Mahwah, NJ: Erlbaum.

Leslie, L., & Caldwell, J. (2006). *Qualitative reading inventory-4.* Boston: Allyn & Bacon.

Morris, D., Ervin, C., & Conrad, K. (1996). A case study of middle school reading disability. *The Reading Teacher, 49,* 368–377.

Spache, G. D. (1981). *Diagnosing and correcting reading difficulties.* Boston: Allyn & Bacon.

Spear-Swerling, L., & Sternberg, R. J. (1996). *Off track: When poor readers become "learning disabled."* Boulder, CO: Westview Press.

3

The Structure of Intervention Sessions

- **THE IMPORTANCE OF CONSISTENT STRUCTURE**

- **INDIVIDUAL TUTORING STRUCTURES AT THE ELEMENTARY LEVEL**
    Reading Recovery
    Early Steps
    Book Buddies
    Reading Rescue
    Howard Street Tutoring Model

- **INDIVIDUAL TUTORING STRUCTURES AT THE MIDDLE LEVEL**
    Case Study of a Sixth Grader

- **GROUP TUTORING STRUCTURES AT THE ELEMENTARY LEVEL**
    First Grade Intervention
    The Boulder Project
    Early Intervention in Reading
    Reading Club
    Literacy Booster Groups
    Cross-Age Tutoring
    The Anna Plan
    Third Grade Intervention
    Project Success

- **GROUP TUTORING STRUCTURES AT THE MIDDLE LEVEL**
    Readers' Workshop
    Cross-Age Tutoring

- **GROUP TUTORING STRUCTURES AT THE HIGH SCHOOL LEVEL**
    Cross-Age Tutoring
    Literacy Tutoring for Adolescents

- **CLASSROOM INTERVENTION STRUCTURES**
    Intervention as Part of the Literacy Block
    Classroom Structures That Foster the Growth of Struggling Readers
    The Four Block Model

The Importance of Consistent Structure

A lesson plan has three main components: objectives, an overall structure, and activities designed to meet the objectives that fill in the structure. In Chapter 2, we examined objectives for intervention as suggested by general patterns of reading problems. We offer suggestions for specific activities in successive chapters. Our purpose in this chapter is to examine what we know about the overall structure of intervention sessions.

What do we mean by the overall structure of a lesson plan? It is how you divide the amount of time you will spend with a student into broad categories such as word study, fluency, and comprehension. Perhaps an analogy will help. Suppose that your objective is to plant a garden. Where do you begin? After deciding where the garden will be located and how large it will be, you decide what part of the garden will be set aside for vegetables and what part for flowers. You will probably divide your flower section into areas for annuals and perennials. This is the overall structure of your garden. Once you have determined it, you can begin to focus on the specific vegetables and flowers that you will plant. These specifics are analogous to lesson plan activities.

In the past, educators believed that both the overall structure of the lesson plan and the activities it contained should be individualized. As a result, the structure of instructional sessions varied from student to student and from day to day. That is, not only did educators present different activities on different days, they emphasized these for different lengths of times. As a result, there was little consistency of structure across sessions. Perhaps the only constant was the total amount of time that the educator met with the student.

The successful interventions discussed in Chapter 1 point out the importance of a consistent lesson structure. Each lesson looks approximately the same as far as the amount of time given to categories of instruction and the sequences for presenting these categories. These successful interventions all incorporate a balanced structure—that is, each lesson in some way addresses word study, fluency development, and comprehension. But what if a student pronounces words effectively and reads fluently? Can you devote an entire lesson to comprehension? Of course you can, but we still emphasize the importance of balance. You want not only to augment word pronunciation and fluency but also to maintain present skill levels. Balance does not mean that all receive equal emphasis. In a balanced structure, you address all three components but one or more receive greater focus depending on the needs of your students.

When planning instructional interventions for one student or a group of struggling readers, you first need to design your overall structure and approximate how much time you will spend on each category of activities. You also need to decide on your sequence. Which will come first, second, and last? Before you choose specific instructional activities to introduce to a student, you must design your structure and stick to it.

Why is a consistent structure so important? First, it makes lesson planning much easier. Because you know exactly how much time you can allot to each activity, you choose only the instructional activities that fit within your structure. This makes you a very discriminating lesson planner. You will not be tempted to include something in the lesson because it appeals to you or because you want to try it out. Your reason for including a specific activity is always whether or not it meets the needs of the student and fits into the structure.

Perhaps an example might help. Suppose you attend an in-service and learn about a new strategy for developing comprehension. It sounds like a lot of fun, and you think the students would enjoy and profit from it; you are eager to give it a try. The first question that you have to ask, however, is whether it fits into the lesson structure. Will it take too much time? Will you have to delete some other component in order to fit it in? If the answer is yes, then this strategy, however enticing, is not appropriate.

Isn't a consistent structure in opposition to individualized instruction? Don't struggling readers need individualization? Of course they do. And an effective educator will provide this within the lesson plan structure. First, remember that you have designed the structure to meet the specific needs of your students. Second, realize that different instructional activities can fit within each part of your structure. Here is where much individualization takes place. If one word study activity does not seem to work, you can choose another. If your student does not seem to profit from your chosen comprehension strategy, you can try a different one. Individualization also occurs with your choice of texts for the student to read. Will you present a narrative, or will you expose the student to expository text? What level of difficulty will be appropriate? Matching a student to just the right type of reading material is perhaps the most important component of individualization.

It will probably take a few lessons before you are totally satisfied with the structure of the intervention. You may need to adjust the sequence or the timing of each component. You may find that some components take less time than you expected and some take more. Make adjustments as needed, but aim for a consistent and workable structure as soon as possible.

Won't the students become bored with a consistent structure? It has been our observation that students often thrive in a consistent framework. They know what is coming next and they are comfortable in that knowledge. There is less off-task behavior when the teacher moves to a new category of activity because the students expect the change and know what the activity involves. We recall one teacher who felt that her students were bored with the structure and decided to begin the lesson in a different way. Her students loudly protested, "That's not how we start!"

Won't you become bored with the same basic structure day after day? We do not think so. In fact, consistent structure will provide a comforting support. Instead of worrying about what comes next in the lesson, your familiarity with the structure will allow you to pay more attention to the students and their needs. Instead of checking your lesson plan book, you will be engaged in observing and responding to your students.

There is another pragmatic reason for designing and maintaining a consistent lesson structure. You may need to use volunteers or aides to implement your intervention. It is easier to train volunteers if you ask them to do the same basic things every time. They will feel more competent and be more willing to stay involved. The high retention rate of community volunteers in the Book Buddies program, mentioned in Chapter 1 and described in more detail in this chapter, was probably due to the consistent structure. There were no surprises; the tutors were not asked to do something new, something for which they might have felt unprepared.

You may create your own structure, adopt the structure of a published program, or you may borrow the structure of successful interventions. Remember, we are concerned with overall structure at this point—the categories of instruction that you will emphasize and the amount of time you will allot to each—not the specific ways you will do it. Let's examine some successful lesson structures. The table at the end of this chapter provides an overview and summary of these structures. In Chapter 13, we will return to the topic of lesson structure and share various intervention arrangements that were designed to meet the needs of students and fit within the time and scheduling constraints of the school or classroom.

Individual Tutoring Structures at the Elementary Level

Reading Recovery

Students in Reading Recovery (Clay, 1993; Lyons & Beaver, 2007; Pinnell, 1989; Pinnell, Deford, & Lyons, 1988; Pinnell, Lyons, Deford, Bryk, & Seltzer, 1994) receive individual tutoring for 30 minutes each day. The lesson structure involves the following sequence of activities. First, the student rereads familiar books, after which the teacher and student engage in letter identification or word analysis. The teacher then guides the student to accurately write a sentence or "story" using the instructional strategy of writing to sound. The teacher cuts up the sentence, and the student reassembles it and then reads it. Finally, the teacher introduces a new book and supports the student in initial reading.

Early Steps

Early Steps (Morris, Shaw, & Perney, 1990; Santa, Ford, Mickley, & Parker, 1997; Santa & Hoien, 1999) also provides daily 30-minute lessons in a format that is very similar to Reading Recovery. For half of the class time, the student reads books at his or her level, progressing gradually to more advanced text. The first part of the lesson is spent rereading books read in previous lessons. Next, the tutor and student sort words according to letter and sound patterns, focusing on the development of phonemic awareness and on strategies for identifying words. Daily writing involves writing and reassembling cut-up sentences, after which the tutor introduces a new book.

Book Buddies

Book Buddies (Invernizzi, Juel, & Rosemary, 1996/1997; Invernizzi, Rosemary, Juel, & Richards, 1997) is a program in which community volunteers individually tutor first-grade struggling readers. The structure of the 45-minute tutoring lesson involves rereading familiar text, word study, writing, and reading a new book. Activities in the word study segment include word sorts and using words from the reading to form a word bank. For writing, the tutor dictates sentences or the students compose their own text using the writing-for-sounds strategy. In the final component, the tutor introduces the new selection using pictures and titles as a basis for prediction and employs choral and echo reading to support the student's first attempts at reading.

Reading Rescue

Reading Rescue (Ehri, Dreyer, Flugman, & Gross, 2007) is an intervention program for low-socioeconomic-status (SES) language minority first graders. Each lesson lasts for 30 to 40 minutes and involves five components taught in the following order: fluency, word analysis and comprehension strategies, phonological awareness and word study, writing, and comprehension and vocabulary development with a new book. The entire tutoring sequence proceeds in phases that gradually present more difficult concepts and materials as students develop their skills. Students begin each lesson by rereading familiar books to increase accuracy, fluency, and expression. Students then reread a book presented in the previous lesson and are introduced to and practice word analysis and comprehension strategies. A third lesson segment involves systematic phonics instruction and attention to phonemic awareness employing both analytic and synthetic approaches as well as decoding by analogy using key words. With the assistance of the teacher, students then write one or more sentences they had produced in conversation about the books read in class. The final lesson segment is introduction of the new book, providing the opportunity to develop oral language by talking about the book and learning the meaning of new words.

Howard Street Tutoring Model

The Howard Street model can be implemented during the school day or after school hours (Morris, 2005; Brown, Morris, & Fields, 2005). Volunteers tutor low-reading second and third graders twice a week for 45 minutes under the supervision of a reading specialist. The tutoring structure begins with an 18-minute segment in which the tutor supports the child in reading and understanding instructional-level stories, using echo reading, partner reading, or independent reading depending on the skill of the child. For 10 minutes, the tutor uses word categorization activities and games to develop understanding of basic spelling patterns. For the next 10 minutes, the child reads easy books or rereads previously read selections for the purpose of building sight vocabulary, fluency, and confidence. At the end of the session the tutor reads a quality selection to the child for approximately 7 minutes.

Individual Tutoring Structures at the Middle Level

Case Study of a Sixth Grader

A sixth grader struggling at a first- or second-grade reading level moved to a fourth-grade reading level over a two-year span (Morris, Ervin, & Conrad, 1996). The structure of the one-hour tutoring session suggests a possible model for intervention with older students reading at low levels. It consists of four components: reading for meaning, word study, writing, and fluency drill. The activities in the reading-for-meaning session are a combination of oral and silent reading of chapter books with frequent informal comprehension checks. Word study involves word sorts, word games, and a spelling focus. The student selects topics for writing, and the teacher helps edit and revise. The fluency drill section involves reading easy material, rereading familiar and previously practiced text, and graphing reading accuracy.

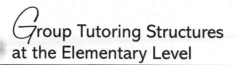

Group Tutoring Structures at the Elementary Level

First Grade Intervention

A group intervention for struggling first graders (Hedrick & Pearish, 1999) described as "fast-paced, tightly structured and balanced" (p. 716), involves daily sessions that last for 30 minutes. Each group consists of eight students who are released from their classrooms during independent reading time. The structure of the lesson involves the following components: reading aloud by the teacher (two minutes), word study and phonics (six minutes), shared reading (two minutes), guided reading (ten minutes), writing aloud/shared writing (two minutes), guided writing (three minutes), and independent reading (five minutes). Activities in the phonics segment focus on letter and sound identification, using a word wall for high-frequency words, and remaking words with magnetic letters. In shared reading, children read sentences from the story, pointing to individual words as they do so. Activities in guided reading include the weekly introduction of a new book and repeated reading using various formats such as choral reading. Shared writing focuses on sequencing and reading cut-up sentences. Activities in guided writing move from simple copying to independent writing. In the final component, children read familiar texts on their own, albeit monitored by the teacher.

The Boulder Project

This intervention (Hiebert, 1994; Hiebert, Colt, Catto, & Gury, 1992) incorporates 30 minutes of instruction for groups of three first graders. The first part of the lesson involves shared and individual rereading of the book from the previous lesson and a review of words that were the focus of that lesson. Then the teacher introduces a new book. The children read it aloud, talk about it, and take turns reading individually. The teacher next moves into word study by asking the children to select words in the book. They write the words, transform them by substituting letters and letter patterns, engage in rhyming activities, and use the words in new sentences. Then, guided by the teacher, the children write one or two sentences about their personal experiences related to the book.

Early Intervention in Reading

This intervention (Taylor, Frye, Short, & Shearer, 1992; Taylor, Short, Shearer, & Frye, 2007; Taylor, Strait, & Medo, 1994) involves supplemental instruction for 20 minutes a day for five to seven struggling readers. The classroom teacher delivers the instruction in the classroom based on a three-day cycle. On the first day, the teacher reads a book to the entire class. He or she uses a 40- to 60-word retelling of the book printed on chart paper as the instructional text. The teacher and the students read and reread this retelling over the next three days. On day one, the teacher uses phonetically regular words from the retelling to develop phonemic awareness and knowledge of consonant sounds. On days two and three, the children write sentences about the story guided by the teacher. In addition to the 20 minutes with the teacher, the students practice rereading the story with an aide, volunteer, or partner. The length of the retelling gradually increases, and eventually actual books are used.

Reading Club

The Reading Club (Kreuger & Townshend, 1997) is a group intervention for first and second graders. Based on the structure and design of Reading Recovery, it involves daily 30-minute sessions. The session is carefully structured to include phonics, rereading, work with sentence strips, and the introduction of new reading. Each of these components is actually taught by different individuals. Because of the lack of adequate personnel, Kreuger and Townshend use retired educators, university students, and volunteers as coaches. However, each coach teaches the same daily segment, which simplifies training by the designers and allows the coaches to develop expertise and confidence in their coaching ability.

Literacy Booster Groups

Literacy Booster Groups (Mackenzie, 2001) are small-group interventions for first and second graders formed to review and apply strategies learned in Reading Recovery. The groups meet weekly for 30 to 45 minutes, each with two teachers. The lesson begins with one teacher helping the students choose four books to read during the week. While students choose books, write in their journals, or read independently, the teachers meet with them individually to check their oral reading proficiency. The teachers then present a minilesson based on the needs of the group and help the students engage in independent practice of the minilesson strategy.

Cross-Age Tutoring

This interesting and effective program (Taylor, Hanson, Justice-Swanson, & Watts, 1997) links small-group intervention with cross-age tutoring. Second-grade struggling readers participate in a seven-week intervention class that meets daily for 45 minutes. The first 30 minutes involve activities rotated according to a three-day cycle.

- On day one, the teacher reads a selection aloud, the students participate in choral reading, and the group discusses the selection.
- On day two, the students read chorally and with a partner and write sentences prompted and coached by the teacher.
- Day three includes more partner reading and sentence writing as well as independent reading. (This three-day cycle has been incorporated by teachers into their regular classroom activities.)
- For the last 15 minutes of the class, the teacher and students engage in language development activities, such as researching seasonal activities and creating a calendar.

The second graders also participate in a twice-weekly cross-age tutoring program. Fourth-grade tutors who are themselves struggling readers listen to the second graders read, coach them in word recognition, and read stories to them. The tutors spend two days preparing for the tutoring session, two days tutoring and debriefing, and one day writing about their experience. The cross-age tutoring continues for 14 weeks. Block and Dellamura (2000/2001) expand on this notion of cross-age tutoring and offer suggestions for journals, reflection forms, strategies checklists, and charting progress through records of reading and goal books.

The Anna Plan

The Anna Plan (Miles, Stegle, Hubbs, Henk, & Mallette, 2004) involves daily 25-minute instructional periods for all first and second graders. The classroom teacher and the class join three reading specialists in the "Reading Room." Students are grouped according to instructional reading levels and four groups operate simultaneously during the 25-minute session. The teacher and the three specialists each teach a group. Students remain with a teacher for two weeks and then move to another teacher. Groups are fluid and students move into and out of them based on their progress. At midyear, the second grade is discontinued and kindergarten children move into the program. Anna Plan activities are divided into days. On day one, the teacher introduces a new book. The students softly read aloud at their own pace and discuss their performance and the book's contents. The day two session focuses on reading comprehension, includes a language minilesson, and involves rereading of the day one book. The emphasis on day three is working with words using a variety of different activities. Day four involves journal writing. The teacher begins with a modeled minilesson and the students are encouraged to write about their own experiences. Day five allows for collaborative team planning. One of the specialists takes over the classroom so the teacher can come to the Reading Room during the regularly scheduled period to discuss student progress and plan for the next week's sessions.

Third Grade Intervention

The Third Grade Intervention (McCormack, Paratore, & Dahlene, 2004; McCormack & Paratore, 1999) goes against the assumption that struggling readers should be taught using text at their instructional level. While instructional text allows students to read words with relative ease, such text "may bar access to concepts and ideas otherwise acquired by reading grade-appropriate text" (McCormack, Paratore, & Dahlene, 2004, p. 119). Students may not acquire the concepts, vocabulary, and syntactical structures needed for success in later grades. The instruction is delivered outside of the regular classroom but is described as "pull-aside" rather than "pullout." Students read the regular classroom texts and, after returning to the classroom, are "reintegrated into ongoing literacy instruction" as full participants (p. 123). The hour-long instruction involves the following components: review and retelling of previously read material, introduction of essential vocabulary, word study including practice with sight words and strategies for decoding, previewing the new selection, teacher read-alouds using think-alouds to model comprehension strategies, discussion of the new text, rereading using a variety of oral reading strategies, and self-selected reading. After approximately a year of instruction, a majority of the students performed at grade level on several assessment measures.

Project Success

Project Success (Cooper, 1997) is an intervention for struggling readers in third grade and above. A group consists of approximately seven students who have daily 45-minute lessons that emphasize expository text. The students begin by reading a familiar book silently or orally with a partner. They then discuss the selection read on the previous day and construct a graphic organizer to demonstrate how the ideas in the text are connected. Before reading a new selection, the teacher prepares the students by using prereading strategies. The students read the new text silently, and then the teacher and students engage in reciprocal teaching. Reciprocal teaching is a format in which students take turns acting as the teacher and guiding their peers through the strategies of questioning, summarizing, clarifying, and predicting. Finally, the students write in response to the selection or as a reflection on their learning.

Group Tutoring Structures at the Middle Level

Readers' Workshop

This Readers' Workshop model (Williams, 2001) is for adolescent struggling readers. Groups of seven to eight students meet daily. For two days a week, Williams uses a traditional reading workshop format. The session begins with the teacher reading aloud to the students for 10 to 15 minutes, often employing a think-aloud strategy during this time. The next step is the 8- to 10-minute minilesson that focuses on strategy instruction. Each minilesson involves five components:

- A statement of what the strategy is and why it is important
- Teacher modeling
- Group or partner practice
- Reminders to use the strategy during silent reading time
- Silent reading for 15 minutes of self-selected texts

A final component involves students' sharing what they have read or what they have learned.

For the other three days, William structures the lessons around peer assisted learning strategies. Students work with partners, reading for five minutes each and helping each other with word identification and retelling. The partners again read for five minutes each, construct a short main idea statement, and summarize each paragraph. They then predict what will come next and read to check the accuracy of their predictions.

Taylor and Nesheim (2000/2001) used children's literature in an innovative application of the workshop model with adolescents in an alternative school. The model is driven by four goals: to present children's literature as enjoyable for readers of all ages, to provide motivation for reading children's literature, to model techniques for sharing reading, and to promote reading as a valued activity. Minilessons address such concepts as print conventions, procedures for small-group sharing, comprehension strategies, strategies for reading aloud, and techniques for fostering reader response.

Cross-Age Tutoring

A cross-age tutoring program (Jacobson, Thrope, Fisher, Lapp, Frey, & Flood, 2001) for seventh-grade less-proficient readers involves a five-day plan. On the first day, the teacher introduces and models the lesson that the tutors will use with their third-grade tutees. On the second day, the tutors are paired with students who practice reading the selection as well as learning the meaning of five difficult words. On days three and four, the tutors teach the lesson to two students in two different third-grade classrooms. On the last day, the tutors discuss the successes and challenges of the lesson. Jacobson et al. report that, as the year progressed, tutors began to devise their own lessons with the assistance of the teacher.

Group Tutoring Structures at the High School Level

Cross-Age Tutoring

Paterson and Elliott (2006) designed a cross-age tutoring program for ninth- and tenth-grade struggling readers with the express purpose of overcoming "the attitudinal barriers of the older student by placing them in a leadership role as tutors for younger children thus implying high academic status and competence" (p. 379). The tutees were struggling second- and third-grade readers. The tutoring occurred within the context of a year-long high school remedial course. Prior to the cross-age tutoring, students practiced expressive reading of the books they would share. They were taught some basic strategies for tutoring reading and received a lesson plan to follow. Eventually the high school students wrote their own lesson plans involving phonics, context clues, sight words, paired and echo reading, and assorted comprehension strategies such as prediction, questioning, and summarizing.

Literacy Tutoring for Adolescents

Chandler-Olcott and Hinchman (2005) suggest a framework for tutoring sessions based on the belief that such programs "are most effective when sessions have a consistent structure and when tutors model the use and enjoyment of reading and writing strategies at each session" (p. 59). Based on a 30- to 40-minute session, they recommend four different approaches that allow tutors to help their student in various ways. The first section (5–10 minutes) involves the tutor reading aloud and thinking aloud with a focus on one or two strategies. In this segment, the tutor models and demonstrates a literacy strategy that will be helpful to students. The next 10–15 minute section entails guided practice in the strategy modeled by the teacher. Then for 10 or 15 minutes, the students engage in independent reading or writing. The session closes with a 5-minute oral or written reflection by the student describing what was learned and what is still not understood.

Classroom Intervention Structures

Intervention as Part of the Literacy Block

An in-class intervention program for struggling third graders (Short, Kane, & Peeling, 2000) is part of the daily literacy block. While the teacher meets with a small group, other students listen to taped books, write, work on making words, or read alone or with a partner. The structure of the daily 25-minute group work involves three components: rereading of familiar texts, shared and guided reading, and shared and guided writing. Students first re-read previously read selections for about 7 minutes. The next component, shared and guided reading, takes about 15 minutes and involves several steps. First, the children again reread familiar text. Next, the teacher chooses a new book at their instructional level and introduces it using the strategy of prediction. The children read the first page silently and then aloud, with the teacher reinforcing cues for word identification and comprehension. In this way, word study is integrated into the guided-reading process. Then the students read independently while the teacher works with an individual student. In the 10-minute shared writing segment, the teacher guides the students to compose a sentence about the story. While the teacher writes the sentence on chart paper guided by student input on letters, word chunks, and punctuation, the students transfer it to their journals. They then reread the sentence, pointing to each word.

Classroom Structures That Foster the Growth of Struggling Readers

Interventions are specifically designed to meet the needs of students and are based on an informal reading inventory assessment or some other assessment tool. Unfortunately, there are always situations that prevent a student from receiving individualized assessment and some form of specialized literacy intervention. Some students do not meet school or district criteria for special instruction, and roadblocks such as budget, scheduling, and availability of personnel often interfere. This is why it is so important to design our classrooms to provide the best possible instruction for all readers. Like an intervention, the classroom should provide a balanced approach to literacy instruction. Direct or explicit teaching of strategies for word identification, vocabulary, and comprehension should be balanced with authentic reading and writing activities. Teachers should read to students every day and provide extended time for them to select and read texts at their instructional or independent reading levels. Although a variety of programs exemplify these principles, we include descriptions of those that offer concrete models that a teacher can implement without extensive training or the purchase of specialized materials. The following programs are not interventions as we have defined the term, but they effectively support the needs of struggling readers in the classroom.

The Four Block Model

This model (Cunningham, Hall, & Defee, 1991; Cunningham, Hall, & Defee, 1998; Hall, Prevatte, & Cunningham, 2007) is an extremely successful structure for accommodating readers of widely varying ability levels. Originally designed for first grade, it has been expanded to other grade levels. The model involves four 30-minute blocks of time, each with a different focus: guided reading, self-selected reading, writing, and working with words. In the guided-reading block, the teacher emphasizes comprehension. Using a basal anthology or multiple copies of trade books, the students read alone, with partners, in groups, or as an entire class while the teacher focuses on comprehension strategies. In the self-selected reading block, the students choose their own books to read. In the writing block, the teacher thinks aloud and writes in full view of the students. Following this explicit modeling, the students write independently. The working-with-words block focuses on a display of high-frequency words called a *word wall* and manipulation of letter tiles to make words.

Fluency Oriented Instruction

This model (Stahl & Heubach, 2005; Stahl & Heubach, 1993) involves restructuring a second-grade classroom to accommodate students of varying reading levels. For each selection in the basal anthology, the teacher follows a prescribed sequence. First, he or she reads the story to the class and guides their discussion. Then the students reread the entire selection or parts of it at least five times before moving to the next selection. Students engage in shared reading with partners or in small groups, and they echo-read with the teacher. They practice favorite parts to read orally to their peers, and they dramatize some selections, with individual students or small groups taking different parts. Students also take books home to read to their parents. Self-selected reading at the students' independent and instructional reading levels is also an important and daily component of this classroom structure.

Reader's Workshop

A popular classroom structure that allows for a balanced and individualized approach, Reader's Workshop (Atwell, 1998; Caldwell & Ford, 2002) is built around five components: focus lessons that are often called minilessons, sustained reading, student response, conferencing, and sharing. Focus lessons are relatively brief, about ten minutes in duration, and are whole group and teacher directed. There are three general kinds of minilessons. Procedural lessons center on instruction about workshop procedures such as how to fill out a response log or different ways to share reading with peers. Literary lessons can focus on different titles and authors and strategies for book choices to expose students to different genres and stylistic techniques. Skill/strategy lessons focus on direct instruction of word identification, vocabulary, and comprehension strategies. Following the minilesson, students engage in sustained reading of text they can handle successfully. Sometimes all students are reading different texts, and sometimes small groups are reading the same text. The next step is response time, during which students respond to their reading in a variety of ways. A common format for this is the response journal or the reading log. Conferencing involves peer conferences, in which students talk about their reading with peers, and teacher conferences with individual readers. Finally, students share their reading with the entire class. The reader's workshop format has been shown to be effective with students of all ages.

Sixth Grade Reading Class

Ahrens (2005) designed and implemented a structure for sixth-grade reading classes because of teacher dissatisfaction with the existing reading program. Students were grouped according to instructional level into nine separate classes which included two classes of students reading at or above level and seven classes that included below-level readers. The daily schedule included five components. At the beginning of the class, 20 minutes was spent in independent reading of self-selected books. Following this, one student engaged in a 5-minute book talk. For students reading at or below a third-grade level, 10 minutes focused on systematic instruction in phonics. All students participated in 5 minutes of spelling instruction that centered on morphemes and syllabication as opposed to memorization. Comprehension instruction took 10 minutes with a focus on one comprehension strategy for at least two to three weeks. The times for these activities were adjusted depending on reading level. Students above third-grade level spent 5 additional minutes in self-selected independent reading and comprehension instruction. Those minutes were devoted to phonics instruction for students below the third-grade level.

Memphis Comprehension Framework

This model focuses on achieving higher expository comprehension for middle school students (Flynt & Cooter, 2005). It involves three steps: preplanning, focused read-alouds and discussion, and three levels of retellings. In the preplanning stage, teachers assess student reading and create a profile of student strengths and needs. They choose a comprehension skill objective and agree to focus on this for a minimum of three weeks. In step two, teachers read aloud daily for at least 10 to 15 minutes for the purpose of expanding the students' listening and speaking vocabularies. The teacher reads expository selections at least twice a week and narratives at least once a week. Then the teacher initiates an active discussion of the text focusing on the comprehension skill objective and using teacher modeling, graphic organizers, key questions, and attention to new vocabulary. The final step focuses on three forms of retelling: guided oral retelling, graphic organizer retelling, and written retelling. In guided oral retelling, students retell the text. In graphic organizer retelling, the students place written words in a graphic organizer. The final step is using the graphic organizer as a tool for completing a written summary of the selection.

Schoolwide Intervention

Reading Acceleration Program

The Reading Acceleration Program (RAP) is a K–8 schoolwide intervention aimed at low-income English language learners (Feazell, 2004). It specifically focuses on teaching decoding and fluency skills and not the total language arts program; comprehension skills are addressed elsewhere in a language arts block. An important component of the program is use of the neurological impress method (Heckelman, 1969) in which a fluent reader and a struggling reader read orally together. Special education and general education teachers at each grade level collaborate in choosing students to participate and the instructional groups maintain a 7:1 student–teacher ratio.

The program involves six components. Each session begins with phonemic awareness training involving a musical or rhythmic activity. The next activity involves dictation of ten phonetically similar words and one to three sentences. Teachers offer ongoing feedback during practice sessions and assess student progress on a weekly basis. The group of seven students and the teacher then read books containing the sound practiced each week. They read together orally using neurological impress strategies. After rereading each page three times, the teacher asks two or three students to read aloud together. RAP also fosters exposure to grade-level literature. Students listen to the current literature session at their grade level on audiocassettes and read along with the tape using the impress method. This allows RAP students to participate in discussion and vocabulary activities with their classmates during their regular language arts block. The students take the audiotapes home for additional practice. Throughout the instructional sequence, teachers attempt to elicit positive emotion in the students through feedback, frequent encouragement, and modeling of their own enjoyment of reading.

Designing Your Own Structure

We have summarized a variety of different intervention structures, indicating their format as pullout or in-class and as individual or group. We have indicated the length of the instructional session and the number of weekly meetings. We have described the broad categories of activities that make up each lesson. Now it is time for you to design the structure that best fits your needs.

Perhaps your first decision will involve format. The majority of structures involve a pullout format, and their success suggests that pullout interventions can be very effective under certain circumstances. However, an educator can easily incorporate these structures into the classroom as part of a flexible grouping arrangement. Any of these intervention structures can be used by the classroom teacher on a daily basis. Reading specialists and other support personnel can also use a chosen structure to implement within the classroom and work with the classroom teacher to deliver needed intervention without pulling students out. In other words, pullout structures can become pullin structures if such an arrangement best fits your needs. If you decide on a pullout format, hopefully it will not replace the student's regular classroom literacy activities.

Perhaps the most important issue is the structure itself. What are those broad categories of instruction that you will address during each lesson, and which will receive the greatest emphasis? Which framework will best suit the needs of your students? The interventions that focus on first and second graders are designed to move logographic readers into the alphabetic stage or to expand knowledge of letter and sound relationships for alphabetic readers. They blend word identification with fluency development and reading for meaning. Interventions designed for older students emphasize comprehension strategies but with a strong focus on self-selected reading of new and familiar text.

Some decisions regarding intervention structure will be constrained by budget considerations, availability of resource personnel, and school scheduling. However, you should make every effort to schedule your intervention lessons as frequently as possible and with the smallest possible group size. Caldwell, Fromm, and O'Connor (1997/1998) had only a limited amount of resources to devote to an intervention program. They wanted to schedule daily lessons for 45 minutes, but in order to do this they would have had to work with groups of five students. Because they felt that smaller groups would be more effective, they settled for two students for 30-minute sessions four days a week. In other words, they compromised their preferences but still designed an effective intervention program.

Perhaps you have decided to use volunteer tutors. Wasik (1998) delineates several principles of effective volunteer programs. First, it is important that you carefully and consistently supervise and support the tutors. You must train them, regularly observe them, and provide supportive feedback. It is your role to design the tutoring structure, decide on specific instructional activities, and provide needed materials. Carefully structure and balance the tutoring session to contain basic components such as word analysis, writing, rereading, and introducing new stories. Materials should be appealing, and assessment of students should be ongoing. Tutoring should be intensive and consistent. It is important that tutors attend regularly and be aware of the commitment that they are making. Finally, if at all possible coordinate the tutoring with classroom instruction. Does all this sound somewhat daunting? It probably does. However, tutoring programs can be very effective and often allow you to service a larger number of struggling readers.

Once you have the structure in place and you have dealt with scheduling and resource issues, you can turn your attention to specific activities to fill each time slot. Table 3.1 on pages 38–40 provides a summary of the intervention structures that we discussed in this chapter. The next chapters will offer suggestions for a variety of activities for developing word identification, fluency, and comprehension within your chosen structure.

Application to English Language Learners

Two of the structures described in this chapter were specifically designed for English language learners, notably Reading Rescue and the schoolwide Reading Accelerated Program. However, because of their focus on a balanced approach to literacy intervention, other structures could also be used effectively to build the literacy competence of English language learners. Such structures emphasize reading and writing for meaning, use of text that

TABLE 3.1   Structures for Instruction of Struggling Readers

Intervention	Format	Grade	Time	Lesson Structure					
Reading Recovery	Individual pullout	First grade	Daily for 30 minutes	Rereading familiar books	Letter identification and word analysis activities	Writing to sounds	Reading cut-up sentences	Introduction of new book using prediction	Reading of new book
Early Steps	Individual pullout	First grade	Daily for 30 minutes	Rereading familiar books (8 to 10 minutes)	Picture and word sorting (5 to 6 minutes)	Writing to sounds (5 to 8 minutes)	Reading cut-up sentences	Introduction of new book using prediction	Reading of new book
Book Buddies	Individual pullout	First grade	Twice a week for 45 minutes	Rereading familiar books	Using words from reading to form a word bank	Word sorting	Writing to sounds	Introduction of new book	Choral and echo reading of new book
Reading Rescue	Individual pullout	First grade	Daily for 30 to 40 minutes	Rereading familiar books	Word analysis and comprehension strategies	Phonological awareness and phonics instruction	Writing	Comprehension and vocabulary	Language development with new book
Howard Street Tutoring Model	Individual pullout	Second and third grade	Twice weekly for 45 minutes	Instructional-level reading: echo, partner, independent (18 minutes)	Word categorization and games (10 minutes)	Easy reading (10 minutes)	Reading to the child (7 minutes)		
Morris, Ervin, & Conrad, 1996	Individual pullout	Sixth grade	Summer: one hour a day for 14 days; school year: one hour a week	Teacher and student alternate reading; informal comprehension checks	Word sorts, spelling, and word games	Student selects writing topic; teacher helps with revision	Rereading of easy material and graphing of reading accuracy		
Hedrick & Pearish, 1999	Group pullout	First grade	Daily for 30 minutes	Teacher reads aloud	Word study	Shared and guided reading	Independent reading		
Boulder Project	Group pullout	First grade	Daily for 30 minutes	Shared and individual reading of previously read book	Review of words from previous lesson	Introduction of new book	Reading and discussion of new book	Transforming words	Writing sentences related to book

Program	Setting	Grade	Frequency							
Early Intervention in Reading	Group in class	First grade	Daily for 20 minutes	Day one: Teacher reads retelling of book previously read to entire class; students reread	Day one: word study using phonetically regular words from retelling	Days two and three: Students reread retelling and write sentences guided by teacher	Daily: Students practice rereading with volunteer, aide, or partner			
Reading Club	Group pullout	First and second grade	Daily for 30 minutes	Phonics	Rereading	Working with sentence strips	New reading			
Literacy Booster Groups	Group pullout	First and second grade	30 to 45 minutes once a week	Book choice	Journal writing or independent reading	Individual assessment of students	Minilesson	Minilesson practice		
Taylor, Hanson, Justice, Swanson, & Watts, 1997	Group pullout	Second grade	Daily for 45 minutes for seven weeks	Day one: Teacher reads aloud; students chorally read; students discuss	Day two: choral reading, partner reading, and sentence writing	Day three: partner reading, sentence writing, and independent reading	Language development activities	Participation in cross-age tutoring twice a week		
Anna Plan	Group pullout	Kindergarten, first and second grade	Daily	Day one: Introduction of new book	Day two: Discussion of new book	Day three: Word work	Day four: Journal writing	Day five: Team planning		
Third Grade Intervention	Group "pull-aside"	Third grade	Daily for one hour	Review and retelling of previously read text	Introduction to essential vocabulary	Word study: sight words and decoding strategies	Teacher read-aloud with modeling of comprehension strategies	Student discussion	Rereading	Self-selected reading
Cooper	Group pullout	Third grade and above	Daily for 45 minutes for seven weeks	Students read a familiar book	Students discuss previous day's selection and construct a graphic organizer	Teacher introduces new selection using prereading strategies	Students read new text silently	Teacher and students engage in reciprocal teaching		

(continued)

TABLE 3.1 *Continued*

Intervention	Format	Grade	Time	Lesson Structure				
Williams	Group pullout	Middle school	Daily for the school year	Days one and two: Teacher reads aloud	Days one and two: Teacher presents minilesson	Days one and two: self-selected silent reading	Days three, four, and five: peer-assisted learning	
Tutoring Session for Adolescents	Individual or group pullout	Middle and high school	30–40 minutes per lesson, as needed	Read-alouds and think-alouds by the teacher (5–10 minutes)	Guided practice of the modeled strategy (10–15 minutes)	Independent reading or writing (10–15 minutes)	Oral or written reflection (5 minutes)	
Jacobson, Thrope, Fisher, Lapp, Frey, & Flood, 2001	Group pullout	Middle school	Daily	Day one: Teacher introduces and models tutoring lesson	Day two: Students practice the lesson	Day three: Students tutor third graders	Day four: Students tutor third graders	Day five: Students discuss lesson success and challenges
Short, Kane, & Peeling, 2000	Group in class	Third grade	Daily for 25 minutes	Rereading of familiar text	Introduction of new book	Reading of new book with teacher coaching on word identification	Independent reading	Shared writing
Sixth Grade Reading Class	Group in-class	Sixth grade	Daily for 50 minutes	Independent reading for 20–25 minutes	Book talk for 5 minutes	Systematic phonics instruction for 10 minutes for students below a third-grade level	Spelling instruction for 5 minutes emphasizing morphemes and syllabication	Comprehension instruction for 10–15 minutes emphasizing one strategy for at least two to three weeks
Reading Acceleration Program	Group pullout	K–8	Daily	Phonemic awareness training using music and rhythm	Dictation of words and sentences	Oral reading of phonics readers using neurological impress	Oral reading of grade-level text using neurological impress	

students can read or comprehend successfully, and provision of time for word study and fluency development.

Application to Adolescent Learners

Since the first edition of this book, interest in intervention for adolescent learners has increased. Deshler, Palincsar, Biancarosa, and Nair (2007) closely examined 48 adolescent literacy programs and grouped them by the following categories: types of students served, program features, and methods of program evaluation. For each program, they describe the instructional approach, the professional development needed to implement the program, and the nature and extent of program evaluation. This is a valuable resource for schools and districts who intend to purchase an already designed program. In addition, a number of articles and books have described successful strategies for helping older struggling readers and we will include these in subsequent chapters.

Response to Intervention

A consistent intervention structure is a critical component of the Response to Intervention model. In RTI, a student who is not performing at an acceptable level in the classroom moves into tier two instruction. At this point, additional assessment identifies specific needs and small-group instruction is designed to support the student in meeting these needs. The teacher carefully and frequently monitors student progress. The RTI model requires that instruction be based on research—that is, have a proven track record. The small-group interventions described in this chapter have been carefully evaluated for effectiveness with struggling readers and could be used in RTI tier 2 or tier 3 tutoring. In addition, the Deshler, Palincsar, Biancarosa, and Nair text (2007) can provide valuable insight into the extent of a program's research base.

A consistent structure offers an added advantage in RTI. Student progress or lack of it is often a function of the class structure as opposed to the class activities. That is, conflicting, variable, and unpredictable class structures may negatively affect student progress. By maintaining a consistent tutoring structure, the teacher can be relatively certain that it is the instruction that is affecting student growth.

Summary

A lesson plan has three components: objectives, an overall structure, and instructional activities for meeting the objectives. The overall structure is how you divide the plan into broad categories such as word study, fluency, and comprehension. It is important to maintain a consistent lesson structure, not only to make planning easier but also to provide a comforting support. Instead of worrying about what comes next in the lesson, you can devote your attention to the students and their needs. Students often blossom in a consistent framework and, if you use tutors, consistency fosters their confidence and effectiveness.

Isn't a consistent framework opposed to individualization? No: Individualization occurs through the time allotted to each category of activities, the instructional activities you employ, and the materials you choose.

A variety of structures exist. Some provide individual tutoring; others are designed with small groups in mind. The majority use a pullout format, and their effectiveness suggests that pullout can work under certain circumstances. Several structures focus on the entire class and on supporting struggling readers in their own classroom.

REFERENCES AND RECOMMENDED READINGS

Reading Recovery

Clay, M. M. (1993). *Reading recovery: A guidebook for teachers in training.* Portsmouth, NH: Heinemann.

Lyons, C. A., & Beaver, J. (2007). Reducing retention and learning disability placement through Reading Recovery: An educationally sound cost-effective choice. In R. L. Allington & S. A. Walmsley (Eds.), *No quick fix, the RTI edition: Rethinking literacy in America's elementary schools* (pp. 116–136). New York: Teachers College Press.

Pinnell, G. S. (1989). Reading recovery: Helping at-risk children learn to read. *The Elementary School Journal, 90,* 161–183.

Pinnell, G. S., Deford, D. E., & Lyons, C. A. (1988). *Reading recovery: Early intervention for at-risk first graders.* Arlington, VA: Educational Research Service.

Pinnell, G. S., Lyons, C. A., Deford, D. E., Bryk, A. S., & Seltzer, M. (1994). Comparing instructional models for the literacy education of high-risk first graders. *Reading Research Quarterly, 29,* 9–30.

Early Steps

Morris, D., Shaw, B., & Perney, J. (1990). Helping low readers in grades 2 and 3: An after school volunteer tutoring program. *Elementary School Journal, 91,* 133–150.

Santa, C. M., Ford, A., Mickley, A., & Parker, D. (1997). *Reading intervention for primary students: First steps.* Paper presented at International Reading Association Convention, Atlanta, GA.

Santa, C. M., & Hoien, T. (1999). An assessment of Early Steps: A program for early intervention. *Reading Research Quarterly, 34,* 54–79.

Book Buddies

Invernizzi, M., Juel, C., & Rosemary, C. A. (1996/1997). A community volunteer tutorial that works. *The Reading Teacher, 50,* 304–311.

Invernizzi, M., Rosemary, C. A., Juel, C., & Richards, H. C. (1997). At-risk readers and community volunteers: A three year perspective. *Journal of the Scientific Studies of Reading, 3,* 277–300.

Reading Rescue

Ehri, L. C., Dreyer, L. G., Flugman, B., & Gross, A. (2007). Reading Rescue: An effective tutoring intervention model for language-minority students who are struggling readers in first grade. *American Educational Research Journal, 44,* 414–448.

Howard Street Tutoring Model

Brown, K. J., Morris, D., & Fields, M. (2005). Intervention after grade 1: Serving increased numbers of struggling readers effectively. *Journal of Literacy Research,* 61–94.

Morris, D. (2005). *The Howard Street tutoring manual: Teaching at-risk readers in the primary grades.* New York: The Guilford Press.

Case Study of Sixth Grader

Morris, D., Ervin, C., & Conrad, K. (1996). A case study of middle school reading disability. *The Reading Teacher, 49,* 368–377.

First Grade Intervention

Hedrick, W. R., & Pearish, A. B. (1999). Good reading is more important than who provides the instruction or where it takes place. *The Reading Teacher, 52,* 716–726.

The Boulder Project

Hiebert, E. H. (1994). A small-group literacy intervention with Chapter I students. In E. H. Hiebert & B. Taylor (Eds.), *Getting reading right from the start: Effective early literacy interventions* (pp. 85–106). Boston: Allyn & Bacon.

Hiebert, E. F., Colt, J. M., Catto, S. L., & Gury, E. C. (1992). Reading and writing of first-grade students in a restructured Chapter I program. *American Educational Research Journal, 29,* 545–572.

Early Intervention in Reading

Taylor, B. M., Frye, B. J., Short, R., & Shearer, B. (1992). Classroom teachers prevent reading failure among low-achieving first-grade students. *The Reading Teacher, 45,* 592–597.

Taylor, B. M., Short, R., Shearer, B., & Frye, B. J. (2007). First grade teachers provide early reading intervention in the classroom. In R. Allington & S. Walmsley (Eds.), *No quick fix, the RTI edition: Rethinking literacy programs in America's elementary schools* (pp. 159–176). Newark, DE: International Reading Association.

Taylor, B. M., Strait, J., & Medo, M. A. (1994). Early intervention is reading: Supplemental instruction for groups of low-achieving students provided by first grade teachers. In E. H. Hiebert and B. M. Taylor (Eds.), *Getting reading right from the start: Effective early literacy interventions.* Boston: Allyn & Bacon.

Reading Club

Kreuger, E., & Townshend, N. (1997). Reading clubs boost second-language first graders' reading achievement. *The Reading Teacher, 51,* 122–128.

Literacy Booster Groups

Mackenzie, K. K. (2001). Using literacy booster groups to maintain and extend Reading Recovery success in the primary grades. *The Reading Teacher, 55,* 222–234.

Cross-Age Tutoring

Block, C. C., & Dellamura, R. J. (2000/2001). Better book buddies. *The Reading Teacher, 54,* 364–370.

Jacobson, J., Thrope, L., Fisher, D., Lapp, D., Frey, N., & Flood, J. (2001). Cross-age tutoring: A literacy improvement approach for struggling adolescent readers. *Journal of Adolescent and Adult Literacy, 44,* 528–535.

Paterson, P. O., & Elliott, L. N. (2006). Struggling reader to struggling reader: High school students' responses to a cross-age tutoring program. *Journal of Adolescent and Adult Literacy, 49,* 378–389.

Taylor, B. M., Hanson, B. E., Justice-Swanson, K., & Watts, S. M. (1997). Helping struggling readers: Linking small-group intervention with cross-age tutoring. *The Reading Teacher, 51,* 196–209.

The Anna Plan

Miles, P. A., Stegle, K. W., Hubbs, K. G., Henk, W. A., & Mallette, M. H. (2004). A whole-class support model for early literacy: The Anna Plan. *The Reading Teacher, 58,* 318–327.

Third Grade Intervention

McCormack, R. L., & Paratore, J. R. (1999). *"What do you do there anyway," teachers ask: A reading teacher's intervention using grade-level text with struggling third grade readers.* Paper presented at the National Reading Conference, Orlando, FL.

McCormack, R. L., Paratore, J. R., & Dahlene, K. F. (2004). Establishing instructional congruence across learning settings: One path to success for struggling third grade readers. In R. L. McCormack and J. R. Paratore (Eds.). *After early intervention, then what? Teaching struggling readers in grades 3 and beyond* (pp. 117–136). Newark, DE: International Reading Association.

Project Success

Cooper, J. D. (1997). *Project success: Literacy intervention for grades 3–6.* Paper presented at International Reading Association Convention, Atlanta, GA.

Reader's Workshop

Atwell, N. (1998). *In the middle: New understandings of writing, reading, and learning.* Portsmouth, NH: Boynton/Cook.

Caldwell, J. S., & Ford, M. P. (2002). *Where have all the bluebirds gone? How to soar with flexible grouping.* Portsmouth, NH: Heinemann.

Taylor, S. V., & Nesheim, D. W. (2000/2001). Making literacy real for "high-risk" adolescent emerging readers: An innovative application of reader's workshop. *Journal of Adolescent and Adult Literacy, 44,* 308–318.

Williams, M. (2001). Making connections: A workshop for adolescents who struggle with reading. *Journal of Adolescent and Adult Literacy, 44,* 588–602.

Literacy Tutoring for Adolescents

Chandler-Olcott, K., & Hinchman, K. A. (2005). *Tutoring adolescent literacy learners: A guide for volunteers.* New York: The Guilford Press.

Intervention as Part of Literacy Block

Short, R. A., Kane, M., & Peeling, T. (2000). Retooling the reading lesson: Matching the right tools to the job. *The Reading Teacher, 54,* 284–295.

The Four Block Model

Cunningham, P. M., Hall, D. P., & Defee, M. (1991). Nonability-grouped, multilevel instruction: A year in a first grade classroom. *The Reading Teacher, 44,* 566–571.

Cunningham, P. M., Hall, D. P., & Defee, M. (1998). Nonability-grouped, multilevel instruction: Eight years later. *The Reading Teacher, 51,* 652–654.

Hall, D. P., Prevatte, C., & Cunningham, P. M. (2007). Eliminating ability grouping and reducing failure in the pri-

mary grades. In R. Allington & S. Walmsley (Eds.), *No quick fix, the RTI edition: Rethinking literacy programs in America's elementary schools* (pp. 137–159). New York: Teachers College Press.

Fluency Oriented Reading Instruction

Stahl, S. A., & Heubach, K. (1993). *Changing reading instruction in second grade: A fluency oriented program.* University of Georgia: National Reading Research Center.

Stahl, S. A., & Heubach, K. M. (2005). Fluency-oriented reading instruction. *Journal of Literacy Research, 37,* 25–60.

Sixth Grade Reading Program

Ahrens, B. C. (2005). Finding a new way: Reinventing a sixth-grade reading program. *Journal of Adolescent and Adult Literacy, 48,* 642–654.

Memphis Comprehension Framework

Flynt, E. S., & Cooter, R. B. (2005). Improving middle-grades reading in urban schools: The Memphis Comprehension Framework. *The Reading Teacher, 58,* 774–780.

Reading Acceleration Program

Feazell, V. S. (2004). Reading Acceleration Program: A schoolwide intervention. *The Reading Teacher, 58,* 66–72.

Heckelman, R. G. (1969). A neurological impress method of remedial reading instruction. *Academic Therapy, 5,* 277–282.

Other Recommended Readings

Caldwell, J., Fromm, M., & O'Connor, V. (1997/1998). Designing an intervention for poor readers: Incorporating the best of all worlds. *Wisconsin State Reading Association Journal, 41,* 7–14.

Deshler, D. D., Palincsar, A. S., Biancarosa, G., & Nair, M. (2007). *Informed choices for struggling adolescent readers: A research-based guide for instructional programs and practices.* Newark, DE: International Reading Association.

Diehl, H. L. (2005). Snapshots of our journey to thoughtful literacy. *The Reading Teacher, 59,* 56–69.

Massey, D. D. (2007). "The Discovery Channel said so" and other barriers to comprehension. *The Reading Teacher, 60,* 656–666.

McKenna, M. C. (2002). *Help for struggling readers: Strategies for grades 3–8.* New York: The Guilford Press.

Morrow, L. M., & Woo, D. G. (2001). *Tutoring programs for struggling readers: The America reads challenge.* New York: The Guilford Press.

Schnorr, R. F., & Davern, L. (2005). Creating exemplary literacy classrooms through the power of teaming. *The Reading Teacher, 58,* 494–506.

Wasik, B. A. (1998). Using volunteers as reading tutors: Guidelines for successful practices. *The Reading Teacher, 51,* 562–573.

4

Phonological Awareness

What Is Phonological Awareness and Why Is It Important?

Phonological awareness is the understanding that our language contains units of sound (phones) that vary in size. Some of the units include many phones (i.e., the syllable), and others include only one. Children learn to distinguish larger units before smaller units. There are three types of phonological structure that are important for reading development (Goswami, 2000):

1. *Syllable*—a phonological unit of sounds that must include a vowel sound
2. *Onset-rime*—two phonological units of sound *within* a syllable defined by the phonemes that precede the vowel sound (i.e., onset, such as *bl*) and the vowel sound and the sounds that follow it (i.e., rime, such as -*ack*)
3. *Phoneme*—the smallest unit of sound represented by a single letter (e.g., /p/)

The terms *phonological awareness* and *phonemic awareness* have often been used interchangeably. However, phonological awareness is the larger category in which phonemic awareness, the recognition that words can be segmented into constituent sounds, is one component (Goswami, 2000).

The development of phonological awareness at the syllable, onset-rime, and phoneme levels has been studied extensively in the past 30 years. Liberman and colleagues (1974) gave students wooden dowels and asked them to tap the number of syllables or phonemes heard, ranging from one to three. They found that 46 percent of the four-year-old students were able to tap the number of syllables correctly six consecutive times, but were unable to tap the number of phonemes. However, 70 percent of six-year-old students were able to correctly tap the number of phonemes six consecutive times. The six-year-olds had been learning to read for a year. Liberman and colleagues (1974) concluded that syllable awareness develops prior to phonemic awareness and that the development of phonemic awareness is partially dependent on being taught to read.

The same–different judgment has been used to measure young children's phonological awareness at all three levels of phonological structure: the syllable, onset-rime, and phoneme. Students were asked to say whether spoken pairs of words shared sounds at the beginning or the end. Words could be alike at the first syllable (*play*ground–*play*thing), the onsets (*br*ake–*br*ain), or the initial phoneme (*f*arm–*f*eed), or they could be alike or at the ending syllable (susp*end*–up*end*), rime (m*ake*–t*ake*), or final phoneme (sto*p*–fla*p*). A comparison of the performance of four-, five-, and six-year-olds showed that all could correctly distinguish the similarity or difference between words differing at the syllable level, but only six-year-olds who had been learning to read for a year could correctly identify the similarity or difference at the onset-rime or phoneme level (Treiman & Zukowski, 1991). These results suggest that the development of phonological awareness occurs first at the syllable level, then at the onset-rime level, and finally at the phoneme level, which seems to require learning to read to develop (also see Goswami, 1999, for a review).

Phonological awareness is important because students who understand these abstract language components learn to read more quickly than students who do not. For example, several longitudinal studies have found that early rhyming skills are highly correlated with later reading and spelling ability (Bradley & Bryant, 1983; Bryant, Maclean, Bradley, & Crossland, 1990; Maclean, Bryant, & Bradley, 1987). The research on whether onset-rime segmentation and blending constitute a necessary intermediate stage between syllable awareness and phonemic awareness has yielded mixed results. According to Goswami (1999), the apparent contradiction in results is due to the early reading instruction of the participants. If children are being instructed at the phoneme level, they are better able to segment words into phonemes than at the onset-rime break. However, instruction in onset-rime segmentation and blending yields faster learning than does similar instruction at the phoneme level. Therefore, for children with little phonological development, the instructional progression of syllable to onset-rime to phoneme is recommended.

How Is Phonological Awareness Developed?

Many children learn about the phonological structure of language through oral interactions with their families. As they learn to speak, the type of oral language stimulation they receive influences not only the development of vocabulary but also of phonological awareness. The student whose family reads *A Children's First Book of Poetry* prior to bedtime exposes him or her to the rhyme and rhythm of our language. One of us received such a book from a colleague and had great fun reading many poems to her son, complete with expression and movement. To this day, if his mother begins a poem from this book, he can finish it. When students have been exposed to rhyming literature, you will hear them making up nonsense words that rhyme and laughing uproariously. Rich language exposure seems to lead to children's playing with the sounds of language. Rap is poetry and is found in music, so engaging children in learning lyrics of *some* songs is another way to develop awareness of rhyme. There is a wonderful poem by Eloise Greenfield (1988), called "Nathaniel's Rap," that children in an after-school tutoring program run by one of us loved. Like much of young children's language learning, the development of phonological awareness often occurs through oral language exposure, not through explicit instruction.

But what if students don't have those years of exposure? Although it is likely that when these children enter school they will have a less developed sensitivity to phonological structure (Elbro, Borstrum, & Petersen, 1998), a large body of research indicates that phonological awareness even at the most difficult level—the phoneme—can be taught (Ehri, Nunes, Willows, Schuster, Yaghoub-Zadeh, & Shanahan, 2001). The instruction can be playful and engaging, and it should be part of any preschool curriculum even if the teacher never refers to letters. Later on we will explain how instruction at various phonological levels should be connected to learning letter sounds, but in the preschool years much language learning can occur completely aurally.

Phonological Awareness and the Emergent Reader

Although phonological awareness continues to develop as students learn to read, the most important time for teachers to understand their students' phonological awareness is when the students are just learning to read. If a student cannot read even the simplest preprimer material with 90 percent accuracy and at least 70 percent comprehension, she or he is considered an emergent reader, independent of age. Students in this stage may understand many important aspects of the reading process, yet may not be able to read in the conventional sense. For example, students may be print aware (Clay, 1985)—that is, they may understand that print is read from left to right and from top to bottom. However, they may not be able to point to a word or point to a letter. Emergent readers may also have varying levels of understanding of the phonological structures of our language. They may or may not be able to rhyme or segment at the onset-rime break; they may know the phonemes represented by a few letters. Only by assessing these skills directly can we determine what is known.

As you can tell, the stage of emergent reading is quite broad and you *cannot* assume that if a student has developed print awareness she or he will have also developed phonological awareness. The development of these skills depends on the child's exposure to written versus oral language. The important components of phonological awareness to be assessed in emergent readers include

- *Rhyme*—words such as *man* and *can* sound alike at the end.
- *Alliteration*—the words *talk, terror, tell, table* all begin with the same sound.

● *Segmentation*—the sounds in words can be divided into units of varying sizes (syllables, onset-rime, phonemes).
● *Blending*—the component sounds in words (syllables, onset-rime, phonemes) can be joined to form words.

The Importance of Rhyme

The ability to recognize when words sound the same at the end is critical to learning to read. Rhyme is important because if a child understands it he or she can predict the words that are likely to come next in many books. You can probably think of a favorite nursery rhyme from your childhood. Why is it so easy to remember? In addition to having heard it many times, its rhyming pattern allows you to guess at words that you may not have stored in memory. For example, in "Humpty Dumpty" we remember that Humpty broke, so when we start the rhyme "Humpty Dumpty sat on a wall, Humpty Dumpty had a great _____," if we forget the exact word we at least know that it rhymes with *wall.* One of the books most frequently read to young children is *Goodnight Moon* (Brown, 1947). Many parents can recite that book without looking at it. Students who are read to learn these patterns of language and generate rhyming words and nonwords, which are often followed by peals of laughter. The books written by Dr. Seuss rhyme, and children love to hear them over and over.

Another rhyming book titled *Is Your Mama a Llama?* (Guarino, 1989) is often used when teaching students to read. This pattern-predictable book makes use of rhyming patterns and pictures to predict what animal will be on the next page. It shows students that they can use different types of picture and sound clues to predict what will come next. Perhaps we've convinced you that rhyming patterns are common in English. Is there another reason why learning to rhyme is advantageous to learning to read? Yes, the rhyme-rime connection.

The Rhyme–Rime–Spelling Pattern Connection

The relationship between the sound of words and their spellings is important in learning to read. If students understand that some words sound the same at the end, presumably it will be easier to teach them that words that sound the same at the end (rimes) are often spelled the same at the end as well. The written equivalent of the rime is called a *spelling pattern,* and it consists of the vowel and the letters within the syllable that follow it. If students understand that *cat, mat, flat,* and *bat* rhyme, it should be easier for them to learn to read and spell those words using the *-at* spelling pattern. This is one example of a reciprocal relationship between phonological awareness and learning to read. We know that being phonologically aware is beneficial for learning to read and that learning to read increases phonological awareness. Techniques for teaching students how to use rhyme to read words with the same spelling pattern will be explained in depth in Chapter 5, on word identification.

Assessment of Rhyme Knowledge

There are many ways to assess whether the student understands what it means for words to sound alike at the end. One of the most commonly used is a same–different task, in which the student is asked to tell the examiner whether or not two words rhyme. The definition of rhyme and examples of rhyming words are given (e.g., *can, man*), as well as examples of nonrhyming words (e.g., *dog, stone*). Then the examiner reads a list of word pairs and asks the student if they rhyme. For example, "Do *make* and *bake* rhyme?" "Do *flag* and *pot* rhyme?" Yopp (1988) presents data demonstrating the reliability and validity of this rhyming task—it was the easiest of the phonological tasks that Yopp investigated with kindergarten children. However, the average (mean) score was only about 70 percent correct on the twenty items, indicating that children's rhyming knowledge is not complete by the end of kindergarten. For this reason, teachers should assess all beginning readers' knowledge of rhyme.

The Informal Reading Inventory as an Indicator of Rhyme Knowledge

If you gave a preprimer word list and story on an informal reading inventory and the student did not read accurately enough to have a preprimer instructional reading level, then it is important to assess his or her awareness of the phonological structure of language. This recommendation applies regardless of the age of the student. Students in the later elementary grades who have severe reading problems still do not have well-developed phonological awareness (Brady, 1997; Elbro, Borstrøm, & Petersen, 1998). You can obtain a copy of Yopp's (1988) 20-item rhyming task, or you can design your own using words from the *Qualitative Reading Inventory-4* word list (Leslie & Caldwell, 2006). To ensure that the teacher-made test is reliable, choose a minimum of 15 items.

Assessing Rhyme Using Informal Reading Inventory Words

Several words on the preprimer and primer word lists in the *QRI-4* would be familiar to children. A teacher might make up a same–different rhyming task by saying, "I'm going to say two words, and I want you to tell me if they sound the same at the end. For example, *cat* and *fat* sound the same at the end because both have the *-at* sound. But *cat* and *walk* don't sound the same at the end. I'm going to say two words, and I want you to tell me if they sound the same at the end."

*can–make	(no)	*keep–sheep	(yes)
*at–bat	(yes)	need–neat	(no)
*he–go	(no)	*not–plot	(yes)
in–pin	(yes)	*thing–thin	(no)
*make–cake	(yes)	saw–paw	(yes)
place–plant	(no)	*like–height	(no)
see–we	(yes)	live–give	(yes)
help–shelf	(no)		

Assessing Rhyme Production

The teacher might also assess rhyme by asking the student to say a word that sounds the same at the end using a subset of the words just listed and marked with an asterisk. For example, the teacher would say, "I'm going to say a word, and I want you to tell me another word that sounds the same at the end. For example, if I said *frog* you could say *dog* or *hog*. Can you give me a word that sounds the same as *keep* and *bat* at the end?" The same–different rhyming task and the rhyme production task are two methods that tap somewhat different aspects of rhyming. If the student does well or poorly on them, we know that he or she does or does not understand rhyme. If the child does well on one task and poorly on the other, the teacher should explain the concept and give examples and nonexamples. He or she might say, "When two words sound the same at the end, we say they rhyme. So the words *cat* and *fat* rhyme, but the words *cat* and *fan* do not. Other words that rhyme with *cat* are *sat, flat, pat,* and *mat.* And some words that rhyme with *fan* are *man, pan, can, tan,* and *van.*" After such instruction the teacher should reassess the student's understanding.

Activities That Teach Rhyme Aurally

Yopp and Yopp (2000) describe an entertaining game for learning rhymes that follows a reading of the book *The Hungry Thing* (Slepian & Seidler, 1967). The creature in the book wears a sign that says FEED ME, but has trouble pronouncing words, so the townspeople try to figure out what it wants to eat. For example, it says, "schmancakes" and a boy in the town says two nonsense words that rhyme with "schmancakes," then says the correct word, pancakes. The structure of the boy's sentence is the *monster's word;* sounds like *nonsense word;* sounds like *new nonsense word;* sounds like *correct word.* Students in an intervention group or in the classroom are encouraged to predict what the creature wants to eat while the teacher reads the book. Afterwards they are encouraged to choose a picture from a bag (e.g., a hamburger) and make up nonsense rhyming words (e.g., *samburger, bamburger*) that are clues to the real word. The students then have to guess each other's word (*hamburger*).

There are many songs that can be used to teach rhyme aurally (Yopp & Yopp, 1996). For example, students can modify "Down by the Bay." The format of the verse is "Did you ever see a _____ with a _____?" The first blank refers to an animal, and the second blank refers to some characteristic. For example, "Did you ever see a cat wearing a fireman's hat?" The students can make up their own lines: *Did you ever see a dog riding on a frog?* This encouragement to make up their own rhymes allows students to develop a sense of rhyme through enjoyable activities.

Reading books can also be a natural way for parents and teachers to encourage rhyme. When reading a rhyming book, stop before the second rhyming word and ask the child what word she or he thinks is coming next. With each success in guessing the correct word, the child will gain confidence. Table 4.1 is a list of books that are useful for teaching phonological awareness, including rhyme.

Connecting Rhyme and Spelling Patterns: Analytic Phonics

An understanding of rhyme can be a powerful tool for teaching reading. Once students understand that words can *sound* alike at the end, it is easier to teach them that these words are often *spelled* the same at the end, too. For example, once students understand that *cat, bat,* and *hat* rhyme, we can teach them that these words are spelled the same at the end with the -*at* spelling pattern. Because some spelling patterns occur much more often than others, it has been recommended that students learn the most common ones first (Leslie & Calhoon, 1995), as listed in Table 4.2 on page 52. As an example, because -*at* is common, a teacher can begin by teaching the student the word *cat,* a high-frequency word with that spelling pattern. Then the student can participate in an activity called *word building,* which involves giving him or her the spelling pattern written on an index card, along with single consonants that, when added to the spelling pattern, yield real words. The teacher might give -*at* with the consonants *h, m, f,* and *b,* and then either ask the student to make as many words as he or she can or provide a clue and ask the student to build the correct word. For example, "This is a word that rhymes with *cat,* and I wear it on my head." The student should build the word *hat.* The use of known words with common spelling patterns to read and spell unfamiliar words with the same spelling patterns is called *reading by analogy.* This method of teaching phonics utilizes words that are already familiar to the student as a basis for instruction.

Techniques for teaching students how to decode unknown words by analogy to known words with the same spelling pattern will be explained in depth in Chapter 5, on word identification.

𝒫honological Awareness Instruction

- Be sure that you are clear on your goals for the lesson. If you are teaching rhyme, all of the words must end with the same sounds, and there should be no other skills required that the student doesn't know.
- Lessons should be short and move at a rapid pace. That is, you should explain briefly and clearly the concept being taught and then involve students right away to see if they understand what was explained.

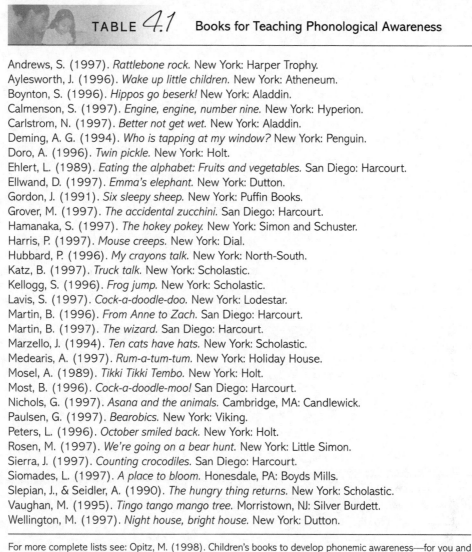

TABLE 4.1 Books for Teaching Phonological Awareness

Andrews, S. (1997). *Rattlebone rock*. New York: Harper Trophy.
Aylesworth, J. (1996). *Wake up little children*. New York: Atheneum.
Boynton, S. (1996). *Hippos go beserk!* New York: Aladdin.
Calmenson, S. (1997). *Engine, engine, number nine*. New York: Hyperion.
Carlstrom, N. (1997). *Better not get wet*. New York: Aladdin.
Deming, A. G. (1994). *Who is tapping at my window?* New York: Penguin.
Doro, A. (1996). *Twin pickle*. New York: Holt.
Ehlert, L. (1989). *Eating the alphabet: Fruits and vegetables*. San Diego: Harcourt.
Ellwand, D. (1997). *Emma's elephant*. New York: Dutton.
Gordon, J. (1991). *Six sleepy sheep*. New York: Puffin Books.
Grover, M. (1997). *The accidental zucchini*. San Diego: Harcourt.
Hamanaka, S. (1997). *The hokey pokey*. New York: Simon and Schuster.
Harris, P. (1997). *Mouse creeps*. New York: Dial.
Hubbard, P. (1996). *My crayons talk*. New York: North-South.
Katz, B. (1997). *Truck talk*. New York: Scholastic.
Kellogg, S. (1996). *Frog jump*. New York: Scholastic.
Lavis, S. (1997). *Cock-a-doodle-doo*. New York: Lodestar.
Martin, B. (1996). *From Anne to Zach*. San Diego: Harcourt.
Martin, B. (1997). *The wizard*. San Diego: Harcourt.
Marzello, J. (1994). *Ten cats have hats*. New York: Scholastic.
Medearis, A. (1997). *Rum-a-tum-tum*. New York: Holiday House.
Mosel, A. (1989). *Tikki Tikki Tembo*. New York: Holt.
Most, B. (1996). *Cock-a-doodle-moo!* San Diego: Harcourt.
Nichols, G. (1997). *Asana and the animals*. Cambridge, MA: Candlewick.
Paulsen, G. (1997). *Bearobics*. New York: Viking.
Peters, L. (1996). *October smiled back*. New York: Holt.
Rosen, M. (1997). *We're going on a bear hunt*. New York: Little Simon.
Sierra, J. (1997). *Counting crocodiles*. San Diego: Harcourt.
Siomades, L. (1997). *A place to bloom*. Honesdale, PA: Boyds Mills.
Slepian, J., & Seidler, A. (1990). *The hungry thing returns*. New York: Scholastic.
Vaughan, M. (1995). *Tingo tango mango tree*. Morristown, NJ: Silver Burdett.
Wellington, M. (1997). *Night house, bright house*. New York: Dutton.

For more complete lists see: Opitz, M. (1998). Children's books to develop phonemic awareness—for you and parents, too! *The Reading Teacher, 51*, 526–528.

Yopp, H. (1995). Read-aloud books for developing phonemic awareness: An annotated bibliography. *The Reading Teacher, 48*, 538–542.

- Be sure to involve students as much as possible by using manipulatives and having them create something. Students' attention lasts longer if they are doing something, such as matching pictures whose names rhyme. For example, if given a set of pictures of a *dog*, a *frog*, a *cat*, a *bat*, a *can*, and a *fan*, the student is to put them into rhyming pairs.

Sample Lesson: Rhyming

Let's assume that the group of students you are teaching knows which letters are consonants and which are vowels. The goal of the lesson is to teach them the concept of rhyme and to associate it with making real words. The materials required for the lesson include the alphabet posted in the room, index cards with *-at*, and three blank index cards for each pair of students.

Explicit Instruction and Modeling from the Teacher. "Today you are going to learn what the word *rhyme* means. When words sound alike at the end, we say that they rhyme.

TABLE 4.2 Basic Spelling Patterns Based on Frequency of Pattern in Our Language

Week	Spelling Pattern			
1	in	and	up	
2	king	long	jump	
3	let	pig	day	will
4	truck	black	not	
5	cat	it	go	look
6	red	fun	he	
7	name	swim	my	map
8	car	vine	see	can
9	tent	round	skate	ten
10	old	frog	right	
11	slide	stop	tell	her
12	am	smash	brave	
13	cow	sleep	scout	
14	for	all	saw	
15	had	kick	snail	glow
16	boat	think	nest	
17	treat	make	thank	
18	mice	little	more	
19	ship	station	clock	wash
20	skunk	whale	boy	baby
21	squirt	school	could	
22	caught	coin	talk	
23	page	flew	flu	
24	use	bug	rain	
25	phone	queen	write	
26	knife	plane	guess	
27	babies	tax	delicious	

Note: Key words taught in group sequence according to the week of instruction.

Source: Benchmark School, 2107 N. Providence Road, Media, PA 19063. Reprinted by permission.

For example, the words *bat* and *cat* rhyme because at the end of each word you hear the /at/ sound. Now I am going to try to think of another word that rhymes with *cat* and *bat*. I look up here at the alphabet and try out each consonant. We already have *bat* and *cat,* so I look at the next letter, *d. Dat* rhymes with *cat* and *bat,* but it isn't a real word, so I'm going to the next consonant, *f. Fat* rhymes with *cat* and *bat!*"

Guided Practice.   "Let's find another consonant that will make a real word that rhymes with *cat* and *bat.* Not *g* because it gives us *gat,* which isn't a word, but how about *h?* Yes, if we put the letter *h* in front of *-at* we get *hat!*"

Paired Practice.   "Now I am going to put you into pairs [or some other size group], and I want you to find three other real words that rhyme with *cat* and *bat.* Remember to use the alphabet, and only make real words! When you have come up with a word, take turns writing it on a card."

Check on the progress of each pair or group. Assist where necessary by repeating the rhyming words *cat* and *bat* and helping the students use the alphabet on the wall to find consonants that will make real words.

Outcome.   Have each pair share a word that they made. Put a tally on the board to see how many students made the same words. The real words to be made are *mat, pat, rat,* *sat,* and *vat.* Now each pair of students has a set of word cards to be used for later activities.

Sample Lesson: Onset-Rime Awareness: Segmenting and Blending

In this lesson the goal is to teach students how to segment and blend onset-rimes. The materials needed are large sets of letters that represent the onsets and rimes to be used—for example, the onsets *f-, fl-, m-, r-, br-,* and *s-* and the rime *-at*—and a feltboard.

Explicit Instruction and Modeling from the Teacher.   "Today we are going to use the spelling pattern *-at* that you learned yesterday to pronounce new words. I will say the beginning of the word, and you will say, /at/; then we will put these sounds together to make a word. Let me show you what I mean. I say /f/ and you say /at/. Put them together and you get *fat.* Here's another one. I say /fl/ and you say /at/. Put them together and you get *flat.*

Guided Practice.   "Let's try one together. I'll say the first sound, you say the /at/ sound, and then we'll put them together and you say the new word. Okay, I'll say /m/ and you say [the students should say] /at/. Put them together and you get [students should say] *mat.*"

You could provide visual support for the blending concept by having two sets of letters: the onset and the rime. These sets should be large enough for all students in the group to see them. The teacher asks two students to come to the front to move the letter sets as the group chants the blending activity just described. One student has to find the correct letter set when the teacher says the onset; the other student places the rime set (e.g., *-at*) near the onset and then moves them together when the new word is formed.

It goes like this:

Teacher: I say /br/ [Student 1 puts the *br* letter set on the feltboard] and you say . . .

Students: /at/. [Student 2 puts the *-at* set near the *br* set on the feltboard]

Teacher: Put them together [Students 1 and 2 move letter sets together] and you get . . .

Students: *Brat!*

This visually supported activity provides students with a concrete example of what they are doing with the sounds when they blend them. As they move the letter sets together, they also blend the sounds to make a new word.

Paired Practice.   Provide pairs of students with their own letter sets so they can move them as they chant other onset-rime patterns.

The Importance of Phonemic Awareness

The most difficult level of phonological analysis is phoneme awareness, the recognition that words can be segmented into constituent sounds. Much of the research of the past ten years has been on phonemic awareness. The National Reading Panel (2000) was commissioned by the U.S. Department of Education to examine the research base in reading ranging from phonemic awareness to comprehension. The panel's summary of research on phonemic awareness yielded the following conclusions:

1. Phonemic awareness can be taught and learned.
2. Teaching one or two phonemic awareness skills at a time is more effective than teaching three or more skills.
3. Phonemic awareness teaching sessions of about 30 minutes are most effective.
4. Computers are effective in teaching phonemic awareness.
5. Phonemic awareness instruction is most effective with pre-K and kindergarten students and students at risk.
6. Phonemic awareness taught with letters is more effective than phonemic awareness taught without letters.

These findings should direct the development of phonemic awareness instruction.

It may not be necessary to conduct lessons of 30 minutes if you are working in a small group because the lesson will go much faster and you will be easily able to monitor students' understanding. Recall the tips for implementing phonological instruction earlier in this chapter. They apply to instruction in phonemic awareness as well. Yopp and Yopp (2000) describe three additional important features of good instruction:

1. Instruction should be age appropriate. For preschool students, songs, chants, and word–sound games are appropriate for developing sensitivity to the sound structure of language. For older students who need instruction, you will want to make the activities appropriate by using more sophisticated songs, rap, and poetry. Instruction can be designed as interactive so that students can play with language among themselves after the instruction is completed.

2. Phonemic awareness instruction should be deliberate and purposeful. Although the playful approach to learning recommended previously should be utilized, your goals for the instruction should be clear. You must understand the level of phonological awareness of your students so that the chants and games will help them develop more advanced awareness. For example, if the students have shown mastery in segmenting onset and rime, the games should focus on developing *phonemic* segmentation.

3. Phonemic awareness instruction should be viewed as only one part of a much larger literacy program. It is important that students continue to hear stories and poetry read in the classroom. Also, writing is an excellent way to both advance and assess students' phonemic development.

Assessment of Phonemic Awareness

What aspects of phonemic awareness need to be taught to specific students? In order to answer this question, a teacher must be able to assess the various components of phonological awareness. We have discussed the assessment of rhyme, so now let's turn to other tasks that measure students' ability to isolate and segment sounds.

Yopp (1988) examined the reliability and validity of several measures of phonemic awareness to determine their level of difficulty for kindergarten students. The task most highly correlated with word learning was found to be *sound isolation,* which requires the student to produce the first, middle, or last sound heard in a word. The average percent correct was 58 percent, but the ability to isolate sounds varied in different parts of the word. Identifying sounds heard in the initial part of the word was the easiest: "What sound do you hear at the beginning of the word *jump?*" The next, in order of difficulty, was identifying the last sound heard: "What sound do you hear at the end of *part?*" The most difficult task was isolating the sound heard in the middle: "What sound do you hear in the middle of *pig?*"

A user of the *QRI-4* could make up a sound isolation test using words from the IRI. For example, "What sound do you hear at the beginning of . . .":

    can   bat   not   saw   like

"What sound do you hear at the end of . . .":

    pin   need   go   at   help

"What sound do you hear in the middle of . . .":

    make   not   find   run   bread

Another task studied by Yopp (1988) was *phonemic segmentation.* In it the directions to the student were "I'm going to say a word and I want you to say the word back to me one sound at a time. Let's try one. If I say the word *hat,* you say /h/ /ă/ /t/." The average percent correct was 54 percent among the kindergarteners studied. Yopp's test is widely available (Yopp, 1995; www.wilearns.com), but we can design a similar task using words from the *QRI-4:* "I'm going to say a word, and I want you to say the word back to me one sound at a time. If I say the word *can,* you say /c/ /ă/ /n/. Now you try . . .":

she (*sh-ē*)	said (*s-ĕ-d*)	place (*p-l-ā-s*)	song (*s-ŏ-n-g*)	find (*f-ī-n-d*)
like (*l-ī-k*)	tired (*t-ī-r-d*)	help (*h-ĕ-l-p*)	from (*f-r-ŏ-m*)	
trade (*t-r-ā-d*)	see (*s-ē*)	go (*g-ō*)	keep (*k-ē-p*)	

One of us has used both sound isolation and phonemic segmentation with second-grade and third-grade students reading at no higher than primer level. The scores in general were good on the sound isolation task (except for identifying sounds in the middle of the word), but were often low on phonemic segmentation. It has become clear to us that the differences in these second and third graders' scores are related to the teaching methods of their kindergarten and first-grade teachers. We also see that students can be proficient on these tasks and yet not have made the jump to applying the learned skills to reading. They need to learn how to associate phonemes to letters. When students do not score above chance on these phonemic tasks, however, phonemic segmentation can be taught aurally.

*D*eveloping Phonemic Awareness Aurally

Alliteration

As indicated previously, an awareness of phonological structures from the syllable level through the onset-rime level to the phonemic level can be gained from oral language. Much of this learning is indirect—that is, the student learns it as he or she learns language, not through explicit instruction. However, if language games have not been part of the student's experience, teachers can use them. Yopp (1992) provides many examples of songs and games to develop phonemic awareness. "Jimmy Crack Corn" can be sung with students producing words that begin with a specific sound. For example, "Who knows a name [or word] that starts with /t/, who knows a name that starts with /t/, who knows a name that starts with /t/, it must start with a /t/ sound. *Tom* is one of those names. *Tom* is a name that starts with /t/, *Tom* is a name that starts with /t/, *Tom* is a name that starts with /t/, *Tom* is one of those names." If your students have difficulty thinking of words without clues, have pictures that represent words beginning with the sound that you are teaching that day. Recognize that this activity can involve breaks at the syllable, onset-rime, or phoneme level. An onset-rime application can ask the students to come up with words with the same initial sounds, for example, /br/. "Who knows a word that starts with /br/, who knows a word that starts with /br/, who knows a word that starts with /br/? It must start with the /br/ sound. *Brake* is a word. . . ." Alliteration can also be taught through the game I Spy. "I Spy something that starts with the /s/ sound: *sandwich, snake, stamp. . . .*" This can be played within a group or a class using pictures or other items present in the room.

Sorting Tasks

Another technique for aurally teaching phonemic awareness involves picture sorting. Students are given sets of pictures (if the students have been taught how to work cooperatively, this activity can be done in small groups using one picture set) and asked to sort them by the first sound they hear when they name the object pictured. For example, the teacher might have pictures of a *tent,* a *tiger,* a *table,* a *truck,* a *triangle,* a *school,* a *snake,* a *sandwich, stairs,* and a *sink,* which the students sort into two piles according to the sound of the first letter. Of course, this task can be made more complex by asking them to find three pictures in these sets that end with the same sound (*truck, sink, snake*). The number of pictures and the number of categories should vary to match the students' abilities. For example, students who are learning to distinguish initial phonemes might be given four pictures and asked to group those that sound the same at the beginning. More advanced students might have nine pictures and be asked to sort them into three categories that represent the same final phoneme.

Counting Tasks

This counting technique for aurally teaching phonological awareness is modeled after Liberman and colleagues' (1974) tapping task. Each student is given a number of tokens, coins, or plastic chips—anything that represents the concept of one. The teacher tells the students, " I am going to say some words. Some of them will have two sounds and some will have three sounds. Listen carefully and put a chip out in front of you for each sound that you hear in the word I say." The teacher then says "*dog*" and the students should put three chips or tokens in front of them. This works very well for several reasons: First, it physically involves the children; second, it provides a visual representation for the sounds heard; and third, it allows the teacher to visually check if the students correctly identify the number of phonemes.

Developing Phonemic Awareness Using Letters

As students learn to recognize letters and associate phonemes to them, the teacher can begin to incorporate letters into the tasks just described. This can be as simple as adding letters to the aural activity. For example, when singing "Who has a name that starts with /t/ . . . ," the teacher can present the letter *t.* In this way he or she is using what the students have already learned aurally and associating it with a visual representation of the sound—a letter. As indicated, this method can be used to teach single-consonant phoneme–grapheme associations or more complex ones such as blends, /br/, or diagraphs, /ch/. If a teacher is using picture sorting, he or she can simply ask the students to choose or write the letter that represents the sound that they hear in the names of the pictures. Again, whether the students are asked to choose the letter or write it should vary depending on their abilities.

The tapping task using tokens can also be modified to include letters. Clay (1993) did so with Elkonin's (1963) sound boxes. The purpose of the boxes is to visually represent the separation of sounds in a word. Blachman (2000) and others recommended a *Say-It–Move-It* task, in which the student is given four boxes and several letter cards (*c, t, n, p, a*). The teacher says a word, and the student must say the sound and put a letter in the box that represents it. If the teacher says *can,* the student says /k/ and moves the *c* into the first box, then says /a/ and moves the *a* into the second box, and finally says, /n/ and moves the *n* into the third box.

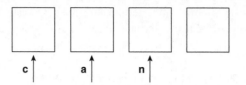

The teacher may decide to take away the extra box or challenge the student to determine how many sounds he or she hears. The teacher may ask the student to remove the letters from the box and then pronounce another word, or ask the student to keep the letters in the boxes but rearrange them to represent another word. In this case the teacher might go from the word *nap* to the word *pan*, illustrating that the same sounds and letters can be rearranged to come up with an entirely different word and thus facilitating the development of the alphabetic principle.

The ability to segment words into their constituent sounds is the cornerstone of phonological awareness. Perhaps that is why it is so important to learning to read. A student will learn to read much more quickly if she or he can mentally remove the sound /n/ in the word *nap* and replace it with the sound /t/ to get the word *tap*. *Blending* is another important aspect of the process because once the substitution of /t/ for /n/ occurs the student must blend the sound of /t/ to /ap/ to produce *tap* and recognize the word's previously stored meaning.

Word Building

When students become successful making words with Elkonin boxes, they are ready to build words using only letter cards. This activity can range in difficulty depending on the students' abilities (Cunningham, 2004). In the simple example above the students can be given only the set of letters (*c, t, n, p, a*). The teacher tells them to start by building the two-letter word *at* and then progresses to three-letter words, giving clues to the words that they should make. For example, "Make the word for the pet who purrs, *cat;* now remove the /c/ and replace it with a letter to make the word that describes how we touch the cat, *pat.*" These activities require students to pay careful attention; the use of manipulatives helps them in doing so.

Sample Lesson: Phonemic Awareness

The goal of the lesson is to teach students how to identify the number of phonemes in a word. The materials needed are Elkonin boxes for each student and poker chips. Note that the Elkonin boxes can be made creatively using a theme or object representing a story to be heard. For example, if you are reading *Brown Bear, Brown Bear,* the boxes can be bear claw prints.

Explicit Instruction and Modeling from the Teacher.   "I'm going to say some words, and I want you to listen carefully and put a chip in a box for each sound that you hear. For example, if I say the word *see* [pronounced in an elongated fashion: *sssss-eeeee*], you put a chip in the first box for the /s/ sound, then another chip in the second box for the /ee/ sound. So you have only two boxes with chips in them." As the teacher explains this example, she or he puts magnets in Elkonin boxes represented on a chalkboard or on any magnetic surface. "If I say *look,* you have a chip in the first box for the /l/ sound, another chip in the second box for the /oo/ sound, and one more chip in the third box for the /k/ sound." Again, as the teacher says these phrases, she or he models placing chips in boxes that are visible to all students. The teacher must be sure to elongate the word's pronunciation so that the students can hear the phonemes distinctly. As they become more proficient, the elongation gets shorter and shorter.

Guided Practice.   The teacher pronounces some words, and the students place chips in the correct number of boxes. The teacher places chips in his or her boxes, too, but waits to reveal each one until after the students have placed one in their first box, second box, and so forth. In this way the students can check their word with the teacher's as they go through it.

Paired Practice.   As in the other tasks described, pairs of students can work together to place chips in boxes, and they must be able to explain to each other why they chose the number of chips they did. This reteaching by students helps them understand more deeply what they are doing.

Sample Lesson: Connecting Letters and Sounds

The goal of this lesson is to associate the number of phonemes in the word with the letters that represent them. As the students become more and more proficient with two- or three-phoneme words, it is time to replace the chips with the letters that represent the phonemes. This activity is identical to the one just described except that the students have to place the correct letter in the boxes, not just the poker chip. When starting with this more difficult task, be sure that the students have a limited number of letters available to them so that they aren't overwhelmed by having to choose among them. For example, if the words have two phonemes, have the students choose the letters as you state their names; then proceed with the phoneme-counting task.

The only materials needed are letter sets *s, ee, l, oo,* and *k.*

Explicit Instruction and Modeling from the Teacher.   "Find the letters *s* and *ee.* Now listen to me say a word, and put those letters in the correct boxes. The word is *sssss-eeeee.*" The teacher puts the letter *s* in the first box and the letters *ee* in the second box.

Guided Practice.   "Now find the letters *l, oo,* and *k.* Listen to me as I say the word *l-oo-k.* Watch as I put the letter *l* in the first box, the letters *oo* in the second box, and the letter *k* in the third box."

Paired Practice.   Like the activities described earlier, this one has pairs of students work together to put the letters in the boxes as the teacher pronounces the words.

Independent Practice.   If teaching in a large classroom, the teacher can set up stations where the students can listen to tapes of him or her saying words and then put letters in the correct boxes. The teacher can have pretaped feedback for them (after a pause on the tape while they are putting letters in boxes, the teacher says, "You should have the letter *r* first, then the letter *u,* then the letter *g.*"). Alternatively, the teacher can hide a written copy of the correct letter sequence somewhere and say on the tape, "Look under the _____ to see if you are correct." There are computer programs that provide this kind of practice. Pressley (2002, p. 113) recommends *Daisy Quest* and *Daisy Castle* (previously published by Pro-Ed of Austin, Texas; now sold in both MAC and PC versions on the Internet. Use the Google search engine and type in *Daisy Quest.*) Also, *Wiggleworks,* by Scholastic, has been cited as an excellent program for a beginning reader (Block, 2004).

*A*pplication to English Language Learners

Whether the instructional strategies presented above are applicable to teaching ELLs to read depends on the native language of the student because the development of phonological analysis is influenced by the orthography of the language (Bear, Templeton, Helman, & Baren, 2003). Alphabetic orthographies can be rated on a continuum of depth by examining the degree of phoneme–grapheme correspondence. A highly consistent phoneme–grapheme relationship is called a shallow or transparent orthography, whereas a language in which the same phoneme can be represented by several different graphemes is termed a deep orthography. Shallow orthographies exist in Spanish and Finnish, but English has a deep orthography. Teachers should be aware of the complexities of the English orthography, especially the vowel sounds, and bring some regularity to decoding in English using the spelling pattern approach discussed in the next chapter.

Of greater challenge to the teacher of ELLs is when the native language differs greatly from English. A contrastive analysis of English and Arabic illustrates such challenges (Palmer, El-Ashry, Leclere, & Chang, 2007). A few examples from the Palmer et al. article will suffice to make the point. Arabic is written from right to left and noun sentences do not contain a verb (e.g., Woman beautiful). Arabic letter forms are of different shapes depending where they are placed in the word. Furthermore, whether a vowel appears in Arabic depends on its sound. Long vowels are expressed in Arabic by using letters; however, short vowels are diacritical marks attached to consonants. Therefore, when a long vowel is present, one letter equals one phoneme and so Arabic would be classified as having a shallow orthography. However, when vowels are not part of the word (i.e., are diacritical marks), then Arabic would be considered to have a deep orthography.

Research has also documented that languages vary in the frequency of use of phonological structures. For example, the syllabic phonetic structure of Spanish may facilitate its speakers in learning to segment syllables (Westby, 2004). In contrast, because Spanish has fewer CVC patterns, Spanish-speaking children may be not be familiar with the onset-rime demarcation that is so prominent in English. The teacher will need to use the syllable as the unit or teach the onset-rime division by demonstrating with letters as described previously in this chapter.

We found no research indicating that the *procedures* for teaching consonant sounds to English language learners should be any different from native speakers (Shanahan & Beck, 2006). However, there are programs for developing early phonological abilities that teach ELLs as well as native speakers. *Jolly Phonics* (cited in Cummins, 2003), a program designed to develop phonemic awareness and letter–sound correspondence, was presented to English-speaking and ELL kindergarten students in Canada. Exposure to the program resulted in superior performance on a variety of phonological measures among both English speakers and English learners, and the ELLs outperformed the English-speaking students who did not take part in the program (cited in Cummins, 2003). Phonemic awareness (phonemic discrimination and phonemic segmentation and blending) and letter–sound correspondence were part of a more complete curriculum designed for ELLs who were taught either in English or Spanish (Vaughn, Mathes, Linan-Thompson, & Francis, 2005). The curricula were identical except that the Spanish version focused on the syllable as the unit of instruction because of the phonetic structure of Spanish. First graders who received this seven-month curriculum outperformed those who did not on phonological analysis, but not on letter naming. Other components of the Vaughn et al. study will be presented in Chapter 5.

Although we have no evidence that different teaching methods are required, the order of consonant sounds that are taught to ELLs could potentially be different. It is recommended that the order of teaching consonant sounds should be consistent with their native language. For example, consonant sounds such as *ch, p, b, t,* and *s* (plus others) occur in both English and Spanish, so the Spanish-speaking ELL student should learn those consonants first when they have the same sound in English and Spanish (Gonzalez-Bueno, 2003; Helman, 2004). In addition, Gonzalez-Bueno (2003) recommends that the letter sounds should be represented by concrete objects so the students can easily image them (e.g., *coche/car*).

There are many English consonant blends that do not occur in Spanish and students' pronunciation of those blends will be affected. For example, because Spanish does not allow "s" blends at the beginning of words, a word such as *swim* could be pronounced by adding an /e/ sound as in "eswim." Spanish speakers also may drop the "s." This applies to other languages as well. For example, Hmong children often have difficulty with the consonants *b, g,* and *j.* A sample of consonant sounds and vowel sounds from several languages and their relationship to English may be found in Echevarria, Vogt, and Short (2008).

These illustrations from several languages portray the complexity of teaching phonological awareness to ELLs, especially those who have not learned to read in their native language. The teacher of a beginning reader must understand how English is similar and different from the student's native language, particularly if the child has learned to read in that language. With such knowledge the teacher can adjust how phonological awareness and letter–sound correspondence are taught to the beginning reader.

Application to Adolescent Learners

Although the vast majority of adolescents have mastered the various components of phonological awareness, students diagnosed as dyslexic at a young age have been found to continue to have phonological weaknesses in adolescence both with spelling and reading rate when compared to average and superior readers of the same age (Shaywitz et al., 1999). Similar results have been found using a cross-sectional research design (Fawcett & Nicholson, 1995).

So do we teach these severely disabled readers phonological awareness yet again in high school and middle school? A review of programs designed to promote phonological awareness (Torgesen & Mathes, 2000) identified only one program, the Lindamood Phonemic Sequencing Program for Reading, Spelling and Speech (Lindamood & Lindamood, 1998), with research evidence demonstrating that it was effective in improving the phonological awareness and the phonemic reading skills of older children with reading disabilities. Yet research on "older" readers is compromised by the fact that the students in these studies range in age from 6 to 13. Torgeson, Wagner, Rashotte, Alexander, and Conway (1997) demonstrated improved phonemic awareness and subsequent word identification and word attack in students within the same age range. In conclusion, although we have evidence that some older disabled readers still have phonological weaknesses and there is a program that could help develop those skills, the highest age of the students in any of these studies is 13, the beginning of adolescence. Teaching older severely disabled readers to read is a complex and intensive process (Torgesen et al., 1997) and the instruction of these children will not likely be the purview of the reading teacher or specialist, but rather the special education teacher who has specialized training in phonological processes and severely disabled readers.

Response to Intervention

At the present time and given the relative newness of RTI, most instruction and assessment focuses on early reading skills. The importance of phonological awareness has been established by research (National Reading Panel, 2000), and research has validated that phonological awareness can be trained. Students who receive such training outperform their peers in later reading skills (Lundberg, Frost, & Peterson, 1988). However, although a variety of instructional suggestions abound in the literature (Adams, Foorman, Lundberg, & Beeler, 1998; Yopp & Yopp, 2000), research has not established which specific instructional activities are more effective than others.

Many published assessments of phonological awareness lend themselves well to the structure of Response to Intervention. That is, they are short, easily administered measures of rhyme awareness, initial and final sound awareness, auditory blending, and auditory segmentation. It is not the purpose of this book to identify and critique such published assessments but only to offer words of caution. Phonological awareness is only one aspect of the complex process we call reading and while it is an important element, teachers must not mistake a part for the whole. Instruction and assessment should also focus on the other components of reading identified by the National Reading Panel (2000): phonics, fluency, word meaning, and comprehension. There is also another concern: Phonological awareness activities do not always resemble real reading. Stretching out words, playing rhyme games, and segmenting words may be important for developing students' awareness of sounds but they should not be the whole lesson. Students need to be actively involved in real reading, and teacher read-alouds coupled with student discussion are just as important as phonological activities in developing reading proficiency.

Summary

This chapter explained phonological awareness and why it is important in learning to read. We explained how phonological abilities normally develop, how they are assessed, and how they are taught. We described the importance of rhyme and how students' understanding of rhyme is used to connect to spelling. Then tips for implementing phonological instruction were provided, and two sample lessons, one on rhyme and one on onset-rime awareness, were presented. We then introduced the importance of phonemic awareness, how it is assessed, how it develops, and how to connect it to letters. Again, two sample lessons were provided, one on phonemic awareness and the second on connecting letters and sounds. The research reviewed by the National Reading Panel indicates that phonemic awareness is most effectively taught when letters are used. Therefore, many of the instructional recommendations made in this chapter related letters with phonemes. We examined whether our recommended procedures would be appropriate for English language learners and concluded that an appropriate application would be determined by the orthographic and phonological relationship of the student's native language to English. The next chapter will continue to associate levels of phonological analysis and learning to read as we focus on word identification.

REFERENCES AND RECOMMENDED READINGS

Adams, M. J., Foorman, B. R., Lundberg, I., & Beeler, T. (1998). *Phonemic awareness in young children: A classroom curriculum.* Baltimore: Brookes.

Blachman, B. (2000). Phonological awareness. In M. L. Kamil, P. B. Mosenthal, P. D. Pearson, & R. Barr (Eds.), *Handbook of reading research* (Vol. III, pp. 483–502). Mahwah, NJ: Erlbaum.

Blachman, B. A., Ball, E. W., Black, R., & Tangel, D. M. (2000). *Road to the code.* Baltimore: Brookes.

Block, C. C. (2004). *Teaching comprehension: The comprehension process approach.* Boston: Allyn & Bacon.

Bradley, L., & Bryant, P. E. (1983). Categorizing sounds and learning to read: A causal connection. *Nature, 310,* 419–421.

Brady, S. (1997). Ability to encode phonological representations: An underlying difficulty of poor readers. In B. A. Blachman (Ed.), *Foundations of reading acquisition and dyslexia: Implications for early intervention* (pp. 21–47). Mahwah, NJ: Erlbaum.

Bryant, P. E., Maclean, M., Bradley, L., & Crossland, J. (1990). Rhyme, alliteration, phoneme detection, and learning to read. *Developmental Psychology, 26,* 429–438.

Clay, M. M. (1985). *The early detection of reading difficulties* (3rd ed.). Portsmouth, NH: Heinemann.

Clay, M. (1993). *Reading Recovery: A handbook for teachers in training.* Portsmouth, NH: Heinemann.

Cunningham, P. M. (2004). *Phonics they use: Words for reading and writing* (4th ed.). New York: Allyn & Bacon.

Ehri, L. C., Nunes, S. R., Willows, D. M., Schuster, B. V., Yaghoub-Zadeh, Z., & Shanahan, T. (2001). Phonemic awareness instruction helps children learn to read: Evidence from the National Reading Panel's meta-analysis. *Reading Research Quarterly, 36,* 250–287.

Elbro, C., Borstrum, I., & Petersen, D. K. (1998). Predicting dyslexia from kindergarten: The importance of distinctiveness of phonological representations of lexical items. *Reading Research Quarterly, 33,* 36–60.

Elkonin, D. B. (1963). The psychology of mastering the elements of reading. In B. Simon & J. Simon (Eds.), *Educational psychology in the U.S.S.R.* (pp. 165–179). London: Routledge & Kegan Paul.

Goswami, I. (1999). Phonological development and reading by analogy: Epilinguistic and metalinguistic issues. In

J. Oakhill & R. Beard (Eds.), *Reading Development and the Teaching of Reading.* Oxford, UK: Blackwell Publishers.

Goswami, I. (2000). Phonological and lexical processes. In M. L. Kamil, P. B. Mosenthal, P. D. Pearson, & R. Barr (Eds.), *Handbook of Reading Research* (Vol. III, pp. 251–267). Mahwah, NJ: Erlbaum.

Leslie, L., & Caldwell, J. (2006). *Qualitative reading inventory-4.* Boston: Allyn & Bacon.

Leslie, L., & Calhoon, J. A. (1995). Factors affecting children's reading of rimes: Reading ability, word frequency and rime neighborhood size. *Journal of Educational Psychology, 87,* 576–586.

Liberman, I. Y., Shankweiler, D., Fischer, F. W., & Carter, B. (1974). Explicit syllable and phoneme segmentation in the young child. *Journal of Experimental Child Psychology, 18,* 201–212.

Lundberg, I., Frost, J., & Peterson, O. (1988). Effects of an extensive program for stimulating phonological awareness in preschool children. *Reading Research Quarterly, 23,* 263–284.

Maclean, M., Bryant, P. E., & Bradley, L. (1987). Rhymes, nursery rhymes, and reading in early childhood. *Merrill-Palmer Quarterly, 33,* 255–282.

National Reading Panel. (2000). *Report of the National Reading Panel: Teaching children to read: An evidence-based assessment of scientific-based literature on reading and its implications for reading instruction.* Washington, DC: National Institute of Child Health and Human Development.

Notari-Syverson, A., O'Connor, R. E., & Vadasy, P. F. (1998). *Ladders to literacy: A preschool activity book.* Baltimore: Brookes.

Pressley, M. (2002). *Reading Instruction that Works* (2nd ed.). New York: The Guilford Press.

Treiman, R. (1985). Onsets and rimes as units of spoken syllables. *Journal of Experimental Child Psychology, 39,* 161–181.

Treiman, R., & Zukowski, A. (1991). Levels of phonological awareness. In S. Brady & D. Shankweiler (Eds.), *Phonological processes in literacy* (pp. 67–83). Mahwah, NJ: Erlbaum.

Yopp, H. (1988). The validity and reliability of phonemic awareness tests. *Reading Research Quarterly, 21,* 253–266.

Yopp, H. (1995). A test for assessing phonemic awareness in young children. *The Reading Teacher, 49,* 20–29.

Yopp, H. K. (1992*).* Developing phonemic awareness in young children. *The Reading Teacher, 45,* 696–703.

Yopp, H. K., & Yopp, R. H. (1996). *Oo-pples and boo-noo-noos: Songs and activities for phonemic awareness.* Harcourt Brace School Publishers.

Yopp, H. K., & Yopp, R. H. (2000). Supporting phonemic awareness development in the classroom. *The Reading Teacher, 54,* 130–143.

Children's Literature

Brown, M. W. (1947). *Goodnight moon.* New York: Harper.

Greenfield, E. (1988). *Nathaniel talking.* New York: Black Butterfly Children's Books.

Guarino, D. (1989). *Is your mama a llama?* New York: Scholastic.

Martin, B. (1967). *Brown bear, brown bear, what do you see?* New York: Henry Holt & Co.

Slepian, J., & Seidler, A. (1967). *The hungry thing.* New York: Scholastic.

English Language Learners

Bear, D., Templeton, S., Helman, L., & Baren, T. (2003). Orthographic development and learning to read in different languages. In G. G. Garcia (Ed.), *English learners: Reaching the highest level of English literacy* (pp. 71–95). Newark, DE: International Reading Association.

Cummins, J. (2003). Reading and the bilingual student: Fact and friction. In G. G. Garcia (Ed.), *English learners: Reaching the highest level of English literacy* (pp. 2–33). Newark, DE: IRA.

Echevarria, J., Vogt, M., & Short, D. J. (2008). *Making content comprehensible for English learners: The SIOP Model* (3rd ed.). Boston: Allyn & Bacon.

Gonzalez-Bueno, M. (2003). Literacy activities for Spanish-English bilingual children. *The Reading Teacher, 57,* 189–192.

Helman, L. (2004). Building on the sound system of Spanish: Insights from the alphabetic spellings of English language learners, *The Reading Teacher, 57,* 452–460.

Palmer, B. C., El-Ashry, F., Leclere, J. T., & Chang, S. (2007). Learning from Abdallah: A case study of an Arabic-speaking child in a U.S. school. *The Reading Teacher, 61,* 8–17.

Shanahan, T., & Beck, I. (2006). Effective literacy teaching for English-language learners. In D. August & T. Shanahan (Eds.), *Developing literacy in second-language learners* (pp. 415–488). Mahwah, NJ: Erlbaum.

Vaughn, S., Mathes, P. G., Linan-Thompson, S., & Francis, D. J. (2005). Teaching English language learners at risk for reading disabilities to read: Putting research into practice. *Learning Disabilities Research and Practice, 20,* 58–67.

Westby, C. (2004). 21st century literacy for a diverse world. *Folia Phoniatrica et Logopaedica, 56,* 254–271.

Woodcock, W. L. (1991). Woodcock Language Proficiency Battery–Revised. Chicago: Riverside Publishing.

Adolescents

Fawcett, A. J., & Nicolson, R. I. (1995). Persistence of phonological deficits in older children with dyslexia. *Reading and Writing, 7,* 361–376.

Lindamood, P., & Lindamood, P. (1998). *The Lindamood phoneme sequencing program for reading, spelling and speech.* Austin, TX: ProEd.

Shaywitz, S. E., Fletcher, J. M., Holahan, J. M., Shneider, A. E., Marchione, K. E., Stuebing, K. K., Francis, D. J., Pugh, K. R., & Shaywitz, B. (1999). The persistence of dyslexia: The Connecticut longitudinal study at adolescence. *Pediatrics, 104,* 1351–1359.

Torgesen, J., & Mathes, P. G. (2000). *A basic guide to understanding, assessing, and teaching phonological awareness.* Austin, TX: ProEd.

Torgeson, J. K., Wagner, R., Rashotte, C., Alexander, A. W., & Conway, T. (1997). Preventative and remedial interventions for children with severe reading disabilities. *Learning Disabilities, 8,* 51–62.

5

Word Identification Instruction: Phonics and More

Word identification is one of the most important components of reading. Comprehension is the goal, and identifying words is critical to it. Word identification can occur through several psychological processes. If a word is well known, it is recognized. That is, when a student sees the word and recognizes it as familiar, she or he pronounces it correctly. If the pronunciation is immediate (within one second), we refer to the word as being in the student's *sight* vocabulary; it is recognized automatically. If a student doesn't recognize a word, she or he must rely on decoding strategies:

1. Trying to sound out the word, pronouncing the sound for each letter in sequence—for example, *f-l-ă-t.*
2. Looking for familiar spelling patterns within the word and trying to decode the word with reading by analogy. For example, *strain*—the student recognizes *rain,* adds the sounds /st/ to *rain* and gets *strain.*
3. Saying the first sound of the word, then reading the rest of the sentence, then going back to the unknown word and thinking of what makes sense in the sentence that starts with that initial sound.

The focus of this chapter is on effective instructional methods to teach word identification. Although we can support teaching the consonant sounds as individual letter–sound associations, we advocate the second strategy in the previous list as the most effective way to teach vowel letter–sound relationships.

Phonics is the understanding that there are predictable relationships between the sounds of spoken language (i.e., phonemes) and the letters that represent those sounds in written language (i.e., graphemes). Literacy experts agree that students must understand phonics in order to read and spell. Where they disagree is the manner in which phonics should be taught. For example, should phonics be taught synthetically—that is, each letter sound taught separately and then blended into a word? Or should it be taught using larger units, such as frequent spelling patterns? A recent review of the results of the National Reading Panel (Ehri et al., 2001) concluded the following:

1. Systematic phonics instruction (i.e., letter by letter, onsets and rimes, and other methods in which a sequence of phonic elements is taught) makes a more significant contribution to students' growth in reading than do alternative programs providing unsystematic phonics instruction or none at all.
2. Specific systematic phonics programs (synthetic and larger-unit programs) are all more effective than nonphonics programs, and they do not appear to differ significantly in their effectiveness.
3. Systematic phonics instruction produces the biggest impact on growth in reading when it begins in kindergarten or first grade, before students have learned to read independently.
4. Systematic phonics instruction is effective when delivered through tutoring, small groups, or whole-class instruction.
5. Systematic phonics instruction is significantly more effective than unsystematic phonics instruction, or none at all, in helping prevent reading difficulties among at-risk students and in helping to remediate reading difficulties in readers with disabilities.

What Is Systematic Phonics Instruction?

When teachers plan a sequence of phonic elements to be taught, explicitly state the relationship between the letters and sounds, and assess the student's growth in understanding these relationships, the phonics instruction is systematic. It differs from a spontaneous, off-the-cuff response to a specific student's momentary need. This is not to say that the spontaneous response is not helpful; in fact, it is often referred to as the teachable moment. However, for phonics to be taught systematically, a planned sequence of elements and explicit instruction are required. But how do we know that students need phonics instruction?

The Informal Reading Inventory as an Indicator of Problems with Word Identification

There are two ways to assess a student's ability to recognize familiar words and identify unfamiliar ones. One is to have them read a list of increasingly difficult words; the other is to have them read stories of various levels of difficulty. If the student cannot read 70 percent of the words on the list at his or her grade level, some weakness in word recognition or identification is suggested. Informal reading inventories (IRIs) have graded word lists; the higher the list, the less frequent and more difficult the words. Although this is *not* a test of knowledge of individual letter–sound relationships, it serves as a beginning indicator of word identification difficulties. There are two scores that can be obtained from graded word lists:

1. The percentage of words on a given list read correctly within one second (i.e., automatically)
2. The total percentage of words read correctly on the same list (i.e., counting automatically read words *and* words identified more slowly or by decoding strategies)

If a student does not know many words automatically but has been taught decoding strategies, the automatic scores and total accuracy scores will be very different. For example, a student might read 75 percent correctly on the third-grade list, but recognize only 50 percent of the words automatically. The instructional program for this student might focus on developing *automatic* word recognition rather than decoding strategies.

The second way to assess a student's ability to recognize familiar words and identify unfamiliar ones is to give him or her progressively harder material to read. The goal of such an assessment is to identify the highest level at which the student can read with at least 90 percent accuracy and at least 70 percent comprehension. This level is called the student's instructional reading level, and to find it the assessor must have the student read harder and harder materials until he or she fails to meet both criteria for the instructional level: 90 percent oral reading accuracy or at least 70 percent comprehension. When the student does not meet the criteria at a level, it is important to examine why, because the implications for instruction will vary. The examples that follow are students with different word identification patterns.

Student A does not meet either the oral reading accuracy score or the comprehension score required for an instructional reading level at his or her grade level. The examiner must determine the problem area by seeing if the student can understand a story at grade level if it is read to him or her (i.e., listening comprehension). In other words, if word identification is assumed to be sufficient, will the student comprehend the text?

Word identification is also the culprit for Student B, who comprehends 70 percent of the story but reads with less than 90 percent accuracy at a level at or below grade placement. In this case the student shows strength in comprehension in the face of problems in word identification.

A different kind of problem occurs when Student C reads with sufficient accuracy but does not comprehend at least 70 percent of the story at grade level. He or she appears to have difficulty comprehending the text. Instruction for this student will be addressed in Chapters 9 through 12.

Miscue Analysis

A more detailed understanding of the student's difficulty with word identification is available with miscue analysis (Goodman, 1969). This procedure is very useful because it may provide clues to the best instructional strategy. Miscue analysis requires the examiner to analyze what the student does when she or he comes to unknown words. For example, does the student attempt to decode an unknown word, self-correct miscues that significantly change the meaning of the story, or just keep reading? The following students show different patterns as a result of miscue analysis.

Student 1. This student stops on coming to an unknown word, looks at the teacher, and makes no attempt at decoding. Despite likely having a corpus of words known automatically, that is, by sight, when faced with an unknown word, he or she doesn't know what to do. This also suggests that the student hasn't figured out (or been taught) letter–sound associations because, if even just the consonants were known, the student could use that knowledge to employ phonetic cue reading (see Chapter 2) to guess at the word using only some of the letter–sound relationships in it. Student 1 needs to be taught a variety of strategies for decoding unknown words.

Student 2. When this student comes to an unknown word she or he reads what the pictures and prior text indicate would make a good story. In this case the miscue has no resemblance to the word in print. This student is in the logographic stage described in Chapter 2. That is, he or she is using pictures and knowledge of how our language works (i.e., syntax) to "read" the text and has not figured out that readers use the printed text to construct meaning.

Student 3. If, after making a miscue that changes meaning, the student keeps on reading, she or he is not monitoring meaning and will have comprehension problems at some point. The student needs to be taught how to check different sources of information to see if what they say makes sense. This is also called *cross-checking,* a technique explained later in this chapter.

Student 4. Does the miscue always look like the word in print at the beginning? At the end? If it looks like the beginning of the word in print but not like the end, the student is focusing solely on initial letters and should be taught to look for spelling patterns when faced with unknown words. Instructional techniques to teach decoding using spelling patterns (i.e., reading by analogy, analytic phonics) will also be explained in this chapter. Miscue analysis informs the teacher of how the student understands the reading process. This information is vital to planning intervention instruction.

Some students can read regularly pronounced words (e.g., *cat, bag,* and *ship*) but cannot read words such as *thought, there, want,* and *through.* Look at the words that the student did not read correctly on the word list or in texts from an IRI. For example, the preprimer and primer grade lists on the *QRI-4* contain words that do not follow the regular patterns listed previously: *write* (silent *w*), *was* (*a* is pronounced as *schwa*), *they* (sounds like *thay*), *were* (shouldn't it have the /ē/ sound?), *want* (schwa sound of /a/ again), *said* (pronounced /sĕd/), *live* (shouldn't the /ī/ sound be there?), *comes* (where's the /ŭ/?). If students have learned to pronounce words by applying letter-by-letter pronunciations and they have been taught certain decoding rules (e.g., when there are two vowels in a syllable the first one "says its name" and the second one is silent), then they will have difficulty reading the irregular words listed previously. At the end of this chapter you will find procedures for teaching students how to read words that are hard to decode.

Student 5. Another interesting diagnostic pattern is a student who can successfully read stories at a particular level, but the highest word list on which she or he can read 70 percent of the words correctly is levels lower. For example, we had a student in an intervention program who after three semesters of tutoring met the criteria for instructional reading level at third grade; however, the highest list on which she scored at least 70 percent was first grade. This student used the context of the story to identify words. Her reading rate at this level was slow (less than 70 WPM), but she could read accurately enough and comprehend the story. She needed to reach a higher automatic word recognition level, so her intervention included lots of reading, writing, and other methods discussed in Chapter 6, on fluency. The following sections will provide recommendations for how to teach word recognition and identification to students who demonstrate difficulties in these areas.

Phonological Awareness versus Phonics

At this point you are likely able to explain the relationship between phonological awareness and phonics. Phonological awareness is the understanding that there are units of spoken language smaller than the word; the smallest unit is the phoneme. Phonics, on the other hand, is the understanding that there are *predictable relationships* between the sounds of spoken language (i.e., phonemes) and the letters that represent them in written language (i.e., graphemes). If the student can segment the phonemes within a word, the teacher's next job is to explain the relationship between them and the letters that represent them.

The heading of this section is The Informal Reading Inventory as an Indicator of Problems with Word Identification. Note the word *indicator*. Certainly we do not believe that any IRI is a sufficient measure of a student's understanding of letter–sound relationships. Rather, phonics knowledge can be assessed with tests that directly measure a student's understanding of letter–sound relationships (Eckwall & Shanker, 2000). These tests ask students to pronounce the sounds represented by an isolated letter or groups of letters (e.g., /bl/). Understanding of letter–sound relationships can also be assessed through spelling (Bear, Invernizzi, Templeton, & Johnston, 2007).

Guidelines for Exemplary Phonics Instruction

What are the elements of good phonics instruction? Stahl (1990) presented nine instructional guidelines:

1. It builds on a student's rich concepts about how print functions. This recommendation is based on the idea that the student must have some basic understanding about how reading works; that is, he or she must understand that print is the primary source of information that readers use in addition to pictures. The student must have had enough exposure to the language of story (that stories have characters with goal-directed event sequences) to value learning to read.

2. It builds on a foundation of phonemic awareness. Chapter 4 explained this important component in depth and hopefully convinced you that phonemic awareness and early phonics instruction go hand in hand.

3. It is clear and direct. A teacher's explanation of the letter–sound relationship is critical to understanding phonics. The teacher should explicitly state the goal for the lesson, model the strategy or skill to be taught, guide the students through an application of the skill, and then provide for independent or paired practice. Simple and direct language will be easier for students to understand. Examples of such language are found in the lesson plans in Chapter 4 and will be used in the lesson plans in this chapter.

4. It is integrated into a total reading program. This principle has separated types of phonics instruction for decades. Many of us associate phonics with skill and drill and the use of worksheets that have little relationship to reading. If phonics instruction is incorporated into a reading program that emphasizes the use of quality literature, students will understand the role of phonics as a key to helping them unlock this literature. Stahl (1990) suggests that no more than 25 percent of total instructional reading/language arts time be spent on phonics instruction and practice. Applied to a 30-minute intervention period, this means 7.5 minutes. In a 45-minute block this is roughly 11 minutes. The rest of the time should be spent reading poetry and stories that contain the phonic elements being taught as well as writing.

The problem in many basal texts is that the phonics instruction is independent from the literature passage, so students may never understand the relationship between phonics and reading. One of us had the following conversation many years ago with a second-grade student who had completed many pages of a phonics workbook but wasn't using any of that knowledge when she came to words that she didn't know. I told the student and her mother that I thought that she left all of her phonics knowledge in the workbook when she was reading. The student assured me that, in fact, she tore out the pages and brought them home every night! (Her mother understood my point.) This type of unconnected knowledge occurs when students see no relationship between skills and reading. It is critical that we as teachers make the reasons for our skills lessons transparent.

5. It focuses on reading words, not learning rules. In the 1920s psychologists found that frequent words are recognized more quickly than less frequent ones. This fact formed the basis for the frequency basal readers of the 1950s and 1960s, including the infamous *See Spot Run* stories that contained frequent words with much repetition: "Look! Look! See Spot run! Run, Spot, run!" over and over. Because of the repetition, students learned these words more quickly than words not as commonly used in their books. In addition, words with spelling patterns that occur more frequently are learned more quickly (Leslie & Calhoon, 1995). Those that include the spelling pattern *-ain,* for example, are learned more quickly than those with the *-oach* spelling pattern because many more words contain *-ain* (e.g., *main, pain, rain, vain, stain, plain, retain, maintain, explain*) than do *-oach* (*coach, roach, approach*). Rather than teach rules, which apply less than 50 percent of the time, we should teach vowel pronunciation based on spelling patterns—that is, the vowel and the consonants that follow in that syllable. Consider the rule "When two vowels go walking, the first one does the talking." It applies to words such as *meat, clean, goat,* and *tied,* but is violated in the words *piece, ground, bread,* and *deaf.*

In contrast to the variability of vowel sounds, of the 286 phonograms (spelling patterns) that appear in primary grade texts, 95 percent are pronounced the same way in every word in which they appear. These statistics have led many to recommend that vowel sounds be taught only in the context of spelling patterns. The least consistent vowel pattern is *-ea,* which, for example, is pronounced differently in *bread* and *meat.* Teaching a student the rule that when two vowels occur together (as with *-ea*) the first vowel is pronounced with its long sound and the second one is silent leads to success less than 50 percent of the time. However, when the six consonants that follow *-ea* are considered, the rule becomes much more regular. The long sound /ē/ is heard in *-eat, -ean, -eak, -eal, -eam,* and *-eap.* The inconsistencies occur when *ea* is followed by *d, f,* or *r.* The short sound /ĕ/ is heard in *-ead* (*bread*), *-eaf* (*deaf*), and *-ear* (*bear*), but the long sound /ē/ is heard in *-ead* (*bead*), *-eaf* (*leaf*), and *-ear* (*hear*).

6. It may include onsets and rimes. Reading programs have been developed to capitalize on the fact that vowel sounds are more consistently pronounced when the consonants that follow them are considered. Gaskins and colleagues (1988, 1997) developed a program in which students are taught to use words that they already know to figure out unknown words. The Benchmark Word Identification/Vocabulary Development Program (Gaskins, Downer, & the Teachers of Benchmark School, 1997) has been researched and revised several times since its inception. The program teaches students a compare–contrast strategy that uses the known word (e.g., *meat*) to read a new word (e.g., *treat*). When the student is reading the sentence *After school come to my house and have a treat,* he or she thinks, if *m-e-a-t* is *meat,* then *t-r-e-a-t* must be *treat.* Then the student rereads the sentence to see if the word she or he pronounced makes sense in the story. A more detailed examination of teaching phonics through onset and rime will follow later in this chapter.

7. It may include invented spelling practice. The major point here is that when students write they work out their understanding of letter–sound relationships, so writing provides the opportunity for such development.

8. It develops independent word recognition strategies, focusing attention on the internal structure of words. As explained in guideline six, students learn to read words by matching them to letter patterns in memory. Therefore, when they come to words that they do not recognize they need strategies that encourage them to look at the internal structure of the word for clues. The onset-rime unit provides the foundation for such a structure. More complex words such as compounds and words with many syllables provide a natural bridge for using rimes to decode longer words. Polysyllabic words with prefixes (e.g., *un*able and *in*destructible) and suffixes (nation*al,* beautiful*ly,* transporta*tion*) can also be used to draw a student's attention to internal word structure.

9. It develops automatic word recognition skills so that students can devote their attention to comprehension, not word identification. The ultimate goal of phonics instruction is for students to recognize words automatically so that little attention is paid to the decoding process and most of the student's cognitive resources are used to develop meanings from the text. The major way that students become fast and automatic at word recognition is to read a lot, as described fully in Chapter 6 on fluency. Completing phonics worksheets will not develop speed and accuracy of word identification. The instruction of sound–symbol relationships is a means to an end, not the end in itself.

There is no agreed-on order of phonic elements that should be taught. However, it is agreed that consonant letter–sound relationships are easier to learn because consonants are usually pronounced in the same manner in all words. Thus, the letter *b* is pronounced /b/ with little variation (except when it is silent in *lamb*). Also, when students are in the early stages of learning to spell, it is consonants that they represent first, omitting the vowel; the word *pan* is spelled *pn, bug* is spelled *bg,* and so forth. Because we want to teach from the student's knowledge base, we begin with what they know something about.

Teaching Consonant Sounds Using Shared Reading

How does a teacher know what letter–sound relationships need to be taught? There is one method that appears in any test of early literacy knowledge: Show the student a letter and ask him or her to name it and then make its sound. If the student just renames the letter, ask him or her to pronounce a word that begins with it. Clay (1985) includes a task like this in her early literacy assessment test, and other researchers consistently find that letter–sound knowledge is one of the best predictors for learning to read. Begin assessing consonant knowledge by choosing the most common consonants: *r, n, s, l, m,* and *t,* and systematically assess the others according to frequency of occurrence. If our students didn't know the majority of the consonant sounds, we wouldn't assess vowel sound knowledge thoroughly, as in all likelihood these relationships would not be known. Also, we would be teaching vowel sounds through spelling patterns, so whether they knew /ā/ and /ă/ as isolated sounds would be of less importance.

Allen (1998) presents an integrated strategy for teaching word identification that embeds planned phonics into quality students' literature. One of the first important steps is finding literature that contains the phonic element to be taught. Generally, students learn the sounds represented by the consonants quite easily because they are pronounced the same way in most words (exceptions are the silent *k,* as in *knock* and the silent *g,* as in *gnaw*). There are many approaches to teaching consonant sounds, but the methods that we find most engaging for students flow from shared-reading activities.

1. The teacher selects a developmentally appropriate book that the students will enjoy.

2. The teacher chooses letters that occur frequently in the book to focus on. For example, *Brown Bear, Brown Bear* (Martin, 1967) has the repeated story line "Brown bear, brown bear, what do you see? I see a [animal name] looking at me." This suggests a focus on the letters *b* [*bea*r], *m* [*m*e], and *s* [*se*e]. The letters are chosen based on their frequency within the story so that students will have maximum exposure to them.

3. The teacher reads the story to the students and then has them read as much of it as they can chorally along with him or her.

4. The teacher focuses on consonant sounds that are the goal of instruction. "What do you hear at the beginning of the word *bear*? That sound is written with the letter *b*. Let's see if anyone in this group has a name that starts with *b*." For that day the focus is on the recognition of the letter *b* and its sound, /b/, in as many words as possible. The big book *Brown Bear, Brown Bear* is made available to the students as they engage in writing activities that relate to their science unit on large mammals, for example. The teacher finds as many ways as possible for the students to engage with the letter *b* and the /b/ sound in many contexts. These experiences provide the students with a context in which to understand why they are learning the letter–sound correspondence between *b* and /b/. This continued application may occur in the student's regular classroom.

5. The next day the teacher chooses to focus on one of the other consonants for that week, *m*. Again, the teacher reads the book; then the students read chorally.

6. The teacher draws attention to the word *me*. It is fortunate that one of the animals in the book is a mouse. However, if the book didn't contain an animal with the /m/ sound, the teacher could bring in a picture of a mouse or a monkey and place it in the book over of one of the author's animal pictures. The teacher would write the animal's name, *mouse* or *monkey,* in place of the original name in the book. Then, when the students get to it, they read, "Brown bear, brown bear what do you see? I see a little *monkey* looking at me!"

7. A writing activity could involve the students rewriting the book using only animals with names that start with /m/. The teacher could have already printed copies of the repeated sentences, "Brown bear, brown bear, what do you see? I see a little _____ looking at me" and sets of pictures of a monkey, a moose, a muskrat, and a macaw. The students would place the pictures in the new book and write the name of the animal in the blank. Obviously the students couldn't spell the entire names, but they could focus on the /m/.

8. On another day the focus shifts to the letter *s,* as in *see.* The teacher may or may not read the book to the students again, depending on the time since the last lesson. The book is read chorally and then attention is drawn to the letter *s*. Activities like those just listed follow.

9. Another book-writing activity could be included, only this time the students would have to think of animal names that start with the letter *s* (*snake, shark, snail*). The teacher would already have pictures of the animals, so that when the students named one, the picture would be available for them to insert into their books.

Using the same book for three consonant sounds allows good books to be well used, and at the rate of three sounds per week the students will have been taught all the consonants within seven weeks. For an intervention group that attends daily sessions, all consonants (except the infrequently occurring *x*) will have been taught in four weeks. Also, the learning of letter–sound correspondences will have been reinforced through reading and writing. Keeping the books available allows students to access the words when they are in the initial stages of writing. Having the books and poetry gives them confidence that they can spell some words correctly, so they are more likely to take chances with invented spelling of other words (Wagstaff, 1997).

What about the Older Student Who Is a Nonreader?

If you have taught older students with severe reading difficulty, you may be thinking that they would never stand for reading *Brown Bear, Brown Bear.* So how do we teach consonant sounds to older nonreaders? First, we explain how sounds can be isolated, as in the first sound of his or her first and last name. That's two letters, but what about the others? There are two instructional methods that we can recommend.

1. Language experience stories can be used. This form of instruction requires the student to tell a story to a teacher, who writes it down as the student tells it. Then the student and teacher each pick out words from the story to learn. The teacher chooses high-frequency words that the student will encounter in many books. The student is likely to choose words of high interest. The teacher should begin with the words that the student wants to learn and isolate the initial sound in each. This provides a set of consonants to learn based on the student's interest. Next the teacher can use the words that she or he has chosen and again isolate the consonant sounds for study. If the words are nouns, the student or teacher can find pictures of them to use (with the consonant written beneath them) as a key to the consonants' pronunciation. These pictures should be displayed so that, if the student is attempting to read a word and can't remember a letter's sound, she or he can look at the pictures, say the word, and isolate the initial sound. It won't take many language experience stories to provide enough words for most of the consonants to be learned.

In using the language experience approach, we find that students often say that they don't have anything to tell that would make a story. What we do is ask them which special classes they have had that day (e.g., art, music, gym) and then have them explain what happened during that class. We write down what they say and ask questions to expand their thoughts and make their sentences more interesting. Students are amazed that their language and experiences can make a story!

2. Use simple nonfiction text. Because the student is limited in his or her reading ability, many narrative texts sound babyish to them. One way to avoid this is to use simple nonfiction. In science series written for beginning readers called *Let's Read and Find Out* (HarperCollins), one of the books, *The Sun* (Branley, 2002), describes the sun as Earth's closest star, its size and its distance from Earth, its temperature, and its value to living things on earth. Although it is too difficult for a nonreader (isn't everything?) it can be used in shared reading to provide a context in which the student can learn consonant sounds. Another book that is interesting, particularly for boys, is *Trucks That Build* (Klove, 1999), which comes from the *Ready-to-Read* series (Simon & Schuster) and describes the different trucks used for building (e.g., backhoe, front loader, bulldozer, excavator). Initial consonant sounds can be chosen from among the many types of trucks in the book. Scholastic also publishes a Science Series for beginning readers that includes *Shadows* (Otto, 2001). This book presents one sentence and a photograph on each page. Although the first few pictures illustrate children at about six years of age, later pictures show objects and older students. It even contains a glossary of five words: *clouds, electricity, light, shadow,* and *shapes.*

Nonfiction provides us with an opportunity to expose older students to information that they can't read on their own, and it makes the learning of letter–sound relationships more palatable for these sensitive young people.

Adjusting Hard Material for Older Students with Low Reading Ability

Sometimes our students are interested in a topic on which we cannot find a book. Or we wish to connect a story with a nonfiction text. One of our undergraduate students was teaching a young man in third grade who was able to read at a second-grade instructional level. With sufficient instruction and support he could read *Stellaluna* (Cannon, 1993), a story about a bat that lives with birds. The teacher wanted to develop the concept of bats, but the only material that she found was too hard for him. So we asked her to rewrite the material she found using as many words as possible that he could read. She also went to the Internet and downloaded pictures to accompany her story. The student loved it. With permission of Sara Ziolkowski, we present the text.

BATS!!!!

Many people are afraid of bats because they've heard things about them that are not true. People think bats fly into people's hair, turn into vampires, or hurt people. None of this is true. Bats are peaceful and interesting animals.

First, bats are not furry birds. They are mammals just like cats, dogs, and people. This means they have fur or hair and feed their babies with their own milk.

Bats have been around for many, many years. Some people have found bat bones that are 50 million years old. There are over 900 different kinds of bats on Earth. They are all different shapes and sizes. Some are very small and have a wingspan of 6 inches. Others are very big and have a wingspan of 79 inches!

Bats' wings are very interesting. Their wings are a lot like our hands. Bats' fingers are the long, thin bones found in their wings. Then there are flaps of skin that connect their fingers together to make up their wings. Bats even have thumbs on the top of their wings that help them crawl around in their homes.

Bat homes are dark, hidden places called roosts. Bat roosts can be caves, holes in trees, bushes, old buildings, and even attics. They find dark places to rest so they can blend in and be safe from other animals. Also, bats are very small so they can fit into small holes in buildings and attics. Some people are afraid of bats because they are nocturnal. This means they come out at night. During the day, bats like to rest, clean themselves, and sleep, but at night they hunt for food. Many people think that bats cannot see. This is not true. Bats can see very well, even in the dark. Being able to see in the dark helps them to hunt at night.

Bats also use their senses of smell and hearing to find food. Different bats eat different things. Some eat fruit or juices from plants. Others eat insects, and some catch fish. There are also vampire bats in Mexico and South America that bite cows and horses and drink their blood. Do not worry though, they do not turn into vampires or bite people!

Bats also hibernate in the winter. They find roosts to keep them warm in the winter and sleep until spring. Their bodies live off of the fat from the food they eat in the spring, summer, and fall.

As you can see, bats are not scary animals. They are very good at flying, so they won't get stuck in your hair. Most bats eat fruit or insects, so they won't hurt you. Finally, the only time you will see vampires is in books and movies, so you do not have to be afraid of them. Bats are like any other animal. They eat, sleep, and try to stay away from others that might hurt them.

Rewriting text takes a lot of time, but if teams of teachers got together they could produce many such materials that could be used year after year.

Teaching Vowel Sounds: Using Spelling Patterns to Read by Analogy

There are four reasons for recommending that vowel patterns be taught by analogy. First, as indicated earlier, vowel sounds are much more regular when you consider the consonants that follow them, so they should be easier to learn by analogy. Second, students learn to segment at the onset-rime level before the phonemic level; therefore, a teacher can begin to teach decoding by analogy earlier than synthetic phonics, which requires the ability to segment at the phoneme level. Third, if students are able to rhyme, it should be easier for them to understand the relationship between the sounds they hear at the end of a single-syllable word and the letters that represent them. Fourth, teaching by analogy requires students to use their existing knowledge to decode unknown words. We believe that building on such knowledge is important for students' understanding of themselves as readers and writers. Finally, we find the compare–contrast strategy used in reading by analogy to be a helpful tool for students' memory.

Notice that there are three prerequisites to reading by analogy implied in the last paragraph:

1. Students should understand the concept of rhyme. That doesn't meant that they must be able to distinguish pairs of words that rhyme and those that do not accurately 100 percent of the time, but they should be able to name a word that rhymes with common words (e.g., *cat, dog, can*).

2. Students should know which letters are vowels and which are consonants so that the teacher can define a spelling pattern as the vowel and the letters that come after it.

3. Students must have a small number of words that they recognize immediately. Often we call these *sight words,* that is, words that students can recognize immediately—within one second, or at sight, without having to decode them. Some words must be known by sight because students must use them as key words in reading by analogy. For example, they must know the word *cat* so that they can use it to decode *mat.* If students know no words by sight, the teacher must teach the key words necessary for them to begin reading by analogy. He or she should use the highest-frequency word (easier to learn because it will be seen more often) with that spelling pattern. For example: *cat* for the *-at* spelling pattern, *rain* for the *-ain* pattern, *dog* for the *-og* pattern.

Let's see how reading by analogy works. A student reads the sentence *Fox and Mouse watered the seeds every day* and stops at the word *seeds.* If the student knows the word *need,* we want him or her to be able to mentally say, "If *n-e-e-d* is *need,* then *s-e-e-d* must be *seed.*" If the student isn't aware of knowing a word that would help to decode the unknown one, the teacher prints the word *need* above the word *seed* and says, "Do you know this word?" If the student answers affirmatively, the teacher prompts use of the compare–contrast strategy. If the student doesn't know, the teacher tells him or her the word and prompts the compare–contrast strategy. The teacher should then make note that instruction of the spelling pattern *-eed* using the common word *need* is in order. A recent study indicates that in addition to reading by analogy, struggling beginning readers will progress more quickly in word reading on lists, pseudoword reading, and spelling during the first two years of instruction if they are also taught to analyze the phoneme–grapheme components of the key word, discuss what they discovered about grapheme–phoneme relationships, and use spelling to reinforce phonemic segmentation skills (Ehri, Satlow, & Gaskins, in press). You will note that the sample lesson on the next pages includes spelling as part of the teaching reading by analogy lesson. Later in this chapter we will illustrate how reading by analogy can be used in words with multiple syllables.

Is There an Order to Teaching Spelling Patterns?

Spelling patterns occur with varying frequency. As indicated earlier, *–ain* is more common than *–oach,* so the most frequent spelling patterns should be taught first because the students are more likely to meet them as they read stories. The Benchmark School has developed a list of common spelling patterns ordered by occurrence, reproduced in Table 4.2. All experts agree that these should be taught first. There is no agreement, however, on whether spelling patterns that contain short vowel sounds should be taught before those with long vowel sounds.

Johnston (1999) makes the case that students' spelling provides clues about when to begin spelling pattern instruction and which types should be taught first. She concludes that when the student is consistently representing both initial and final consonants in the spelling of words, the teacher should introduce one spelling pattern at a time, starting with patterns that contain the same short vowel sound. For example, she recommends that the teacher begin with *-at, -an,* and *-ap.* When students begin to include single vowels in their writing but confuse the short vowel sounds, she recommends teaching spelling patterns with different vowels, such as *-og* and *-ug.*

On the other hand, Allen (1998) recommends that the frequent spelling patterns be taught based on their occurrence in children's literature. To our knowledge there is no evidence to support any specific order of teaching frequent spelling patterns. Teachers must decide on the basis of the availability of reading materials that will provide students with practice reading words with specific patterns. Table 5.1, which appears later in the chapter, lists students' books and the spelling patterns that are used in a rhyming format. It should also be recognized that reading by analogy is a strategy, so we aren't teaching spelling patterns alone but a strategy by which students can use words that they already know to decode unknown words.

Sample Lesson: Reading by Analogy

The goal of this lesson is to teach the spelling pattern *-own* and have the students apply it to reading unknown words in the context of a story or poem. A children's literature book or poem that uses the *-own* spelling pattern in a rhyming format is selected. It must include at least two words that have that spelling pattern used in sentences that rhyme so the student will have practice in applying the spelling pattern to more than one word. For example, a good book for teaching the spelling pattern *-own* is *Silly Sally* (Wood, 1992). The first sentence describes how Sally went to town in a strange way, including upside down. So right away the students are presented with two examples of the *-own* spelling pattern: *down, town.* Each student should have index cards: one with the key word written on it (in this example it will be the common word *down*), one with the *-own* spelling pattern, and others with the single consonants *t* and *g* and consonant blends *br* and *cr.*

Procedure:

1. Read the big book *Silly Sally.*

2. Review or teach the key word *down* by having the first sentence of the story written on a large sentence strip. Remember to underline the spelling pattern in the key word, *down.*
   a. Read the sentence.
   b. Draw attention to the word *down* by saying, "This word is *down.* Remember it? You learned it when we read the book."
   c. If the students have learned the word and have a file box that contains all their known words alphabetized, the teacher says, "Look through your file box and find all the words that begin with the letter *d.* Now find the word *down.*"

3. "Look at the letters that I have underlined [*-own*]. Does anyone remember what we call those letters? That's right, *-own* is a spelling pattern, and it is the vowel and the letters that come after it."

4. "Today I am going to teach you how to use the word *down* to read some new words. Look at the word *town.* It is the same as *down,* except for the first letter. So, if *d-o-w-n* is *down,* then *t-o-w-n* must be . . . [*town*]!"

5. "Let's do some word building. I am going to give you a hint to the meaning of the word, and I want you to use your consonants and the spelling pattern *-own* to make the word. This word rhymes with *down* and is a color. Choose letter cards that, when you put them with the spelling pattern *-own,* will spell the word. [The teacher checks the students' cards for *brown.*] Now write the word on a blank card."

6. "The word rhymes with *down* and is the look on your face when you are not happy. Choose letters that, when you put them with the spelling pattern *-own,* will spell the word. [The teacher checks the students' cards for *frown.*] Now write the word on a blank card."

7. "The word rhymes with *down* and is what a queen wears on her head." Choose letters that, when you put them with the spelling pattern *-own,* will spell the word." [The teacher checks the students' cards for *crown.*] Now write the word on a blank card."

Now the students return to reread the book or, even better, a poem with the *-own* spelling pattern. The following poem is one example.

FALL
Red, yellow, and then to brown.
Leaves change color, then fall down.
From sun and warmth to less light.
Days end early into night.

Steps in Teaching Reading by Analogy

1. Find a poem or story that uses a common spelling pattern in a rhyming format (e.g., *Is Your Mama a Llama* [Guarino, 1989], *Sheep on a Ship* [Shaw, 1989]).

2. Choose a high-frequency word that contains the common spelling pattern to be taught and write down the sentence from the book that contains it. (If the book has a common spelling pattern but does not include a high-frequency word with the pattern in it, you can write your own sentence to introduce the word.)

3. Read aloud the sentence that contains the key word in it.

4. Review or introduce the key word with the spelling pattern underlined. If this is the first time you are teaching spelling patterns, you must define what the spelling pattern is: the vowel and the letters that come after it (in a syllable). Begin with one-syllable words and then move into polysyllabic words later.

5. Model using the compare–contrast strategy (if *d-o-w-n* is *down*, then *t-o-w-n* must be *town*).

6. Have the students build words with index cards: one that has the key word, one that has the spelling pattern, and others each with either a single or a double consonant that, when added to the spelling patterns, will make a real word.

7. Make up clues that will help the students build words. The clue should always begin: "It rhymes with [key word] and is [meaning clue]."

8. Check that the students have made the correct word, and then have them write the word on another card.

9. Reread the book with the students, or better yet, bring in a poem that includes that spelling pattern. Don't be afraid to make up your own poem, as we did. It doesn't need to be publishable to make the point to your students that reading by analogy involves taking a word that they know and using it to read a word that they don't know.

Notice that we have used students' books rather than specific basal readers to teach students how to use spelling patterns to read by analogy. The reason for this is that many good books are written in a rhyming pattern that lend themselves to these methods. We list several of them by their spelling patterns in Table 5.1. The list is by no means exhaustive, but it provides a starting point. It doesn't matter whether you use big books, easy-to-read books, or basal readers. However, it should be interesting to keep students motivated to learn to read. Rather than teaching these skills in isolation, we advocate the use of materials that students will want to read as we demonstrate decoding strategies to them.

Poetry is another good source of text to teach spelling patterns. We recommend three books that provide poetry with spelling patterns: *Phonics through Poetry* (1998) and *More Phonics through Poetry* (2007), both authored by Babs Bell Hajdusiewicz and published by Goodyear Books; and *70 Wonderful Word Family Poems* (2002) by Jennifer Wilen and Beth Handa, published by Scholastic.

How to Read Polysyllabic Words by Analogy

One of the benefits of teaching students to decode unfamiliar words by using familiar ones is that the same strategy applies to longer words. Because each syllable must have a vowel sound, it must therefore have a spelling pattern. Students can be taught to look for the spelling patterns in a word and to decode each syllable using the same compare–contrast strategy they use to read single-syllable words. Of course, not all syllables allow direct comparison, so many prefixes and suffixes must be taught as separate chunks; still, they are usually regularly pronounced. Consider the *-ly* ending. Students can be explicitly taught that /le/ is pronounced /lē/, or you can explain that the letter *y* often sounds like /ē/ at the end of words. Take the common polysyllabic word *suddenly*. The teacher demonstrates reading by analogy by writing common words above each syllable. For example, *mud-hen-ly* would be written above *sud-den-ly*.

The student is encouraged to apply the compare–contrast strategy to each spelling pattern, so if *m-u-d* is *mud,* then *s-u-d* must be *sud*. For the next syllable, if *h-e-n* is *hen,* then *d-e-n* must be *den*. Now the student must blend these two syllables to get *sudden* and then add the already known /lē/, and blend *sudden* with it to get *suddenly*. At this point the student should reread the sentence to be sure that what has been read makes sense.

The Importance of Cross-Checking

It is important for students to know that reading *must* make sense. We have seen too many poor readers who read to "get done," without regard to meaning. So, as we teach students to read by analogy, we always have them *reread* the sentence to see if it makes sense. For example, in the following sentence the student stops at the word *seeds:* "Fox and Mouse watered the seeds every day." As indicated earlier in this chapter, the student employs the analogy strategy, using a known word, *need,* to figure out *seeds,* but then must reread the sentence for sense. In other words, the student must ask him or herself if it makes sense that someone would water *seeds* every day. If the word makes sense, the student continues reading. If it doesn't, he or she should try another word.

We believe that no matter what strategy the student uses to decode an unknown word, she or he should always reread to make sure it makes sense. Therefore, we teach cross-checking using the following steps:

1. Say the first sound or sounds.
2. Finish reading the sentence.
3. Go back and think of a word that has the same first sound or sounds.
4. See if the word has a spelling pattern that you know. If it does, use the compare–contrast strategy to figure out the word.
5. When you think you know the word, say it and finish the sentence.
6. Reread the sentence with the word to make sure it makes sense.

TABLE 5.1 Rhyming Books with Spelling Patterns
(The books listed have at least two words with the same pattern)

Spelling Pattern	Author	Title	City, Publisher	Date
-ace	Shirley Neitzel	*The Dress I'll Wear to the Party*	New York: Scholastic	1992
	Arnold Lobel	*The Rose in my Garden*	New York: Scholastic	1984
	Barbara Gregorich	*Jace, Mace, and the Big Race*	Grand Haven: School Zone	1992
-ack	Shirley Neitzel	*The Dress I'll Wear to the Party*	New York: Scholastic	1992
-ad	Reeve Lindbergh	*The Day the Goose Got Loose*	London: Puffin	1995
-ail(s)	Marilyn Janovitz	*Can I Help?*	New York: North-South Books	1996
	Nancy Shaw	*Sheep on a Ship*	New York: The Trumpet Club	1989
-ain	William H. Hooks	*A Dozen Dizzy Dogs*	New York: Bantam Books for Young Readers	1990
	Laura McGee Kvasnosky	*See You Later Alligator*	New York: Red Wagon Books	1995
-ake	B. G. Hennessy	*Jake Baked the Cake*	London: Puffin	1992
	Mark Tolon Brown	*Pickle Things*	New York: Parents Magazines Press	1980
	Margaret Blackstone	*This Is Maine*	New York: Henry Holt	1995
	Dayle Ann Dodds	*Wheel Away*	New York: Scholastic	1989
-alk	Felicia Bond	*Tumble Bumble*	New York: Harper Festival	1999
-all	Robert Louis Stevenson	*The Moon*	New York: Harper and Row	1984
	Judy Hindley	*Little and Big*	Cambridge: Candlewick Press	1986
-and	Shirley Neitzel	*The Dress I'll Wear to the Party*	New York: Scholastic	1992
	Leah Komaiko	*Earl's Too Cool for Me*	New York: Harper and Row	1988
-ap	Nancy Shaw	*Sheep on a Ship*	New York: Trumpet Club	1989
	Marilyn Janovitz	*Can I Help?*	New York: North-South Books	1996
	Margaret Blackstone	*This Is Maine*	New York: Henry Holt	1995
-ar	Crescent Dragonwagon	*Half a Moon and One Whole Star*	New York: Macmillan	1986
	Edith Baer	*This Is the Way We Go to School*	New York: Scholastic	1992
-ars	Laura Numeroff	*Chimps Don't Wear Glasses*	New York: Scholastic	1995
-art	Susan Arkin Couture	*The Biggest Horse I Ever Did See*	New York: HarperCollins	1997
	Edith Baer	*This Is the Way We Go to School*	New York: Scholastic	1992

(continued)

TABLE *5.1*   *Continued*

Spelling Pattern	Author	Title	City, Publisher	Date
-at	Wendy Cheyette Lewison	*Buzzzz Said the Bee*	New York: Scholastic	1992
	Brian Wildsmith	*Cat on the Mat*	New York: Oxford University Press	1982
	Bill Martin, Jr., and John Archambault	*The Ghost-Eye Tree*	New York: Scholastic	1985
	Joanna Cole	*Mixed-Up Magic*	New York: Scholastic	1987
-ath	Marilyn Janovitz	*Can I Help?*	New York: North-South Books	1996
-ay	Raffi	*Five Little Ducks*	New York: Crown Books for Young Readers	1999
	Bill Peet	*Kermit the Hermit*	Boston: Houghton Mifflin	1973
	Razvan	*Lemon Whip*	New York: Atheneum	1995
	Marcia Vaughan	*Snap*	New York: Scholastic	1994
-eam	Jane Yolen	*Beneath the Ghost Moon*	New York: Little Brown	1998
	Reeve Lindbergh	*The Day the Goose Got Loose*	London: Puffin	1995
-eeds	Marilyn Janovitz	*Can I Help?*	New York: North-South Books	1996
-eep	Nancy E. Shaw	*Sheep in a Jeep*	Boston: Houghton Mifflin	1997
-ell	Bill Peet	*Kermit the Hermit*	Boston: Houghton Mifflin	1973
	David McPhail	*Pigs Aplenty, Pigs Galore*	New York: Dutton Children's Books	1993
	Angela McAllister	*Sleepy Ella*	New York: Doubleday Books for Young Readers	1994
-est	Eileen Spinelli	*Naptime Laptime*	New York: Scholastic	1995
-ide	Rita Golden Gelman	*Hello, Cat You Need a Hat*	New York: Scholastic	1979
-ig	Wendy Cheyette Lewison	*Buzzzz Said the Bee*	New York: Scholastic	1992
	James Young	*The Cows are in the Corn*	New York: Scholastic	1996
-ight	Angela McAllister	*Sleepy Ella*	New York: Doubleday Books for Young Readers	1994
	Razvan	*Lemon Whip*	New York: Atheneum	1995
	Marc Gave	*Monkey See, Monkey Do*	New York: Cartwheel Books	1993
	Crescent Dragonwagon	*Half a Moon and One Whole Star*	New York: Macmillan	1986
	William H. Hooks, Joanne Oppenheim, and Barbara Brenner	*How Do You Make a Bubble?*	New York: Byron Preiss Visual Publications	1992
	Duncan Bell	*Grandfather's Wheelything*	New York: Simon and Schuster	1994
	Tom Paxton	*The Animals' Lullaby*	New York: Morrow Junior Books	1993
	Jane Yolen	*Beneath the Ghost Moon*	New York: Little Brown	1998
	Kathleen Hague	*Calendar Bears*	New York: Henry Holt	1997

TABLE 5.1   *Continued*

Spelling Pattern	Author	Title	City, Publisher	Date
-ill	David McPhail	*Pigs Aplenty, Pigs Galore*	New York: Dutton Children's Books	1993
	Dayle Ann Dodds	*Wheel Away*	New York: Scholastic	1989
	Bernard Most	*Four and Twenty Dinosaurs*	New York: Scholastic	1990
	Deborah Chanara	*Miss Mabel's Table*	New York: Browndeer Press	1994
-in	Cheryl Willis Hudson and Bernette G. Ford	*Bright Eyes, Brown Skin*	New York: Scholastic	1990
	Rita Golden Gelman	*Hello, Cat You Need a Hat*	New York: Scholastic	1979
-ind	Laura Numeroff	*Chimps Don't Wear Glasses*	New York: Scholastic	1995
	Ellen Blonder	*Noisy Breakfast*	New York: Scholastic	1994
-ing	David McPhail	*Pigs Aplenty, Pigs Galore*	New York: Dutton Children's Books	1993
	Etta Wilson	*Music in the Night*	New York: Cobblehill Books	1993
	Gail Jorgensen	*Crocodile Beat*	Adelaide: Omnibus Books	1988
	Stephanie Calmenson	*Engine, Engine Number Nine*	New York: Hyperion Books for Children	1996
	William H. Hooks, Joanne Oppenheim, and Barbara Brenner	*How Do You Make a Bubble?*	New York: Byron Preiss Visual Publications	1992
	Karla Kuskin	*City Dog*	New York: Clarion Books	1994
	Karla Kuskin	*City Noise*	New York: Harper Collins	1994
	Bill Peet	*Kermit the Hermit*	Boston: Houghton Mifflin	1973
	Marcia Vaughan	*Snap*	New York: Scholastic	1994
	Joanne Oppenheim	*Have You Seen Birds?*	New York: Scholastic	1968
-ip	William H. Hooks, Joanne Oppenheim, and Barbara Brenner	*How Do You Make a Bubble?*	New York: Byron Preiss Visual Publications	1992
	Bill Peet	*Kermit the Hermit*	Boston: Houghton Mifflin	1973
	Nancy Shaw	*Sheep on a Ship*	New York: Trumpet Club	1989
-irt	Barbara Hill	*The Wind*	Wellington: Government Printer	1984
	Dayle Ann Dodds	*Wheel Away*	New York: Scholastic	1989
-ite	William H. Hooks, Joanne Oppenheim, and Barbara Brenner	*How Do You Make a Bubble?*	New York: Byron Preiss Visual Publications	1992
-iv	Bill Martin, Jr.	*The Maestro Plays*	New York: Henry Holt	1970
-oal	Joanna Cole	*Mixed-Up Magic*	New York: Scholastic	1987
	Razvan	*Lemon Whip*	New York: Atheneum	1995
-ock	Leah Komaiko	*Great-Aunt Ida and Her Great Dane, Doc*	New York: Delacorte Press	1994
	Bill Peet	*Kermit the Hermit*	Boston: Houghton Mifflin	1973
-og	Leonard Kessler	*Ghosts and Crows and Things With O's*	New York: Scholastic	1976

(continued)

TABLE 5.1 *Continued*

Spelling Pattern	Author	Title	City, Publisher	Date
-old	Deborah Chandra	*Miss Mabel's Table*	New York: Browndeer Press	1994
-one	William H. Hooks	*A Dozen Dizzy Dogs*	New York: Bantam Books for Young Readers	1990
-ook	Laura Numeroff	*Chimps Don't Wear Glasses*	New York: Scholastic	1995
	Leonard Kessler	*Ghosts and Crows and Things With O's*	New York: Scholastic	1976
	Bill Peet	*Kermit the Hermit*	Boston: Houghton Mifflin	1973
-oon	Crescent Dragonwagon	*Half a Moon and One Whole Star*	New York: Macmillan	1986
-oose	Reeve Lindbergh	*The Day the Goose Got Loose*	London: Puffin	1995
-op	Laura Numeroff	*Chimps Don't Wear Glasses*	New York: Scholastic	1995
	Ellen Blonder	*Noisy Breakfast*	New York: Scholastic	1994
-ose	Marilyn Janowitz	*Can I Help?*	New York: North-South Books	1996
	William H. Hooks, Joanne Oppenheim, and Barbara Brenner	*How Do You Make a Bubble?*	New York: Byron Preiss Visual Publications	1992
-ot	Rita Golden Gelman	*The Biggest Sandwich Ever*	New York: Scholastic	1980
-ound	Arnold Lobel	*The Rose in My Garden*	New York: Scholastic	1984
	Anne Frasier	*Sleep Tight*	London: Onyx Books	2003
-ouse	Jane Yolen	*Beneath the Ghost Moon*	New York: Little Brown	1998
	Mary Ann Huberman	*A House Is a House for Me*	New York: Scholastic	1978
	Robert Louis Stevenson	*The Moon*	New York: Harper and Row	1984
-out	James Young	*The Cows Are in the Corn*	New York: Scholastic	1996
-ow	Edith Baer	*This Is the Way We Go to School*	New York: Scholastic	1992
	Juan Wijngaard	*Going to Sleep on the Farm*	New York: Dial Books for Young Readers	1992
-own	Duncan Bell	*Grandfather's Wheelything*	New York: Simon & Schuster	1994
	Bernard Most	*Four and Twenty Dinosaurs*	New York: Scholastic	1990
	B. G. Hennessy	*Jake Baked the Cake*	London: Puffin	1992
	Maurice Sendak	*Pierre*	New York: Scholastic	1962
	Teddy Slater	*N-O Spells No*	New York: Scholastic	1993
-ub	Leah Komaiko	*Earl's Too Cool for Me*	New York: Harper & Row	1988
	Cathy East Dubowski	*Snug Bug*	New York: Grosset & Dunlap	1995
-ug	Mary Ann Hoberman	*A House Is a House for Me*	New York: Scholastic	1978
	Cathy East Dubowski	*Snug Bug*	New York: Grosset & Dunlap	1995

How to Learn Words That Are Difficult to Decode

Not all single-syllable and polysyllabic words lend themselves to reading by analogy, but by the time a student is reading even a little he or she has confronted inconsistencies in our language. One of the words that appear relatively early in students' literature is *serious*. How do we teach students such a word? This challenge has been faced by any teacher of an intervention group with the following frequent words: *through, thought, there, their, where, was,* and so forth. All of these words occur frequently enough that students must learn to recognize them automatically. But how? Remember the basis for automatic word recognition: frequency and repetition (Chapter 6, on fluency, expands on this concept). It applies equally to high-frequency irregular words. There is no simple way to teach these words, but a few principles can be offered:

1. Introduce them in the context of a sentence, because the meaning of many of them isn't clear. That is, they are abstract words that do not have a concrete referent.
2. Isolate them for study.
3. Use as many ways as you can to provide the students with experience reading and writing them.
4. Use the *See It–Say It–Spell It* chant to keep students engaged. It goes like this. The teacher has the word written in a sentence from the book being used in instruction.
   a. Teacher: "This is one word that you are going to learn today. This word is *thought.*"
   b. "Say it." Teacher and students: "Thought."
   c. Teacher: "Look at the word and spell it, *t-h-o-u-g-h-t, thought.*"
   d. Students: "*t-h-o-u-g-h-t, thought.*"
   e. Teacher: "Clap your hands as you say each letter."
   f. All: "*t-h-o-u-g-h-t, thought.*"
   g. "Now write it." The teacher spells it again as she or he writes each letter and students copy: "*t-h-o-u-g-h-t.*"
5. The students should return to a poem or story that contains the word *thought.* Also, the teacher may want the students to use the word in a journal response or guided writing activity. The prompt for a response activity could include the word, such as "When I read the story *Fox Outfoxed* (Marshall, 1992), I *thought* . . ."
6. Other follow-up activities include "making words" (Cunningham & Cunningham, 1992), in which students are given a set of letter cards (each with a single letter). The teacher asks the students to make two-letter words, then three-letter words, then four-letter words, and so on, until they come close to the "mystery word." In our example here, that could be a frequent word that they just learned (e.g., *thought).* Making words helps students to see the relationship between sounds and letters.

Sample Lesson: Teaching High-Frequency Words by Sight

In this lesson the goal is to teach three high-frequency words that have infrequent spelling patterns or that are difficult to decode: *went, met, walking.* You can use the book *Silly Sally,* which was used before to teach *-own.* Again, have index cards for the students, and have sentences from the story that include the words *went, met,* and *walking.*

Introduction.   "The other day when we were reading *Silly Sally,* there were some words that are important for you to know because you see them in books all the time. Silly Sally *went* to town. The first word that you are going to learn is *went.*"

Teacher Models Chant.   "Say it, *went.* Spell it, *w-e-n-t, went.* Clap it, *w-e-n-t.* Now write it, *w-e-n-t, went.*" The teacher also might say, "*Went* is one of those action words; it tells us that someone is doing something. Let's make up another sentence with the word *went* in it. The teacher writes, "Our class *went* to the zoo in May."

The teacher provides the same introduction and modeling for the other words being taught, perhaps asking the students to make up a new sentence with a word in it but continuing to model writing each one.

Now the teacher finds a new piece of literature in which the students can practice reading the words taught. In a pinch the teacher can write a short story using the words, but rarely are our stories as interesting as those written by children's authors. If the words are truly frequent, it won't be hard to find books that include them.

Practicing Sight Words in Isolation

Students must see words over and over in order to store them in memory. Once this happens, such words become sight words—recognized without matching letter–sound patterns. The best way to store words in memory is through wide reading in which the student meets them again and again in a meaningful and supportive context. However, some struggling readers can profit from additional practice with words in isolation as a means of increasing their sight vocabularies.

Which words should a teacher select for isolated practice? Obviously, you should teach words that students do not know, words that they missed during administration of the informal reading inventory (IRI) word list, or words missed during reading of the IRI passages. Also use words that proved troublesome during past intervention lessons, and provide practice on words that were known but not automatically—that is, words that the students pronounced only after some hesitation. Another source of words for practice in isolation is high-frequency words, such as *the, around,* and *them,* that occur over and over in text. These words should become sight words as quickly as possible. Figure 5.1 provides a list of high-frequency words (Harris & Sipay, 1990).

Many high-frequency words are what we call *function words:* prepositions, articles, and pronouns that have little meaning of their own. For example, try to define *which* or *to.* Function words can be quite confusing because their meanings are abstract. In addition, they tend to look alike (*when* and *then; where* and *were*) and they often represent irregular letter–sound patterns. Because of this, function words are certainly strong candidates for additional practice. Other words for isolated practice are those that are personally important to the student.

Word Cards and Word Sorts

Word cards are a very effective method for providing practice in isolation. Students enjoy manipulating and sorting them in various ways. Word cards also provide evidence of improvement. A growing stack of known word cards is visible and motivating proof of student progress.

Practicing words in isolation should always be tied to meaning in some way. On the back of the word cards, students should draw pictures or write clues to help them remember the word's meaning and they should tie the meaning of the word to their lives in some way. For abstract function words, place the word in a phrase that illustrates its meaning, such as *to* the store or *under* the bed.

What do students do with word cards that help turn words into sight vocabulary? Cards provide an opportunity for multiple exposures to the words as students decide on and construct meaning clues for the back of a card. More exposure occurs as students sort cards in a variety of ways. They can sort into three stacks: words I know, words I almost know, and words I do not know. They can sort according to sound or spelling patterns, according to structural clues such as prefixes, and according to meaning.

Word sorts are of two kinds. In a closed sort, the teacher tells students how to sort the words—for example, all words that end in the same sound or that begin in the same way. In an open sort, students sort the words according to categories of their own choosing. Manipulating word cards into stacks representing different categories can be a motivating and enjoyable experience.

Games are often recommended as a way of extending sight vocabulary. However, we strongly advise that you do *not* use games, for several reasons. First, your instructional time is probably too brief and too precious to allow time for setting up a game and explaining the rules for playing. Second, students tend to focus on winning the game rather than learning words. They pay more attention to the moves than to the words, and they get so caught up

FIGURE 5.1 High-Frequency Words at Preprimer, Primer, and First-Grade Levels

Preprimer

a	but	don't	he	like	out	sit	want
all	by	down	help	little	pet	so	we
am	came	fish	here	look	pig	stop	what
and	can	fly	hide	make	play	that	where
are	can't	for	home	man	read	the	who
at	car	from	I	me	red	they	will
be	cat	game	in	my	ride	thing	with
bear	come	get	is	no	run	this	yes
big	day	girl	it	not	said	time	you
blue	did	go	it's	of	say	to	your
book	do	good	jump	old	see	too	
boy	dog	have	let	on	she	up	

Primer

about	dad	funny	if	much	put	street	two
after	didn't	good-by	into	must	rabbit	sun	under
an	does	got	just	name	rain	surprise	us
animal	door	green	know	need	ran	swim	very
as	duck	grow	lake	new	road	take	wait
ask	each	had	last	next	rock	talk	walk
away	eat	happy	laugh	night	sad	tell	was
back	end	has	liked	nothing	same	thank	water
bad	every	hat	lion	now	sat	that's	way
bag	fall	hello	live	oh	saw	them	well
ball	fast	hen	lived	one	school	then	went
bat	father	her	lost	open	seed	there	were
bed	feel	hid	lot	or	show	think	when
bee	feet	high	made	other	sing	thought	why
bird	find	hill	many	over	sky	three	window
bob	fire	him	may	paper	sleep	today	woman
box	fix	his	maybe	park	slow	took	won't
call	found	hot	more	pat	small	top	work
city	fox	house	mother	people	some	tree	would
could	friend	how	mouse	pick	something	trick	you're
cow	frog	I'll	Mr.	place	sometime	truck	youth
cut	fun	I'm	Mrs.	plant	still	turtle	

(continued)

FIGURE 5.1 *Continued*

First Grade

again	cave	fell	jay	off	smell	tonight
ago	chair	fill	keep	only	smile	town
alone	children	fine	kind	our	smiled	toy
along	class	first	king	outside	snake	track
always	clean	floor	kite	paint	snow	train
another	close	flower	kitten	pan	someday	tried
ant	cloud	food	leave	part	someone	trip
any	clown	gave	leg	party	song	try
anything	coat	give	let's	picture	soon	turn
apple	cold	glad	letter	plan	sorry	TV
aren't	color	glass	light	please	sound	until
around	coming	gold	line	pot	squirrel	use
ate	cook	gone	long	pound	stand	wasn't
bake	couldn't	grandma	love	pretty	star	watch
bark	country	grass	lunch	push	start	we'll
beautiful	cry	great	making	quiet	stay	wet
because	dance	grew	mayor	ready	step	what's
been	dark	ground	mean	real	stick	which
began	dinner	guess	men	right	stone	while
begin	doctor	hand	might	room	store	white
being	doesn't	he's	miss	rope	story	wind
best	don	head	mix	sandy	stuck	winter
better	draw	hear	mom	sang	sure	wish
bike	drink	heard	money	sea	table	without
birthday	drove	helper	morning	seat	tail	wood
bit	even	herself	most	secret	tall	word
bite	ever	hi	move	seen	teacher	worker
black	everyone	hold	moved	sheep	than	yell
boat	everything	hole	myself	shoe	their	yellow
bone	everywhere	hop	named	shop	there's	zoo
breakfast	eye	horse	near	should	these	
brother	face	hungry	never	shout	those	
brown	family	hurt	nice	side	tiger	
bus	far	I've	noise	sign	tire	
cake	faster	inside	nose	sister	together	
care	feed	isn't	note	six	told	

Source: Adapted from Harris & Sipay, 1990.

in winning and losing that they pay scant attention to the purpose of the activity—learning words.

If you have taught the words using the *See It–Say It–Spell It* method, the students will have them ready for sorting. If you are using other words, make the word cards for the students. This will reduce the amount of time needed before the sort begins and avoid spelling errors or penmanship that cannot be easily read. If you are working with an individual or a small group, you will be able to carefully match the cards to the students' needs. That is, you can choose words that were missed during oral reading or words that are personally meaningful to the students. This is extremely difficult to do with a large group—for that we suggest the following procedure. Choose words from the reading selections that you feel are important for students to know, words that were missed in spelling or writing, and words that students stumbled over during practice reading. Make some duplicate cards and put them all in a tub or bucket. When you want students to engage in word sorts, give each student or group a number of words from the bucket to use for the sorting process. Students often receive some words that will not fit in a closed sort. When this occurs, they can suggest a category for these words and for other words that would fit in the same category. When the sorting is over, return the words to the bucket and shuffle the contents. The teacher can use word cards and word sorts to provide practice in sight word development. High-frequency words and function words often need additional practice by struggling readers.

Letter and Sound Word Sorts

Words with two letters, three letters, etc.

Words with one syllable, two syllables, etc.

Words that start with a consonant, two consonants, a vowel, two vowels, etc.

Words that have double letters that make one sound

Words that have silent letters

Words with two vowels that make one sound

Words with a long vowel sound, a short vowel sound, etc.

Words with the same vowel pattern

Words with a prefix, a suffix, or a foreign root

Words that rhyme

Meaning Word Sorts

Words that stand for something you can touch, see, hear, taste, etc.

Words that stand for something you can buy, sell, own, trade, learn, make, etc.

Words that stand for something that is in your house, locker, book bag, kitchen, bedroom, classroom, etc.

Words that stand for something your mother will/will not let you bring home

Words that stand for something you can do, be, etc.

Words that stand for something you saw someone do on TV, in the movies, in your neighborhood, etc.

Words that stand for something an animal, plant, machine, etc., can be or do

Words that can describe a person, animal, plant, food, sport, etc.

Words that make you feel happy, sad, angry, etc.

Glue words (articles, prepositions, helping verbs, conjunctions, etc.)

Putting It All Together: Guided Reading

We have described several ways to teach students how to identify words and then to verify that what they have read makes sense. These instructional strategies assume that students are reading connected text, either orally or silently, and that the teacher is providing an introduction (Clay, 1991), feedback, and assistance. The teacher's introduction is crafted based on his or her understanding of the challenges that the students will face when reading the particular text. So the teacher may use specific words in the introduction that she or he believes the children will not know (i.e., cannot accurately read or do not understand). She or he may also use certain phrases in the introduction that will be unfamiliar to the students. Finally, the introduction engages the students in a dialogue as they look at the pictures and discuss what is happening in the story. This type of introduction builds their understanding of the overall structure of the story (but not the climax) and allows them to read the story more easily. As the students read the book, the teacher guides them to different sources of information to use when faced with an unknown word. To illustrate effective feedback and guidance, let's return to a segment of the *Fox and Mouse* passage from the *QRI-4* used earlier. The text is in parentheses, the student's reading is written above the text, and the teacher's responses are in the second column.

Student	**Teacher's responses**
"Fox wanted to plant a /g/ . . ."	"Look at the picture. What could Fox be planting that starts with a *g*?"
(Fox wanted to plant a garden.)	
Student replies: "garden."	"Good, now reread the sentence and see if it makes sense."
"Fox wanted to plant a garden."	"Does it make sense?"
Student: "Yes, it does."	"Okay, keep reading."
"Mouse helped him."	
(Mouse helped him.)	
"They put /ss/ . . . in the garden."	"Do you know another word that has the *-eed* spelling pattern in it?
(They put seeds in the ground.)	
Student says: "need."	"Good! If *n-e-e-d* is *need,* then *s-e-e-d* must be . . ."
Student says: "seed."	"Now reread the sentence and see if *seed* makes sense."
"They put seeds in the garden."	"Does that make sense? Yes, it does! Now, look at the last word in the sentence. You said it was *garden,* and that makes sense, but if you look carefully at all the letters it isn't *garden.* Look at the word *garden* at the end of the first sentence. Now look at this word (points to *ground*). What are the first sounds in the word?"
Student says: "/gr/"	"Okay, so read the sentence and say /gr/ for the last word."
"They put seeds in the /gr/ . . ."	"What would make sense there that starts with /gr/?"
Student says: "ground."	"Great! Now read the sentence again."
"They put seeds in the ground."	"Yes, excellent!"
"They watered the seeds."	
(They watered the seeds.)	
"Then they waited."	
(Then they waited.)	

Note that this example has more words that the student doesn't know than we would recommend for instructional level material. However, we wanted to provide several examples of teacher–student interaction within a short piece of text. These teacher responses provide the student with three sources of information: pictures, letter–sound correspondences, and meaning. They model for the student what she or he can do when faced with unknown words.

Fountas and Pinnell (1996) describe this type of instructional guidance as *guided reading*. Here are some additional characteristics:

1. The instruction occurs in small groups of students with similar reading abilities.
2. Each student reads the whole text silently.
3. The goal is independent reading of books of increasing difficulty.
4. Students are grouped and regrouped as their abilities change.

You might wonder how the teacher can guide the reading if the students are reading silently. What Fountas and Pinnell mean is that the students all read at the same time, as silently as they can. The teacher interacts and guides the reading of one student at a time. Students may read the entire text to themselves, and, while the teacher is listening and guiding one student, the others are engaged in partner reading. This approach attempts to achieve some of the benefits of Reading Recovery, but in small groups. Guided reading differs from round-robin reading, in which only one student reads at a time (and often the others are not paying attention). As we know from decades of research, the more the students are on task (i.e., reading), the more learning takes place.

Teacher Prompting during Oral Reading

So how do we answer the teacher's question: "What do I say when a student gets stuck on a word?" First, all students should be reading material at their instructional level (at least 90 percent oral reading accuracy or 95 percent semantic acceptability) and 70 percent comprehension. When a student pauses at a word or miscues on a word, the teacher should wait until the student has completed a meaningful segment of text (clause or sentence) to see if the student will spontaneously self-correct. If the teacher interrupts too soon, the student will not learn how to check that his or her reading makes sense in the sentence.

Teachers should encourage children to use multiple cues to decode unknown words and the type of clue used should depend on the student's developmental level (Brown, 2003). Emergent readers use primarily picture clues as the teacher points out that the word the child says should begin with the same sound as the initial letter. As the child develops the ability to use multiple cue sources, the teacher will expand prompts. Notice in the guided reading example above that the teacher prompted the child to use picture clues, sound clues (initial and spelling patterns), syntactic clues, and meaning clues often *in concert* with each other. The goal of the teacher's support, or scaffolding, is to "keep the task whole while students learn to manage the parts" (Clark & Graves, 2005, p. 571). Teachers need to scaffold to keep the meaning of the text in focus while the students are trying to figure out the words. There are several good articles in our references that explain how teachers can use students' knowledge and text to successfully prompt students during oral reading (Brown, 2003; Clark & Graves, 2005; Cole, 2006).

We cannot leave this topic without addressing the role of dialect in oral reading. Dialect is a form of a language that differs from what is considered "standard." For example, if a student reads *pumpkin* as *punkin,* it is not considered a reading error or miscue, but rather represents the way the student pronounces the word in speech. This seems simple enough, until one considers African American Vernacular English (AAVE), which some teachers believe (incorrectly) to contain certain pronunciations that are "wrong"—therefore, reading errors. Speakers of AAVE often omit the past tense marker (*-ed*), plural marker (*s*), and the possessive (*'s*) in speech and therefore in reading. Because these forms of language are in their speech they should not be considered reading miscues. Teachers must learn the characteristics of the student's language so that misinterpretations between a speech pronunciation and a reading error do not occur. This issue applies similarly to ELLs whose pronunciation of English will be affected by characteristics of his or her native language.

Application to English Language Learners

The Report of the National Literacy Panel on Language-Minority Children and Youth (August & Shanahan, 2006) concluded that as with native speakers of English, word awareness, letter knowledge, and phonemic awareness are predictors of word identification and reading fluency. Therefore it appears that the basic processes of learning to read are similar across languages. Of interest to teachers is whether the same teaching methods are applicable to ELLs. There have been few studies that compared whether published programs of teaching word identification skills to native English speakers would be as efficient with English language learners. However, like the reference to the *Jolly Phonics* program in Chapter 4, the studies that we found (Gunn, Biglan, Smolkowksi & Ary, 2000; Vaughn, Mathes, Linan-Thompson, & Francis, 2005) indicated that the same supplementary methods using a large decoding emphasis were as effective with children whose native language was Spanish as with native speakers. The Gunn et al. study provided a direct comparison between Hispanic and non-Hispanic students using the same curriculum. In contrast, the Vaughn et al. study developed a curriculum in Spanish to parallel an already established program. The program included several strands: phonemic analysis, letter–sound knowledge, word identification, reading in decodable text, and comprehension of such text. The Spanish version of the intervention program included modifications related to the specific nature of Spanish and language support systems using visual aids, gestures, and facial expressions in teaching vocabulary and clarifying meaning of content, as well as providing explicit instruction in language use and allowing for elaborated responses to words included in the program. Higher scores for the intervention group were found on word attack and reading comprehension on the Woodcock Language Proficiency Battery–Revised (Woodcock, 1991).

The long-term effects of such interventions were documented by Gunn, Smolkowski, Biglan, and Black (2002) who found that the students (Hispanic and non-Hispanic) who received supplementary instruction continued to score higher on measures of word attack, oral reading fluency, vocabulary, and comprehension than students who did not receive the instruction. In fact, Gunn and colleagues reported that ELLs who spoke little English profited as much by the intervention as ELLs who were more proficient in English.

In summary, it appears that the basic tenets of word identification can be taught to ELLs in the same manner as native speakers of English, depending on how each particular native language may be structured. As described in Chapter 4, the teacher must consider the similarities and differences between English and the native language of ELLs. For example, although Spanish is an alphabetic language, its letter–sound correspondences are regular, and the unit of phonetic structure is the syllable. Therefore, if the program for ELLS includes teaching them to read in Spanish, then the syllable would be the unit to focus on (Vaughn et al., 2005). If the student has already learned to read in Spanish, then the similarities and differences between Spanish and English described in Chapter 4 must be considered if the student is a very beginning reader of English. If the student has already mastered the differences in letter formation and the complexity of vowel pronunciations in English, for example, then the teacher can make use of word identification techniques that connect pronunciation to meaning. One such strategy is the use of cognates between the languages, which are words derived from the same original form. For example, *calculate* and the Spanish equivalent, *calcular,* are cognates that share the Latin base. More information about the use of cognates to teach vocabulary can be found in Chapter 8 and in Vogt & Echevarria (2008).

The application of guided reading to English language learners was carefully explained by Cappellini (2006), with the major difference between the guided reading procedure described earlier in this chapter and guided reading for ELLs being an increased emphasis on student talk and discussion. For example, as the students discuss the title and predict what the story will be about, the teacher is cuing into language used in the book that the students need to know. She might ask a question whose answer leads to the specific text language needed. As the teacher guides students through the first reading of the text, she encourages students to "find words on the pages that match their predictions, what they see in the pictures, and what they think the author would say" (Cappellini, 2006, p. 119). The teacher also uses the same tense in discussion as used in the text, hoping that the students will respond using the same structure. It is the teacher's responsibility during the orientation to the book to ask questions that are designed to elicit the vocabulary that students will need to read the text. It is these kinds of adaptations that are most often suggested to teachers instructing ELLs.

In a similar fashion, it has been recommended that teachers analyze the text to identify language that may cause difficulty for ELLs (Avalos, Plasencia, Chavez, & Rascón, 2007/2008). Examples of language likely to cause problems during guided reading are low-frequency words, words not frequently used in speech, figurative language or phrases without literal translations in the student's native language, homophones and homographs, and complex grammar or syntax. Teacher will need to be astute examiners of text used for guided reading with ELLs.

Application to Adolescent Learners

Teaching word identification to an adolescent reader is a complex and highly controversial topic. The National Reading Panel's meta-analysis (Ehri, Nunes, Stahl, & Willows, 2001) concluded that whereas phonics instruction was shown to increase the reading performance of normally developing children in K–1 as well as reading-disabled students, it did not appear to affect low-achieving older readers. The panel's separation of the effects of phonics instruction on reading disabled students versus low-achieving older readers is important. When reading the academic literature surrounding this issue, it becomes clear that some researchers are addressing only the most severely reading disabled (Lovett & Steinbach, 1997; Lovett et al., 2000), whereas others are speaking about a much wider audience of adolescents (Ivey, 1999; Ivey & Broaddus, 2001; Ivey & Baker, 2004). For example, two phonics programs designed for disabled readers found equal improvement between younger (grades 2–3) and older (grades 5–6) students (Lovett & Steinbach, 1997). Students learned what the program had to teach them and transferred their strategies to new material. In this case, the oldest group of students were fifth and sixth graders. In fact all of the studies included in the NRP on reading-disabled students included children ages 6 through 13 or through sixth grade; therefore we only know the effects of word identification instruction on the very youngest adolescents.

The problem is that school personnel may interpret the research results differently. Most middle school or high school administrators are looking for programs to help all below-average readers. Any phonics program selected will be unnecessary for 95 percent of the students who are below-average readers. Although researchers studying severely disabled readers would not agree, some researchers suggest that phonics programs are therefore inappropriate for adolescents. Still other researchers seem uncertain. Despite the title of their article, "Phonics Instruction for Older Students? Just Say No," Ivey and Baker (2004) state: "Some struggling readers need to think more about the structure of words. An interactive and connected approach, such as word study, enables students to manipulate key words from their reading and begin extending generalizations to unfamiliar words" (pp. 37–38). The authors go on to provide an example of teaching students how to spell long vowel patterns in one-syllable words. In our opinion, this is word identification instruction (analytic phonics) that the title of the article seems to dismiss.

The key to this apparent anomaly is the context in which the skill is taught. Ivey and Baker (2004) are saying no to isolated skill-and-drill phonics instruction. They support word identification study that selects words and spelling patterns from the students' reading (as we have advocated for young students also). Ivey and Baker's example also demonstrates their concern for students' particular needs and that instruction ensures that the skill is transferred immediately back to text for the student to apply to figure out unfamiliar words.

Effective teaching of word identification strategies to adolescents depends on a deep understanding of the students' needs; therefore, assessments that help teachers identify the students' strengths and weaknesses are needed (Deshler, Palincsar, Biancarosa, & Nair, 2007). However, an effective program cannot be built on only the academic needs of students. Adolescents have serious motivational and engagement issues that the students explain as lack of choice in what they read and a dislike for the curriculum that they are assigned (Ivey, 1999; Ivey & Broaddus, 2001; Worthy, Moorman, & Turner, 1999). Also, context effects on adolescent readers are demonstrated by students who struggle with literacy in their content areas while being avid readers of other types of materials (Ivey, 1999; RAND Reading Study Group, 2002). At this point you may be thinking, okay, you've told us how complex it is to teach reading to adolescents effectively, but we still have to teach them, so how do we do it?

If the adolescent is a nonreader, you might follow the language experience approach described previously. Get students talking about their interests outside of school and have them dictate a story to you. Type it up and present it as text for the student to read and as the source of word study. However, if the student can read at a second-grade level (and therefore has some knowledge of words with more than one syllable) then our previous description of how to teach polysyllabic words by analogy is an appropriate strategy. Decoding polysyllabic words by analogy is particularly useful because the decoding of larger words is being taught through the application of spelling patterns in each syllable. If the student doesn't know a spelling pattern, it can be taught as a means of identifying a polysyllabic word, so the task doesn't look so babyish. As we emphasized earlier in this chapter, it is important that the words the student is learning to decode are in the texts that he or she is reading. Adolescents who are still struggling with word identification have likely had much isolated phonics instruction, and we don't want to see that repeated.

Word study activities *can* be highly engaging for intermediate and middle school students (Bloodgood & Pacifici, 2004). Their research concluded that given the high coverage demand of the teachers that their approach to word study would best be incidental. "Root of the Day is an incidental learning strategy that involves the teacher choosing a root word from Latin or Greek and the students add words that they think are related" (p. 253). Toward the end of the day the students can discuss their hypotheses about the word's meaning. The Bloodgood and Pacifici article is full of suggestions, such as using word sorts discussed in this chapter but with the sorting based on more complex English orthography. If students are having trouble with homophones, they suggest using a chart to help the students associate the spelling with the correct meaning of the word.

Two chapters in *Informed Choices for Struggling Adolescent Readers* (Deshler, Palincsar, Biancarosa, & Nair, 2007) explain the content of adolescent literacy instruction and the elements common to effective instruction. Because the topic of this chapter is word identification, we will share only two aspects of these chapters. First, it is stated quite directly that decoding instruction via phonics is appropriate content for the particular students that need it (Nair, Deshler, Biancarosa, & Palincsar, 2007). And the only program listed among their instructional programs designed solely to help struggling high school readers with decoding difficulties is the Strategic Instruction Model (Center for Research on Learning, University of Kansas). However, Nair et al. also articulated that such instruction should not be solely relied on. Rather students "need to be supported in the acquisition of higher level literacy skills and of grade-appropriate content in other subject areas" (Nair et al., 2007, p. 38).

Second, they describe one element of effective instruction for adolescents that is particularly appropriate for word identification skills: teaching for transfer (Palincsar, Nair, Deshler, & Biancarosa, 2007). In this particular context, teaching for transfer requires that the effective instruction described must be embedded in content. That means that content area knowledge must be included in English and language arts classes as examples of where and how comprehension strategies can be applied and that content area classes must include good literacy instruction as part of their discipline. Finally, they make the strong point that content-specific strategies should be taught for students to learn each content area. To put it bluntly, students will only learn to apply strategies when the strategies are explained and modeled in all of their classes.

Response to Intervention

The importance of explicit and systematic instruction in phonics has been established by research (Ehri, Nunes, Stahl, & Willows, 2001). Similarly, research has confirmed the effectiveness of the decoding by analogy approach (Ehri, Satlow, & Gaskins, in press). Instructional activities based on these methods would be acceptable for the research-based instruction mandated by RTI.

Like phonological awareness, assessment of phonics can take the form of short, easily administered probes. However, we present the same words of caution that we offered in Chapter 4. Teachers must remember that while phonics is a necessary component of successful reading, it is not a sufficient one. The ability to accurately pronounce words means little if comprehension is absent. Our concern is that tier two and three lessons will focus on phonics to the exclusion of activities that foster and develop comprehension strategies and a valuing of the reading process. While intervention instruction can address and even emphasize phonics, it must also include real reading activities. Students should read or be read to. They should talk about their reading. Pronouncing words is always secondary to understanding them and students should have ample opportunity to discuss and clarify word meaning and connect it to their lives in school and at home.

Summary

This chapter has explained how to assess and teach students' understanding of letter–sound relationships and their ability to recognize and identify words. Using the principles from the National Reading Panel report and the recommendations of Stahl (1990), we have laid a framework from which to teach these important skills. In all cases we encourage the teaching of letter–sound relationships and word recognition and identification in the context of quality students' literature. Using the whole-part-whole framework, the first step involves finding a good book or poem that includes the phonic element or word to be taught. The next step isolates the element or word to be taught. The third step returns to the initial book, or better yet provides the students with experience reading another piece of literature that reinforces the skills that were taught. We recommend teaching phonics using onset-rime units because teaching rimes increases the consistency with which vowels are pronounced. We also showed how decoding by analogy, using onset-rime, can be applied to words with more than one syllable. We also explained how to teach words that aren't easily decoded and discussed procedures that you can use to help students practice sight words in isolation, including how to use word sorts for a variety of purposes. We discussed the importance of teacher coaching during oral reading to ensure that students learn to use multiple sources of information to gain meaning. We also discussed the applications of our recommendations for teaching word identification to ELLs and adolescents. We concluded that word identification strategies should be only a small part of a comprehensive reading program for those adolescents who need it. The use of Response to Intervention assessments were described, as well as cautions about their use in isolation from real reading activities.

REFERENCES AND RECOMMENDED READINGS

Allen, L. P. (1998). An integrated strategies approach: Making word identification instruction work for beginning readers. *The Reading Teacher, 52,* 254–268.

Bear, D., Invernizzi, M., Templeton, S., & Johnston, F. (2007). *Words their way: Word study for phonics, vocabulary and spelling instruction* (4th ed.). Columbus, OH: Merrill.

Brown, K. (2003). What do I say when they get stuck on a word? Aligning teacher prompts with students' development. *The Reading Teacher, 56,* 720–733.

Clark, K. (2004). What can I say besides "sound it out"? Coaching word recognition in beginning reading. *The Reading Teacher, 57,* 440–449.

Clark, K. F., & Graves, M. F. (2005). Scaffolding students' comprehension of text. *The Reading Teacher, 58,* 570–580.

Clay, M. M. (1985). *The early detection of reading difficulties* (3rd ed.). Portsmouth, NH: Heinemann

Clay, M. M. (1991). Introducing a new storybook to young readers. *The Reading Teacher, 45,* 264–273.

Cole, A. (2006). Scaffolding beginning readers: Micro and macro cues teachers use during student oral reading. *The Reading Teacher, 59,* 450–459.

Cunningham, P., & Cunningham, J. (1992). Making words: Enhancing the invented spelling-decoding connection. *The Reading Teacher, 46,* 106–115.

Eckwall, E., & Shanker, J. (2000). *Ekwall-Shanker reading inventory* (4th ed.). Boston: Allyn & Bacon.

Ehri, L., Satlow, E., & Gaskins, I. (in press). Graphophonemic enrichment strengthens keyword analogy instruction for struggling young readers. *Reading and Writing Quarterly.*

Fountas, I., & Pinnell, G. S. (1996). *Guided reading.* Portsmouth, NH: Heinemann.

Gaskins, I., Downer, M., and the Teachers of Benchmark School. (1997). *The Benchmark word identification/vocabulary development program.* Media, PA: Benchmark Press.

Gaskins, I., Downer, M., Anderson, R., Cunningham, P., Gaskins, R., & Schommer, M. (1988). A metacognitive approach to phonics: Using what you know to decode what you don't know. *Remedial and Special Education, 27,* 36–41.

Goodman, K. S. (1969). Analysis of reading miscues: Applied psycholinguistics. *Reading Research Quarterly, 5,* 9–30.

Hajdusiewicz, B. B. (1998). *Phonics through poetry PK–1.* Tucson, AZ: Goodyear Books.

Hajdusiewicz, B. B., & Grant, D. L. (2007). *More phonics through poetry 2–3.* Tucson, AZ: Goodyear Books.

Harris, A. J., & Sipay, E. R. (1990). *How to increase reading ability* (9th ed.). New York: Longman.

Johnston, F. (1999). The timing and teaching of word families. *The Reading Teacher, 53,* 64–75.

Leslie, L., & Calhoon, J. (1995). Factors affecting children's reading of rimes: Reading ability, word frequency, and rime-neighborhood size. *Journal of Educational Psychology, 87,* 576–586.

Stahl, S. (1990). Saying the "p" word: Nine guidelines for exemplary phonics instruction. *The Reading Teacher, 45,* 618–625.

Wagstaff, J. M. (1997). Building practice knowledge of letter-sound correspondences: A beginner's word wall and beyond. *The Reading Teacher, 51,* 298–304.

Wilen, J., & Handa, B. (2002). *70 wonderful word family poems.* New York: Scholastic.

Children's Literature References

Branley, F. M. (2002*). The sun: Our nearest star.* New York: HarperCollins.

Cannon, J. (1993*). Stellaluna.* New York: Scholastic.

Guarino, D. (1989). *Is your mama a llama?* New York: Scholastic.

Klove, L. (1999*). Trucks that build.* New York: Simon and Schuster.

Marshall, J. (1992). *Fox outfoxed.* New York: Puffin.

Martin, B. (1967). *Brown bear, brown bear.* New York: Holt.

Otto, C. B. (2001). *Shadows.* New York: Scholastic.

Shaw, N. (1989). *Sheep on a ship.* New York: Houghton-Mifflin.

Wood, A. (1992). *Silly sally.* New York: Harcourt Brace.

English Language Learners

August, D. L., & Shanahan, T. (2006). *Developing literacy in second language learners: Report of the national literacy panel on language-minority children and youth.* Mahwah, NJ: Erlbaum.

Avalos, M. A., Plasencia, A., Chavez, C., & Rascón, J. (2007/2008). *The Reading Teacher, 61,* 318–329.

Cappellini, M. (2006). Using guided reading with English learners. In T. A. Young & N. L. Hadaway (Eds.), *Supporting the literacy development of English leaders: Increasing succession all classrooms* (pp. 113–131). Newark, DE: International Reading Association.

Gunn, B., Biglan, A., Smolkowski, K., & Ary, D. (2000). The efficacy of supplemental instruction in decoding skills for Hispanic and non-Hispanic students in early elementary school. *Journal of Special Education, 34,* 90–103.

Gunn, B., Smolkowski, K., Biglan, A., & Black, C. (2002). Supplementary instruction in decoding skills for Hispanic vs. non-Hispanic students in early elementary school: A follow-up. *Journal of Special Education, 36,* 69–79.

Shanahan, T., & Beck, I. (2006). Effective literacy teaching for English-language learners. In D. August & T. Shanahan (Eds.), *Developing literacy in second-language learners* (pp. 415–488). Mahwah, NJ: Erlbaum.

Vaughn, S., Mathes, P. G., Linan-Thompson, S., & Francis, D. J. (2005). Teaching English language learners at risk for reading disabilities to read: Putting research into practice. *Learning Disabilities Research and Practice, 20,* 58–67.

Vogt, M. E., & Echevarria, J. (2008). *99 ideas and activities for teaching English learners with the SIOP model.* Boston: Allyn & Bacon.

Woodcock, W. L. (1991). *Woodcock Language Proficiency Battery–Revised.* Austin, TX: ProEd.

Adolescents

Bloodgood, J. W., & Pacifici, L. C. (2004). Bringing word study to intermediate classrooms. *The Reading Teacher, 58,* 250–263.

Deshler, D. D., Palincsar, A., Biancarosa, G., & Nair, M. (2007). *Informed choices for struggling adolescent readers: A research based guide to instructional programs and practices.* Newark, DE: International Reading Association.

Ehri, L. C., Nunes, S. R., Stahl, S., & Willows, D. M. (2001). Systematic phonics instruction helps students learn to read: Evidence from the National Reading Panel's meta-analysis. *Review of Educational Research, 71,* 393–447.

Ivey, G. (1999). A multicase study in the middle school: Complexities among young adolescent readers. *Reading Research Quarterly, 34,* 172–192.

Ivey, G., & Baker, M. I. (2004). Phonics instruction for older students? Just say no. *Educational Leadership, 40,* pp. 35–39.

Ivey, G., & Broaddus, K. (2001). "Just plain reading": A survey of what makes students want to read in middle school classrooms. *Reading Research Quarterly, 36,* 350–370.

Lovett, M. W., Lacerenza, L., Borden, S. L., Frijters, J. C., Steinbach, K. A., & De Palma, M. (2000). Components of effective remediation for developmental reading disabilities: Combining phonological and strategy-based instruction to improve outcomes. *Journal of Educational Psychology, 92,* 263–283.

Lovett, M. W., & Steinbach, K. A. (1997). The effect of remedial programs for reading disabled children of different ages: Does the benefit decrease for older children? *Learning Disabilities Quarterly, 20,* 189–210.

Nair, M., Deshler, D. D., Biancarosa, G., & Palincsar, A. (2007). The content of adolescent literacy instruction. In D. Deshler, A. S. Palincsar, G. Biancarosa, & M. Nair (Eds.), *Informed choices for struggling adolescent readers: A research based guide to instructional programs and practices* (pp. 37–48). Newark, DE: International Reading Association.

Palincsar, A. S., Nair, M., Deshler, D. D., & Biancarosa, G. (2007). Characteristics and supports of adolescent literacy instruction. In D. Deshler, A. S. Palincsar, G. Biancarosa, & M. Nair (Eds.), *Informed choices for struggling adolescent readers: A research based guide to instructional programs and practices* (pp. 49–60). Newark, DE: International Reading Association.

RAND Reading Study Group. (2002). *Reading for understanding: Toward an R & D program in reading comprehension.* Santa Monica, CA: RAND.

Worthy, J., Moorman, M., & Turner, M. (1999). What Johnny likes to read is hard to find in school. *Reading Research Quarterly, 34,* 12–27.

Other Readings of Interest

Mesmer, H. A., & Griffith, P. L. (2006). Everybody's selling it—But just what is explicit, systematic phonics? *The Reading Teacher, 59,* 366–376.

Torgeson, J. K., Wagner, R., Rashotte, C., Alexander, A. W., & Conway, T. (1997). Preventative and remedial interventions for children with severe reading disabilities. *Learning Disabilities, 8,* 51–62.

6

Word Identification Instruction: Fluency

The Importance of Fluency

Good readers are fluent readers. What does it mean to be fluent? Fluency involves three things: accuracy, speed, and expression. Fluent readers are accurate, correctly identifying

95

both familiar and unfamiliar words (familiar words are words they have seen before). When they first meet new words, they may analyze them by matching letters and sounds but eventually they are able to identify them from memory. We call words that are recognized without analysis *sight words*. Good readers are also able to recognize unfamiliar words very quickly because they are skilled at matching letter–sound patterns. Note how fast you are able to pronounce the following word, which we suspect you may never have seen before.

rebarbative

Good readers do not have to think about word identification. They just do it. Because they do not have to pay conscious attention to pronouncing words, they can read at an appropriate rate of speed. The National Reading Panel (2000) defined fluency as reading with speed, accuracy, and proper expression without conscious attention on the reader's part.

What role does speed or reading rate play? Appropriate reading rate is usually a signal that the reader is automatically identifying words either from memory or as a result of efficient letter–sound matching. Because the reader does not have to focus on identifying words, she or he can pay attention to meaning; and because the reader is concentrating on meaning, she or he can read with expression, using proper intonation and a rhythm that approximates natural speech. Good readers read smoothly, and we enjoy listening to them. Poor readers who are not fluent read slowly, often in a monotone. They pause frequently and often repeat words, seldom reading with expression. In contrast to good readers, they are painful to listen to as they stumble their way through a selection.

In order to be fluent, readers need three things. First, they must have a large store of sight words, those that are automatically recognized from memory. Second, they must have effective strategies for analyzing unfamiliar words. And third, they must understand that the purpose of reading is comprehension, which allows them to read with expression. Because they understand what they are reading, they are able to "project the natural intonation and phrasing of the spoken word upon the written text" (Richards, 2000, p. 535).

How do readers develop fluency? Obviously, they must learn effective strategies for matching letter–sound patterns so they can identify unfamiliar words. However, this is only a small part of becoming fluent. Quite simply, readers become fluent by reading, reading, and more reading. As students read, they meet and identify new words. They meet these new words again and again until identification becomes fixed in memory, and as a result their sight vocabulary grows. Because they do not have to analyze every word, they can direct their attention to meaning, and because they understand what they read, they enjoy and appreciate reading and are motivated to read more. Effective identification of unfamiliar words, a large sight vocabulary, and attention to meaning all interact in a wonderful way to produce a fluent reader, and being fluent may be a "necessary condition for good comprehension and enjoyable reading experiences" (Nathan & Stanovich, 1991, p. 176).

The Informal Reading Inventory as an Indicator of Lack of Fluency

Oral Reading

How do you know if fluency is a problem? You will know a nonfluent reader when you hear him or her. Your first indication comes from listening to a student orally read at his or her independent or instructional levels. It is important to assess fluency in instructional materials because you can expect some lack of fluency in frustration level text. For example, we suspect you might not be too fluent reading a book on advanced statistics.

There are various types of nonfluent readers: the choppy reader, who sounds as if he or she is reading a list of unconnected words; the hesitant reader, who pauses often, tends to repeat words and phrases, and frequently loses his or her place; and the monotone reader, who shows little variation in voice tone or expression and ignores punctuation and sentence breaks. Most nonfluent readers represent a combination of these patterns.

Reading Rate

Reading rate is another indication of lack of fluency. It indicates reading speed and is measured in words per minute (WPM). Most informal reading inventories have procedures for measuring WPM for both oral and silent reading. Reading speed is not an instructional goal in itself. That is, it means nothing if there is no comprehension. Reading speed is rather an indicator of two things: that the reader is able to recognize words automatically and that he or she can process meaning at an acceptable rate. To understand how these differ, consider what might happen if you were reading on a very unfamiliar topic, such as the structure and function of the kidneys. You would probably automatically pronounce all the words; however, because you would not know all their meanings and because you have no background in anatomy, you would read much more slowly than you normally do in an attempt to process or comprehend the selection.

Often, teachers do not consider reading rate an important issue if students understand what they read. However, chronic slow reading, even if coupled with some understanding, can lead to problems. First, slow readers have to put more time and energy into reading than do their more fluent classmates. It takes them longer to complete assignments, and they are often painfully aware that their peers have finished reading although they are only halfway through. This may cause them to avoid reading, and, as we mentioned earlier, fluency primarily develops through wide reading. Thus, slow readers may avoid the very thing that would contribute to reading improvement.

If reading rate is used to indicate an instructional focus, there are several issues to consider. First, reading rate varies according to the passage that is being read. It also varies according to our interest in and purposes for reading. We tend to read more slowly in difficult and unfamiliar text, whereas we generally read faster when we are interested in the topic or when we want to find out how the story or novel ends. Also, we tend to read more slowly if the result of our reading has personal consequences. Think about your reading rate when perusing directions for filling out your income tax form or studying for a test. Finally, there are no uniform reading rates that students at a specific level should attain. Good readers at the same instructional reading level often display very different rates. The *QRI-4* contains some suggestions for reading rates. Other informal reading inventories provide similar guidelines.

Given these considerations, how can we interpret reading rate? There are several principles to keep in mind. First, interpret desired reading rates in a general way and realize that many factors can cause variation; use published reading rates only as rough estimates of where your student should be. Second, always determine rate in independent or instructional level text that represents the student's best performance and recognize that reading rates are naturally affected by a variety of factors. Third, do not compare individual students; once you have determined a student's rate in independent or instructional level text, use this as a guideline for measuring progress—in other words, compare a student to him- or herself, not to other students.

Do oral and silent reading rates differ? Yes. Silent reading is and should be faster than oral reading, and some young students experience difficulty moving from oral to silent reading. However, students who are comfortably fluent in oral reading generally make a successful transition to silent reading fluency. If a student exhibits a slow rate when reading silently, first determine if this is due to lack of automatic word identification. Some students do well recognizing unfamiliar short words but lack effective strategies for dealing with long ones. If word identification is not a problem, the student is probably experiencing difficulty in processing the text or comprehending during reading. He or she can profit from many of the comprehension strategies that we will discuss in following chapters.

General Principles for Developing Fluency

The ability to quickly and accurately recognize unfamiliar words is one aspect of fluency. Chapter 5 offered a variety of suggestions for helping students identify unfamiliar words, always within the context of reading for meaning. The primary purpose of this chapter is to suggest instructional activities for developing a large store of automatically recognized sight words and for guiding students to read expressively and with attention to meaning.

According to The National Reading Panel (2000), fluency instruction is appropriate for students in grades 2 through high school and is equally effective for good and poor readers. In Chapter 1, we mentioned that accommodating the needs of struggling readers in the regular classroom is just as important as designing and implementing effective individual and small-group intervention lessons. The principles that guide fluency instruction apply to both the classroom setting and the intervention lesson. They also apply to achieving as well as struggling readers and provide a framework for helping all readers to become fluent and engaged.

Linking to Meaning

Fluency instruction should always be linked to meaning because, after all, the whole purpose of reading is to comprehend. Isolated drill activities aimed at fixing words in memory may actually do more harm than good in that they may reinforce the student's belief that reading is saying words. This means that even when the instructional focus is fluency development, students must talk about what they have read. They must be guided to comment on the selection, to laugh at or empathize with the characters, and to connect the content to their own lives and interests. If students are working with single words such as when sorting word cards or building a word bank, there must still be a focus on meaning. It is not enough to pronounce the word. Students must be able to say what the word means and to connect it to other words and to their own experiences.

Providing Guidance and Feedback

Fluency develops through supportive activities that provide guidance and feedback before, during, and after students read orally. The National Reading Panel (2000) concluded that repeated and monitored oral reading significantly affects word recognition, fluency, and comprehension. Support can come from teachers, tutors, parents, or peers, all of whom the panel found to be effective. Students need to listen to models of fluent reading. All too often, struggling readers listen only to their nonfluent peers. They need support as they read a text for the very first time, and they need the support of different practice activities such as repeated reading.

Encouraging Wide Reading

Fluency develops through practice, and the best practice is wide reading of meaningful and enjoyable text. The classroom teacher should provide daily opportunities for all students to independently read selections that they have chosen, selections that appeal to their needs and interests. The short time frame of many intervention lessons may not allow for much independent reading within the lesson structure; however, you can and should encourage your students to read on their own. And when they do, it is important that they are successful or they will not continue. Let them take books that you have introduced and those they have practiced back to their regular classroom for independent reading time. Encourage them to take these books home to read to their parents. During the intervention lesson, employ reading materials that appeal to the students' reading interests. Many struggling readers associate reading with failure and difficulty and do not see reading as a worthwhile activity. Entice them with selections that pique their interest and engage their attention. Choosing appealing materials is just as important for the classroom teacher, who must maintain the attention and engagement of an entire class as opposed to a small group of intervention students.

Although common sense and our own experience with good and poor readers tell us that wide reading enhances fluency, according to the National Reading Panel (2000) there is little evidence that encouraging independent and recreational reading is sufficient. Wide reading cannot substitute for well-designed and regular instructional activities that focus on fluency development.

Considering Student Reading Levels

Consider your students' independent and instructional reading levels when choosing books. When students read on their own, they should read easy books at their independent reading level. This allows them to experience success and keeps them reading. Students who struggle when reading independently, whether in class or at home, will soon stop and move to other pursuits. If the teacher is providing support to students through activities that we will describe later in this chapter, instructional level text can be used. In this way students develop fluency in manageable text and, at the same time, have some opportunities for meeting the challenge of new words and new linguistic structures. Because students in a single class vary widely in reading levels, it is important that the classroom be stocked with a variety of books at different levels and on different topics.

Avoiding Unpracticed Reading

Avoid two unfortunately common practices: asking students to orally read a selection for the first time cold—that is, without practice—and round-robin oral reading. The only time a student should be asked to read something without practice or support is during the assessment process, such as when being administered an informal reading inventory. Reading something for the first time without support or practice can produce much anxiety and affirm the student's perception that he or she is a poor reader. This can happen even if the only individual listening to the student is a sympathetic and caring teacher. University students often comment on the apprehension and embarrassment they felt when asked to read orally in front of their peers. Some can even remember the words they stumbled over.

The old practice of round-robin oral reading can also do more harm than good. In this practice, each student in a group takes a turn and reads part of the selection while the other students listen and wait their turns. Usually, students are reading the text for the very first time with no opportunity for practice, and their peers are witness to mistakes, confusion, and overall lack of fluency. This is an unfair situation. Would you like to read a strange selection to your peers without some practice first? The primary focus of round-robin oral reading is saying words correctly as opposed to making meaning. Even if the teacher intervenes between students to discuss the text, the unsuccessful reader, all too conscious of his or her poor performance, will have little to say. Those who are waiting their turns will also have little to say. Many are probably estimating what page will fall to them and are reading ahead in preparation or dread. This is certainly not a practice to foster understanding or love of reading. Table 6.1 summarizes the general principles for developing fluency.

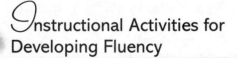

Instructional Activities for Developing Fluency

Reading Aloud to Students

One of your authors remembers with fondness being read to each night before bed. My mother read poetry ("Paul Revere's Ride" by Longfellow was a favorite), short stories, and

TABLE 6.1   General Principles for Developing Fluency

Always link fluency instruction to meaning.

Provide support that offers guidance and feedback during oral reading activities.

Encourage wide reading of meaningful and enjoyable text.

Consider the independent and instructional reading levels of students when choosing materials for practice.

Avoid unpracticed reading and round-robin oral reading.

chapter books such as *The Wizard of Oz*. We described our feelings about the selection, we laughed at the characters, and sometimes we cried at what happened to them. Occasionally, we read poems together, and to this day I can still recite with expression the first stanzas describing Paul Revere's noble intention on that long-ago night. By reading to me, my mother introduced me to the world of books and the joys of reading. I saw reading as something to be valued, and I understood that reading was making meaning, not just saying words. I read and reread most of the selections introduced during those nightly read-alouds and never, at the time, realized how very fortunate I was. Reading aloud introduced me to "the joy of reading and the art of listening" (Fisher, Flood, Lapp, & Frey, 2004).

Many children today do not experience being read to on a regular basis. Parents often hold down multiple jobs and are not always available for reading aloud. Some do not value reading themselves, and there are few reading materials in the home. Television and video games can easily entice children away from books. This is unfortunate because reading aloud is uniformly recommended as a way of enhancing language development and encouraging literacy. It introduces students to the world of books and to motivating materials that they might read on their own. Reading aloud to students also provides a model of fluent reading and is a strong factor in fluency development.

Reading aloud can take place in the regular classroom or in the intervention session. There are several things to keep in mind when choosing read-aloud materials. Obviously, you want interesting selections that grab and hold your listeners' attention. If the students do not enjoy the selection or begin to lose interest, stop and move on to other things. Continuing to read something that students find boring will only reinforce the idea that reading is an activity to be avoided. Read selections that students might choose to read on their own. An effective read-aloud can often motivate a student to choose that book for independent reading. Choose a variety of reading materials from very easy selections to more difficult ones; by choosing easy materials you dignify such selections for struggling readers; by choosing more complex texts, you challenge the thinking processes of all students.

Read the selection to yourself first. You may want to practice a bit, especially in exciting or emotionally charged parts. You do not have to begin on page one and move sequentially through a selection. Instead, you might select an especially exciting part that actually occurs later in the book. Explain what led up to it in your own words and then read it. Of course, you do not want to give away any surprise endings, but you can use reading aloud to entice students into reading the selection on their own.

How long should you read? Fifteen minutes works well. It is better to stop while students are still involved so they will be motivated for the next read-aloud session. Encourage comments about the selection, but do not require them. Sometimes intense enjoyment or appreciation is lessened if one is forced to comment or share.

In summary, reading aloud to students is an effective strategy for developing fluency. It provides a model of fluent reading and often entices students to read the selection on their own. In addition, it is enjoyable for both teacher and students. Moreover, reading aloud to students has other benefits. Discussion during and after reading aloud can encourage students to become active learners and challenge them to higher levels of thought (Lane &

Wright, 2007). The teacher can use open-ended questions to lead students to draw inferences, examine the meanings of unfamiliar words, and connect the selection to their own lives. Open-ended questions elicit greater language production on the part of the students and encourage elaboration (Beck & McKeown, 2001). McGee and Schickedanz (2007) suggest a process for reading the same selection three times. At the first read-aloud, the teacher introduces the book, offers any needed background support, and reads using gestures and expressive voice intonation. At the second reading, the teacher stops during the reading, asks analytic questions, models acceptable answers, and draws the students into the discussion process. After the third read-aloud, the teacher only reads selected parts and the students retell and reconstruct. Reading aloud is a powerful instructional tool for the literacy classroom as well as the intervention session and fosters both fluency and higher-level comprehension processes.

Fostering Wide Reading

The first and perhaps most successful method for developing fluency is wide reading of easy text. Students should read, read, read. Many struggling readers avoid reading, however, and it is easy to understand why. No one likes to do things that are difficult or that lead to repeated failure. Given the importance of developing fluency and the crucial role of reading in doing so, your first activity should be to locate reading materials at your students' independent and instructional reading levels that they can read successfully. This applies equally to the regular classroom or to the intervention lesson.

You may have to begin with a book with one or two words on a page or with predictable and repeated refrains. Read the book to the students and talk about it. Then you can read it together several times. When the students feel comfortable and successful, you can mark this book for independent reading and move to another. Gradually, you and the students will build up a store of books that they can handle on their own. Reading and rereading them will help to expand the students' store of automatically recognized words. Teachers often worry that a book may be too "babyish" for some older readers, but it all depends on how you introduce it. If you demonstrate enthusiasm and enjoyment, the students will be more inclined to follow your lead. Taylor and Nesheim (2000/2001) cleverly used children's literature selections with older struggling readers and trained them to read these to younger students. The older students were captivated by the opportunity to read and share with children and, as a result, were not offended by the simple texts.

You do not always have to use books. Many students are motivated to read other forms of text, so provide a wide variety. In our experience, interest in a topic can often motivate a student to read and reread materials that might, at first glance, seem too difficult. One instructor regularly cut out headlines from the sports section of the local newspaper and stapled them in manila folders along with the first paragraphs from the accompanying stories. She found these to be very appealing to her students, who read and reread accounts of their team's victories and losses. Because of their interest, they were very careful to determine the pronunciation of any unfamiliar words. She also cut out portions from popular magazines about favorite entertainers, which proved equally attractive.

Providing Support through Modeling and Feedback

The teacher can use a variety of activities to model fluent oral reading and provide feedback to the student. These can occur during the introduction and first reading of a selection or during oral reading practice. Table 6.2, on pages 108–109, lists these activities and indicates how they can best be used. All of them can be adapted to fit into the structure of a regular class or an individual or small-group intervention session.

Assisted Reading. In assisted reading, the teacher and the students read orally together. The teacher can read with a single student or with several students, or he or she can employ assisted reading with the entire class. Assisted reading provides the struggling reader with a model of fluency. As the teacher sets the pace, students hear how reading should sound. Assisted reading is also very nonthreatening. Word recognition is not a problem: If a student meets an unknown word, she or he hears it pronounced practically at the same time. There is no censure or embarrassment for not knowing the word. Indeed, the other students in the group or class may not even be aware of the situation. Assisted reading provides effective practice in contextual reading.

Assisted reading is a good choice for introducing a new selection, considering that, even if the selection is at the students' instructional level, asking them to read aloud can be disturbing. It is hard to do what we think we cannot do successfully even in the presence of someone we trust. Reading orally with students and stopping occasionally to talk about the selection is far more enjoyable and effective. Once the teacher and students have read the selection together, the students may be more motivated to attempt it on their own. Assisted reading can also be used as practice and is particularly applicable if students continue to experience difficulty with a specific selection.

When engaging in assisted reading, remember that you set the pace. Resist any temptation to slow down to match the reading rate of the student, because they will always be slightly behind. If you slow down, the students will do the same, and eventually the reading will become slow, labored, and nonfluent. If they stop reading with you, pause and determine why. Talk about what has been read so far. Perhaps reread the last page at which they were actively involved and then begin again and stop after shorter segments of text to talk about the selection.

Assisted reading can work for all ages and selections, depending on any modifications you may have to make. If the selection is relatively short, you can employ assisted reading for its entirety without losing the attention of the students. However, if your chosen selection is long, you may want to choose assisted reading for certain parts. For example, you can read some parts to the students, summarize other parts in your own words, and use assisted reading with others.

Intersperse assisted reading with discussion. It is important to talk about the text with your students, perhaps to laugh at it or wonder about it and to do what all good readers do—tie the content of the reading to their own lives. Talking about the selection keeps the students engaged and provides important modeling of reading as making meaning, not just saying words.

When assisted reading is used to introduce a selection, it can be combined with other forms of supported oral reading. After a particularly exciting part, for example, you might engage in echo reading. Once you have read a part using assisted reading, you might ask students to chorally read it without your support. When planning for assisted reading, we encourage you to think ahead and use sticky notes to mark how you and your students will read each part and the questions or comments you might use as discussion starters.

Echo Reading.   Echo reading is a form of assisted reading in which the teacher models fluent oral reading of very short segments of text and then asks the students to imitate or echo. It can take place during a first reading, but it is perhaps most effective as a form of practice reading. You can use echo reading throughout an entire selection or just for certain parts. For example, modeling how characters might say something is very effective as echo reading, and students learn to pay attention to question and exclamation marks. Using echo reading for repeated refrains is also effective.

Echo reading works best in short segments. If the segment is too long, students will forget how you modeled the first part by the time their turn comes. It can work with an individual, but it is particularly effective with groups. A single student may be embarrassed or reluctant to imitate a teacher, but doing so in a group is nonthreatening. Echo reading is also very effective as practice for various forms of performance reading.

Paired Reading.   In paired reading, a more capable reader is joined with a struggling reader. Both read the selection together at a pace that is relatively comfortable for the struggler. The capable reader models fluent reading, supports the struggler with word identification, and fosters comprehension through questions and discussion. Paired reading was originally developed as a strategy for parents and children (Topping, 1987, 1989). However, it can be effectively incorporated into intervention lessons, with the more capable reader being the teacher, a tutor, an aide, a volunteer, a parent, or even an older student. Topping recommends sessions that are 15 to 30 minutes long, but you will have to determine length based on your chosen lesson structure.

The process begins with the student selecting the material to be read, which is ideally at his or her instructional level. The student and the tutor then read together orally, with the tutor maintaining a reasonable pace and resisting the temptation to slow down to meet the student's pace. As in assisted reading, the student will always be slightly behind. If the student mispronounces a word, the tutor says the word correctly and asks the student to repeat it. Then the pair continues reading. If the student wants to read independently, he or she signals this to the tutor. At the signal, which is agreed on beforehand and can be a tap or a nudge, the tutor stops reading. If the student meets an unfamiliar word during independent reading, the tutor waits approximately five seconds. If the student is not able to pronounce the word within that time, the tutor supplies it and the pair resumes reading together. This continues until the student once again signals a desire to read alone. After reading, the pair talks about the selection and the tutor notes any good reading behaviors exhibited by the student, such as self-correcting miscues, reading at an appropriate rate, and reading with good expression.

Paired-reading scenarios can be set up within the structure of the regular classroom. It is important that student preference and social relationships be considered when forming pairs. One pair who is carefully trained can work independently while the teacher trains another pair. Three pairs operating at the same time represent an optimal situation that allows the teacher to carefully monitor and evaluate progress. During paired reading, the other students can engage in independent or partner reading.

The regular structure of paired reading makes it ideal for use with aides, volunteers, parents, and tutors such as older students. Training is relatively simple. The teacher acts as the tutor and models the process while the intended tutor watches. Then the tutor and students who are paired read while the teacher observes and offers feedback. By engaging the prospective tutor in paired reading, after one or two attempts he or she should generally feel comfortable implementing this with struggling readers. Very often teachers are unsure how best to utilize aides and volunteers. Setting up paired-reading formats provides an effective program of fluency development and frees the teacher for other pursuits.

Partner Reading.   There are several variations of partner reading. In one version, students read orally to each other, usually by alternating pages. In another version, partners engage in repeated reading of the same selection to their partner several times in succession. In still another model, partners read orally together, helping each other with difficult words, coaching each other in becoming more fluent and expressive, and complimenting each other on a job well done. The teacher must model partner reading and help students understand the process, but once in place, the strategy is an effective way of providing reading practice for both students.

Partner reading is less scripted than paired reading. In paired reading, a more capable reader takes the lead and generally controls the flow of activity. In partner reading, both partners are equally involved in setting the direction of the lesson. When students are engaged in partner reading, the classroom or the intervention teacher has time to work with other individuals.

There are certain things to remember when using partner reading. It is better to choose relatively easy text, such as frequently read and familiar selections. However, if the selection is relatively new, allow students to practice it first to avoid any embarrassment or frustration in the presence of their partners. The teacher should model the process to the entire group and realize that careful monitoring and regular feedback are important in the early stages.

Choosing the right partners is another issue. Some students are comfortable with a friend, even if the friend is a better reader. Others are more comfortable with a partner of similar ability. We suggest not wasting valuable instructional time choosing partners or letting students choose partners. Instead, set up a simple device such as drawing names from a bowl. Keep partners together for a short time and then choose new ones. In this way, all the students will have a chance to partner-read with everyone in the class or group.

We recall one teacher who met daily with a group of fifteen struggling readers. Each day, she introduced a short poem or a stanza from a longer poem using assisted, echo, and repeated reading. Then, while she worked with an individual student, the other members of the group engaged in partner reading of the previous day's selection. Partner reading was a regular part of every lesson that the students expected and looked forward to, and they knew exactly how to proceed. The partners were rotated every week, and their names were posted on the board so there was no confusion about partner choice or matching. Students were expected to work cooperatively with their partners and, if the selection was not their preferred choice, they knew they would have another partner within a short time.

Structured Repeated Reading.   All of the activities just described can involve some form of repeated reading as students reread the same selection or parts of it. However, the term *repeated reading* usually refers to a more structured format in which the student orally re-reads a short selection until a certain level of accuracy, speed, or expression is attained, with the teacher providing guidance and feedback after each reading. Often the teacher and student jointly fill out a chart that shows visible evidence of progress over time. They can record the number of words read within a set time limit, such as three minutes, the number of seconds it took the student to read the selection, or the number of miscues or errors in pronunciation that were made.

Structured repeated reading is most commonly used with oral reading, but it can involve silent reading. It can be used with older students who are slow readers and can be quite effective in increasing their reading rate.

After choosing a selection of 50 to 200 words in length, the teacher begins by reading to the student first and providing assisted reading support until the student can read somewhat independently. (These first steps may not be necessary with older students who are attempting to increase their silent reading speed.) At that point, the student rereads the selection until attaining the desired fluency level. The student does not have to chart progress after every reading and can practice the selection between charting sessions.

As with other fluency development activities, choice of text is important, with instructional level text appropriate for structured repeated reading. Which evidence of progress is better to chart: number of words read, pronunciation errors, or reading speed? All have their place, and it is up to the teacher to decide which best fits the student's needs. However, it is important that the student do the actual charting of progress using information provided by the teacher. This ensures awareness of his or her growing fluency. We suggest that you chart only one measure of improvement in the beginning. The intent of charting is to offer visible proof of progress, and you do not want the student to become confused by conflicting measures.

Structured repeated reading usually requires the active involvement of the teacher. You cannot expect the student to keep track of his or her own mispronunciations, count number of words read, and efficiently handle a stopwatch. Because of this limitation, repeated reading tends to be focused on a single individual and does not always fit well within a small group or a regular classroom setting. An exception is the older student attempting to increase silent reading rate, who can be trained to practice independently, use a stopwatch to time length of reading, and figure out word-per-minute scores.

As with paired reading, tutors, aides, and volunteers can be trained to implement structured repeated reading. Some students find repeated reading and charting to be very motivating, whereas others find it incredibly frustrating. If a student falls into the latter category, try something else and do so very quickly.

Using Performance Reading to Develop Fluency

In performance reading, students practice reading with the ultimate goal of performing for peers, other teachers and students, or parents.

Choral Reading.   Choral reading involves groups of students reading in unison, and it can be set up in a variety of ways. In the beginning, the teacher can be part of the process; however, the goal is for the students to function independently. Students may read the entire selection chorally, or they may read only a certain part such as a repeated stanza or refrain. Alternatively, small groups of students can practice different parts of the same selection. The teacher's role is to move around to each group, offer suggestions, and perhaps model how the text might best be read. The students practice their part until they are fluent, and when each is satisfied as to his or her performance they come together and perform the entire selection. Poems or stories with predictable refrains lend themselves very well to choral reading.

Choral reading can easily get out of control if the groups are too large or the text segments too small. Each group should have enough practice material to keep it occupied for the allotted amount of time. Be sure that they have something else to do if they feel they have practiced enough. In fact, each student should have not only his or her choral reading part but also a book for independent reading if the group finishes before the others. In addition, the noise level can be deafening unless the students are shown how to practice using whisper reading.

Reader's Theater.   In reader's theater, students perform a script without costumes, props, or memorization. They read their parts with a focus on expressive reading appropriate to the character or situation, not on facial expressions, body movements, or specific acting techniques. The script can be a poem, a speech, a play, or a story that is dramatized with students playing the characters and acting as narrator. They practice their parts and rehearse until the final performance. Usually, students play solitary parts; that is, they perform alone. Choral reading can be an effective part of reader's theater, however.

Students need to know their designated parts, and just telling them does not work. Forgetting is very easy, and confusion soon reigns. Each student must have a copy of the entire script with his or her part clearly marked. Using colored highlighters is particularly effective for this.

Reader's theater works only if students have ample time to practice their parts until they can read them fluently. Many struggling readers will need extra support and the comfort of practicing with a teacher, tutor, or friend. It is important to stress to students that all actors and actresses engage in many rehearsals before the final performance and amount of practice time has nothing to do with reader ability. It is the teacher's role to schedule that performance at a point at which all participants are ready. Admittedly, reader's theater seems more suited to the regular classroom setting because it takes more time than is generally available in intervention sessions. However, some very short scripts might lend themselves to practice over a series of lessons, culminating in a final performance.

Radio Reading.   Radio reading is similar to reader's theater in that a student reads a selection as opposed to memorizing it. One student takes the part of the radio announcer and reads a selection while peers act as the audience. Only the teacher and the announcer have a copy of the text; the other students listen just as they would if they were listening to the radio. The teacher retains a copy of the script in order to help the announcer should difficulties occur. Usually they do not, as long as the following guidelines are followed.

Choose text that is at the student's independent or instructional reading level and that is of interest to the student. Allow for ample practice time. Use your knowledge of the student to determine if she or he should read to the entire class, to a small group, or to a friendly audience of one. Very often, students will begin by practicing for a single friend and, as their confidence grows, gradually move up to a small-group and then a whole-group performance.

Radio reading is a bit easier than reader's theater to fit into an intervention structure. The key to success is the students' initial comfort level. You need to set up a very successful first performance or students will not want to continue, so choose text that may seem too easy in order to guarantee this. Students do not have to read a long selection. They can read one or two sentences, perhaps as radio commercials, and gradually move to more lengthy segments.

The text for radio reading usually involves factual materials that do not necessarily require dramatic expression. The focus is on clearly conveying a message with suitable expression and at a rate that is appropriate for listener comprehension. Accounts of sports or news events are effective and motivating choices for radio reading, as are selections from history books. The announcer can also act as a critic and read book or movie reviews.

Lesson Procedures for Developing Fluency

All of the activities described can be combined in a variety of ways to promote fluency. However, there are some already developed lesson procedures a teacher can use that can be easily incorporated into a classroom setting or an intervention structure. Three procedures are quite similar: the fluency development lesson, the oral recitation lesson, and supported oral reading. All three combine various forms of support for initial reading, discussion of the content, and student oral reading practice.

The Fluency Development Lesson.   The fluency development lesson (Rasinski & Padek, 1996; Rasinski, Padak, Linek, & Sturtevant, 1994) involves a combination of reading to students, reading with students, and reading by students and takes about 10 to 15 minutes to complete. First, the teacher reads a short text of 50 to 150 words while students follow along with their own selections. Then the teacher and students discuss both the selection and the teacher's expression during reading. Following this, the teacher and class read the text chorally several times. The students then form prearranged pairs and take turns reading the selection and helping each other. Finally, individual or group volunteers perform the selection for the class.

The Oral Recitation Lesson.   The oral recitation lesson (Hoffman, 1985; Reutzel & Hollingsworth, 1993; Reutzel, Hollingsworth, & Eldridge, 1994) is very similar to the fluency development lesson. The teacher reads a selection to the class and after discussing it the class summarizes it. Then they talk about expressive reading and how punctuation marks signal voice changes. The students read the selection chorally. Individuals practice by softly reading the text to themselves. Students also practice reading in pairs. Finally, the selection is performed for the class. This procedure can be used for long selections. The teacher breaks the selection into manageable parts and repeats the lesson on successive days.

Supported Oral Reading.   Supported oral reading (Morris & Nelson, 1992) involves a three-day sequence. The teacher reads a selection, stopping occasionally to discuss the content. The teacher and students then read it chorally. On the second day, pairs of students practice reading alternate pages to each other. Each pair is then assigned a specific part to practice. On the third day, individuals read their assigned part to the teacher.

A tip for successful implementation of these three lesson structures is to choose one and stick with it. You want the students to become so comfortable with the format that they can pay attention to developing fluency. Realize that first attempts may seem disorganized and somewhat confusing. However, as soon as students learn what they are expected to do, things will improve.

Choice of text is, as always, important. You want short segments that pack a wallop, so to speak. If students are interested in the selection, they will be motivated to follow the procedure and practice. If they find the selection dull, they will find other things to do during the practice sessions.

If you are implementing these procedures in an intervention structure, you may want to use segments from the content texts that students are no doubt struggling with in the regular classroom. If you coordinate this carefully with the classroom teacher, students may find it very motivating to read, discuss, and practice this material.

Very often, support personnel come to the regular classroom to work with struggling readers. These lesson procedures provide a consistent structure for such in-class support.

Making Grade Level Text Manageable with Repeated Reading. We have repeatedly stressed the importance of using materials for fluency development that are at the students' independent or instructional reading levels. Unfortunately, these levels are often far below that of the classroom reading assignments. Many struggling readers are just not able to read the content textbooks used in their classes, and they are thus denied access to the concepts and language patterns present in grade level material. McCormick and Paratore (1999) see this as a concern and have devised an effective procedure for using grade level materials in intervention sessions.

First, the teacher introduces essential vocabulary and helps the students to identify and review decoding strategies for pronouncing it. The students preview the text, predict possible content, and formulate questions. The teacher then uses assisted reading and reads the text aloud while the students follow along. Discussion takes place, and the students talk about their predictions and pose answers to previously raised questions. Then they reread the selection with a peer. They may read chorally, use echo reading, or work as partners. Finally, the students reread the selection to the teacher in pairs or individually. This process can be employed with a whole section of text, or the teacher can a break a longer section into smaller parts.

To achieve success, the intervention teacher must carefully coordinate the readings with the classroom curriculum. Ideally, the students should work with the grade level material before it is addressed in class so that they can take an active part in classroom discussion—something that can be extremely motivating to students who are used to remaining silent and avoiding participation.

It is important not to overload the intervention session with too much text. Choose carefully those paragraphs that are probably the most important (the classroom teacher can help you with this), and summarize the others. We will address ways of structuring discussion in later chapters.

Fluency Oriented Reading Instruction (FORI). Fluency Oriented Reading Instruction (Stahl, Heubach, & Cramond, 1997; Stahl & Kuhn, 2002; Stahl & Heubach, 2005). was developed for second-grade classrooms and involves three components: a redesigned basal lesson, a daily free reading period in the classroom, and a home reading program. The redesign of the traditional basal lesson allows students reading below grade level to profit from it. The teacher first reads the basal selection to the students and leads them in an active discussion focused on comprehension. Following completion of vocabulary review and comprehension exercises, the teacher might reread parts of the selection using echo reading or have students orally practice parts, and then send the story home so parents can read it with their children. The home reading program is carefully monitored through the use of reading logs. On the second day, the students reread the selection as partners, alternating pages and monitoring each other until the selection is finished. Each day, the students also read easy or comfortable materials of their own choosing, with independent reading sessions ranging from 15 to 30 minutes. This program has been extremely effective, with students gaining an average of two years' growth in one year.

Morrow, Kuhn, and Schwanenflugel (2006/2007) conducted a five-year study of the Fluency Oriented Reading Program involving over 300 second-grade students. Children who participated in FORI demonstrated greater improvement in reading fluency than children who did not, and struggling readers benefited at similar rates as normal readers. The home reading program was expanded to include three evening workshops "to heighten awareness about the importance of fluency, describe the school program, and discuss activities that parents could do with their children at home to enhance fluency" (p. 326). Parent surveys and interviews suggested the effectiveness of the enhanced home program.

There are many aspects of this program that you can incorporate into your classroom or intervention structure, but don't try to do it all at once. Begin with one element that seems easiest: the redesigned basal lesson, independent reading in the classroom, or the home reading program. When you are comfortable with that, move to a second component. It may take all year to fully implement the structure, but it is better to move slowly and meet with success than to attempt too much and end up with nothing.

Table 6.2 provides a summary of the various fluency activities that we explained in this chapter.

Application to English Language Learners

Donovan and Ellis (2005) established a paired reading tutorial program for all second-grade students and all third- through fifth-grade students who participated in basic skills improvement or English as a second language programs. The target tutor population was

TABLE 6.2 Instructional Activities to Develop Fluency

Fluency Activity	Description	Appropriate for
Assisted reading	Teacher reads orally with one or more students.	First reading of a selection. Practice reading of previously read and perhaps difficult selection. Can be combined with other forms of oral reading support. Should be interspersed with discussion about the selection.
Echo reading	Teacher reads orally. One or more students imitate or echo the teacher's expression.	Practice reading of previously read selection. Can be used as practice for performance reading. Works best with short segments of text.
Paired reading	Capable reader reads with one student. Student signals desire to read alone. Shared reading resumes if word pronunciation error occurs.	First reading of a selection. Practice reading of previously read selections. Aides, volunteers, and tutors can be trained for this.
Partner reading	Partners read alternating pages to each other, repeatedly read a selection to each other, or read chorally together.	Practice reading of previously read and easy selection. Monitoring and feedback are essential while students learn the process.
Structured repeated reading	One student practices and charts progress guided by the teacher; can be used to increase silent reading speed.	Practice reading of previously read selection. Chart number of words, number of seconds, or number of errors. Chart one at a time. Aides, volunteers, and tutors can be trained for this.
Choral reading	Single group of students reads the same text together, or groups of students read different texts together.	Practice reading of previously read selection. Students must learn to whisper read.

the children's parents. Parents and children participated in five workshops throughout the school year. During the first workshop, they learned about the importance of fluency and watched a demonstration of paired reading. The children chose books to read at home and they and their parents practiced paired reading. In following workshops, parents shared success stories and parents and children engaged in a variety of literary activities.

Roser, May, Martinez, Keehn, Harmon, and O'Neal (2004) and Rea and Mercuri (2006) recommend reader's theater as a way of fostering the language development of English language learners. Reader's theater, as described in this chapter, involves reading (not memorizing) a script and performing it without scenery, makeup, or props. However, Rea and Mercuri suggest adding props and gestures as additional supports for English language learners. They caution that English language learners should not rehearse lines that have no meaning for them and the teacher should carefully assign roles based on the student's current facility with spoken English. An English language learner can also pair up with another student and share the same role. Roser et al. (2004) combined reader's theater with comprehension minilessons. They divided the class into five "repertory groups" and rotated activities so that each day included introduction of a new text or revisiting an old one with a performance by one of the groups.

In a similar vein, Mohr (2004) recommends using the following strategies to accelerate competence in academic language: reading aloud, rereading, choral reading, and

Fluency Activity	Description	Appropriate for
Reader's theater	Students or groups of students take different parts and practice for a performance.	Practice reading of previously read selection. Can use choral reading as practice. Parts should be clearly marked.
Radio reading	One student reads as the "announcer" and other students act as listeners.	Practice reading of previously read selection. Make certain the first experience is successful.
Fluency development lesson	Teacher reads to students. Teacher and students discuss selection and expression. Students read chorally. Students read as partners.	First reading of a selection. Can be a structure for in-class support.
Oral recitation lesson	Teacher reads to students. Students discuss and summarize selection. Students chorally read. Students practice in pairs or individually.	First reading of a selection. Can be used for in-class support.
Supported oral reading	Teacher reads to students and stops for discussion. Teacher and students read chorally. Students read as partners.	First reading of a selection.
Repeated reading of grade level text	Teacher reviews vocabulary. Teacher and students preview selection. Teacher reads. Teacher and students discuss selection. Students read with peers.	First reading of a selection using grade level content text.
Fluency Oriented Reading Selection	Teacher reads basal selection. Students discuss. Teacher and students practice rereading all or part of selection. Students daily read independently in easy text.	First reading of a selection.

reader's theater. Lenters (2004/2005) also encourages teachers to foster rereading in English language learners and suggests a three-step process involving teacher read-alouds, shared reading, and independent reading. Herrell and Jordan (2008) offer detailed explanations and model lessons for implementing interactive read-alouds and shared reading with English language learners.

Application to Adolescent Learners

Fluency development is primarily associated with primary or elementary reading. However, Rasinski, Padek, McKeon, Wilfong, Friedauer, and Heim (2005) investigated whether lack of fluency represented an issue in the reading difficulties of high school struggling readers. They asked over 300 ninth graders to read grade level materials and retell what they read. While the students were basically accurate readers, their reading rate scores were well below normal for their grade level. Their fluency rates were significantly correlated with scores on a standardized reading comprehension test; that is, as fluency rates increased so did test scores. Rasinski et al. concluded that "improvements in fluency could account for significant and substantial gains in students' reading comprehension" at the high school level (p. 25). They suggest wide reading of independent level material, repeated readings, performance activities, and assisted reading as effective methods for incorporating fluency development in the high school classroom.

McKenna (2002) suggests several principles for teaching fluency to adolescent learners. Students will need assistance in order to become fluent and practice is critical. Teachers should model fluent reading and maximize the amount of time that students spend reading. McKenna recommends many of the strategies described in this chapter: repeated reading, paired reading, echo reading, choral reading, reader's theater, peer tutoring, and self-selected reading.

Chandler-Olcott and Hinchman (2005) offer several suggestions for tutoring adolescent learners who lack fluency. Teacher modeling of fluent reading is effective, especially with content area texts that may contain many unfamiliar words. Repeated reading can also be useful, working best when done for a real-world purpose such as reading to younger children or practicing for a performance. Independent reading of easy text is another suggestion. The authors caution, however, to keep fluency lessons short, focused, and connected to the real-world interests of the student.

Response to Intervention

The most widely used assessment probe in Response to Intervention focuses on oral reading fluency. The student reads aloud for one minute and the teacher calculates the number of words read correctly in that time. Wright (2007) suggests that the teacher repeat this procedure with three passages, rank them in terms of scores, and choose the middle, or median, score as the best indicator of the student's reading rate. In RTI, identifying and recording oral reading errors is very similar to the process used during administration of an informal reading inventory. Determining the acceptability of the fluency rate involves comparing the student's score to class norms or to norms from other sources (Caldwell, 2008; Leslie & Caldwell, 2006; Hasbrouck & Tindal, 1992, 2006).

Despite its popularity, we are not convinced that a one-minute reading evaluation of number of correct words per minute is truly representative of a student's fluency. Fluency is more than speed and accuracy; it also involves voice expression or prosody and, of course, comprehension. Of what use is fluency in the absence of comprehension? Our concern is shared by Samuels (2007), Johns (2007), and Marcell (2007). Granted, a one-minute accuracy probe is a fast and relatively easy method of assessment and may have its uses. However, if it suggests tier 2 instruction, the student's fluency should be assessed in a more complete and natural way by asking the student to read and comprehend an entire passage.

If fluency scores suggest that a student should move into tier 2 or 3 three instruction, the teacher can use the activities described in this chapter for fluency improvement. It is important to remember, however, that fluency without comprehension is meaningless. Any assessment of fluency improvement should also involve some evaluation of student comprehension. If speed and accuracy are the primary components that are assessed, students will soon figure this out. They will then concentrate on saying the words correctly as fast as they can and pay less attention to the process of understanding and enjoying what they read.

Summary

Fluent readers are accurate. They read at an appropriate rate of speed and with expression. In order to be fluent, students must have a large store of automatically recognized sight words as well as effective strategies for pronouncing unfamiliar words. They also must understand that the purpose of reading is comprehension.

Lack of fluency can be determined by listening to students read orally in independent or instructional level text. Reading rate, measured as words per minute, can also indicate lack of fluency.

Certain principles govern fluency development in the intervention session or in the regular classroom. Always link fluency instruction to meaning. Support the students by providing guidance and feedback before, during, and after oral reading, and encourage wide reading of meaningful and enjoyable text. Pay attention to students' independent and instructional reading levels when choosing books and other reading materials. Finally, avoid unpracticed reading and round-robin oral reading.

Instructional activities for developing fluency include reading aloud to students and fostering wide reading. Various activities can provide support to students through modeling and feedback: assisted reading, echo reading, paired reading, partner reading, and structured repeated reading. Performance reading can take the form of choral reading, reader's theater, and radio reading. There are also various lesson procedures for developing fluency: the fluency development lesson, the oral recitation lesson, and supported oral reading. A classroom structure for fostering fluency is fluency-oriented reading instruction.

Reading to, with, and by ELLs is important. Daily read-alouds provide ELLs with the opportunity to experience literature and gain information from text before they can read it independently. Reader's theater is effective in developing fluency in ELLs. Fluency development may be just as important with adolescent readers and is best fostered through opportunity to engage in self-selected reading. With regard to Response to Intervention, we caution that fluency assessment without assessment of comprehension may present a distorted picture of progress.

REFERENCES AND RECOMMENDED READINGS

The Definition of Fluency and the Importance of Fluency

Hudson, R. F., Lane, H. B., & Pullen, P. C. (2005). Reading fluency assessment and instruction: What, why and how? *The Reading Teacher,.58,* 702–713.

Johns, J. (2007). Monitoring progress in fluency: Possible unintended consequences. *Reading Today,* June/July, 18.

Johns, J. L., & Berglund, R. L. (2002). *Fluency: Questions, answers, evidence-based strategies.* Dubuque, IA: Kendall/Hunt Publishing Company.

Kuhn, M. R., Schwanenflugel, P. J., Morris, R. D., Morrow, L. M., Woo, D. G., Meisinger, E. B., Sevcik, R. A., Bradley, B. A., & Stahl, S. A. (2006). Teaching children to become fluent and automatic readers. *Journal of Literacy Research, 38,* 357–388.

Marcell, B. (2007). Fluent to fault: Put fluency in the passenger seat and let comprehension take the wheel! *Reading Today,* June/July, 18–19.

Nathan, R. G., & Stanovich, K. E. (1991). The causes and consequences of differences in reading fluency. *Theory into Practice, 30,* 176–184.

National Reading Panel. (2000). *Report of the National Reading Panel: Teaching children to read: An evidence-based assessment of the scientific-based literature on reading and its implications for reading instruction.* Washington, DC: National Institute of Child Health and Human Development.

Peebles, J. L. (2007). Incorporating movement with fluency instruction: A motivation for struggling readers. *The Reading Teacher, 60,* 578–581.

Pikulski, J. J., & Chard, D. J. (2005). Fluency: Bridge between decoding and reading comprehension. *The Reading Teacher, 58,* 510–519.

Rasinski, T. (2004). Creating fluent readers. *Educational Leadership, 61,* 46–50.

Rasinski, T. V. (2000). Speed does matter in reading. *The Reading Teacher, 54,* 146–151.

Richards, M. (2000). Be a good detective: Solve the case of oral reading fluency. *The Reading Teacher, 53,* 534–539.

Samuels, S. J. (2007). The DIBELS tests: Is speed of barking at print what we mean by reading fluency? *Reading Research Quarterly, 42,* 563–566.

Walczyk, J. J., & Griffith-Ross, D. A. (2007). How important is reading skill fluency for comprehension? *The Reading Teacher, 60,* 560–569.

Assisted Reading and Echo Reading

Jennings, J. H., Caldwell, J. S., & Lerner, J. W. (2006). *Reading problems: Assessment and teaching strategies.* Boston: Allyn & Bacon.

Taylor, S. V., & Nesheim, D. W. (2000/2001). Making literacy real for "high-risk" adolescent emerging readers: An innovative application of reader's workshop. *Journal of Adolescent and Adult Literacy, 44,* 308–318.

Paired Reading

Caldwell, J. S., & Ford, M. P. (2002). *Where have all the bluebirds gone? How to soar with flexible grouping.* Portsmouth, NH: Heinemann.

Donovan, H., & Ellis, M. (2005). Paired reading: More than an evening of entertainment. *The Reading Teacher, 59,* 174–177

Topping, K. (1987). Paired reading: A powerful technique for parent use. *The Reading Teacher, 40,* 608–614.

Topping, K. (1989). Peer tutoring and paired reading: Combining two powerful techniques. *The Reading Teacher, 42,* 499–494.

Repeated Reading

Samuels, S. J. (1979). The method of repeated reading. *The Reading Teacher, 34,* 511–518.

Performance Reading

Worthy, J., & Broaddus, K. (2001/2002). Fluency beyond the primary grades: From group performance to silent, independent reading. *The Reading Teacher, 55,* 334–342.

Worthy, J., & Prater, K. (2002). "I thought about it all night": Reader's theatre for reading fluency and motivation. *The Reading Teacher, 56,* 294–297

Lesson Procedures

Griffith, L. W., & Rasinski, T. V. (2004). A focus on fluency: How one teacher incorporated fluency with her reading curriculum. *The Reading Teacher, 58,* 126–137.

Hoffman, J. V. (1985). *The oral recitation lesson: A teacher's guide.* Austin, TX: Academic Resource Consultants.

Kuhn, M. (2004/2005). Helping students become accurate expressive readers: Fluency instruction for small groups. *The Reading Teacher, 58,* 338–344.

McCormack, R. L., & Paratore, J. R. (1999). *"What do you do there anyway," teachers ask: A reading teacher's intervention using grade-level text with struggling third grade readers.* Paper presented at the National Reading Conference, Orlando, FL.

Morris, D., & Nelson, L. (1992). Supported oral reading with low-achieving second graders. *Reading Research and Instruction, 31,* 49–63.

Morrow, L. M., Kuhn, M. R., & Schwanenflugel, P. J. (2006/2007). The family fluency program. *The Reading Teacher, 60,* 322–333.

Rasinski, T. (2006). Reading fluency instruction: Moving beyond accuracy, automaticity and prosody. *The Reading Teacher, 59,* 704–706.

Rasinski, T., & Padak, N. (1996). *Holistic reading strategies: Teaching students who find reading difficult.* Englewood Cliffs, NJ: Merrill.

Rasinski, T. V., Padak, N. D., Linek, W. L., & Sturtevant, E. (1994). Effects of fluency development on urban second graders. *Journal of Educational Research, 87,* 158–165.

Reutzel, D. R., & Hollingsworth, P. M. (1993). Effects of fluency training on second graders' reading comprehension. *Journal of Educational Research, 86,* 325–331.

Reutzel, D. R., Hollingsworth, P. M., & Eldridge, L. (1994). Oral reading instruction: The impact on student reading comprehension. *Reading Research Quarterly, 29,* 40–62.

Stahl, S. A., & Heubach, K. M. (2005). Fluency-oriented reading instruction. *Journal of Literacy Research, 37,* 25–60.

Stahl, S. A., & Kuhn, M. R. (2002). Making it sound like language: Developing fluency. *The Reading Teacher, 55,* 582–584.

Stahl, S. A., Heubach, K., & Cramond, B. (1997). *Fluency-oriented reading instruction.* (Research Report No. 79). Athens, GA: National Reading Research Center.

Assessing Fluency

Caldwell, J. S. (2008). *Reading assessment: A primer for teachers and coaches.* New York: The Guilford Press.

Hasbrouck, J. E., & Tindal, G. (1992). Curriculum-based oral reading fluency norms for students in grades 2 through 5. *Teaching Exceptional Children,* Spring, 41–44.

Hasbrouck, J., & Tindal, G. A. (2006). Oral reading fluency norms: A valuable assessment tool for reading teachers. *The Reading Teacher, 59,* 636–643.

Leslie, L., & Caldwell, J. (2006). *Qualitative reading inventory-4.* Boston: Allyn & Bacon.

Wright, J. (2007). *RTI toolkit: A practical guide for schools.* Port Chester, NY: Dude Publishing.

Reading Aloud

Beck, I. L., & McKeown, M. G. (2001). Text talk: Capturing the benefits of read-aloud experiences for young children. *The Reading Teacher, 55,* 10–20.

Fisher, D., Flood, J., Lapp, D., & Frey, N. (2004). Interactive read-alouds: Is there a common set of implementation practices? *The Reading Teacher, 58,* 8–17.

Lane, H. B., & Wright, T. L. (2007). Maximizing the effectiveness of reading aloud. *The Reading Teacher, 60,* 668–674.

McGee, L. M., & Schickedanz, J. A. (2007). Repeated interactive read-alouds in preschool and kindergarten. *The Reading Teacher, 60,* 742–751.

English Language Learners

Donovan, H., & Ellis, M. (2005). Paired reading: More than an evening of entertainment. *The Reading Teacher, 59,* 174–177.

Herrell, A. L., & Jordan, M. (2008). *Fifty strategies for teaching English language learners.* Upper Saddle River, NJ: Merrill/Prentice Hall.

Lenters, K. (2004/2005). No half measures: Reading instruction for young second language learners. *The Reading Teacher, 58,* 328–336.

Mohr, K. A. J. (2004). English as an accelerated language: A call to action for reading teachers. *The Reading Teacher, 58,* 18–26.

Rea, D. M., & Mercuri, S. P. (2006). *Research-based strategies for English language learners.* Portsmouth, NH: Heinemann.

Roser, N. L., May, L. A., Martinez, M., Keehn, S., Harmon, J. M., & O'Neal, S. (2004). Stepping into character(s): Using reader's theatre with bilingual fourth graders. In R. L. McCormack and J. R. Paratore (Eds.), *After early intervention, then what? Teaching struggling readers in grades 3 and beyond* (pp. 40–69). Newark, DE: International Reading Association.

Adolescent Learners

Chandler-Olcott, K., & Hinchman, K. A. (2005). *Tutoring adolescent literacy learners: A guide for volunteers.* New York: The Guilford Press.

McKenna, M. C. (2002). *Help for struggling readers: Strategies for grades 3–8.* New York: The Guilford Press.

Rasinski, T. V., Padek, N. D., McKeon, C. A., Wilfong, L. G., Friedauer, J. A., & Heim, P. (2005). Is reading fluency a key for successful high school reading? *Journal of Adolescent and Adult Literacy, 49,* 22–27.

7

Prior Knowledge and Concept Development

How Prior Knowledge Affects Comprehension

Models of text comprehension agree that comprehension requires the reader to be an active processor of text. Put simply, that means that the reader must *think* while reading. But what should the reader be thinking about? Some models focus on one aspect of comprehension more than others, but overall it is agreed that readers must *construct* meaning; that is, they must use their knowledge base to interpret text information in specific ways. This is not usually a conscious process; readers don't say to themselves, "What do I know about beavers? Oh, I know that they have big teeth and chew on wood." Rather, if a student had such knowledge about beavers and read the title of the passage, "Busy Beaver" (Leslie & Caldwell, 2006, p. 243), a visual image might be evoked—that of a beaver with large teeth chewing on wood. Another student with less knowledge about beavers might know only that they are animals and have no image of what they look like. A student with a lot of knowledge about beavers might know that they are animals that live near water and cut down trees with their teeth to build homes for their families. When these students read a passage about beavers, they each construct a personal understanding of the text, and because of knowledge differences their personal understandings differ. Let's look at "Busy Beaver" (see Figure 7.1) and the meanings that each student described above might construct (see Table 7.1).

The student who knows only that beavers are animals may learn that beavers live near water and use their teeth to collect sticks and cut down wood to build their houses. The student who already understands that beavers use their teeth to cut wood might develop a deeper understanding of how they build a dam to form a pond, and learn that a beaver's home is in the middle of the pond and that it uses its teeth to gather sticks for his house. The student who already knows what the previous student has just learned from reading the passage might confirm that knowledge and learn the impact of the beaver's activities on the environment. Each of these students gains new knowledge from the text, but the specifics of the new knowledge differ. This example demonstrates how important it is that *teachers assess* what their students already know about a topic before reading about it. Notice that prior knowledge does *not* mean simply a definition of the word *beaver*. The student with the least amount of knowledge in the example knows that a beaver is an animal. The student with more knowledge about beavers knows not only that they are animals but also about their behavior and habitat—a more specific knowledge. Knowing what students already know about a topic provides the teacher with a window to understanding why they have learned varying types of information, or why one student might have difficulties understanding the intricacies of "Busy Beaver" and another does not. In this chapter we will discuss how to assess prior knowledge and what to do with the varying levels of knowledge that are bound to appear in a small group of students and in the classroom.

FIGURE *7.1*   Busy Beaver from *Qualitative Reading Inventory-4* (Leslie & Caldwell, 2006)

Have you ever heard someone say, "Busy as a beaver"? Beavers are very busy animals and they are master builders. This furry animal spends its life working and building. As soon as a beaver leaves its family, it has much work to do.

First, the beaver must build a dam. It uses sticks, leaves, and mud to block a stream. The beaver uses its two front teeth to get the sticks. The animal uses its large flat tail to pack mud into place. A pond forms behind the dam. The beaver spends most of its life near this pond.

In the middle of the beaver's pond is a large mound. This mound of mud and twigs is the beaver's lodge or house. The beaver's family is safe in the lodge because it is well hidden. The doorway to the lodge is under the water. After the lodge is built, the beaver still cannot rest. More trees must be cut down to be used as food for the coming winter. Sometimes there will be no more trees around the pond. Then the beaver has to find trees elsewhere. These trees will have to be carried to the pond. The beaver might build canals leading deep into the forest.

All this work changes the land. As trees are cut down, birds, squirrels, and other animals may have to find new homes. Animals that feed on trees lose their food supply. The pond behind the dam floods part of the ground. Animals that used to live there have to move. However, the new environment becomes a home for different kinds of birds, fish, and plants. All this happens because of the very busy beaver.

TABLE 7.1 The Relationship between Student Prior Knowledge and New Learning from "Busy Beaver"

Student	Prior Knowledge	New Learning
1—Little knowledge	Beavers are animals.	Beavers are animals that *live near water, use their teeth to collect sticks, and cut down wood to build their houses.*
2—Some knowledge	Beavers are animals that cut down wood to build houses.	Beavers are animals that *use their teeth* to cut down wood and *collect sticks* to build houses *behind a dam in the middle of a pond.*
3—A lot of knowledge	Beavers are animals that use their teeth to cut down wood and collect sticks to build houses behind a dam in the middle of a pond.	When beavers cut down trees *to build their homes, other animals may have to find new homes. The pond behind the dam floods land so animals that cannot live in water must move. Other animals that can live in the flooded land move in.*

Knowledge Activation

In addition to having knowledge about a topic, students need to know that their knowledge is relevant to what they are reading or why it is. In some cases, what they are thinking might be irrelevant to the specific topic. Knowledge activation is the process of being aware of knowledge related to the topic. Sometimes this knowledge is relevant, as in the three examples discussed previously. Other times it is irrelevant. For example, there are multiple meanings of many English words, so a reader can have knowledge activated that is unrelated to the specific meaning of the word in the text. The word *groom* when used as a noun refers to the male of a couple being married, whereas the word *groom* when used as a verb, as in *to groom,* means to clean. If a student knows the noun *groom* and activates the wedding schema, it will not help him or her understand an article about how chimpanzees groom each other or the statement "The man is well groomed." A teacher must assess conceptual prior knowledge to determine if the knowledge the student possesses is appropriate or adequate for the new information to be learned.

Prior knowledge is closely tied to our knowledge of word meaning or vocabulary. We often think of word meaning in a limited way. We believe that students understand a word if they can provide us with a definition or a synonym. But conceptual knowledge is so much more. Words represent concepts, and a concept is much broader and richer than a definition. Think again of *groom.* What is your concept of *groom,* the male half of a wedding couple? Is it appropriately described by such a limited definition? We suspect that it is not. Your concept likely includes what the groom wears, typical groom behavior at the reception, and so forth. It includes grooms you have personally known as well as those you have seen on television and in the movies. Your concept may even include historical grooms, such as the much married King Henry VIII.

What is the point? Assessment and development of prior knowledge can be closely tied to our development of vocabulary, but only if we regard words as representing concepts, not just definitions. In other words, we can expand a student's knowledge base through vocabulary instruction if we remember that a single word can actually represent a broad concept.

How to Assess Prior Knowledge

There is substantial research that describes different methods of assessing a student's knowledge base. Holmes and Roser (1987) and Valencia and Stallman (1989) summarize the research on several methods:

1. Oral or written definitions of important concepts and vocabulary: What is a beaver?
2. Oral free association to important concepts and vocabulary: What do you think of when you hear the word *beaver*?
3. Multiple choice tests to measure important concepts and vocabulary: A beaver is
   a. A bird
   b. A mammal
   c. An insect
   d. A fish
4. Judgments of the likelihood that statements would be included in an article on a certain topic:

   Which of the following statements would likely occur in a passage about a beaver? Mark all those that apply.
   a. A beaver swims through the water to find sticks.
   b. A beaver builds a lodge to house his family.
   c. A beaver walked down the alley behind my house.
   d. On a boat ride in the ocean we saw a beaver.
5. Written predictions of content given topical prompts or pictures:

   Write what you think the passage will be about if it includes the following words: *Lodge, beaver, flat tail, pond,* and *sticks.*
   This picture is shown in the passage that you will read. What do you think the text will be about?

All of these ways of assessing prior knowledge have been shown to correlate with comprehension, yet no single method captures all a student knows about a topic. Certainly knowledge of critical concepts is important, but what *level* of knowledge is necessary for comprehension? And what if the reader understands a concept but not the word or words being assessed? There is no research answer for these questions at present. However, the measurement of prior knowledge, by whatever method you choose, is important to determine if

- A student is not understanding the text because of a lack of knowledge
- The student's knowledge is inconsistent with the content of the text
- The student is not activating the knowledge she or he possesses and using it to construct meaning

Using an Informal Reading Inventory to Assess Prior Knowledge

One purpose of informal reading inventories (IRIs) is to diagnose a student's reading problems, not simply to determine that the student is having problems—most teachers know that before an IRI is given. Rather, the goal is to determine what aspects of the reading process are troublesome. If a student is reading accurately and fluently but does not comprehend the text, we need to look for the reasons. As discussed previously, students may not comprehend because they lack a knowledge base consistent with the topic. How do we know? IRIs may include measures of prior knowledge that can be used to determine if the student knows concepts important to the passage. The *Basic Reading Inventory* (Johns, 2005) asks the student to respond to concepts related to the text, and the examiner is to make a judgment as to the level of familiarity student's with the topic. The *QRI-4* (Leslie & Caldwell, 2006) contains concepts that the student is asked to define: *What is _____? or What does _____ mean to you?* The examiner scores the student's responses on a 3-2-1-0 scale, and if the score is above 55 percent, then the passage is considered familiar. This percent was determined by examining the average prior knowledge score associated with comprehension at 70 percent or higher. The average percentage across all passages above second grade was 55 percent.

However, more important than the percentages are the student's responses to the concepts. Some concepts are more important to the overall story than others. For example, it is one thing to have never heard of Patricia McKissack (a children's author) and yet another not to know what a biography is. One concept is measuring a specific piece of knowledge, whereas the other is measuring a class of narrative text. We would rather have our students understand what a biography is so that when they begin to read one they expect the common elements of biographies: information about the person's childhood and how it influenced who she or he became, what she or he is known for, and so forth.

Teachers should examine prior knowledge measures on IRIs to determine general familiarity with text concepts and to note which concepts are the most important to an overall sense of the text. What if an IRI doesn't contain a prior knowledge measure? The procedures described in the following paragraphs, which explain how to assess prior knowledge before instruction, are applicable. That is, the teacher must first identify the important text information necessary for the students to understand it, and then decide which forms of prior knowledge assessment are most appropriate given the knowledge required for comprehension. This is a time-consuming task, which is why it is helpful for IRIs to contain reliable and valid measures of knowledge necessary for comprehension.

Assessing Prior Knowledge before Instruction

Teachers should always assess prior knowledge before students read a piece of text, and this can be accomplished with any of the methods described previously. It also can be done while activating students' knowledge just before reading a text. Let us return to our "Busy Beaver" example and the three students that we described earlier. We will assume that you are teaching a group of six students. Pair them and ask them to take three to five minutes to discuss with each other and write down what they know about beavers. At the end of that time, draw a semantic map using the ideas that the students have generated so that they see the relatedness among the concepts (Blachowicz & Fisher, 2000). Consider an example in which the students generate something about where beavers live, what they eat, and how they build their homes. The semantic map shown in Figure 7.2 illustrates the organization of the ideas. You write these categories in the boxes and have the students fill in the specific knowledge that they have generated.

FIGURE 7.2 Semantic Map for Beavers

Semantic maps provide an excellent way to activate prior knowledge important to understanding the text. Also, you can correct any misconceptions that would interfere with student learning. From this semantic map students can also make predictions about the kinds of information that the author will present in the text. After reading the text, the students can fill in the boxes and add more if appropriate. Doing this gives them a visual representation of what they read and may serve as a study aid. Other examples of graphic aids can be found in Chapter 10 on retelling expository text.

*B*uilding a Knowledge Base: Concept Development

Although the previous discussion was under the heading of activating prior knowledge, it should be clear that developing a semantic map from students' knowledge and adding to it after they have read a text is also adding to their knowledge base. Some students may only learn new terms for concepts that they already know, others will learn a few new specifics about beavers, and others will learn many specifics.

Determining Critical Concepts

One of the most important questions that a teacher must ask regards which concepts are critical for students to know in order to comprehend the major ideas and which are used repeatedly in the text. Probably the best example of this occurs in science. Because of the number of new and often abstract scientific concepts, writers of elementary grade science texts mark important concepts by bolding them, using headings that indicate what the section will be about, and providing a glossary of important terms. The bolded terms are usually those that the students will need to understand for later chapters. Also, charts can provide an excellent way to recognize how concepts are related, and figures can often explain a concept or concepts better than any words can. In these cases teachers have a variety of information sources for activating and building background knowledge.

Unfortunately, not all content texts are so reader friendly. Social studies texts have notoriously demanded inferences that students cannot make because of insufficient prior knowledge (Loxterman, Beck, & McKeown, 1995). Let's look at two paragraphs from one of the examples used by Loxterman and colleagues. The passage is about *El Niño*:

> From time to time the warm current that flows along the coast of Ecuador moves south and pushes the Peru Current away from the coast. This event is called El Niño because it happens around Christmastime. El Niño means "the child," which is what Spanish-speaking people call the baby Jesus. When El Niño comes, it brings bad times to Peru's coast. Heavy rains cause flooding and landslides. Millions of fish die because the warm water has less oxygen and food. When the fish die, thousands of birds starve to death too. (p. 367)

Consider what would happen if a student was asked why fish die during an *El Niño*. The only answer that is directly stated in these paragraphs is something like, "The water is warm" or "Because they get less food and oxygen." A more complete answer is "The water is warm, and it has less oxygen and food." What does this have to do with *El Niño*? The paragraph tells us that warm water from Ecuador pushes the Peru Current away from the coast. But what it doesn't say is that the Peru Current is normally cold and it is the rapid change in water temperature that affects the fish. How is a student going to make this connection? Would you expect your students to know that the Pacific Current near Peru is normally cold? We doubt it. So what do we do?

Loxterman and colleagues studied the effects of revising the text to provide clearer connections among ideas and found significant improvement in students' comprehension.

For example, they add a sentence to the first paragraph: "Every three to five years, the Pacific Ocean's current changes abruptly along the western coastline of South America and causes serious economic hardships for the people of Peru." They go on to tell us, "This sudden change is called El Niño, which means 'the child Jesus,' because it occurs right after Christmastime." Notice that they told us that *El Niño* is a sudden change, which reinforces the concept of abruptness stated earlier. In the next paragraph they state: "When El Niño happens two very important climate changes occur. The usually cool Pacific waters become warmer close to the coast, and there is 10 times the normal rain" (p. 367).

Loxterman and colleagues' revised text tells us directly what happens during *El Niño*. In the next paragraph they include information about the fish dying because of the shift in the water temperature. Although their revision is somewhat longer than the textbook version, the causal connections are made much more explicit. The revised text assumes less background knowledge and reduces the inference load by explaining why changes in the water temperature cause problems. Now, we can't all rewrite our social studies texts, but we can and must examine these materials to see what they are assuming that our students know. The concepts won't be labeled for you, and the only bolded words are probably *El Niño*.

Another text aid to help students understand the relationship of the ocean currents and *El Niño* is a picture of the western coast of South America with the countries of Ecuador and Peru labeled and the movement of the warm and cold water currents illustrated. Of course, the students will need the teacher to explain how the map illustrates what is said in the text; however, this is usually necessary for students to make effective use of a visual aid. Even the most advanced readers will not use a visual aid unless taught how to do so effectively. Think about readers who are struggling with the text; they probably view the visual aid as great because they don't have to read it at all!

Building a Knowledge Base: Connecting to Unschooled Knowledge

It is believed that we learn new knowledge only by connecting it to something that we already know. This is one reason that examples and analogies (e.g., baseball to cricket) are so useful in teaching. We take the student's knowledge base and develop connections between it and the new information. As we learn what they know about a topic, we see that students have knowledge that is not taught in formal schooling, but rather develops during everyday experiences. Readers increase their knowledge through newspapers, magazines, television, movies, and interactions with friends and acquaintances. Alexander and Jetton (2000) describe students as participating in "millions of information exchanges" (p. 286) that build an extensive knowledge base on a variety of topics. Such knowledge should be used to teach the new, more school-based information. For example, although students may have little knowledge of the Vietnam War or World War I, they probably have extensive knowledge of wars in general gleaned from newspapers, magazines, television, and movies. The teacher should activate what they know about the general concept of war and then connect that to the specific concepts related to the war that they will be reading about.

The accompanying semantic map illustrates one student's knowledge base about war. Similar examples can be found in Chapter 10 on retelling expository text. The students had been asked to write down all of the words that they thought about when they heard the term *war*. The following words and sentences were written: *guns, bombs, 2 sides and there are winners and losers. When it is over changes happen in the losing country, like maybe its government. There are a lot of reasons why war happens.* From that information the teacher formatted the semantic map in Figure 7.3.

From the semantic map, the students then went on to read about World War I. They were encouraged to look for the causes of the war, which countries were on opposite sides in the war, what kinds of weapons were used, and the changes that occurred in the participating countries, especially the losers. As they read they were asked to fill in the semantic map with

FIGURE 7.3   Semantic Map for War

details learned. Working from the information that they already knew, they could more easily learn the new information. If all of the important categories hadn't been generated through group discussion, the teacher was free to add it. Let's say that the students didn't mention causes. The teacher could ask, "What do you know about how wars get started?" and then write the word *causes* in a box on the map. This would provide the students with a reminder to look for that important information in the text.

Perhaps prior knowledge *assessment* and *development* should center on more general or universal, as opposed to specific, concepts. Most prior knowledge measures tend to focus on the specific, but Narvaez (2002) suggests that "prior knowledge often comes in the form of general knowledge structures" or scripts (p. 159). It may be that teachers should concentrate more on the "big picture" of understanding. For example, prereading expectation guides might help students to access and expand their principled knowledge prior to reading unfamiliar material (Jennings, Caldwell, & Lerner, 2006). Chapter 10 illustrates how expectation guides are used to help students discuss what they know about a topic and how that will likely relate to what they are going to read.

Building a Knowledge Base: The Internet, Movies, CDs, and Other Visual Methods

The Internet is a marvelous source of pictorial information. Once during a tutoring session, a young girl asked, "Where do frogs go in the winter?" Her teacher said, "Well some of them dig deep in the mud under a lake," but that was all she knew, so they went to the Web and typed "Where do frogs go in the winter?" in the search engine. Up came many marvelous websites that explained how frogs survive, complete with pictures. They printed it out, and *voila*! The teacher had instant information just when it was needed. Of course, if you have Internet access in your room, the students can use it to research topics themselves.

Returning to social studies, it is often difficult for students to imagine a time long ago when people lived in structures far different from ours, without electricity, running water, and so forth. Fortunately, we have movies that depict these times very well and can serve to expand students' knowledge base. You don't have to show the entire movie, just enough to build the necessary background knowledge. These recommendations are directed toward a classroom in which most or all of the students have insufficient prior knowledge.

You may be thinking, okay, all of that is nice, but I am tutoring a group of six students, and I don't have time to use the Internet or movies. What can I do? Use objects or pictures. Students love it when teachers bring something in from the "real world." For example, the "Busy Beaver" selection described earlier can be enhanced if it includes a picture of a beaver's lodge showing how the dam holds back the water. If your text doesn't include important pictures, find them. The Internet is a great source.

What about Narrative Text?

When textbooks do not label and explain the concepts critical for understanding, the teacher must examine the text and ask what his or her students need to know so that they will understand it. In fiction, the important concepts are rarely directly indicated, so the teacher is left to identify them. And even if books do identify some critical concepts, the teacher must consider whether or not his or her students will know them. For example, in the *Autobiography of Malcolm X,* Malcolm X is described as being *articulate.* That section of text is describing his verbal communication skills, so if students don't understand the idea of being *articulate,* the only help from context is that it has something to do with a way of talking. This concept is important to this section of the autobiography because it sets up the contrast between Malcolm's facility in oral language and his inability to read and write well. Teachers should explain this before students read the text.

Application to English Language Learners

The research on the effects of prior knowledge on ELLs is minimal, but the results support previous research with native speakers of English. One study of second language reading comprehension found that students understood more when they read material that was consistent with their background knowledge (Droop & Verhoeven, 1998). Therefore, the content and teaching recommendations previously presented in this chapter apply similarly to ELLs. However, developing content knowledge in native speakers versus ELLs may differ in that there may be content knowledge differences among ELLs of which the teacher is unaware, particularly if there were students from many different countries in the class. Therefore, the teacher must face not only the challenge of improving students' linguistic knowledge, but also improving prior knowledge related to experience and culture. It is important for the teacher to assess prior knowledge using the techniques described earlier to determine what the students know about the topic.

Returning to the earlier example of *El Niño,* students' experience with the concept of currents may vary considerably, depending where they lived prior to immigrating. The major concept to be learned is that *El Niño* is caused by a change in the temperature of the water, which is caused by a change in the movement of currents. All students will need conceptual development in current activity, but ELLs may need additional concept development about *currents.* A video clip of moving currents would be the best way to illustrate how the *El Niño* effect occurs, but a drawing depicting the moving currents could also be effective. It has also been suggested that the teacher prepare ELLs for content vocabulary by working with them a day or two ahead of time, providing examples of the concepts, and perhaps letting them get a head start on reading the text (Fitzgerald & Graves, 2003).

It is important that teachers recognize that parents of students in their classrooms can be important resources for demonstrating concepts, whether they are culturally specific or not. Perhaps a parent has fishing experience and has learned how the fish behave in currents during spawning season. This parent's personal experience could help bring the concept of changing currents home to the students in ways that texts cannot. Using parents' knowledge also acknowledges the parents' talents and helps the teacher learn about the culture (Fitzgerald & Graves, 2003). Once the teacher has more knowledge, he or she can do a better job of connecting the content to be taught to something in the ELL's background, an important feature of the SIOP model discussed in Chapter 12 (Echevarria, Vogt, & Short, 2008).

A suggestion for how to negotiate both language development and content learning is having students work "with a buddy who could assist in translation or clarification in the language" (Hurley & Tinajero, 2001, p. 69). In this example the student is having difficulty with aspects of English in addition to the concept being taught. A similar idea would be groups of three ELLs at different levels of English proficiency. This arrangement could encourage the student who is least proficient in the language to believe that he or she *will* learn English and will show the more proficient English language learners how far they have come.

A somewhat easier issue emerges if the student understands the concept that is being taught, but only knows the word for it in his native language. In this case it is simply a matter of connecting the concept in their native language to the English word. Pictures are very helpful for concrete objects. An excellent example of a student knowing a concept but not the English word for it occurred during the *QRI-4* testing of a seventh grader from Bosnia. His classroom teachers thought that he was learning disabled, but he had been observed by one of us while being tutored in a group of three and no evidence of learning disability was observed. He read two eighth-grade-level passages on immigration, an experience he had vivid knowledge of; however, the type of item used to measure prior knowledge varied. His prior knowledge scores on the two sections of the immigration passages represent a marked contrast. On the first section assessing his understanding of the words *immigrant, persecution, hardship,* and *oppression,* he answered "I don't know" to all of these words, yet certainly he conceptually understood *immigrant* based on his story of immigrating to the United States. The words above are technical words from social studies material that would not be known from only social language development in English. In contrast, the second text asked for an explanation of the following concepts: *symbol, to explain the difference between a dream and reality, culture,* and *why it might be difficult to move to another country.* In this situation he was able to explain all the concepts. For example, for *symbol,* he said "it presents (represents) something." When asked for an example, he gave *flag.* When asked what is meant by culture, he responded, "religions, people, and languages," which are all aspects of culture. He had personal examples to explain why it would be difficult to move to another country. This example illustrates both that how we assess prior knowledge influences the outcomes and therefore the inferences that we make, and second, that there is a difference between understanding a concept and knowing a particular word used to describe it. This distinction is particularly important for ELLs.

One area of reading comprehension most affected by cultural and linguistic knowledge is figurative language. Figurative language interpretation is based on a person's schema; therefore, without appropriate cultural experiences comprehension will suffer. Several examples given by Palmer, Shackelford, Miller, and LeClere (2007) illustrate how one English word can have a variety of meanings. Consider the many meanings of the word *hot* in the following contexts: A fire is *hot;* a *hot rod* doesn't mean a burning car, but rather a cool one; someone who is *hot under the collar* is angry; and *hot off the press* describes a newly printed newspaper. Consider the confusion of an ELL when faced with the many difficulties of figurative language. Palmer et al. recommend four steps in finding meaning in figurative language (p. 263).

1. Identify the figurative language in written text
2. Determine if the literal meaning in the text makes sense
3. Find the intended meaning of the figurative language expression
4. Make connections between the figurative language and real life, or how it is applied

A sample poster in the Palmer et al. article illustrates how to apply these four steps in learning the meaning of *beeline.* Figurative language will be a major stumbling block for ELLs unless teachers are aware of its difficulty and address it directly.

Application to Adolescent Learners

The research on prior knowledge and practical implications of it apply similarly to readers of all ages. In fact, the early research on prior knowledge effects on comprehension was conducted using college students (e.g., Anderson, Reynolds, Schallert, & Goetz, 1977) and adults (Steffensen, Joag-Dev, & Anderson, 1979). There are no recent studies of prior knowledge effects on comprehension, but instructional programs designed to improve comprehension of adolescents include the building or activating of prior knowledge within their programs (Echevarria, Vogt, & Short, 2008; Fitzgerald & Graves, 2003). Content teachers are challenged to recognize students' potential gaps in knowledge so they can teach these concepts and how they relate to other concepts within the knowledge domain.

We will address the role of prior knowledge in learning content within the strategies for teaching ELLs presented in Chapter 12. All of the research and methods on assessing and teaching conceptual learning described in this chapter apply directly to adolescent learners who spend much of their school day trying to use what they know to learn new information in content areas.

Response to Intervention

In tier two and tier three instruction, teachers must take account of the powerful role of prior knowledge. It is quite possible that a student's comprehension or lack of it may be due to background knowledge and not the ability to pronounce the words or engage in comprehension strategies. Let us consider the student who knows a lot about a specific topic. The ability to answer questions or complete class activities may be a function of that knowledge. We well recall a youngster who was passionately interested in snakes and was able to answer many questions about the text solely based on that knowledge. In the opposite scenario, the student who knows very little about the topic reflects this in the quality of his or her comprehension. In piloting for various editions of the *Qualitative Reading Inventory,* time and time again we have encountered students who read at grade level in familiar text but encounter difficulties in text with an unfamiliar structure and on unfamiliar topics. In assessing progress in RTI, the teacher should make every effort to negate the effect of prior knowledge by choosing texts that represent a similar level of familiarity—either all very familiar, all moderately familiar, or all very unfamiliar. Unless topic familiarity is addressed, the teacher cannot be certain if progress or lack of it is due to reading skill or prior knowledge.

Summary

This chapter has provided the rationale for teaching concepts critical for understanding a particular piece of text. In order to know whether the students understand these concepts, prior knowledge of them must be assessed. Examples of how to assess prior knowledge, how to activate prior knowledge, and how to use these techniques to develop a conceptual foundation for text were provided. We extended our discussion to include issues related to teaching ELLs and concluded that the same approaches apply, although the student is learning English in addition to conceptual knowledge. The importance of prior knowledge and the methods of assessment and instruction presented apply similarly to adolescent readers. We caution that measuring a response to intervention using connected text must attempt to negate the effects of prior knowledge. The next chapter will connect conceptual knowledge with learning vocabulary and will examine how to provide effective vocabulary instruction.

REFERENCES AND RECOMMENDED READINGS

Alexander, P. A., & Jetton, T. L. (2000). Learning from text: A multidimensional and developmental perspective. In M. L. Kamil, P. B. Mosenthal, P. D. Pearson, & R. Barr (Eds.), *Handbook of reading research* (Vol. III, pp. 285–310). Mahwah, NJ: Erlbaum.

Beck, I., McKeown, M. G., & Worthy, J. (1995). Giving a text voice can improve students' understanding. *Reading Research Quarterly, 30,* 220–238.

Blachowicz, C. L. Z., & Fisher, P. (2000). Vocabulary instruction. In M. L. Kamil, P. B. Mosenthal, P. D. Pearson, & R. Barr (Eds.), *Handbook of reading research* (Vol. III, pp. 503–524). Mahwah, NJ: Erlbaum.

Holmes, B. C., & Roser, N. (1987). Five ways to assess readers' prior knowledge. *The Reading Teacher, 40,* 646–649.

Jennings, J. H., Caldwell, J. S., & Lerner, J. W. (2006). *Reading Problems: Assessment and Teaching Strategies* (4th ed.). Boston: Allyn & Bacon.

Johns, J. (2005). *Basic reading inventory* (8th ed.). Dubuque, IA: Kendall/Hunt Publishing.

Leslie J., Caldwell, J. (2006). *Qualitative reading inventory-4.* Boston: Allyn & Bacon.

Loxterman, J. A., Beck, I. L., & McKeown, M. G. (1995). The effects of thinking aloud during reading on students' comprehension of more or less coherent text. *Reading Research Quarterly, 24,* 353–367.

Narvaez, D. (2002). Individual differences that influence reading comprehension. In C. C. Block & M. Pressley (Eds.), *Comprehension instruction: Research-based best practices.* New York: The Guilford Press.

Valencia, S. W., & Stallman, A. C. (1989). Multiple measures of prior knowledge: Comparative predictive validity. In S. McCormick & J. Zutell (Eds.), *Cognitive and social perspectives for literacy: Research and in-* struction (pp. 427–436). Chicago: National Reading Conference.

English Language Learners

Droop, M., & Verhoeven, L. (1998). Background knowledge, linguistic complexity, and second-language reading comprehension. *Journal of Literacy Research, 30,* 253–271.

Echevarria, J., Vogt, M., & Short, D. J. (2008). *Making content comprehensible for English learners: The SIOP model* (3rd ed.). Boston: Allyn & Bacon.

Fitzgerald, J., & Graves, M. F. (2003). Scaffolding reading experiences for multilingual classrooms. In G. G. Garcia (Ed.), *English learners: Reaching the highest level of English literacy* (pp. 96–124). Newark, DE: International Reading Association.

Hurley, S. R., & Tinajero, J. V. (2001). *Literacy assessment of second language learners.* Boston: Allyn & Bacon.

Palmer, B. C., Shackelford, V. S., Miller, S. C., & Leclere, J. (2007). Bridging two worlds: Reading comprehension, figurative language instruction, and the English-language learner. *Journal of Adolescent and Adult Literacy, 50,* 258–267.

Adolescent Learners

Anderson, R. C., Reynolds, R. E., Schallert, D. L., & Goetz, E. T. (1977). Frameworks for comprehending discourse. *American Educational Research Journal, 14,* 367–382.

Steffensen, M. S., Joag-Dev, C., & Anderson, R. C. (1979). A cross-cultural perspective on reading comprehension. *Reading Research Quarterly, 15,* 10–29.

8

Vocabulary Learning

The Importance of Vocabulary Learning

As we discussed in Chapter 7, prior knowledge and concept development are closely tied to vocabulary knowledge. Vocabulary knowledge, in turn, is closely related to comprehension (Stahl & Fairbanks, 1986; Stahl & Nagy, 2006). It makes sense that knowledge of word meanings helps the reader to understand the text. One of us recalls struggling through a chapter on the structure and function of the kidneys, meeting word after word whose meaning was unknown, and having little comprehension of what was written.

How do we learn new vocabulary? Certainly the world we live in plays an important part. A child raised on a farm will probably learn different words than a child raised in the city. Interest also plays a role. An individual who enjoys watching the History Channel and reading history books will learn different words than one who prefers to watch and read about sports.

We learn words in different ways. We learn them by listening. Much of young children's rapid vocabulary development occurs through exposure to rich oral language and literature. When we hear a new word, we may determine its meaning through the context of the dialogue or situation, or we may ask the speaker for a definition. The meaning we learn is the one we attach to the word when we see it in print, but only if our pronunciation of the word matches the pronunciation we have stored in memory.

We also learn words through reading. As we encounter new words, we determine their meaning from context or in some other way. Upon encountering the word *animadvert* in a historical novel, one of us asked family members what it meant. No one knew. The context of the selection indicated only that it was something that a character did that was not well received. She was puzzled enough to put down the book and locate a dictionary, where she learned that a person who animadverts makes a critical remark. Actually, readers use a dictionary less than we might suppose. As they encounter the same word multiple times in different contexts, they develop a fairly accurate and extensive notion of its meaning. Had she been willing to let this natural process happen, the author would probably have come to a fairly specific meaning of *animadvert* over the course of time. Some researchers estimate that students who are exposed to normal amounts of text may learn from 1,000 to 5,000 new words each year through reading alone (Nagy & Herman, 1984). Anderson and Nagy (1991) suggest that word learning occurs primarily through means other than direct teaching. Unfortunately, if a student does little reading, this avenue of word learning is closed. Good readers have substantially larger vocabularies than struggling readers.

We also learn words through instruction, and vocabulary instruction has always been prevalent in our classrooms. You probably remember being given a list of words to look up in the dictionary and use in a sentence; however, we doubt you remember it with much fondness. How many words do students learn through instruction? If the teacher teaches 10 to 12 new words each week, that probably equates to about 400 new words each year—assuming, of course, that all of the 10 or 12 taught words are actually unknown prior to teaching and that the student actually learns them!

For any word, we can know a little about it or a lot (Beck, McKeown, & Kucan, 2002), and we learn more about a word each time we encounter it (Harmon, Hedrick, Soares, & Gress, 2007). We may be able to provide a definition or synonym; however, these can be memorized, and the ability to memorize does not always indicate understanding. We may recognize a word in a general sense as being something good or bad. We may understand its meaning in a supportive context but be unable to recall the meaning when someone asks us. We probably know many words that we would find hard to define but, if someone asks us what a word means, we resort to an explanation by placing the word in a specific context and describing its meaning in that way. We also have extensive knowledge of many words that allows us to use them appropriately and effectively in speaking and writing.

What is involved in knowing the meaning of a word? At the lowest level, it involves being able to provide a definition. At a higher level, it involves understanding how that word fits into a variety of contexts. The student can provide examples of the word and tie it to his or her life. Let's return to *animadvert*. We have provided you with the definition, but we are certain that you have moved far beyond this. You have probably thought of situations in which individuals tend to animadvert, such as when they are asked for an opinion or when they comment on a political candidate or event. You may have thought of people who naturally animadvert because of their personality or their job, such as coach, movie or theater critic, or teacher. You may have recalled a time when you animadverted with perhaps disastrous results. You may have catalogued one who animadverts in a negative light or recalled when such a remark actually helped you. In short, you have gone beyond matching a word with a definition and moved to the level of concept. Because they are remembered and used long after definitions have been forgotten, concepts should be the focus of vocabulary instruction.

The Informal Reading Inventory as an Indicator of Vocabulary Learning

Some informal reading inventories include vocabulary as part of the questions that follow reading of the passage. The reader is asked what a specific word means, and this may involve one or two questions. The answers to these questions then become part of the total score that determines independent, instructional, or frustration level in comprehension. However, what do the answers tell you with regard to intervention strategies? Actually, very little. You know that the student knows or does not know the meaning of one or two words in the passage. The words themselves may or may not be critical to overall comprehension. If you have administered several passages, you may see a pattern with vocabulary questions being regularly answered or missed. However, whether or not a student knows a few words offers little specific direction for planning intervention.

Some informal reading inventories, such as the *Qualitative Reading Inventory-4* (Leslie & Caldwell, 2006), assess knowledge of word meanings as part of the prereading prior knowledge assessment. This tells you a bit more, allowing you to estimate if the student is relatively familiar with the topic of the selection and helping you to judge if a low level of prior knowledge may have influenced comprehension.

It is impossible to target vocabulary knowledge as the primary cause of poor comprehension on an informal reading inventory. That a student demonstrates acceptable word pronunciation and fluency but experiences difficulty in comprehension can be the result of a variety of things, and vocabulary knowledge may play a part. So may the student's prior knowledge on the topic and his or her interest in it. Lack of workable comprehension strategies may also be a factor, as well as the structure of the text itself.

What does this mean for intervention? Comprehension involves knowing the meanings of words and using them to construct meaning. Therefore, intervention for struggling readers, as well as classroom instruction for all readers, should address vocabulary learning and include regular attention to word meaning.

General Principles for Developing Vocabulary Learning

The National Reading Panel (2000) suggests that preteaching words and repeated exposure to words in different contexts improve vocabulary learning. A meta-analysis by Stahl and Fairbanks (1986) suggests that focusing vocabulary instruction on both word definitions and learning words in context is superior to instruction that emphasizes only one of these components. Furthermore, Stahl and Fairbanks describe three levels of learning a word. At the lowest level, the student learns an association between a word and a definition or a single context; for example, the student learns that the definition of *court* is "a smooth surface for playing tennis or handball." Such associative learning can be and often is accomplished by rote memorization, and it may involve minimal understanding. The next level is comprehension; the student does something with the word, such as showing understanding of the word when meeting it in a sentence, supplying a synonym or antonym, or placing the word in a category such as place or sports. The highest level is generation; the student produces a novel response to the word by restating its definition in his or her own words or producing an original sentence. We suggest that vocabulary instruction focus on the generation level but move far beyond it to the concept level, where the student uses and understands the word in multiple and novel contexts.

A word may be unfamiliar at two levels (Blachowicz & Ogle, 2001). It may be a new word for an already known concept. It is much easier to learn and remember the meanings of such words because we can attach them to what we already know. For example, *animadvert* fits easily into the concept of criticism. Other words may represent entirely new concepts and obviously are more difficult. Many of these words are ones that students encounter in content area reading such as *isotope, nebula,* and *assimilation.* Helping students to learn these words requires more time and effort because the teacher is developing a brand new concept as opposed to drawing on one already developed.

Nagy (1988) lists three properties of effective vocabulary instruction.

1. *Integration:* The words that are taught should come from the material that students are reading.
2. *Repetition:* It takes much repetition of words in various contexts before meanings become apparent. Instruction must be "deep"; that is, it must include the word used in many different sentences and paragraphs. The teacher must also use the word orally in the instructional group or classroom. Vocabulary activities that review previously learned words can provide such meaningful repetition. We describe some of these later in this chapter.
3. *Meaningful use:* Students need to use the new words in order to remember them. These words must be used in discussions with other students, in writing assignments, and in the world outside of school. Whenever possible, they must be specifically tied to the student's life and concept base.

Teach Vocabulary before, during, after, and between Reading

Because vocabulary is such an important component of comprehension, it should pervade the intervention or classroom literacy session. Present important vocabulary before reading to develop or expand student knowledge of the coming selection. As you read with students, draw attention to vocabulary during reading discussion. After reading, include vocabulary as part of the final discussion or as part of the comprehension activity that follows. Between reading selections, structure short and fast-paced vocabulary lessons that review words previously addressed and present new words. The real issue is not when to draw attention to word meanings, but doing it as often as possible.

Choose Meaningful Words for Vocabulary Instruction

It would be nice if there were a valid list of words that students should know at each grade level. Unfortunately there has never been such a list and there probably never will be (Biemiller, 2004), although two interesting attempts have been made. Hirsch collected a list of terms and phrases that he felt every American should know as part of "cultural literacy" (Hirsch, 1987; Hirsch, Kett, & Trefil, 1993) and chose key vocabulary items for each grade level, involving almost 5,000 terms across grades K–8. Marzano, Kendall, and Gaddy (1999) used state benchmarks and standards to craft a list of essential vocabulary in 14 content areas: mathematics, science, history, language arts, the arts, civics, economics, foreign language, geography, health, physical education, technology, behavioral studies, and life skills. They grouped almost 7,000 words into four levels: K–2, grades 3–5, grades 6–8, and grades 9–12. A teacher may find these lists helpful in choosing words for instruction.

In the absence of a definitive grade level vocabulary list, let the following principles guide you in selecting words for instruction. First, words to be taught should be important, that is, words that the reader or listener needs to know in order to understand the text (Harmon, Hedrick, Soares, & Gress, 2007). "Words that are related to the selection, the content, or to a thematic unit have instructional potential and should be considered high on the list of candidates for explicit instruction" (Kamil & Hiebert, 2005, p. 12).

Second, the word should be a useful word, that is, be frequent enough that the students are likely to see it again. Beck, McKeown, and Kucan (2002) describe words as comprising three tiers. The first tier includes familiar words such as *walk, mother, animal,* and so on. Students generally know the meanings of these words, so they rarely require instructional attention. The second tier of words are high-frequency useful words that appear in diverse and multiple contexts across a variety of content areas, such as *compromise, diligent,* and *fortunate.* Students may not know their meanings and because they occur over and over, they deserve instructional attention. The third tier of words are those limited to specific content areas, such as *polygon, ecosystem,* and *urbanization.* In order to understand mathematics, science, and social studies topics, among others, the teacher must address these third-tier words.

Let's examine how these two principles apply to the story *Peter's Chair* (Keats, 1967). The author uses the words *whispered* and *muttered* to describe how Peter spoke. This usage conveys that Peter is unhappy about his parents' focus on his baby sister. Although these words are not used frequently in primary grade reading material, they are important to the story. So, as part of our activation of background knowledge, we include them, explaining how they describe ways of talking and their purpose in the book. In this way, we build important prior knowledge. We also show the students what these words look like so that when they came to them, they are more likely to read them correctly and understand what they mean. After reading, we might structure a short review activity focusing on these words. We describe semantic feature analysis as one such activity later in the chapter.

Students in fourth grade and higher have demonstrated that they learn words more effectively (remember the meanings and spellings) when they, rather than the teacher, select the words to learn. These students also choose words at or above their grade level (Blachowicz, Fisher, Costa, & Pozzi, 1993; Fisher, Blachowicz, & Smith, 1991).

Rapp-Rudell and Shearer (2002) describe how a vocabulary self-collection strategy was helpful for readers who were having difficulty comprehending text. These middle school students were enrolled in a daily 45-minute small-group intervention program. Each student with the teacher selected one word per week that she or he wanted to study and nominated it for the class list. Students had to explain where they found the word, what they thought it meant, and why they thought it should be on the list; there were no restrictions on the source of the word. They studied the words throughout the week using a variety of interactive activities. At the end of the week, they were tested on their ability to spell the word, explain its meaning, and write a meaningful sentence using it. Every three weeks a few "old" words were reviewed, and there was retesting of five words randomly selected from the weekly lists. The collection of words that the students chose was quite difficult and included such words as *exhilarating, rendezvous, laccolith,* and *terracotta.* Many of them came from content area classes; however, students described discussing the words with family members and friends. The authors describe students who were excited about word learning and how it helped them "read better."

Immerse Students in Words

The National Reading Panel (2000) suggests that most vocabulary is learned through reading or through listening to others read. If we consider that preschool children learn vocabulary through exposure to oral language and through being read to, it is logical to conclude that older children do as well. What this means for the teacher is that the room should be a literacy-rich environment, one in which there are ample reading materials of various levels of difficulty and content and in which students regularly read and are read to. It is an environment in which word learning is modeled, encouraged, and celebrated, and creative writing is frequent.

Research also suggests that students learn new vocabulary better when they are exposed to it in many contexts and when their exposure involves active discussion and participation. Asking students to memorize definitions, match words to definitions on a worksheet, or use unfamiliar words in sentences is ineffective in developing word knowledge at the conceptual level. Students need to talk about words and actively discuss how they are connected to their own lives.

Teach Students How to Learn Word Meaning through Context

Although students learn the meanings of words incidentally, they are not always able to derive word meaning from context (Nagy & Scott, 2000). Some sentences provide rich context from which a student can derive meaning. Others are not helpful at all, and some may actually mislead the student (Carver, 1994). Even in sentences with relatively rich context, it takes many exposures before students learn a word's meaning. When a student meets a new word in context, Dale (1965) proposes four possible reactions:

1. The student has never seen it. This was the reaction of one of us when faced with *animadvert.*
2. The student has heard it, but does not know what it means. For example, the student has heard the word *proton* but is not interested enough or able to determine its meaning.
3. The student recognizes that the word is somehow connected to the reading—for example, that a *proton* is part of or has something to do with an atom.
4. The student knows the word well and uses this knowledge to construct meaning.

What does knowing a word well mean? Paribakht and Wesche (1997) suggest that the student is able to use the word in a sentence. But not just any sentence. A student who knows a word well can use it in a sentence that indicates she or he understands its meaning. We know that children can use a word "correctly" in a sentence, but many other words would be correct in the same location. Consider the word *audition.* A sentence using the word correctly would be: "Sara went for an *audition.*" But the words *ice cream* or *book* would also fit there. A sentence that illustrates the user's understanding of the word would be: "Sara went to *audition* for the play" or "After the *audition,* the director selected the lead actor." If you ask students to use vocabulary words in a sentence, it is important that you accept only sentences that actually demonstrate students' knowledge of them. This is often difficult to do, and we are not convinced that writing words in sentences is as helpful for word learning as other activities that we describe later in the chapter.

Teachers and students must realize that context provides clues but seldom offers rich definitions. Context clues may be vague at first, and students need to know this. They should realize that context works best over time. The first time a student meets a word, she or he must be satisfied with a minimal and often vague understanding of its meaning. Of course, the student may be so inquisitive that she or he asks someone or goes to a dictionary or thesaurus (as one of us did with *animadvert*). However, let us be frank. Using a dictionary or asking questions breaks the flow of reading, and context can offer an acceptable substitute if we understand its limitations.

Context clues to word meaning can come from words within the sentence or may require the student to infer connections between sentences. Consider the following examples from the *Qualitative Reading Inventory-3:*

From "The City of Cahokia" (Leslie & Caldwell, 2001): "Cahokia was discovered because of a group of mounds or hill." In this example, the student needs to recognize a way that authors can signal the meaning of a word to a reader. After naming the new word, *mounds,* the writer then provides a synonym indicated by the word *or.*

Adapted from "Margaret Mead" (Leslie & Caldwell, 2001): "Margaret Mead took a course in anthropology, the study of how people lived a long time ago." In this example, the author defines the new word *anthropology* by setting it off with a comma.

In *Nugget & Darling* by Barbara Joosse (1997), Darling, the kitten, is shivering. The following sentence indicates that Nell wraps a sweater around the kitten. In this example the student must infer that wrapping a sweater around the kitten had something to do with the word *shivering.* Specifically, the student would need to know that we wear sweaters when we are cold. Nell put the sweater around the kitten because it was cold; therefore, the word *shivering* must be something that the kitten does when it's cold.

Unfortunately, many materials that attempt to teach students to use context ask them to memorize a variety of context clues or offer artificially constructed sentences where the meaning of the word is readily apparent. It is unfair to expose students to materials that do not parallel the real world of books and may set up expectations for effective use of context that the student can never meet. Use of context is best developed through discussion in which the teacher guides the students to discover what they know and don't know about the meaning of the new word. Students generally enjoy puzzles, so present context as if it were a wonderful puzzle. We suggest that you regularly present short selections of one or two sentences containing an unfamiliar word and ask the students what they can figure out about the word's meaning from the context. This can take a relatively short time and is a great filler activity for those times when you are waiting to leave for recess, lunch, gym, and the like. One teacher we knew had a large store of such short selections that she brought out during instructional downtimes.

Consider this sentence from "The Lifeline of the Nile" in the *Qualitative Reading Inventory-4* (Leslie & Caldwell, 2006): "Other times, the Nile did not flood enough and crops could not grow. When this happened, Egyptians used the food they stored from surplus harvests." What can we learn about the meaning of *surplus* from the context of those two sentences? We know it is a describing word because it comes before the noun *harvests.* We know the harvests had been stored and were available for the Egyptians. So *surplus* could mean a variety of things, such as *stored, plentiful, helpful,* or *extra.* The context is not detailed enough to indicate that the meaning of surplus is *extra* or *excess.* Students must learn to attach the best meaning possible and read on.

Use Morphological Analysis to Expand Vocabulary Learning

What is morphological analysis? Words are made up of morphemes, which are the smallest units of meaning in a word. For example, *walk* contains one morpheme but *walked* contains two: the root word, *walk,* and the past tense marker, *-ed.* The word *relocking* contains three morphemes: *lock,* the prefix, *re-,* and the present tense marker, *-ing.* Recently one of us observed a student teacher explain to her small group of third graders that the ending of a word (i.e., *-ing* and *-ed*) told when the action occurred. The children had no idea that word endings affected the meaning of a word.

Nagy and Scott (2000) suggest that the meanings of words with more than one morpheme are often transparent from knowledge of the individual morphemes. Thus it is important to teach morphemes that students might not know. Let's examine this assertion.

Mary walked down the street. In this sentence only *walked* contains more than one morpheme: the root word, *walk,* and the past tense marker, *-ed.* Therefore, if a student knows the meaning of *walk* and understands that *-ed* indicates past tense, he or she can infer that *walked* must refer to a walk that occurred prior to now. A sentence from *Nugget & Darling* (Joosse, 1997) describes a swirly cape and a sparkly wand. If the student knows the meaning of *swirl* and that adding *-y* to a word makes it describe something, then he or she can infer that *swirly* must refer to a cape that swirls around. Similarly, if the student knows what *sparkle* means and that adding *-y* to a word makes it describe something, then he or she can infer that *sparkly* must indicate that the wand sparkles. Again, we are advocating teaching prefixes and suffixes using children's reading material to show students that we *use* these affixes to construct meaning when we read. Even books that are written at the second-grade level have a few affixes. Take, for example, *Jamaica's Find* (Havill, 1986). In addition to having the very common *-ed* and *-ing,* the book also includes *-ly* (*cuddly, quietly, closely*) and *-est* (*biggest*). Because there are three words that contain *-ly,* this is the suffix that we would teach if we were reading *Jamaica's Find.*

Bear, Invernizzi, Templeton, and Johnston (2004) provide guidance on which prefixes and suffixes to teach. They suggest that plurals and inflectional endings should be taught first because, as just indicated, they are the first to appear in children's reading materials. This makes it easy for teachers to find words in their reading selections that can be used as examples of how the meaning of the word changes when these suffixes are added. The next set recommended by Bear and colleagues includes common prefixes, such as *un-, re-,* and *dis-,* and suffixes, such as *-er, -ful, -ly, -ness, -less, -ion,* or *-tion.* Bear also provides examples of word sorts and materials that can be used to reinforce students' understanding of these affixes. For example, you could have your students sort by prefix and then explain how the meaning of the root word changes with the prefix added. Or you could have them sort by meaning of the root word, such as ways of speaking—*yelled, muttered, whispered, talked, cried*—versus ways of moving—*walking, skipping, jumping, strolling, sauntering, strutting.* Knowledge of root words is also helpful in expanding a student's conceptual base. If a student understands that *tele-* means *far,* this can be a powerful aid in unlocking the meaning of unfamiliar words containing that root. Consider the word *audition:* The root *aud-* means *hear.* Think about how this could transform a student's understanding of *audience, auditorium, auditory,* and *audible.* We suggest that a simple and effective method of dealing with morphology is to present students with three or four words that share a common prefix, suffix, or root and use these to generate discussion of meaning. For example, given *suicide, homicide,* and *pesticide,* what might the root *cide* mean?

In Tables 8.1, 8.2, and 8.3, we present common prefixes, suffixes, and roots. If students understand the meaning of these affixes, they can use them to unlock the meanings of unfamiliar words.

Instructional Activities for Fostering Word Learning

Teachers often worry about which words to teach. We have made the case that you should teach words that are critical to an understanding of the story or selection. But is there any rationale for teaching vocabulary that may be unconnected to a specific story or expository text? We are talking about a vocabulary lesson. Can this be effective for struggling readers in the classroom or intervention session? We suspect that it can, given certain conditions.

In considering how to teach a vocabulary lesson unrelated to a specific selection, let us examine first what not to do—specifically, the old and traditional vocabulary lesson that did not work very well. The teacher presented a series of unconnected words to the students. The teacher and students then discussed the meanings of the words and possibly used them in sentences. Remember the old assignment that asked students to look up or write definitions of words and then use the words in sentences? The lesson would often end with a vocabulary test of some sort, usually in multiple-choice format in which the students chose one synonym or definition from a group of four or five. One of us followed this format quite a few years ago and was always chagrined to discover that students could often pass the test but not really learn the words, evidenced by their confusion and lack of understanding when they met them at a later time. This lack of learning is particularly problematic for readers struggling to comprehend because of insufficient background knowledge.

An effective vocabulary lesson is a thinking activity. Students talk about words and do something meaningful with them, such as classifying or sorting or adding prefixes or

TABLE *8.1* Common Prefixes

Prefix	Meaning	Example
un-	not	unhappy
in-	not	incorrect
re-	again	reread
anti-	against	antibiotic
mis-	wrong	mistreat
pre-	before	predict
post-	after	postgame
dis-	opposite	disadvantage
circum-	around	circumference
inter-	between	interstate
intra-	within	intramural
sub-	under	submarine
super-	above	supernatural
uni-	one	uniform
bi-	two	bicycle
tri-	three	tripod

TABLE *8.2* Common Suffixes

Suffix	Meaning	Example
-ed	past	jumped
-ing	present	jumping
-ful	full of, like	careful
-ly	like	sadly
-ness	condition	sadness
-less	without	hairless
-tion, -ion	state of	participation
-ism	belief	egotism
-logy	science	geology
-ician	specialist	pediatrician

TABLE *8.3* Common Roots

Root	Meaning	Example
aud-	hear	audition
chron-	time	chronicle
-cide	kill	homicide
dict-	tell, say	dictate
-duct	lead	conduct
flu-	flow	fluent
-gress	step	progress
-ject	throw	project
leg-	law	legal
man-	hand	manipulate
-mit	send	omit
mort-	death	mortician
ped-	foot	pedal
-pel	drive	expel
phil-	love	philosophy
-port	carry	transport
-rupt	break	erupt
-scrib	write	inscribe
-sect	cut	dissect
-spec	look	inspect
tele-	far	telescope
-tort	twist	distort
-trac	draw	distract
-vert	turn	convert
voc-	voice	vocal

suffixes. They determine how two or more words are alike or different. We remember a teacher who mourned that her students seemed to get a glazed look in their eyes when she said "vocabulary." The activities in the following paragraphs promote excitement about words, not resigned boredom. They can form the kernel of a brief and informal discussion about words, or they can be the focus of a formal lesson. All of the activities described are extremely adaptable. The teacher can flexibly use them to suit the needs of the students and to fit within a variety of intervention and classroom structures.

Using Words in Sentences

Creating sentences using the target word is a common method of vocabulary instruction. Students are asked to look up the meanings of words in a dictionary and use them in a sentence. Teachers inherently realize that the ability to do this represents a high level of vocabulary knowledge (Stahl & Fairbanks, 1986); unfortunately, it is seldom effective. Why?

We do not teach students how to write such sentences and so we seldom get sentences that tell us much of anything.

One of us remembers assigning *extrovert* as a word for middle school students to define and use in a sentence and receiving the following sentences.

I saw an extrovert. The student recognized *extrovert* as a noun but nothing more.

I extroverted down the hall on my birthday. The student seemed to have some idea of the meaning of *extrovert* but used it as a verb, not a noun.

An extrovert is happy. An extrovert may or may not be happy and the student's understanding of the word is ambiguous.

Before the teacher can assign using vocabulary words in sentences as a way of developing word meaning, students have to learn how to write such sentences. Perhaps an analogy will help. Playing tennis can increase muscle and agility but first you have to learn to hit the ball. Similarly, students need to learn how to construct sentences that illustrate the meaning of a word. Once they catch on, not only will their sentences begin to make sense but they will be effective vehicles for expanding vocabulary knowledge. Show students how to compose meaningful sentences by modeling the process and helping them create their own sentences. Use their sentences as a focus for discussion and explain how they reflect word meaning and how they might be improved

First, identify each word as a noun, verb, or adjective or use the following alternatives: thing word, action word, or describing word. If the word is a noun, the student explains what it does or does not do, or writes one or two sentences describing it.

- Sometimes *myths* were used to explain things like an angry god throwing lightning off a mountain.
- People think that *myths* are true but many are just made up stories.
- The *merchant* sold old clothes and shoes and funny hats in order to make money.
- *Merchants* have to know how to be nice to customers and how to choose the right things to sell.

If the word is a verb, the student writes one or two sentences that tell who or what would perform the action or how they might do it.

- My mother always *insists* that I clean my room on Saturday. If I don't, I can't go to my friend's house until I do.
- A thief might *covet* a fancy car but he can't afford it so he tries to steal it instead.
- Friends *banter* with each other all the time. They kid each other and even insult each other but it's all in fun.
- Our teacher *circulates* around the room all the time checking that we know what we are doing.

If the word is an adjective, the student writes one or two sentences telling who or what this word describes.

- My brother is very *reluctant* when it's his turn to take out the garbage. He waits as long as he can until my mother yells at him.
- The quarterback's performance was *dazzling*. He threw for four touchdowns and had no interceptions.
- Dad said the food at the restaurant was only *tolerable* and not worth the money. We ate it because we had already ordered it.
- When lunch comes, I am *ravenous* and can't wait to eat.

What about adverbs? Adverbs are basically adjectives with *-ly* added on. A student who understands the meaning of an adjective will readily transfer this to the adverb form.

Students enjoy this form of sentence construction, and they often incorporate their own experiences in sentence composition. It is wonderful if they do so because people build new knowledge based on what they already know, and tying a new word to personal experience helps students learn and remember it.

Personalizing Word Learning

If we consider a new word as representing a rich concept as opposed to a short definition, we need to tie it to concepts that students already know. However, students have such differences in their prior knowledge that a teacher may struggle to realistically do this. Help students personalize the word in a very individual way by tying it to their own lives. If they can do this, they will have a good chance of remembering the word. And because everyone does this in different ways, students will enjoy sharing and comparing what they have done.

After introducing a word and explaining what it means, guide the students to see this word in active operation in their lives. One teacher did this by constructing what she called Word in My Life cards, shown in Figure 8.1. In the first box, the student writes what she or he learned about the word from the teacher, class discussion, glossary, and the like. In the second box, the student writes or draws the word as part of his or her life. The following comments from students about the word *mercenary* illustrate how different students can take the same word and tie it to their lives in different ways.

My brother is mercenary because he won't do anything I want unless I give him something. I wanted him to help shovel and he said only if I give him $5.00. I said he could go take a flying leap.

I saw a mercenary guy on TV called Scrooge. He was real stingy and everybody hated him and then he changed and gave money away.

My dog is named Boodles. Can dogs be mercenary? She won't do any tricks unless I give her a treat. Not one trick. And she has to see the treat first!

FIGURE 8.1 Word in My Life Card

Word: _____	
What I Learned about the Word	The Word in My Life

*See reproducible figure at end of chapter.

> There was that bug-like guy in Star Wars who owned the kid and I can't remember his name but he wouldn't let the kid go without getting a lot of money. And he wouldn't let the mother go either. So he was really mercenary.

> There is a mercenary guy on our block. He has lots of flowers in his garden and I asked if I could have some for my grandmother and he said only if I paid him. I didn't have any money and he had so many flowers. Big old mean person.

Sharing these Word in My Life comments is much more motivating to students than looking up definitions and using a word in a contrived and usually dull sentence.

Clustering Word Learning

If you are teaching a vocabulary lesson that is unrelated to a specific piece of text, what words should you choose? There are few guidelines for this. As we have said, it is a good idea to choose high-utility words, ones that you expect the students to meet over and over again. But there are so many of these that choosing is a difficult task. One way to avoid having to choose is to teach words in clusters.

A word has a specific meaning but, as we discussed earlier, that meaning is embedded in a concept of much broader proportions. Consider the word *mutter,* which means "to speak in a low tone, to grumble, or to complain." Our concept of *mutter* probably includes why one might do this, times when we have muttered to ourselves or heard others mutter, the effects of muttering on others, and so forth. But, thinking more broadly, the concept *mutter* is part of an even greater concept. It represents a form of oral communication and is thus part of a larger cluster of words that includes *explain, argue, whisper, yell, complain, talk,* and *cry.* So, instead of teaching *mutter* by itself or with other unrelated words, teach several words that all represent forms of communication. Instead of teaching *plunge* alone, teach it as part of a cluster that focuses on kinds of movement, such as *shrink, chase, grow,* and *expand.* This is effective because it is easier to remember items of information if we can place them in a pattern of some sort. Six words that all deal with size are easier to remember than six words that are completely unrelated.

Some time ago, Marzano (1984) suggested teaching vocabulary in clusters related to word frequency. He examined the most frequent words in our language and classified them into semantic clusters. In Table 8.4, we list the first 25 of Marzano's 61 "superclusters," a suggested starting point for your design of isolated vocabulary instruction. However, you can build your own clusters. How? Let's go back to *mercenary,* which describes a human charac-

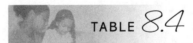 **TABLE 8.4**   Semantic Word Clusters

Occupations: *manager, coach, doctor*	Location/direction: *here, there, inside*
Types of motion: *pull, plunge, toss*	Literature: *story, novel, poem*
Size and quantity: *tiny, many, large*	Liquid: *rain, dew, river*
Animals: *pet, dog, snake*	Clothing: *shirt, cap, shawl*
Feelings/emotions: *terror, shame, love*	Places: *town, state, country*
Food: *vegetables, meat, supper*	Noises: *clatter, peep, scream*
Time: *noon, month, year*	Land: *territory, planet, desert*
Machines/tools: *engine, hammer, spoon*	Dwellings: *home, hospital, igloo*
People: *woman, boy, child*	Materials: *canvas, burlap, metal*
Communication: *explain, argue, command*	Human body: *eye, throat, spine*
Transportation: *ship, rocket, bicycle*	Vegetation: *shrub, branch, spruce*
Mental actions: *search, think, reason*	Groups: *network, gang, committee*
Nonemotional human traits: *nice, lazy, stubborn*	

teristic. What other words do the same thing? What about *generous, intelligent, stupid, reckless, cautious,* and *frugal*? You can generate word clusters alone or with students. Of course, students may already know some of the words, but they will expand their understanding of them through the activity. And if you have the students generate words, always have several of your own to include that you know are new and unfamiliar. Clusters provide opportunity for practice that requires students to sort by the categories in Table 8.4 or provide synonyms and antonyms. This type of practice fosters students' general understanding of the words.

Semantic Feature Analysis.   An effective instructional strategy that parallels clustering is semantic feature analysis. Developed by Johnson and Pearson (1984), it offers students the opportunity to think about words and note the similarities and differences of words within a cluster. Select a cluster such as transportation, and choose five to ten words that are part of it. The number of words depends on the age of the students and the time you have for this activity. You might choose *car, bicycle, rocket, stagecoach, snowmobile, canoe,* and *raft.* List them in a column and then, in a row, list features that they may or may not share: *moves on land, has a motor,* and so forth. The students examine each word in relation to the features and mark it with a plus if it shares that feature and with a minus if it does not (see Figure 8.2).

There are many activities you can use to expand this simple matrix. Students can generate more examples of transportation, such as *surfboard, balloon,* and *sled,* and they can add additional features, such as *used in winter, not too common, is dangerous,* and *can be carried.* The matrix then becomes a stimulus for discussion. Sometimes students are reluctant to choose a plus or minus, saying that it depends on the circumstances. In this case they place a check under the feature to signal their need to explain more fully. Perhaps they do not know if the item shares a feature. In that case, they mark *DK* and eagerly wait for discussion that will expand their word knowledge.

It is easy to construct a blank feature analysis matrix on the computer and have a store of blanks for later use. We suggest that you first introduce and work with feature analysis as a group. When students understand the procedure (and this happens fast), ask them to fill out the matrix as a small group. It can be an individual activity, but the completed matrix is always shared so that students can learn from each other. This is not an activity in which answers are right or wrong, but one in which answers naturally change as a result of student discussion. It has been our experience that after being exposed to semantic feature analysis, a common next step for students is to work together to generate their own matrix.

FIGURE *8.2*   Semantic Feature Analysis

	Moves on land	Has motor	Uses muscle	Uses fuel
car				
bicycle				
rocket				
stagecoach				
snowmobile				
canoe				
raft				

*See reproducible figure at end of chapter.

Building Words

Earlier, we said that you should focus on prefixes, suffixes, and roots. One simple way to do this is to take a word and make it grow. We have found that students enjoy this activity, and it promotes spelling as well as understanding of prefixes and suffixes. In the following example, students begin with *check*.

> check
> checks
> checked
> checking
> checker
> checkers
> checkout
> checkerboard
> checkbook
> recheck

Another group begins with *thunder*.

> thunder
> thunders
> thundered
> thundering
> thunderer
> thunderous
> thunderstorm
> thunderclap
> thunderstruck
> thundercloud

Students enjoy a competition in which two or more groups see who can find the most words. An interesting side effect is that students eagerly use the dictionary to add to their list. They also add suffixes to new words to increase their total number, such as making *thunderclap* and *thunderstorm* plural.

Comparing Word Meaning

We have stressed the importance of developing vocabulary concepts as opposed to vocabulary definitions. Determining how two things are alike is a basic categorization activity that we use every day to make sense of our world. For example, we categorize vehicles as automobiles, SUVs, or trucks based on shared likenesses. We categorize plants as flowering or nonflowering, fragile or hardy, and poisonous or edible based on likenesses. It just makes sense to use this common activity to foster word learning.

All you need is a store of words, which can be from previous readings or previous lessons. They can be new or old, familiar or unfamiliar. They can be words from today's headlines or words that students have chosen to learn or that give them difficulty. We suggest that you keep a running account of all the words you emphasize or include in lessons by writing them on small index cards. This can usually be done in a few minutes at the end of the day when your memory of class or intervention activities is relatively fresh. Put the cards in a bucket or container of some sort.

To begin comparing words, reach into the container, shuffle the contents, and draw out two cards, or have a student do this. Show the two cards to the students or write the words on the board. Then ask the students how the two words are alike. As in semantic feature analysis, this is not a right or wrong exercise but a way of generating discussion about word meaning. Consider the following examples of student reactions to word pairs selected at random from a store of word cards:

hungry and *heavy*

Both have two syllables.

Both start and end with the same letter.

Both can describe something, maybe someone who likes to eat.

They go together. If you're always hungry you'll get heavy.

You can be both. You can be hungry and you can be heavy.

reluctance and *nourishment*

Both end in a suffix.

They're both nouns.

I really don't see how they are alike unless it's because they're both long words.

I guess they would fit with people, but I'm not sure how 'cause I don't know the meaning of *reluctance*.

spike and *twine*

They're both things.

You can buy both of them.

You would probably get them in a hardware store.

My grandpa has both in his garage. I know 'cause I saw them.

They are short words.

They have the same vowel sound.

They're tools.

They are useful.

You can tie twine around a spike.

A spike is hard and twine really isn't but it's hard to break both of them.

strut and *twirl*

They are something you can do.

People in a band at halftime do both of them.

They are both movements.

They both take energy.

You have to be pretty sure of yourself to do either one.

I think dancers do both or rock bands.

I don't think they are something that animals do.

As you can see, some students focus on the sound or spelling of the word and others focus on the meaning. Both are valuable comments. Some word pairs generate only a few comments; other generate many more. You should participate in the discussion along with students and offer suggestions as to how the words may be alike. This offers a valuable opportunity to teach word meanings. For example, the teacher who presented the word pair *reluctance* and *nourishment* briefly defined *reluctance* after one student complained that he did not know what it meant. As a result, the student offered the following comment: "I guess a person could have reluctance to eat nourishment especially if it's peas or broccoli!"

Why are you focusing on how words are alike rather than how they are different? The differences between two randomly chosen words are obvious, but it is much harder to note likenesses, and this forces a greater depth of thought. Like other activities we have described, comparing words can be a regular part of intervention or class activities, or it can be a fast-paced filler exercise that profitably uses time waiting for a transition to a different school activity or setting.

Application to English Language Learners

Like all students, ELLs must develop vocabulary knowledge in their native language by learning new meanings for familiar words and first meanings for unfamiliar words. But ELLs also face an additional burden, that of expanding their vocabulary in English. Many ELLs have limited breadth of vocabulary knowledge in English; they just do not know as many word meanings as their English-speaking peers. They also lack depth of vocabulary knowledge, that is, knowledge of the multiple meanings of many words (August, Carlo, Dressler, & Snow, 2005).

Unfortunately, little research has focused on effective vocabulary instruction for ELLs. After reviewing these few studies, Shanahan and Beck (2006) concluded that activities that promote deeper processing of word meaning are as effective for ELLs as for native speakers. All the activities described in this chapter foster such deep processing. "These strategies include providing definitional and contextual information about each word's meaning; actively involving students in word learning through talking about, comparing, analyzing, and using the target words; providing multiple exposures to meaningful information about each word; as well as teaching word analysis" (August, Carlo, Dressler, & Snow, 2005, p. 54).

Emphasis on pronunciation and memorization of definitions is less effective than instruction that fosters active processing through words presented in meaningful situations. For ELLs, it is very important that vocabulary development involves or follows concept development; it should never precede it. Learning a word that cannot be readily tied to a familiar concept forces the student to memorize without understanding and what is memorized in this way will be easily forgotten. "Vocabulary instruction is most effective when it is used to label experiences or constructs that have grown out of experiences" (Schifini, 1994). This involves developing word meaning through reading, discussion, classroom pursuits, and a variety of oral language activities. The construction of pictures, semantic maps, and matrices that show the relationships between words is also helpful (Barone & HongXu, 2008; Schifini, 1994). Klinger and Vaughn (2004) recommend that vocabulary maps be kept "alive," that is, available to the students for additions and revisions. They also suggest that teachers present a limited number of words at one time and that words should be presented in semantic units.

August, Carlo, Lively, McLaughlin and Snow (2006) describe a vocabulary improvement program (VIP) for ELLs and English-only students working collaboratively. The program targeted approximately 12 words each week. These were tier 2 words (Beck, McKeown & Kucan, 2002), which are frequent and useful words that cross all content areas. The program combined teacher-directed instruction with cooperative group learning. The teacher initially explained and modeled the vocabulary activity and students practiced it as a whole group followed by cooperative group work. The program focused on four primary activities: inferring word meaning from context, answering questions containing the target word, using cognates where applicable, and teaching roots and affixes. Cognates are words that have similar spellings in English and the native language and are related in meaning, such as *patience* and *paciencia* in Spanish. Deshler et al. (2007) include VIP as one of the 48 programs that target adolescent learners.

It is important to develop academic language in ELL students (Pilgreen, 2006). There are basically two types of academic vocabulary: general and content-specific (Rea & Mercuri, 2006). Content-specific vocabulary is the vocabulary of specific disciplines—for example, *retrovirus* in science, *monarchy* in social studies, and *stanza* in language arts; these need to be taught in context to students. Other academic words cross several disciplines, like *index, chapter, graph, paragraph, boldface,* and so on. Such words are part of the school talk that teachers often use but are not generally part of the listening or speaking vocabularies of many ELL students.

Dutro and Moran (2003) classify vocabulary as involving "brick" and "mortar" words. Content-specific words are "brick" words and "mortar" words are "general-utility vocabulary required for constructing sentences" (p. 240). Brick words are words that teachers traditionally preteach at the beginning of a lesson or unit. Mortar words take several forms, such as connecting words like *therefore, whereas, furthermore,* and *moreover,* which are difficult for all children to learn because they are not easily connected to a picture, concept, or theme. Other mortar words are prepositions and prepositional phrases, basic and irregular verbs, pronouns, and general academic vocabulary as described in the preceding paragraph. Many ELLs do not know mortar words and need explicit instruction. August, Carlo, Dressler, and Snow (2005) also suggest that ELLs need explicit instruction in tier 1 words (Beck, McKeown & Kucan, 2002) like *clock, baby,* and *happy* that are already known by English-only students who do not require explicit instruction. Mortar words and tier 1 words are probably different names for the same entity, words that are not typically understood by ELLs and therefore need instructional attention.

Forrest (2006) describes high school ELLs who speak their first language at home, have been educated in the United States, are familiar with U.S. culture, and appear to be native language speakers. However, while they are fluent in social English, they are less skilled in academic linguistic literacy and teachers should not assume they have low cognitive ability. Forrest recommends higher track classes and a balanced approach to develop skills of academic literacy, including authentic writing, emphasis on vocabulary development, print exposure, and strategy training to develop critical literacy skills.

Using read-alouds is an effective means of teaching vocabulary and expanding language development in ELLs. Cappellini (2005) suggests at least two read-alouds per day. Hickman, Pollard-Durodala, and Vaughn (2004) suggest thematic grouping of narrative and informational trade books in order to promote stronger concept development. Books should be one or two levels above the students' grade placement. On day one, the teacher introduces the book and the new vocabulary words. The teacher reads aloud and students use the "thumbs up" signal when they hear the targeted vocabulary words. The teacher and students talk about the book, review the vocabulary words, and summarize the content of the reading. The teacher may reread certain parts to review, clarify, and check for understanding. On days 2, 3, and 4, the previous day's words are summarized and the process is repeated. On day 5, the teacher rereads the entire selection, students respond to comprehension questions, and engage in a variety of vocabulary activities such as semantic mapping and word family associations. Blachowicz and Obrochta (2005) describe a very similar process for intermediate students. It involves reading aloud five books on a single theme, activating prior knowledge by presenting a list of words related to the theme, engaging in group talk about the words, and reading aloud with the students making a "thumbs up" sign when they hear one of the words. After reading, the students construct a word chart and write what they learned through the read-aloud process.

Application to Adolescent Learners

The importance of vocabulary instruction for struggling adolescent readers is emphasized by the program analysis of Deshler et al. (2007). Of the 48 adolescent literacy programs reviewed, 33 included some form of vocabulary instruction. McKenna (2002) summarized what research suggests about teaching vocabulary to adolescent learners:

- Preteach key vocabulary to improve comprehension
- Teach words systematically and consistently
- Introduce new words in related clusters to make words easier to learn
- Use techniques that help students see the connections between words
- Tie new words to what the students already know
- Realize that word meaning represents more than a definition
- Stress context and structural analysis as tools to acquire word meaning
- Avoid rote copying of definitions
- Foster the independent reading of students because most word meanings are learned incidentally through reading.

Graves (2004) suggests that typical vocabulary instruction for adolescents generally consists "solely of teaching the meanings of a small number of difficult words that come up in the selections students are reading" (p. 443). He believes that adolescents deserve a more comprehensive program of vocabulary instruction that includes word-learning strategies. Such a program should also foster word consciousness as well as interest in and excitement about words. Unfortunately many content teachers equate word knowledge with being able to recognize a word or provide a definition. They do not understand that "knowing words includes a deep understanding of how words interrelate and can be used in multiple ways and have multiple meanings" (Deshler, Palincsar, Biancarosa & Nair, 2007, p. 41). Vocabulary instruction is important for all adolescents, who should be provided with ample and multiple opportunities to discuss, compare, analyze, and use words.

Many of the strategies we have described in this chapter work well for adolescent struggling readers. McKenna (2002) recommends grouping words into categories and using a variety of graphic organizers and semantic maps to display the connections between words in a visual format. Chandler-Olcott and Hinchman (2005) also recommend graphic organizers as a way of visualizing connections between words and concepts. Like Graves (2004), they encourage tutors of adolescents to foster word-learning strategies such as determining word meaning through context and structural analysis.

Response to Intervention

It is difficult to imagine that tier 2 and tier 3 instruction in the Response to Intervention model will not involve some sort of vocabulary instruction. Given the strong relationship between vocabulary knowledge and comprehension, teaching students to read better must involve developing word knowledge. However, as noted in this chapter, because there are no clearly defined lists of words to be taught at any grade level, it makes sense that word selection should focus on frequent and useful words that will be repeatedly encountered in a variety of texts, which Beck, McKeown, and Kucan (2002) describe as tier 2 words.

How can student progress in word learning be monitored? The easiest way is to keep track of all words that are directly taught either prior to, during, or after reading. Periodically use these words to assess the students' understanding of and memory for word meanings. As illustrated in this chapter, there are many strategies that teachers can use to teach these words. We suggest that the same strategies should be used for assessment; that is, the format for instruction should also be the format for assessment. If students construct or fill in a semantic map of some kind, the teacher should use that same activity to assess their progress. Teaching students vocabulary meaning using one activity and assessing their progress in a totally different way can cause confusion. Poor progress may be the result of the new assessment format and not lack of word knowledge.

Summary

Knowing a word is much more than simply matching it with a definition. Truly knowing a word means that the word is embedded in a rich concept base and that the reader can use and understand it in multiple contexts. We learn most words by listening and by reading, but vocabulary instruction can also play an important role in expanding a student's meaning vocabulary. Because knowledge of word meanings is so critical for comprehension, intervention and classroom instruction should include regular attention to word learning. The teacher should direct attention to vocabulary before, during, and after reading and should also provide a variety of short and fast-paced vocabulary lessons. He or she should emphasize words that are important for understanding the selection and those that are relatively frequent and that students are likely to meet again. It is important to immerse students in words. Students should learn how to determine word meaning from context, but this involves their understanding of context's limitations. Word meaning can also be enhanced through discussion of morphemes, such as endings, prefixes, and roots. It is important that students be engaged in activities that contribute to active engagement, such as personalizing word learning, clustering word learning, building words, and comparing words.

Little research has focused on effective vocabulary instruction for ELLs; however, activities that promote deeper processing of word meaning are probably as effective for ELLs as for native speakers. It is important to develop academic language in ELLs. Teachers should also develop general-utility vocabulary that is used for sentence construction. Read-alouds can be particularly effective in expanding the language development of ELLs. Vocabulary development is also important for adolescent learners. Vocabulary instruction should involve more than recognizing or providing a definition; it should foster word consciousness, word learning strategies, and interest in and excitement about words. Vocabulary instruction in RTI should focus on frequent and useful words and the format for monitoring progress should parallel the format used for instruction.

REFERENCES AND RECOMMENDED READINGS

Research Summaries, Instructional Articles, and Books

Allen, J. (1999). *Words, words, words: Teaching vocabulary in grades 4–12*. Portland, ME: Stenhouse Publishers.

Anderson, R. C., & Nagy, W. (1991). Word meanings. In R. Barr, M. Kamil, P. Mosenthal, & P. D. Pearson (Eds.), *Handbook of reading research* (Vol. II, pp. 690–724). New York: Longman.

Baumann, J. F., & Kame'enui, E. J. (2004). *Vocabulary instruction: Research to practice.* New York: The Guilford Press.

Bear, D., Invernizzi, M., Templeton, S., & Johnston, F. (2004). *Words their way: Word study for phonics, vocabulary and spelling instruction.* Columbus, OH: Merrill.

Beck, I. L., McKeown, M. G., & Kucan, L. (2002). *Bringing words to life: Robust vocabulary instruction.* New York: The Guilford Press.

Biemiller, A. (2004). Teaching vocabulary in the primary grades: Vocabulary instruction needed. In J. F. Baumann & E. J. Kame'enui (Eds.), *Vocabulary instruction: Research to practice* (pp. 28–40). New York: The Guilford Press.

Blachowicz, C., & Fisher, P. (1996). *Teaching vocabulary in all classrooms.* Englewood Cliffs, NJ: Prentice-Hall.

Blachowicz, C. L. Z., & Fisher, P. (2000). Vocabulary instruction. In M. L. Kamil, P. B. Mosenthal, P. D. Pearson, & R. Barr (Eds.), *Handbook of reading research* (Vol. III, pp. 503–524). Mahwah, NJ: Erlbaum.

Blachowicz, C. L. Z., Fisher, P., Costa, M., & Pozzi, L. (1993). *Researching vocabulary learning in middle school cooperative reading groups: A teacher-researcher collaboration.* Paper presented at the Tenth Great Lakes Regional Reading Conference, Chicago.

Blachowicz, C. L. Z., & Obrochta, C. (2005). Vocabulary visits: Virtual field trips for content vocabulary development. *The Reading Teacher, 59,* 262–268.

Blachowicz, C., & Ogle, D. (2001). *Reading comprehension: Strategies for independent learners.* New York: The Guilford Press.

Bloodgood, J. W., & Pacifici, L. C. (2004). Bringing word study to intermediate classrooms. *The Reading Teacher, 58,* 250–263.

Bromley, K. (2007). Nine things every teacher should know about words and vocabulary instruction. *Journal of Adolescent and Adult Literacy, 50,* 528–536.

Carver, R. P. (1994). Percentage of unknown vocabulary words in text as a function of the relative difficulty of the text: Implications for instruction. *Journal of Reading Behavior, 26,* 413–437.

Cunningham, P. (2006). What if they can say the words but don't know what they mean? *The Reading Teacher, 59,* 708–711.

Dale, E. (1965). Vocabulary measurement: Techniques and major findings. *Elementary English, 42,* 82–88.

Fisher, P., Blachowicz, C. L. Z., & Smith, J. C. (1991). Vocabulary learning in literature discussion groups. In J. Zutell & S. McCormick (Eds.), *Learner factors/teacher factors: Issues in literacy research and instruction* (pp. 201–209). Chicago: National Reading Conference.

Harmon, J. M. (2002). Teaching independent word learning strategies to struggling readers. *Journal of Adolescent & Adult Literacy, 45,* 606–615.

Harmon, J. M., Hedrick, W. B., Soares, L., & Gress, M. (2007). Assessing vocabulary: Examining knowledge about words and about word learning. In J. R. Paratore & R. L. McCormack (Eds.), *Classroom literacy assessment: Making sense of what students do* (pp. 135–153). New York: The Guilford Press.

Hiebert, E. H., & Kamil, M. L. (Eds.) (2005). *Teaching and learning vocabulary: Bringing research to practice.* Mahwah, NJ: Erlbaum.

Hirsch, E. D. Jr. (1987). *Cultural literacy: What every American needs to know.* Boston: Houghton Mifflin.

Hirsch, E. D. Jr., Kett, J., & Trefil, J. (1993). *The dictionary of cultural literacy: What every American needs to know.* Boston: Houghton Mifflin.

Johnson, D. D. (2001). *Vocabulary in the elementary and middle school.* Boston: Allyn & Bacon.

Johnson, D. D., & Pearson, P. D. (1984). *Teaching reading vocabulary.* New York: Holt, Rinehart & Winston.

Kamil, M. L., Hiebert, E. H. (2005). Teaching and learning vocabulary: Perspectives and persistent issues. In E. H. Hiebert & M. L. Kamil (Eds.), *Teaching and learning vocabulary: Bringing research to practice,* pp. 1–26. Mahwah, NJ: Erlbaum.

Leslie, L., & Caldwell, J. (2001). *Qualitative reading inventory-3.* New York: Longman.

Leslie, L., & Caldwell, J. (2006). *Qualitative reading inventory-4.* Boston: Allyn and Bacon.

Marzano, R. (1984). A cluster approach to vocabulary instruction: A new direction from the research literature. *The Reading Teacher, 38,* 168–173.

Marzano, R. J., Kendall, J. S., & Gaddy, B. B. (1999). *Essential knowledge: The debate over what American students should know.* Aurora, CO: McRel.

Nagy, W. E. (1988). *Teaching vocabulary to improve reading comprehension.* Urbana, IL: National Council of Teachers of English.

Nagy, W. E., & Herman, P. A. (1984). *Limitations of vocabulary instruction* (Tech. Rep. No. 326). Center for the Study of Reading. Champaign: University of Illinois.

Nagy, W. E., & Scott, J. A. (2000). Vocabulary processes. In M. L. Kamil, P. B. Mosenthal, P. D. Pearson, & R. Barr (Eds.), *Handbook of reading research* (Vol. III, pp. 269–284). Mahwah, NJ: Erlbaum.

National Reading Panel. (2000). *Report of the National Reading Panel: Teaching children to read: An evidence-based assessment of scientific-based literature on reading and its implications for reading instruction.* Washington, DC: National Institute of Child Health and Human Development.

Paribakht, T. S., & Wesche, M. (1997). Vocabulary enhancement activities and reading for meaning in second language vocabulary acquisition. In J. Coady & T. Huckin (Eds.), *Second language vocabulary acquisition* (pp. 174–200). Cambridge, UK: Cambridge University Press.

Richek, M. (2005). Words are wonderful: Interactive, time-efficient strategies to teach meaning vocabulary. *The Reading Teacher, 58,* 414–425.

Rapp-Rudell, M., & Shearer, B. A. (2002). "Extraordinary," "tremendous," "exhilarating," "magnificent": Middle school at-risk students become avid word learners with vocabulary self-selection strategy (VSS). *Journal of Adolescent & Adult Literacy, 45,* 352–363.

Spencer, B. H., & Guillaume, A. M. (2006). Integrating curriculum through the learning cycle: Content-based reading and vocabulary instruction. *The Reading Teacher, 60,* 206–219.

Stahl, S. A., & Fairbanks, M. M. (1986). The effects of vocabulary instruction: A model-based meta-analysis. *Review of Educational Research, 56,* 72–110.

Stahl, S. A., & Nagy, W. E. (2006). *Teaching word meanings.* Mahwah, NJ: Erlbaum.

English Language Learners

August, D., Carlo, M., Dressler, C., & Snow, C. (2005). The critical role of vocabulary development for English language learners. *Learning Disabilities Research and Practice, 20,* 50–57.

August, D., Carlo, M., Lively, T. J., McLaughlin, B., & Snow, C. (2006). Promoting the vocabulary growth of English learners. In T. A. Young & N. L. Hadaway (Eds.), *Supporting the literacy development of English learners: Increasing success in all classrooms* (pp. 96–112). Newark, DE: International Reading Association.

Barone, D. M., & HongXu, S. (2008). *Literacy instruction for English language learners, Pre-K–2.* New York: The Guilford Press.

Cappellini, M. (2005). *Balancing reading and language learning: A resource for teaching English language learners, K–5.* Portland, ME: Stenhouse Publishers.

Dutro, S., & Moran, C. (2003). Rethinking English language instruction: An architectural approach. In G. G. Garcia (Ed.), *English learners: Reaching the highest level of English literacy* (pp. 227–258). Newark, DE: International Reading Association.

Forrest, S. N. (2006). Three foci of an effective high school Generation 1.5 literacy program. *Journal of Adolescent and Adult Literacy, 50,* 106–112.

Hickman, P., Pollard-Durodola, S., & Vaughn, S. (2004). Storybook reading: Improving vocabulary and comprehension for English language learners. *The Reading Teacher, 57,* 720–729.

Klinger, J. K., & Vaughn, S. (2004). Strategies for struggling second-language readers. In T. L. Jetton & J. A. Dole (Eds.), *Adolescent literacy research and practice* (pp. 183–209). New York: The Guilford Press.

Pilgreen, J. (2006). Supporting English learners: Developing academic language in the content area classroom. In T. A. Young & N. L. Hadaway (Eds.), *Supporting the literacy development of English learners: Increasing success in all classrooms* (pp. 41–60). Newark, DE: International Reading Association.

Rea, D. M., & Mercuri, S. P. (2006). *Research-based strategies for English language learners.* Portsmouth, NH: Heinemann

Schifini, A. (1994). Language, literacy and content instruction: Strategies for teachers. In K. Spangenberg-Urbschat and R. Pritchard (Eds.), *Kids come in all languages: Reading instruction for ESL students* (pp. 158–179). Newark, DE: International Reading Association.

Shanahan, T., & Beck, I. (2006). Effective literacy teaching for English-language-learners. In D. August & T. Shanahan (Eds.), *Developing literacy in second language learners* (pp. 415–418). Mahwah, NJ: Erlbaum.

Adolescent Learners

Chandler-Olcott, K., & Hinchman, K. A. (2005). *Tutoring adolescent literacy learners: A guide for volunteers.* New York: The Guilford Press.

Deshler, D. D., Palincsar, A. S., Biancarosa, G., & Nair, M. (2007). *Informed choices for struggling adolescent readers: A research-based guide for instructional programs and practices.* Newark, DE: International Reading Association.

Graves, M. (2004). Theories and constructs that have made a significant difference in adolescent literacy but have the potential to produce still more positive benefits. In T. L. Jetton & J. A. Dole (Eds.), *Adolescent literacy research and practice* (pp. 433–452). New York: The Guilford Press.

McKenna, M. C. (2002). *Help for struggling readers: Strategies for grades 3–8.* New York: The Guilford Press.

Literature References

Havill, J. (1986). *Jamaica's find.* Boston: Houghton Mifflin.

Joosse, B. (1997). *Nugget and darling.* New York: Clarion Books.

Keats, E. J. (1967). *Peter's chair.* New York: Scholastic.

APPENDIX 8.1

Word in My Life Card

Word: _____	
What I Learned about the Word	The Word in My Life

Semantic Feature Analysis Grid

9

Comprehension Instruction: Retelling Narrative Text

The Importance of Retelling

Teachers have traditionally assessed comprehension by asking students questions about their reading. If students provide correct answers, teachers assume that they understand the text. This practice continues to be dominant in our classrooms, with teachers rarely asking students to retell what they have read. Should teachers pay attention to retelling? In other words, is it essential that we assess a student's ability to do so? Is it important to provide instruction in constructing coherent and complete retellings? We think retelling is a significant and natural component of good reading and should be actively addressed in the regular classroom as well as in intervention sessions. There is ample research indicating that practice in retelling improves not only retelling itself but students' ability to answer questions (Kapinus, Gambrell, & Koskinen, 1987; Koskinen, Gambrell, Kapinus, & Heathington, 1988; Morrow, 1985).

First, consider how we share our reading once we have left school. We primarily retell. If someone asks us questions, it is usually in response to our retelling. Perhaps an example will help. Suppose you are reading an engaging magazine article. You may find it very entertaining and humorous, or it may make you angry or open up new avenues of thought. You want to share your reactions and get the opinions of others. How do you do this? You seldom wait until your spouse, friend, or colleague has read the article. Instead, you retell the article to give him or her a framework for understanding and responding to your reaction. Your spouse, say, may ask a question or two for clarification, and, of course, you answer them, but the bulk of your sharing is in the form of a retelling.

We also retell to ourselves. For example, you are in the midst of a novel and have not had a chance to read it for several days. When you pick it up, you mentally go over what has happened so far with particular attention to the last chapters read. In other words, in preparation for reading, you briefly retell yourself the contents of your book. You are probably not even aware of doing it. How did this help you? It probably set up a barrage of expectations and predictions and established a focus for comprehension of the next chapters.

An effective retelling has a coherent structure; that is, it flows together in an organized fashion. We have all listened to confused, disorganized, or meandering retellings and wished we could politely stop the speaker. On the other hand, a good retelling is a pleasure to listen to because it makes sense.

How do good readers structure their retellings? By using their knowledge of the topic and the genre to provide a personal rendition of the text. We see great differences in students' ability to retell narrative and expository text. If students read both narrative and expository selections in an informal reading inventory, a common pattern often emerges (Leslie & Caldwell, 1990, 1995, 2001). Students effectively retell a narrative selection but are unable to retell an expository one at the same level. This may be partly due to the unfamiliarity of the expository subject matter, but the greater complexity of expository structure is also a factor. Because narrative and expository texts are so different, we treat retelling of each in separate chapters.

A good retelling is structured according to the type of text being retold. In narrative retelling, the plot is retold. The complexity of the plot varies according to the difficulty of the book. Simple children's stories may include a major character, a few minor characters, a setting (important or not), the major character's goal, the problem in the story, and events that occur as the character attempts to achieve the goal or solve the problem. Finally, the resolution explains how the problem is solved. In more complex stories there are characters with conflicting goals and the plot develops around the problems raised by them. Children's stories occur in a sequential temporal order, in contrast to more complex narratives that have flashbacks that make comprehension more difficult.

Children learn the structure of narrative text by being read to. Studies were conducted with kindergarten children who were read stories and, when asked to retell them, recalled the character, the problem, some events, and some type of resolution. These results illustrate children's implicit understanding of the structure of narratives. However, children who have not been exposed to stories may need explicit instruction in the elements of a story. Techniques for teaching narrative structure are the focus of this chapter.

The Informal Inventory as an Indicator of Ability to Retell Narrative Text

Some informal reading inventories, such as the *Qualitative Reading Inventory-3* (Leslie & Caldwell, 2001), provide retelling forms that list the elements of text that are likely to be recalled. After the student reads the text, the examiner asks him or her to retell everything that he or she can remember. The examiner marks each segment of text remembered and may indicate the sequence of recall by placing a number next to each segment instead of a checkmark. He or she may also write down any inferences made by the student. This record serves to assess the accuracy, completeness, and coherence of a student's retelling.

What Is a Good Retelling?

A good retelling of a narrative text includes the major elements of the story, is sequential, and makes clear causal connections between events in the story. That is, the retelling should make clear how the character's actions relate to achieving the goal or solving the problem. Research on the retelling of simple stories with one major character and goal shows that a good retelling comprises about 33 percent of the idea statements contained in the story. Similarly, Leslie and Caldwell (2001) show that the average retelling of a narrative text by students reading at their instructional level is 33 percent. The narratives in the *QRI-3* at the elementary grade levels range in length from 112 to 487 words.

Let's examine a complete retelling in a second grade story: "What Can I Get for My Toy?" (*Qualitative Reading Inventory-3*). It might look like this:

> It's about a boy named John who wanted some new toys. <u>He had played with his toys so much that he got bored with them.</u> His mother told him that they didn't have the money to buy any-thing new. <u>He decided to see if his friend would trade with him.</u> He asked his friend to trade his car for John's truck. He did and <u>maybe they will trade again later.</u>

An average retelling would include every idea, except those underlined, and represent 36 percent of the idea statements. An excellent retelling would include all of the idea state-ments written, or 64 percent of the statements. Notice that the average retelling includes the character, goal, problem, one event, and the resolution. The excellent retelling includes the reason for the goal and adds more detail to the resolution.

Let's see what a complete retelling looks like in a more involved book, *Peter's Chair* by Ezra Jack Keats:

> The story is about a boy named Peter who had a baby sister. His father was painting all of Peter's baby furniture pink, and Peter wasn't happy about that. When his father was painting his crib pink, Peter took his blue chair and hid it so his father wouldn't paint it pink. Peter's mother told him to be quiet when the baby was sleeping, and Peter felt like his baby sister caused everything to change in the family. He hid from his mother and even ran away from home, but he didn't go far. One day he tried to sit in his blue chair and he was too big for it. So, he brought it to his father and suggested that they paint it pink for his baby sister.

- *Characters:* Peter, his parents, and his baby sister. Even though the sister does noth-ing in the story, her presence is essential to it.
- *Goal/problem:* Peter's goals and problems are complex and implicit. Does he just not want his furniture painted, or is there more to it? As adults we recognize that Pe-ter's life has changed since the birth of his little sister. He doesn't like the change and would prefer things be the way they were. We infer this because of experience or stories of other children's reactions to the birth of a sibling. The author never explic-itly tells us that Peter is unhappy, but we infer it from his behavior and the illustrations.
- *Events:* Peter takes his chair away so his father can't paint it. He hides from his mother and runs away from home. He tries to sit in his chair but doesn't fit.
- *Resolution:* He realizes that his furniture isn't right for him and joins his father in painting the chair pink.

The readability level of both stories is second grade, and both contain narrative struc-tures. However, *Peter's Chair* is far more complex than "What Can I Get for My Toy?"

because of the demand on the reader to make inferences about Peter's goal and problems. Teachers must examine the complexity of the story to understand why children find some stories so much harder to retell than others.

What Is a Poor Retelling?

The retellings just described were good ones. What constitutes a poor retelling? There are both quantitative and qualitative answers to this question. A retelling that doesn't contain most of the elements of a story is of poor quality. Also, retellings out of sequence indicate a less than adequate understanding of the story. Typically, a sequential retelling contains more idea statements and elements of story structure than one out of sequence. This occurs because it is easier to recall any story if the student understands the elements and structure of stories in general. It is believed that knowing the structure provides "slots" to be filled in when reading any story, so for example, if students know that all stories contain problems, they will anticipate a problem as they read and will remember it better than would someone who doesn't know that stories contain problems.

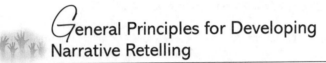

General Principles for Developing Narrative Retelling

Connect with Prior Knowledge

As we previously stated, the most effective instructional strategies begin by connecting the student's knowledge with the new information that we are going to teach. Although students may not have had stories read to them, they have watched TV and experienced stories in their own lives. TV programs are event episodes; that is, they have characters with goals and problems. At the end of a show some resolution occurs, unless there are ongoing episodes of the same story, such as in soap operas. Also, when parents and children get together at the end of the day they often explain the day's events. Look closely at the stories that are told in your family and you will see that many of them include characters, goals (I wanted to . . .), problems (but then . . . happened), events (so then I . . .), and problem resolution.

Focus on Developing an Understanding of Event Structures

Nelson (1984) studied preschool children's understanding of the typical events in their day. In contrast to Piaget's belief that preschool children could not recall events in temporal order, Nelson found that they were highly capable of retelling a typical day. She even found out why, when parents ask their children what happened in school that day, the children say "nothing." What they mean is nothing out of the ordinary. If the events of the day follow the normal routine, there is nothing to distinguish this day from any other. To avoid this problem one of us learned to ask her son what interesting or different things happened in school. She didn't always get an answer, but it served to prompt memory of anything out of the ordinary that might have occurred.

Focus on Text Structure

Students' knowledge of everyday events can be used to show them how stories are structured in similar ways. We can explain that stories have elements similar to events in our lives and on TV shows.

How Is Story Structure (Often Referred to as *Story Grammar*) Taught?
- Begin with a simple, well-structured story that has only a few important characters, a clearly stated goal or problem, and events that relate to the solving of the problem or at-

tainment of the goal. Note that in the following examples there are multiple goals because the characters' goals conflict: "Three Billy Goats Gruff" (the goats want to go up the hillside to eat grass and get fat; the troll wants to eat one of the goats); "The Three Little Pigs" (the pigs want to build houses and live in them; the wolf wants to eat the pigs); and "Goldilocks and the Three Bears" (Goldilocks wants to find food and furniture that is "just right"; the bears want to eat their porridge when they return from their walk).

- Read the entire story to the children.
- Explain the purpose for learning story structure. Stories have parts, and if students know the parts, they will remember and understand them better.
- Begin with teaching that a main character is the person or animal that the story is mostly about. This character appears more often in the story than any other (e.g., Goldilocks). Other characters are important to the story, but don't apppear as often (e.g., the three bears).
- Teach setting: the time and place in which a story takes place. The setting may or may not be important to the story. In "Goldilocks and the Three Bears," there are two settings, the woods and the house. The house is more important because that is where all of the main character's action takes place.
- Teach goal: what the character wants. In some stories the goal isn't stated but must be inferred. Begin with stories in which the goal is explicitly stated. For example, in "Three Billy Goats Gruff" the goats' goal is to get to the mountain, eat grass, and get fat.
- Teach problem: what stands in the way of the character achieving his or her goal. Teach problem on the same day that you teach goal because the two are integrally related.
- Teach events: what happens in the story that explains how the goal is met or the problem is solved. This is where the problems lie: Children tend to recall detailed events but not necessarily the important ones. You will need to model very carefully and frequently which events lead to the solution.
- Teach solution/resolution: whether and how the goal is achieved; whether and how the problem is solved.

Use Visual Aids

To help students remember the meaning of the story elements, you need to create a poster containing the name of each story element, a simple definition, and a picture to cue the children as to the meaning of the element. Make the order of the elements clear on the poster so that you can point to them as you prompt the student to retell a story. Students in our classes find it helpful to use a sports metaphor on their posters because it helps depict the concept of goal. On their posters you might see a soccer or basketball theme, in which team members are the characters, the setting is on a field or court, the goal is shown by a player scoring either a goal or a basket, the problem is the opposing team's defense, the events are the plays in the game, and the resolution is who wins the game.

Recent articles have combined the use of a structured story map with written prompts and outlines to assist struggling fourth graders organize information from a novel (Arthaud & Goracke, 2006). This method has resulted in students learning to use graphic aids and outlines to help them in many subject areas. Several visual interpretations of stories with multiple episodes were discussed by Dymock (2007). This work is helpful to teachers who recognize that their students understand basic narrative structure but are unable to generalize it to more complex stories.

The Importance of Modeling

The previous section provided explicit instruction on the elements of stories. However, as we know, teachers must model how to map a story using them. Many teachers write large story maps on the board, on paper, or on the computer and give the students blank story maps to fill in. Then the teacher retells a story, filling in the map with character, setting, goal, problem, important events, and resolution. There are many visual examples of story maps, but they all contain the same elements. Figure 9.1 is a generic story map, and Figure 9.2 is a story map designed for the book *The Frog Prince, Continued* (Scieszka, 1991).

Mapping More Complex Stories

Shanahan and Shanahan (1997) illustrate how story mapping leads students to look at the story from one perspective and how the choice of main character leads to a very different view of the story being summarized. We indicated that by presenting the goals of Goldilocks versus those of the three bears, the troll versus the billy goats, and the three pigs versus the wolf. Those of you who are familiar with *The True Story of the Three Little Pigs* (Scieszka, 1989) will understand how perspective influences our understanding of stories. Scieszka tells the story and explains the conflict from the wolf's point of view. The wolf is only trying to borrow a cup of sugar to make a cake, and he has allergies so he keeps sneezing at their door. He isn't trying to blow the house down at all. The story is humorous to adults and older children, but we have found that our primary grade students don't accept this view at all. They can't seem to accept more than one perspective. Perhaps if they were taught earlier that most stories have different goals depending on the character you choose to focus on, they would be more willing to see multiple perspectives.

Shanahan and Shanahan (1997) present a character perspective chart that illustrates how differently stories can be summarized depending on the character that we choose to focus on. The chart is made of two columns with the same questions written in each box (see Figure 9.3 on p. 158).

*B*iographies: Bridging Narrative and Expository Text

Biographies are narrative texts that describe someone's life, usually making some mention of the person's childhood and the events that led up to the person doing something extraordinary for which she or he is known. Often the person has a particular goal that is stated in the biography, such as becoming a writer, studying primitive people, flying around the world, or bringing equality to black people. Following the statement of the goal are problems that the person encountered, as in the case of Amelia Earhart, whose plane crashed before she could reach her goal. Biographies such as these are included as narrative text on the *Qualitative Reading Inventory-4* (Leslie & Caldwell, 2006). If students can recall simple story-type narratives but have difficulty with biographies, explicit instruction on how the elements of a story relate to the elements of a biography is in order. It should be straightforward to explain to students that the same elements are in biographies as in any story. There may be more detail in a biography and the author may include information that is not directly relevant to the goal or problem, but the same elements will be included.

The teacher should model how to fill in a story map from a biography. Let's try to identify the story elements from the 263-word biography of Amelia Earhart in the *QRI-4* (Leslie & Caldwell, 2006, p. 251).

> Amelia Earhart was an adventurer and a pioneer in the field of flying. She did things no other woman had ever done before. During World War I, Earhart worked as a nurse. She cared for pilots who had been hurt in the war. Earhart listened to what they said about flying. She watched planes take off and land. She knew that she, too, must fly.
>
> In 1928, Earhart was the first woman to cross the Atlantic in a plane. But someone else flew the plane. Earhart wanted to be more than just a passenger. She wanted to fly a

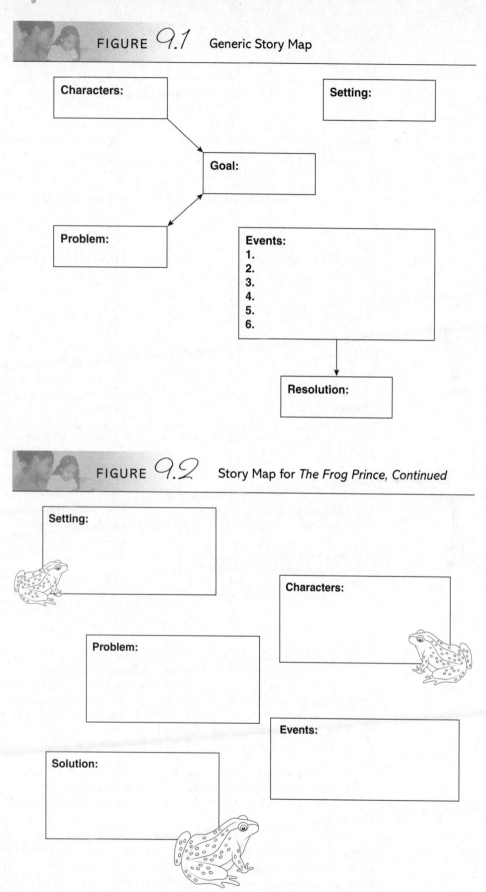

FIGURE 9.1   Generic Story Map

Characters:

Setting:

Goal:

Problem:

Events:
1.
2.
3.
4.
5.
6.

Resolution:

FIGURE 9.2   Story Map for *The Frog Prince, Continued*

Setting:

Characters:

Problem:

Events:

Solution:

FIGURE 9.3   Character Perspective Chart

| Three Billy Goats Gruff |

| **Who are the main characters?** | **Who is the main character?** |
| The three billy goats. | The troll. |

| **Where does the story take place?** | **Where does the story take place?** |
| By a bridge. | By a bridge. |

| **What do the goats want?** | **What does the troll want?** |
| To get to the mountain to eat grass. | To eat the goats. |

| **What is the problem?** | **What is the problem?** |
| The troll tries to stop them from crossing the bridge. | Each goat tells the troll to wait until his larger brother comes so that he will get a bigger meal. The goats trick the troll. |

| **Events:** | **Events:** |
| Each time the goats try to cross the bridge, the troll stops them, but the goats trick him. | Each time the goats try to cross the bridge the troll stops them and says he will eat them, but he doesn't. |

| **Resolution:** | **Resolution:** |
| All of the goats get across the bridge safely because the largest goat kills the troll. The goats reach their goal as they go across the bridge and up the mountain to eat grass and get fat. | The troll waits to eat the last goat, who is very large, and kills him. His goal is not met. |

plane across the ocean herself. For four years, Earhart trained to be a pilot. Then in 1932, she flew alone across the Atlantic to Ireland. The trip took over fourteen hours. Flying may seem easy today. However, Earhart faced many dangers. Airplanes had just been invented. They were much smaller than our planes today. Mechanical problems happened quite often. There were also no computers to help her. Flying across the ocean was as frightening as sailing across it had been years before. Earhart knew the dangers she faced. However, she said, "I want to do it because I want to do it. Women must try to do things as men have tried. When they fail, their failure must be a challenge to others."

Earhart planned to fly around the world. She flew more than twenty thousand miles. Then her plane disappeared somewhere over the huge Pacific Ocean. People searched for a long time. Finally, they gave up. Earhart and her plane were never found.

The main character of this biography is clear—no other character is named. There are several physical settings, none of which is important to an understanding of the selection. The time in which the story took place is important because planes were new. The psychological setting is also important, but can be listed under the problem. How Earhart became the first

FIGURE *9.4*   Map of Amelia Earhart Biography

woman pilot is explained, with experiences that led her to want to be a pilot, followed by her training as cited. Her first goal of becoming a pilot is met. The problems of flying in those days are explained, including the fact that no other woman had become a pilot. Then her second goal of flying around the world is introduced, concluding with the disappearance of her plane over the Pacific Ocean. This biography has two goals, only one of which is met, so the story map will look a little different (see Figure 9.4).

Modeling how to map a biography with one character but more than one goal helps students see the applicability of a story map for more complex stories.

Application to English Language Learners

Cultural influences on story telling and retelling have been studied internationally. Narratives have an oral tradition, and different languages and cultures have different structures for telling stories. Although all cultures have stories with episodic structure, English stories use a three-episode structure, whereas Native Americans often have four-part stories (Westby, 2004). Asian cultures vary with some preferring repetition of two, and Chinese often use five (e.g., *The Five Chinese Brothers*). So, how does the different structure affect how the student either tells or retells a story? When an *expected* narrative structure is violated the reader may reorganize the retelling of the story to fit the expected structure. Recall is affected by reducing the number of episodes or by omitting one or combining two episodes into one (Kintsch & Green, 1978). Therefore, it is likely that if students had been told or read stories with structures different from the typical English structure, they will retell an English story using their culture's format. Teachers might interpret this retelling as incorrect or poorly formed. As ELLs hear and read English stories they will come to learn their plot-based structure.

To consider whether a student's retelling is different from the typical English story in important ways requires the teacher to understand the structure of stories from the student's culture and of course whether it was part of the family tradition to tell stories on a regular basis. If a student was used to hearing a four-episode story and read a three-episode English story, it is likely that the student's recall would be affected. The student might add information or another episode.

So how is a teacher to know the form of stories known by students in the classroom? Scholars who study language development have one possible method. The researcher explains a situation that has happened to him or her and asks the child if he or she has ever had that experience. For example, the researcher might relay an episode involving a visit to the doctor's office. Then the child is asked if he or she has ever gone to the doctor and to tell about it. Language development researchers learn about the oral traditions of cultures from this methodology and that cultural groups vary in the importance that they give to different components of the story. During the height of the story grammar research, Matsuyama (1983) reported that 80 percent of Japanese folktales did not have a goal for the main character. Therefore, it is likely that Japanese children familiar with their cultural folktales might not recall the goal of a story written in English. The situation with speakers of Spanish is complex because there are many cultures that speak Spanish and the same features do not exist in their stories. One common feature, however, is to omit a pronoun when retelling the most important part of the story. It is assumed that the character is easily inferred from the story (Mahecha, 2003). Also, children from several Spanish-speaking and Native American cultures emphasized settings, especially descriptions of family members who were present, and often omitted the event sequence.

An example of embellishing the family members in a story occurred while one of the authors administered the *Qualitative Reading Inventory-4* to a second-grade Mexican American student (whom we'll call Carlita) who had been in the United States for one school year. Carlita read a second-grade story, "A Special Birthday for Rosa," which describes the main character's first birthday after moving to the United States. The character's problem is that all of her family cannot be with her on this birthday. This story depicts several family members as its characters and although the girl and her parents were major characters in the story, the other family members were important to the plot. When Carlita recalled the story she repeated all of the members of the family exactly as they were in the story (uncle, aunt, cousins). In contrast, English students would retell this sequence by referring to her *family,* but not identify uncle, aunt, and cousin. The inference that we made from her retelling was that each member of the extended family was important to her. Because the student's understanding of story comes from hearing them, teachers must be careful not to misjudge the retelling of a story by an ELL. Teachers must be aware of how the student's native language and culture can influence recall of English stories, for example when using the "tell me a story" methodology explained previously.

The knowledge of text structure affect only young school-age children, but rather depends on the student's level of English acquisition (presumably by being exposed to English narrative structure). Chinese freshmen and senior college students recalled text written in the Chinese structure better than in the English structure, especially when the texts were unfamiliar and judged by the students to be difficult. And, as expected, the recall of the seniors was better than that of first-year students (Chu, Swaffar, & Charney, 2002). Therefore, if middle school or high school students come to the United States knowing the structure of narratives in their native language, it will still take them significant time to learn the English structures; we can't assume that because they are older they will learn the structures without instruction.

Teaching Recommendations for ELLs

- Assess the student's knowledge of story using the "tell me a story" methodology.
- Teach story structure: To increase students' knowledge of English story structure, teachers should explain very directly how the English stories will be similar and different to stories from their own culture. In this way, the teacher is using the students' prior knowledge of structure to teach the new structure. Perhaps the teacher would use a Venn diagram to illustrate similarities and differences between the same story written from the viewpoint of different cultures. There are hundreds of variations of the Cinderella stories that could be used, and one story told from different cultural perspectives is *Little Red Riding Hood* and the Chinese version, *Lon Po Po*. The teacher could explain the cultural factors that affect how stories are written. After specific instruction on English narrative structures the student should be exposed to English stories through read-alouds as well as their own reading.
- Use the previewing strategy to increase comprehension: Previewing involves an introduction to the text that includes a question or statement that will attract the students' interest and will connect with something familiar in the students' experience. Then the characters are introduced and the content of the story is given up to the climax. Finally students are given a purpose for reading. Chen and Graves (1998) report that college-age ESL students who read a previewed story scored 40 percent higher on a short-answer test compared to students who did not receive a preview.
- Be patient and scaffold student responses: When the student is learning the new structures for English stories, accept a longer wait time during recall and when asking questions to assess comprehension, using partial answers to help students elaborate ideas into a more complete response. Feedback to students should clarify, connect, and elaborate the verbal interactions between students and teachers (Mohr & Mohr, 2007).
- Emphasize multicultural literature: The selection of literature that the children read is also important. If bilingual children and children of color make up the majority of the students in the classroom, then most of the books that they read should have characters that look like them. This is especially important for young readers who may not have formed a concept of "book." We want students to know that books contain stories with characters like them.

Application to Adolescent Learners

Although there was much research on teaching the structure of narrative text to grade school children, there has been much less conducted on struggling adolescents. The research is dated, and it does not use retelling of narratives as the dependent measure. The initial research-based article on this topic concerning adolescents was conducted at the time of the story grammar research boom. Singer and Dolan (1982) taught story schemata to one group of regular eleventh graders who were not struggling readers and compared their comprehension to students taught traditionally. The story elements taught were character, goal, obstacles, outcome, and theme, along with schema-directed questions (e.g., "What is getting in the way of the character achieving his or her goal?"). The students were also taught to use the schema-directed questions to generate story-specific questions that they would answer after reading the text. The traditional group read and answered questions generated by the teacher. Six short stories typically used in high school curriculum were used over a three-week period. The schema group outperformed the traditional group on the multiple-choice quizzes starting in session 3 and continuing through session 6. Singer and Dolan (1982) concluded that when high school students are reading complex stories and the fit between the schema and the story is not clear, then instruction in story structure can be helpful. It was surprising to see that teaching the simple story structure aided these high school students in understanding high school material. It is likely that the same effects would occur with high school struggling readers.

The only other study we found examined the effects of a generic story grammar instruction compared to genre-specific story grammar instruction on tenth graders' recall of critical elements in science fiction stories (Thomas, 1995). In addition to these groups, two other groups were instructed in either theme or question and answer. The genre-specific story grammar group was taught the critical elements in science fiction and they recalled more critical elements at each of four time periods after the pretest. The other groups' recall did not differ from each other. Students were also asked to write a story using the genre-specific elements of science fiction. Although the theme group began with better constructed stories, at the end of the six-week instructional period, the genre-specific story group wrote stories containing more critical elements of science fiction. These results indicate that teaching high school students specific genre elements improves their recall and story writing of that genre.

Because these were the only studies found that examined the effects of story structure instruction on adolescents' comprehension or recall of narrative text, we broadened our scope to examine other studies that focused on narrative text but taught other aspects of story, specifically theme.

A study of adolescents with learning disabilities examined whether teaching theme would improve their comprehension (Williams, Brown, Silverstein, & deCani, 1994). A group of seventh and eighth graders with severe reading disabilities were taught the concept of theme over a 12-week period. Compared to the traditionally taught group, the theme group was better able to respond to questions on the concept of theme, perseverance, and theme identification. No differences were found on theme application and novel theme generation. The lack of differences on these two measures suggests that these severely disabled readers needed more practice in these more complex skills. It should be noted that both groups performed similarly well on questions related to plot, so general comprehension was adequate. Interestingly, students in the theme group were also better able to recall story details, suggesting that the organizational unit of theme helped the students remember more of the basic story information.

The paucity of research on the understanding of narrative text by adolescents is likely because the focus on the field of adolescent literacy has changed to the study of several new topics. We surmise that the issues in adolescent literacy extend far beyond whether the students benefit from instruction in story structure. Recent research has documented that adolescents have difficulties in several areas: getting the main idea and locating ideas in text (Stine-Morrow, Gagne, Morrow, & DeWall, 2004), as well as higher-level strategies, such as summarization, making predictions, or questioning during and after reading as a means of fostering deep comprehension (Murray & Burke, 2003). The other area of great interest is the role of text choice to motivate and engage adolescent learners (Worthy, Moorman, & Turner, 1999). In fact, a recently published book summarizing the research basis for programs designed to assist struggling adolescent readers (Deshler, Palincsar, Biancarosa, & Nair, 2007) indicates that beyond some students' problems with basic skills and strategies there are several other large issues: student engagement and motivation, the structure of middle schools and high schools, the lack of content area teachers using reading strategies appropriate to their discipline, and the lack of attention to the types of literacy that students are engaging in outside of school. These are the areas that are consuming the time of researchers and classroom teachers.

Response to Intervention

Teaching narrative structure as part of RTI instruction is relatively straightforward. That is, because narratives follow a predictable structure, the teacher can teach a single structure over a series of texts. Assessing a student's knowledge of narrative structure can involve filling out story maps or answering questions that focus on the specific structural elements. The teacher can create a simple rubric for assessing story maps, narrative retellings, or answers to questions by differentiating each element and noting which ones are easily recognized by the student and which are still problematic.

Summary

To improve students' abilities to retell narrative text, they need to be exposed to stories. Teachers should read to children, especially English language learners and to those native speakers of English who have not been read to previously. In addition, explicit instruction in the elements of a story is recommended. Story maps can provide students with a visual representation of story elements. When characters in stories have conflicting goals and problems, a different type of visual representation is warranted. We also explain how story maps can be used to help students understand the structure of biographies, thereby improving their ability to retell them. The next section examined how story telling and retelling may be affected by the structure of stories in the ELL's native language. We presented a method for assessing the student's understanding of story and provided teaching recommendations based on the results. Finally, we addressed the limited research on teaching narrative structures to adolescents. The three studies we examined demonstrated that the retelling, comprehension, and writing of normal achieving and struggling adolescents can be improved by teaching text structures, including more genre-specific texts. A simple plan for using RTI to measure growth in retelling narrative text was provided.

REFERENCES AND RECOMMENDED READINGS

Arthaud, T. J., & Goracke, T. (2006). Implementing a structured story web and outline strategy to assist struggling readers. *The Reading Teacher, 59,* 581–586.

Dymock, S. (2007). Comprehension strategy instruction: Teaching narrative text structure awareness. *The Reading Teacher, 61,* 161–167.

Kapinus, B. A., Gambrell, L., & Koskinen, P. S. (1987). Effects of practice in retelling upon the reading comprehension of proficient and less-proficient readers. In J. Readance & R. S. Baldwin (Eds.), *Research in literacy: Merging perspectives* (pp. 135–141). Rochester, NY: National Reading Conference.

Koskinen, P. S., Gambrell, L. B., Kapinus, B. A., & Heathington, B. S. (1988). Retelling: A strategy for enhancing students' reading comprehension. *The Reading Teacher, 41,* 892–896.

Leslie, L., & Caldwell, J. (1990). *Qualitative reading inventory.* Glenview, IL: Scott Foresman.

Leslie, L., & Caldwell, J. (1995). *Qualitative reading inventory II.* New York: HarperCollins.

Leslie, L., & Caldwell, J. (2006). *Qualitative reading inventory-4.* Boston: Allyn & Bacon.

Morrow, L. M. (1985). Retelling stories: A strategy for improving young children's comprehension, concept of story structure, and oral language complexity. *Elementary School Journal, 75,* 647–661.

Nelson, K. (1984). The transition from infant to child memory. In M. Moscovitch (Ed.), *Infant memory.* New York: Plenum Press.

Shanahan, T., & Shanahan, S. (1997). Character perspective charting: Helping children to develop a more complete conception of story. *The Reading Teacher, 50,* 668–677.

English Language Learners

Chen, H. S., & Graves, M. (1998). Previewing challenging reading selections for ESL students. *Journal of Adolescent and Adult Literacy, 41,* 570–571.

Chu, H. C. J., Swaffer, J., & Charney, D. H. (2002). Cultural representations of rhetorical conventions: The effects on reading recall. *TESOL Quarterly, 36,* 511–541.

Kintsch, W., & Green, E. (1978). The role of culture-specific schemata in the comprehension and recall of stories. *Discourse Processes, 1,* 1–13.

Mahecha, N. (2003). Spanish speaking American children. In A. McCabe & L. Bliss (Eds.), *Patterns of narrative discourse: A multicultural life span approach* (pp. 73–90). New York: Allyn & Bacon.

Matsuyama, U. (1983). Can story grammar speak Japanese? *The Reading Teacher, 36,* 666–669.

Mohr, K., & Mohr, E. (2007). Extending English-language learners' classroom interactions with the response protocol. *The Reading Teacher, 60,* 440–450.

Westby, C. (2004). 21st century literacy for a diverse world. *Folia Phoniatrica et Logopaedica, 56,* 254–271.

Adolescent Learners

Deshler, D. D., Palincsar, A., Biancarosa, G., & Nair, M. (2007). *Informed choices for struggling adolescent readers: A research based guide to instructional programs and practices.* Newark, DE: International Reading Association.

Murray, J. D., & Burke, K. A. (2003). Activation and encoding of predictive inferences: The role of reading skill. *Discourse Processes, 35,* 81–102.

Singer, H., & Dolan, D. (1982). Active comprehension: Problem solving schema with question generation for comprehension of complex short stories. *Reading Research Quarterly, 17,* 166–186.

Stine-Morrow, E. A. L., Gagne, D. D., Morrow, D. G., & DeWall, B. H. (2004). Age differences in rereading. *Memory & Cognition, 32,* 696–710.

Thomas, M. (1995). The effect of genre-specific story grammar instruction on recall, comprehension, and writing of tenth-grade students. Unpublished doctoral dissertation. Milwaukee, WI: Marquette University.

Williams, J. P., Brown, L. G., Silverstein, A. K., & deCani, J. S. (1994). An instructional program in comprehension of narrative themes for adolescents with learning disabilities. *Learning Disabilities Quarterly, 17,* 205–221.

Worthy, J., Moorman, M., & Turner, M. (1999). What Johnny likes to read is hard to find in school. *Reading Research Quarterly, 34,* 12–27.

Children's Literature

Galdone, P. (1972). *The three bears.* New York: Houghton Mifflin.

Keats, E. J. (1967). *Peter's chair.* New York: Harper & Row.

Marshall, J. (1989). *The three little pigs.* New York: Scholastic.

Meltzer, L. (1984). *Three billy goats gruff.* New York: Scholastic.

Scieszka, J. (1989). *The true story of the three little pigs.* New York: Viking.

Scieszka, J. (1991). *The frog prince, continued.* New York: Trumpet Club.

10

Comprehension Instruction: Expository Retelling

Retelling Expository Text

Chapter 9 explained the importance of retelling as an indicator of comprehension. We also commented that students often experience more difficulty retelling expository text than narrative text. This is probably because of the greater unfamiliarity of expository topics, but the complexity of expository text structure is also a factor.

Good readers use their knowledge of a topic to guide comprehension and organize expository retellings. This knowledge may be specific or general. Consider a magazine article about dog training. Someone who owns dogs will approach this article with a fairly good idea of its content before even beginning to read. He or she knows that it will probably explain the latest methods for obedience or show training, describe advantages and disadvantages in relation to specific breeds, illustrate examples of training success in terms of ribbons or prizes won, and offer resources for learning these new methods in terms of training sites, time commitment, and cost. The reader will use these expectations to guide comprehension and structure retelling.

But what if the reader knows very little about dog training? How does this "ignorant" reader approach the text and build a coherent retelling? He or she uses his or her knowledge of "training" in general as a guide. The reader probably approaches the text with the expectation that it will identify who will be trained and the purpose for doing so. The reader expects the author to include a rationale for using the training, delineate the format or steps in the training process, possibly list advantages and disadvantages, and offer examples of successful training. In other words, the skilled reader uses expectations attached to a *general* topic to structure comprehension or retelling of a *specific* topic.

Good readers also use knowledge of expository text structure to construct retellings. Unfortunately, that structure is not as clearly and consistently defined as is narrative structure. Nevertheless, good readers are aware that expository text can possess several distinct structures. It can be a description using key attributes or a sequential, time-ordered format. It can be an explanation of causes and effects or problems and solutions. It can also be a comparison or contrasting of two or more entities, clarifying how they are alike and how they are different. Readers who enjoy exposition are often aware of these patterns as they read and may use them to structure their recall.

The Informal Reading Inventory as an Indicator of Ability to Retell Expository Text

Some informal reading inventories, like the *Qualitative Reading Inventory-4,* provide retelling grids that list explicit segments of the text. After the student has read a passage, the examiner asks him or her to retell what has been read. The examiner then checks each segment that the student remembered and may indicate the sequence of the retelling by placing a number next to each segment instead of a checkmark. He or she may also record any inferences that the student made. The examiner uses this grid to assess the accuracy, completeness, and coherence of a student's retelling.

What does a good expository retelling look like? It may be quite brief, but it is basically accurate and relatively sequential. Its underlying structure consists of the important ideas in the text clarified or amplified by supporting details. Judging the quality of an expository retelling is not an exact science. Retellings come in many forms, and students retelling the same text can offer very different versions. There are no numerical guidelines for the exact number of ideas that should be included in an effective retelling. Similarly, there are no guidelines for how sequential the retelling should be. Should longer passages result in longer retellings? Does one misplaced event turn an acceptable retelling into a poor one? It is impossible to answer these questions. The effectiveness of a retelling should be judged in a general fashion based on the components of accuracy, sequence, and coherence. Trust yourself. Just as you know a fluent reader when you hear one, so you will know a good retelling when you hear one.

How would you judge the following retellings? Even if you have not read the selection, you know which retelling is more complete and coherent.

It was about a giant octopus that changes color. It has enemies. They are in movies and they attack people and they squirt stuff. They have a lot of legs and eat crabs and can turn pink.

An octopus is really shy. They are small and have eight arms. They poison crabs so they can eat them. They can move real fast to get away from an enemy. They also squirt out dark stuff so they can hide. And they can also change color to hide.

Did you notice how disorganized and scattered the first retelling is? The student mentions color in the first sentence and again in the last sentence. She or he states that the octopus has enemies but does not expand on this in any way. Unrelated comments about number of legs, eating habits, and color are strung together in a single sentence. The retelling suggests that the student mentioned details as she or he remembered them but the memory is not organized in any way. The second retelling is more coherent. Descriptive comments are retold together. Poisoning crabs, squirting dark liquid, and changing color are all connected to reasons for each action on the part of the octopus. The structure of the retelling suggests that the student organized recall first around description of physical appearance and then around behavior.

General Principles for Developing Effective Expository Retellings

Expository retellings can be oral or written, and they can follow listening or reading of content area textbooks or informational trade books. Learning how to retell in an organized fashion is a precursor to developing summarization skills (Moss, 2004). As we stated previously, good readers retell using a combination of topic knowledge and text structure knowledge to comprehend, remember, and organize their retellings. Therefore, it makes sense to focus on these two components while helping students to retell more effectively.

Focus on Developing General Topic Knowledge

You want students to acquire underlying structures that can guide both their overall comprehension and their retelling. One way to do this is to focus on developing general as opposed to specific topic knowledge. In fact, it is impossible to teach students all the specific topic knowledge they will need to read their way through school and in the business world. Think, for example, of all the animals, plant forms, and organisms that students can read about; no one can cover all of these. However, teaching students to read about any animal, plant, or organism using general expectations for content can be very effective. When you read about an animal, what do you expect the author to tell you? You expect to learn what the animal looks like and where it lives. You expect to read about its behavior and its eating and mating habits. You expect the author to discuss its predators and the benefits or dangers it poses to people. Teaching students to identify and use general expectations like these before and during reading will help them to better comprehend and remember text.

Focus on Text Structure

A reader can use general topic knowledge to guide comprehension and retelling. He or she can also organize comprehension and retelling according to the structure of the text. Teachers often emphasize narrative structure in the elementary grades by asking students to fill in graphic organizers based on narrative components. They also use narrative components to structure writing. Even if teachers do not focus on narrative structure, narratives are the primary form of reading that students are exposed to. As a result, many readers learn narrative structure on their own simply by listening to and reading stories. This may not be the case for struggling readers, who generally read a lot less than their more able peers, however. In Chapter 9, we presented strategies for helping struggling readers recognize the structure of narrative text and use it for comprehension and recall.

We see a very different pattern for expository text. In comparison with narratives, students read much less exposition in elementary school. Teachers seldom read it to them, preferring poems, stories, and chapters from novels. And they rarely focus on expository text structures as possible frameworks for comprehending or writing. As a result, many able readers experience difficulty both understanding and retelling expository selections in a coherent and complete manner. And, of course, struggling readers fare worse.

Teaching students the structure of expository text can provide a framework for both comprehending and retelling. This is analogous to our daily and often unconscious use of specific structures to guide our actions. For example, if we understand how a familiar store or shopping mall is arranged, we can function more efficiently in a strange one. What about the arrangement of city streets? In some cities, east/west streets are numbered and north/south streets have names. In other cities, this is reversed, but once you catch on to the structure, it is much easier to get around. The same applies to reading. Once you understand and identify a possible structure, it is easier to comprehend even if you are reading unfamiliar material.

Typical expository structures include the following: description, sequence, cause–effect, problem solution and compare–contrast. Moss (2004, 2006) recommends working with one expository structure at a time. Because the sequential structure is easiest, it represents a good beginning point. Introduce the pattern, point out significant words and text features that suggest the structure, and share examples. Present a graphic organizer (see Figure 10.4) to visually represent the structure, such as the idea maps we describe later in this chapter (see Figure 10.1). Then read the expository text aloud, model your own thinking, and involve the class in completing the organizer. Use the processes of rereading and looking back to locate and fill in missing information. Involve the whole group in completing

FIGURE *10.1*   Words That Signal Expository Structures

Type of Word	Use	Signal Words
Sequence	Used to present ordered events	First, second, third, next, last, before, after, during, while, when, finally, soon, later, following, not long after
Description	Used to explain key features	No specific signal words
Compare and contrast	Involves explanation of likenesses and differences	Alike, similar to, same as, resembles, is compared to, unlike, different from, but, yet, either/or, not only/but also
Cause-effect	Describes reasons for events	If, so, so that, because, as a result of, in order to, since, therefore, cause, effect, consequently, nevertheless, if/then
Problem–solution	Explains a problem and offers or critiques possible solutions	Problem, solution, because, so that, as a result, accordingly, thereby, thus

the organizer and gradually move to smaller groups and pairs for construction of the graphic organizer. Ask students to locate other examples of the structure in content textbooks or informational trade books. Graphic organizers/idea maps are the first step to composing effective summaries and they can serve as a template for retelling.

Provide Modeling for Students

Learning through modeling can be very potent. How many times have you learned a skill by watching someone else perform it? Effective modeling is a combination of doing, explaining, and encouraging. The teacher should retell, explain how he or she constructed the retelling, and encourage students to attempt their own retelling. Instead of telling students what to do, the teacher shows how to do it and supports the students' first efforts. The teacher gives them honest and nonthreatening feedback by focusing on what was done well and what could be improved.

Move from a Written Focus to an Oral Focus

When first introducing general topic expectations or text structure, do so in a visible and written form by constructing graphic organizers based on these components. We offered examples of different organizers in Chapters 7 and 9 and will show more later in this chapter. Construct the organizers for and with the students. Assemble them on the chalkboard, on chart paper, on an overhead transparency, or on computer-generated graphics while students watch and contribute ideas. They can dictate while you fill in the graphic organizer or, if you wish, they can add to it themselves. Students may also fill in their own copies of the organizers. Place the organizers in a prominent place in the classroom, where they can act as a reminder of what good readers do when they read. Eventually, you will move from writing to just talking—that is, using the organizers as discussion aids without necessarily filling in the details. The organizers provide a discussion framework that keeps the reader focused and, in time, become a mental model for understanding and remembering.

Encourage and Support Rereading

Struggling readers often have a very inaccurate picture of the abilities of good readers. We have talked with many students who find reading difficult, and we are always dismayed at the unrealistic expectations they hold for good reading. They believe that good readers know all the words and that they can read anything, no matter how difficult, just once and be able to answer any questions the teacher might ask. They seldom think about retelling because they equate comprehension with providing correct answers, but, if asked, they express the belief that good readers will be able to remember and retell everything after a single reading! In fact, they view rereading quite negatively and as a sign of weakness. It is no wonder, given this distorted picture, that they entertain little hope of ever entering the ranks of good readers.

We know that rereading is a natural and necessary activity for good readers and that it enriches our understanding and appreciation of a selection. However, we must demonstrate this for struggling readers. We must model rereading and how it helps add to our understanding and our retelling. We must ask students to reread and add to their retellings. In short, we must remove the stigma associated with rereading and present it as something that all good readers do. Students may reread the entire text, or they may reread parts of it. They may reread to increase their understanding, or they may reread to construct a better retelling. They may simply reread for the sheer enjoyment of saying the words, experiencing the language flow, and visualizing what is going on.

$\mathcal{I}$nstructional Strategies for Constructing Expository Retellings

Expository Expectation Grid

An expository expectation grid is a graphic organizer that serves a dual purpose. It prepares the student to read about a specific topic by activating prior knowledge, and it sets general expectations for the content of the text. We discussed prior knowledge in Chapter 7, and certainly the expectation grid could fit in that chapter. We include it here because it is so well suited to helping students deal with the unfamiliar topics that are so prevalent in expository text. It is these general expectations that then become the structure for remembering and retelling. We all recognize that it is difficult to understand selections on new and unfamiliar topics. This is the case for much expository text that students are required to read in school. The expectation grid helps students comprehend and remember content that is basically unfamiliar. How does it work?

As a good reader, you unconsciously formulate a mental expectation grid prior to reading. You do this so naturally that you are hardly aware of it. For example, suppose you choose to read about a new bill recently signed into law. Although you know nothing about the bill, you have general expectations for the content of the text that come from your past experiences with reading and learning about other bills. You will probably expect to read about the purpose of the bill, the party or individuals who sponsored it, their reasons for doing so, those who opposed the bill, and why they did so. You might also expect to learn about changes or compromises made to the bill in order to ensure its passage. And, of course, you hope to learn how this bill might affect you positively or negatively. Struggling readers must be taught to approach reading with similar expectations. These expectations will improve their comprehension and act as a structure for their recall.

You can construct an expository expectation grid on the chalkboard, chart paper, overhead transparency, or computer. Place a general topic (important person, plant, animal, war, etc.) in the center. Then guide students to identify categories of information that they can expect to encounter in a selection about the topic. (See Figure 10.2.) To do this, tie the topic to something familiar in the students' lives. For example, ask the students to identify an

FIGURE *10.2*   Example: Expository Expectation Grid for Animal

What it looks like

How it behaves

Animal

Where it lives

Its enemies

*See reproducible figure at the end of chapter.

important person in their life or a familiar animal such as a pet. If they were going to write about this person or animal, what information would they include? If a student says that she or he would write that his or her dog is big, has a lot of fur, and is black and brown, help him or her to realize that this type of information can fit under a category such as appearance. Using these familiar items as a guide, brainstorm with the students possible categories of information that they can expect to read about. For example, if they are reading about an animal, they will probably learn what the animal looks like, its habitat, what it eats, its life cycle, how it acts, and its enemies. If they are going to read about a country, they can expect to read about its location, its geographical features, its government, its culture, and its economy. Place these categories around the general topic and separate them by lines. Point out that they can expect to read about similar categories of information whenever they read about an animal or a new country.

How many categories should you place on the grid? This depends on factors such as the age of the students and the text to be read. Two to four categories work well for younger students. Older students can handle more. What categories should you choose? It is wise to know before you lead students to identify them. Use the text as a guide and choose those that are specifically addressed by the author.

Once you and the students have identified the categories, have the students indicate the specific animal or country they will be reading about. You can then use the grid to fill in what they already know about their topic. As explained in Chapter 7, this is a wonderful way to activate prior knowledge in an organized fashion. Often teachers ask students to tell what they know about a subject and write down student contributions as they are offered. The expectation grid allows you to organize student contributions, and it offers students the opportunity to match isolated bits of information to a larger picture. You might want to have the students preview their text and use this as a source of information for the grid. Don't worry if they know very little about the new topic. Explain that this is what makes reading exciting. It gives you the opportunity to learn many new things.

It is critical that the students understand the purpose of the expectation grid. Once the basic grid is constructed, remind them to use these categories of information as they read. Model this by reading the text in segments and stopping to fill in the grid. You can fill in the grid as the students dictate comments and information. The students can also fill in the categories individually or in small groups as they read or after they read. You might use one color of ink for the prereading comments and a second color for the postreading ones. In this way, students can clearly see how much they have learned through reading. You can further use the expectation grid by giving the students opportunities to retell what they have read using the grid categories as guidelines. They can also construct summaries using the grid as a road map.

It is important that students match information to the proper category. Why? Because you are teaching them to use expectations for general categories of information to identify specific content. During discussion, a student will often volunteer a piece of information. Ask him or her to place this information under a specific category and then write it on the grid. In other words, try not to supply the category for the students; that is their job.

We recommend that, at the very least, a brief discussion of general expectations precede all reading of expository text. Learning how to think differently takes a long time, and you will need to constantly remind students of the need to read with general expectations in mind. However, there are many options for using the expectation grid, and you will have to adapt its use to the length of your intervention, the size of the group, and student willingness to write. You may only have time to use it as a written prereading activity. On the other hand, you can also use it during and after reading and spread the activity over several days. You may do the writing or ask the students to do it. Because many struggling readers do not like to write, it may be better for them to dictate and for you to write, at least until they become familiar and comfortable with the grid. Throughout the process, you must constantly remind the students that setting expectations before reading makes remembering easier.

You can also use expectation grids as prewriting brainstorming tools. Once students have identified a topic they want to write about, they can construct grids to first identify important categories of information to include in their composition and then to fill in explanatory details.

Example of an Expectation Grid Lesson

Here is a transcript of a dialogue involving the construction of an expectation grid. The teacher, Donna, met with two struggling middle school readers, Matt and Ethan, several times a week. Both boys were reading below the level of the materials used in their content area classes and, as a result, found it difficult to understand and contribute to class activities. Donna's overall purpose was to prepare them to participate more actively and successfully in their content classes. The week prior to a specific lesson, Donna and the boys would read important parts of the classroom textbook and discuss what they read. Constructing and using an expectation grid was a regular part of this preparation.

Donna's goal was to introduce the boys to a new expectation grid, that of an important event. She began by briefly reviewing past lesson activities and introducing the topic of the new lesson.

Donna: So, you are finishing up the unit on the Civil War. How did it go?

Matt: Pretty good. We saw a neat video.

Ethan: It was okay. The South lost and the soldiers had to give up their rifles but they could keep their horses. And the slaves were freed.

Matt: I think I'm going to get a good grade on my project. I drew a Civil War army camp.

Ethan: My group did a WebQuest on the battle of Gettysburg.

Donna: Well, we are onto the next segment in your book. Let's check it out. It's about something called Reconstruction.

Ethan: What's that?

Donna: You guys know what *re* means. Like in *repackage, rewrite,* or *repaint.*

Matt: Yep, it means do over.

Ethan: And I know what construction is. My brother works for a construction company. They build houses.

Donna: Then how does Reconstruction fit with the Civil War?

Matt: They have to rebuild all the houses that got smashed and burnt, I guess.

Donna: What else might they have to rebuild?

Matt: I don't know. It doesn't sound too exciting.

Donna's next goal was to tie the new topic to an expectation grid. Her purpose was to use events in the boys' life to illustrate the categories of the grid.

Donna: Well, we are going to read and find out what else besides houses might have been rebuilt. And it's always exciting to learn new things. Reconstruction was an important thing that happened after the war. Even if you don't know much about it, I bet you can figure out some of the things you will be reading about.

Ethan: Are we going to make a grid like we did for war?

Donna: Good for you. You are way ahead of me. This grid will be for an important event. So think of an event in your life, one that was pretty important or exciting. Or maybe an event you read about or saw on television.

> **Ethan:** My grandpa's retirement party last weekend. The whole family went.
>
> **Matt:** The Packer game on Sunday. They won!
>
> **Donna:** Okay, now think about these events. If you were going to write about them, what kind of information would you include? You want to think very generally. You want to think of information that could apply to both the party and the game.

Donna's intention was to guide the boys to identify the following categories for an important event: description, sequence, causes and effects, and problems. As she elicited these from Matt and Ethan, she began to construct the grid on a large sheet of chart paper. She first placed "important event" in the center.

> **Matt:** Well, I guess we'll learn about where and when it all happened. And all the people, like who was the quarterback.
>
> **Donna:** Good. You're right. Ethan, would that fit with your grandfather's party?
>
> **Ethan:** Yes. It was at a big restaurant, and there had to be about a hundred people. It happened at night.
>
> **Donna:** We've talked before about information like when, where, and who. We can pull them all together in one category called . . .
>
> **Matt:** I know. It's description!
>
> **Donna:** Good for you.

Donna wrote "description" in one corner of the grid.

> **Donna:** What about how the party happened? What came first, second, third?
>
> **Ethan:** Like first we ate, and then there were speeches, and then Grandpa got gifts. And then there was a video that my dad put together.
>
> **Donna:** When things happen in a certain order, we call that sequence, don't we? Matt, would there be a sequence to the game?
>
> **Matt:** Sure. The quarters and the first half and the second half. And who got the ball and when they made a touchdown.
>
> **Donna:** So if we are reading about an important event, we can expect to learn about where and when it happened and the people who were involved. And we can put these under description. And now we have another category, which is sequence.

Donna wrote "sequence" in another corner of the grid.

> **Donna:** Anything else? Any other categories?
>
> **Matt:** I don't think so.
>
> **Donna:** Matt, why did the Packers win? Did anyone talk about that on television or in the newspaper?
>
> **Matt:** Sure. The other team had a rotten quarterback, and their defense was pretty weak.
>
> **Donna:** Matt, what happened because the Packers won?
>
> **Matt:** They moved into second place! They have a chance at the playoffs!
>
> **Donna:** And how did that make you feel?
>
> **Matt:** Great!
>
> **Donna:** I think we have a new category here called cause and effect. Ethan, would cause and effect fit your party?

Ethan: I don't know how it would fit.

Donna: What caused the party to happen?

Ethan: Well, Grandpa retired, so they had a party. He wanted to and he was old enough.

Donna: You have the cause. And the effect?

Ethan: He won't have to go to work! And he and Grandma are going to travel, and Grandpa says all the fish better watch out 'cause he's going to fish and fish and fish.

Donna: And there are your effects!

Donna wrote "cause–effect" in another corner of the grid.

Donna: Matt, did the Packers have any problems?

Matt: Yeah, a bunch of guys got hurt and the kicker was in a slump.

Donna: Ethan, any problems with the party?

Ethan: Not that I know of. Mom said it went real smooth.

Donna: Well, sometimes we have a category and we don't find any information that fits. I think we have our grid together now.

Donna wrote "problems" in the final corner of the grid.

Donna: And then when we read, how are we going to use the grid?

Matt: Like when we used the grid for war. We're going to look for information that fits in the categories.

Donna: And when I ask you to tell me what you remember?

Ethan: We use the grid for that too. But we haven't done a grid for an important event, so you better hang it up so I can remember the categories.

Donna: You bet!

Donna and the boys then began to read the text orally using shared reading. Donna stopped after several paragraphs; the boys discussed what they had read and identified any information that might fit into the grid. Donna filled in the grid as they dictated what she should write. After completing the first text segment paragraph by paragraph, they had placed these items under each category:

Description
- Plan to bring country together
- A new president, Andrew Johnson

Sequence
- Congress set up the Freedmen's Bureau
- Johnson tried to be fair to South
- Pardoned Confederates
- Abolished slavery with Thirteenth Amendment
- White Southerners took over state governments

Cause–Effect
- South didn't want slaves to be free
- Formed Ku Klux Klan
- Passed black codes

Problems
- Black codes limited rights of former slaves
- Couldn't vote or travel
- Couldn't own certain property or work in certain businesses
- Ku Klux Klan killed people and burned houses

The first time you construct an expectation grid, it may seem to take a very long time and you may feel that the process is just too time consuming. This is a very natural situation. After all, the entire concept is unfamiliar to both you and the students. However, as students get the idea and as you become more comfortable with the process, it goes quite a bit faster.

It is a good idea to save old expectation grids to remind the students about the process. If you are working with the same topic, you don't have to construct a second grid; you can just recycle the old one. This is a good reason for initially drawing the grid on a transparency or chart paper. Expectation grids also make good bulletin board material. We recall one teacher who traveled to several different rooms each day. She took with her a large poster board, the kind that folds in three parts so it can stand up. She used this as a traveling bulletin board, and expectation grids were prominently displayed.

Table 10.1 suggests possible categories for grids as well as possible familiar examples. Don't use all of the suggested categories. Choose those that fit the ages of your students. Older students may be able to handle five or six different categories. Younger ones may be more successful with fewer. Also choose categories that fit the text. Donna previewed the section on Reconstruction and chose categories that were emphasized by the authors.

Identifying categories using familiar elements in the students' lives can be very effective. However, if you are working with a large group, it may be confusing for each student to refer to his or her familiar element as Matt and Ethan did. It is more efficient to choose one familiar element that represents all of the students' choices. For example, a group preparing to fill out a grid on process offered these familiar examples: making a pizza, cleaning your room, washing a car, learning to skateboard, making an airplane model, learning a new game, and packing for a camping trip. The group decided that making a pizza was a good

TABLE *10.1* Topics and Categories for an Expectation Grid

Topic	Categories
Animal	Appearance, behavior, habitat, mating habits, life cycle, food, predators, use to people
Plant	Type, appearance, habitat, uses, life cycle, enemies
Important person	Achievements, obstacles, personal characteristics, sequence of life, friends or associates, enemies
Important event	Causes, why important, description, people involved, countries involved, sequence, effects
Country, city, or state	Location, size, geographical features, government, industry, culture, landmarks
War	Location, time, causes, effects, countries involved, significant events or battles, important people, methods of warfare
Process	Who carries it out, needed organisms, needed materials, end products, possible problems, usefulness
Government	Form, structure, when established, problems, current status

example of a process and, using it, chose the following categories: who does it, what you need to do it, the steps you follow, what can go wrong, and the final result.

You eventually want the expectation grid to become a mental exercise, something students do in their heads as they begin reading. This will not happen overnight, so your role is to constantly remind your students of the importance of approaching reading with general expectations. You will gradually move from a written expectation grid to a grid that is discussed. You will move from a grid that students fill in to their explanation of the categories they used during reading.

Expository Idea Map

An expository idea map is another form of graphic organizer that is based on the organizational patterns present in expository text. Making such patterns visible helps students to understand, remember, and retell. Armbruster (1986) and Armbruster and Anderson (1982) first created idea maps to focus on the expository structures of description, cause–effect, problem–solution, sequence, and compare–contrast. The expository maps that we will present are simplified versions of these. During or after reading, students fill in the maps, which then provide a framework for remembering and retelling.

FIGURE *10.3* Example: Expository Idea Map for Description

FIGURE *10.4* Example: Expository Idea Map for Sequence

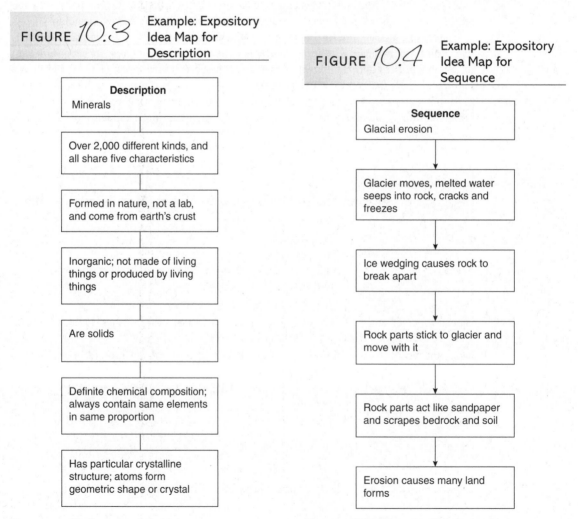

Description
Minerals

Over 2,000 different kinds, and all share five characteristics

Formed in nature, not a lab, and come from earth's crust

Inorganic; not made of living things or produced by living things

Are solids

Definite chemical composition; always contain same elements in same proportion

Has particular crystalline structure; atoms form geometric shape or crystal

Sequence
Glacial erosion

Glacier moves, melted water seeps into rock, cracks and freezes

Ice wedging causes rock to break apart

Rock parts stick to glacier and move with it

Rock parts act like sandpaper and scrapes bedrock and soil

Erosion causes many land forms

*See reproducible figure at end of chapter.   *See reproducible figure at end of chapter.

You may equate filling in idea maps with taking notes. In fact, note taking is very similar to retelling. When we retell, we mainly include important elements of the text. An effective note taker does the same, jotting down the key items that she or he wants to remember. We are amused and often concerned as we watch undergraduates highlight their textbooks as a form of note taking. They highlight almost everything instead of carefully choosing important information, turning expensive textbooks into damp pages of yellow or pink. Idea maps can be used as frameworks for note taking. They are limited in size, which helps students to be more discriminating readers and note takers.

Expository idea maps are a series of rectangles arranged to illustrate the structure of the text and the relationship between ideas. They are built on the categories of description, sequence, cause–effect, problem–solution, and compare–contrast, with the first rectangle in each map indicating the expository structure and the item being explained. Figures 10.3 through 10.7 illustrate different expository idea maps using examples from representative textbooks.

In Figure 10.3 on page 176, one set of rectangles forms the description idea map. Lines join the rectangles to indicate that all the characteristics are clearly related to the item being described. Like the description map, a single set of rectangles forms the sequence map shown in Figure 10.4 on page 176. Down arrows join the rectangles to indicate that the explanatory items follow in a certain order. Figure 10.5 shows the cause–effect map, formed by two sets of rectangles. The first rectangles in each set contain the general cause and the general effect. A horizontal arrow joins them to indicate that causes precede effects. The rectangles under cause and effect list details that describe each one more fully. The problem–solution format, shown in Figure 10.6 on page 178, is similar to the cause–effect

FIGURE *10.5*   Example: Expository Idea Map for Cause–Effect

Cause: Andrew Jackson thought Bank of United States too powerful	→	**Effect:** Jackson closes bank in 1836
Bank controlled loans by state banks		Jackson vetoes renewal of bank charter
Bank undemocratic because run by private bankers		Jackson declares bank unconstitutional
Jackson disliked president of bank, Nicholas Biddle		Jackson re-elected on bank issue
Jackson thought Biddle used bank to benefit the rich		No government money put in bank
Whigs used renewal of bank charter as a strategy to defeat Jackson		Loss of federal money cripples bank

*See reproducible figure at end of chapter.

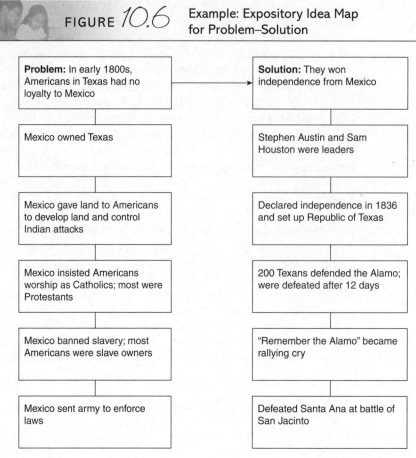

FIGURE *10.6*   Example: Expository Idea Map for Problem–Solution

*See reproducible figure at end of chapter.

map. The first rectangles, joined by an arrow, contain the problem and the solution. The arrow indicates that problems precede solutions. The rectangles under these contain details that describe the problem and solution in more detail. The first rectangles in the compare–contrast map, shown in Figure 10.7 on page 179, indicate the two items being compared. The student may use the descending rectangles to simply describe each item. However, a more advanced form of the compare–contrast map matches the attributes by placing categories of information in adjoining rectangles. Note in the figure how the descriptors are matched with regard to time, title, evolution, land mass changes, and climate.

Students may also indicate the relationship between the descriptors of two contrasted items, showing if they are alike, different, or similar by writing these designations between the descriptors. In order to determine likeness, difference, and similarity, the items must be matched as described above. This may be a difficult task for some students, particularly if the items are not so organized in the text.

The rationale for the similar and different designations in Figure 10.7 are as follows. Both eras are similar in that they occurred millions of years ago. However, a student would be justified in describing them as different because one happened 250 million years ago and the other 66 million years ago. The important thing is that the student can justify why two descriptors are alike, different, or similar. Both eras were called ages, so they might be considered similar, although one can understand if a student marks them as different. Both are similar in that mammals evolved. The next two descriptors are different because different things happened: the evolution of birds and plants versus the evolution of modern mammals. The following two sets of descriptors are similar in that both describe land changes and climate.

FIGURE *10.7*   Example: Expository Idea Map
for Compare–Contrast

Compare–Contrast: Mesozoic Era		Compare–Contrast: Cenozoic Era
250 million years ago	Similar	66 million years ago
Called age of dinosaurs	Similar	Called age of mammals
First mammals evolved	Similar	Mammals evolved into plant and animal eaters
Birds and flowering plants evolved	Different	Ancestors of all modern mammals evolved
Single land mass broke and shaped into continents	Similar	Land was shaped by glaciers
Major changes in environment and climate	Similar	Cool dry climate with ice age at end
		First humans evolved

*See reproducible figure at end of chapter.

You need to structure the idea-mapping experience very carefully so as not to overwhelm the students. In the first stages, mark the text segment to be mapped. This can vary from a single paragraph to multiple paragraphs depending on the level of the text. Identify the underlying structure for the students and give them the appropriate map to fill in. Once they are relatively comfortable with one structure, move to another one. Once you have introduced all the appropriate structures to your students, identify a text segment and present them with two structure choices. Have them choose the appropriate one. Different students will probably choose different maps. If a student can fill in the chosen map, then his or her choice is valid.

Why might two students choose different maps? This is an issue with expository text structure that often confuses teachers. Different readers see different structures or patterns in the same segment of text, but this does not make the use of idea maps less valid. The key component is that readers see any pattern and use it to structure their comprehension. For example, consider a segment in a history text that describes how goods from Asia were transported to Europe during the Middle Ages. One reader may see this as a sequential pattern, moving from overland trade routes to seaports, to Italy, and then to the final destination. Another might regard it as involving a problem–solution structure as traders located new routes, drew new maps, developed a uniform monetary system, and dealt with attacking marauders. Still another might see a description pattern. It is crucial to understand that the important element for struggling readers is to see a pattern, not to identify the pattern that the teacher feels is the correct one.

We have found description, sequence, problem–solution, and compare–contrast to be quite appropriate for younger students, but cause–effect may work better for older students. Cause–effect is especially difficult because in many texts the author begins with the effect and then describes the causes, even though causes precede effects. Some students find this confusing.

The teacher must be aware that expository structures are much more complex than narrative ones. They are not clearly marked; that is, the author does not call attention to the structure but assumes that the reader will identify it. Often the structure is buried in a lot of verbiage. Expository material tends to be very concept dense, and students often struggle with unfamiliar and complex terms. This can obscure the underlying structure of the text itself.

Will you use all of the idea maps? Maybe not. It depends on the level of your students and of the materials that you are using. For younger readers and lower-level texts, description, sequence, and compare–contrast may be sufficient. Older readers struggling with middle school and high school texts will need exposure to problem–solution and cause–effect. Make multiple copies of each idea map so the students can choose the one that they feel is appropriate for the text. The students can also draw the idea maps themselves; however, we have found that this can obscure the purpose of the activity. Some students become more concerned with straight rectangles or attractive arrows than with identifying the important ideas in a selection and the relationships between them. The number of rectangles in any map depends on the complexity of the text and the number of relevant ideas. Students should have the freedom to delete rectangles or add them as needed.

Use the maps as study aids and as retelling or summarizing guides. Assign different segments of text to different students or small groups of students. When they have finished filling in the map, bring them together to share. If you wish, students can illustrate the maps with pictures or other graphic aids. The possibilities are many.

Use idea maps for prewriting expository text, much as you would use the expectation grid. When students write informational text, have them use the idea maps to first decide their structure and then brainstorm the specific content.

Main Idea Map

Perhaps nothing is more elusive for struggling readers than finding the main idea. We teach students that main idea statements are usually the first sentence in a paragraph, but this is often not true. If you examine representative content textbooks, you may find a main idea statement in almost any position in the paragraph. It is more common to find one main idea statement that covers several paragraphs. And sometimes there is no explicitly stated main idea; the author just assumes the reader can generate one.

We are often amused when we ask struggling readers to underline main ideas. Some do this very quickly by underlining the first sentence in each paragraph, often without even reading the text. They have learned their lesson well, but it is not a lesson that helps them in dealing with expository material.

Struggling readers must be aware that main idea statements are not always present and, when they are not, it is their role to generate one or to generate an acceptable substitute. We suggest that an acceptable substitute for a main idea statement is the topic, and we define topic as no more than one or two words. The main idea is longer, usually a statement, that expresses the author's perspective on the topic.

Focusing on the topic has many advantages over attempting to locate a main idea that may or may not be explicitly stated. First, content publishers use topics as headings throughout their text. Second, we have seldom encountered readers who could not identify the topic even in the absence of a heading. On the other hand, even good readers often struggle locating or generating a main idea. Third, the topic can serve as an effective underpinning or connection for all of the details that the author employs in explaining the topic. Fourth, once a student identifies the topic and connects it to relevant details, the main idea is often easily identified or generated. If it is not, the topic and details provide an acceptable structure.

A main idea map is a form of graphic organizer that helps students to identify or, if necessary, generate a main idea (Jennings, Caldwell, & Lerner, 2006). A main idea map requires that the student identify the topic first. As we mentioned, this is often a heading in the text. If there is no heading, the topic is generally the subject of each sentence. Next, the student fills in relevant details. The third step, locating or generating a main idea statement, may or may not occur. If it doesn't, all is not lost. The student still has the topic and details to study or use for a summary.

The main idea map shown in Figure 10.8 was constructed from three paragraphs under the heading *Black Codes*. The main idea statement was the last sentence of the third paragraph, but it could well have been considered an additional detail. In that case, an effective generated main idea statement would be *Black codes were unfair.*

Just like idea maps, main idea maps provide a vehicle for understanding and discussing expository content. Just like idea maps, different students will construct a main idea map differently as well as identify or generate main idea statements in different ways. This

FIGURE *10.8*   Example: Main Idea Map

```
┌─────────────────────────────────────────────────────────┐
│ Topic:                                                    │
│ Black codes                                               │
└─────────────────────────────────────────────────────────┘
                              │
┌─────────────────────────────────────────────────────────┐
│ Detail:                                                   │
│ Laws passed by South limiting rights of freed slaves      │
└─────────────────────────────────────────────────────────┘
                              │
┌─────────────────────────────────────────────────────────┐
│ Detail:                                                   │
│ Couldn't vote, own guns, or serve on juries               │
└─────────────────────────────────────────────────────────┘
                              │
┌─────────────────────────────────────────────────────────┐
│ Detail:                                                   │
│ Could only work as farm laborers or servants              │
└─────────────────────────────────────────────────────────┘
                              │
┌─────────────────────────────────────────────────────────┐
│ Detail:                                                   │
│ Had to sign work contract for one year or be arrested     │
└─────────────────────────────────────────────────────────┘
                              │
┌─────────────────────────────────────────────────────────┐
│ Detail:                                                   │
│ Had some rights: could marry and own property             │
└─────────────────────────────────────────────────────────┘
                              │
┌─────────────────────────────────────────────────────────┐
│ Main Idea Statement:                                      │
│ Black codes kept freed slaves from getting economic       │
│ and political power.                                      │
└─────────────────────────────────────────────────────────┘
```

*See reproducible figure at end of chapter.

is troublesome to some teachers and certainly to struggling readers who tend to believe that there is one and only one main idea. This is not the case. Just read a textbook with a friend and see how main idea identification can vary. What is important is that a reader recognizes the important ideas and the details that explain them. Struggling readers need to be aware that locating a main idea is not always a right or wrong situation, that it is open to some interpretation, and that a topic can be as effective as a main idea statement in understanding and remembering text.

We suggest that you indicate the segments of text for the students to map. For younger students and lower-level text, they will probably be single paragraphs. For higher-level text, use one topic and one main idea, which will probably span several paragraphs.

Fill in the map for the students in the initial stages so they can concentrate on identifying the key elements instead of concerning themselves with writing and spelling. Main idea maps also make fine prewriting organizers. Hopefully you will move from written main idea maps to maps used as a structure for discussion. As we mentioned earlier in the chapter, you want this to become a way of thinking, a mental model for readers to use as they face the challenges of expository text.

Are there any guidelines for choosing an idea map based on expository structure over a main idea map? Not really. Work with the one that you are most comfortable with or the one that your students seem to prefer. However, don't be too quick to change. Mapping expository text is not easy, and it takes a long time before students are comfortable with it. You will have to motivate, encourage, model, and facilitate to keep students involved in something they find difficult, especially struggling readers who have learned to give up easily.

Application to English Language Learners

Expository text represents a challenge for all students, not just ELLs. Expository text is generally acknowledged to be more difficult than narrative text and it is much less frequent in elementary classrooms. Comprehending expository text can be especially challenging for ELLs who must not only learn new vocabulary but also decide how all the text information fits together. Moreover, ELLs probably have less awareness of expository text structures than native language speakers because of less exposure to such texts and different text structure conventions in their native language.

Moss (2006) recommends teaching expository text structures to ELLs because it helps them to "predict and confirm meaning in a passage" (p. 138). Being aware of the structures helps ELLs understand what they are reading and hearing and provides a vehicle for organizing their thoughts. Teaching text structure can be incorporated into a variety of oral and written activities such as guided conversation, picture matching and sequencing, drawing, shared reading, and read-alouds. It is important to teach ELLs the signal words that indicate text structure (Bouchard, 2005). Rea and Mercuri (2006) demonstrate a teacher think-aloud lesson for teaching ELLs to recognize the cause-and-effect structure and create a visual representation of the text ideas.

Graphic organizers offer a structure "through which students can access and organize information and ideas and can actively connect the known to the new" (Farnum, Flood, & Lapp, 1994, p. 146). Lessons using such nonlinguistic representations are especially appropriate for ELLs who may have difficulty demonstrating their understanding through writing or traditional test-taking formats (Hill & Flynn, 2006; Hedrick, Harmon, & Wood, 2003). The use of graphic organizers or idea maps can make expository content more accessible for ELLs "because the process of preparing arrays of symbolic information helps them build a framework for learning key ideas and vocabulary" (Hernandez, 2003, p. 134). Cappellini (2005) comments that ELLs often lose track of the big picture in their efforts to absorb text information. She recommends a form of graphic organizer which she calls a "focus sheet" to help them summarize and identify main ideas. Hill and Flynn (2006) recommend using graphic organizers prior to reading to provide a framework for helping ELLs understand the often confusing relationships presented in the text.

Application to Adolescent Learners

Comprehending expository text is critical for adolescents who struggle with their content area texts. While teachers often expect students to deal successfully with such materials, many struggling readers are unable to do so. Even if they have adequate word identification skills, they may not be able to deal with the heavy vocabulary load and concept density of typical middle and high school textbooks. Consider the example of a typical U.S. history text. The chapter on the first colonies contained four parts, one of which focused on the English colonies. This 10-page segment included the following information: the geography of the colonies; a description of the New England colonies, including biographical information about Puritan leaders; a description of the middle colonies focusing on Pennsylvania; a description of the southern colonies focusing on Georgia; biographical information on William Penn, Roger Williams, and Anne Hutchinson; and a page-length chart comparing and contrasting the thirteen colonies. And this is only one segment of a four-part chapter! In a similar vein, a 350-word segment in a science textbook contained approximately 20 new words, such as *organelles, ribosomes,* and *capsids.* This same short segment also contained a number of relatively familiar words that took on new and unfamiliar meanings, such as *core, protein, complementary,* and *envelope.*

Recognizing different text structures can help struggling adolescent readers identity and summarize important content. Chandler-Olcott and Hinchman (2005) suggest that tutors should ask their students to summarize after each segment of text that they read together. They recommend using graphic organizers to show the relationships between key ideas to help the students "sort out which ideas are important and which are less so" (p. 91).

Response to Intervention

Teaching students to coherently retell what they have read is a worthy strategy for tier 2 or tier 3 instruction. The general principles and the specific strategies outlined in this chapter provide instructional suggestions for doing so. However, we offer several cautions. First, recognizing and using text structure is not a quick fix; progress will become evident over a span of weeks as opposed to days. Second, the teacher will have to resist three very natural temptations. The first is to do too much in the first stages of instruction, that is, teach several text patterns at once. It is more effective in the long run to teach an initial expository pattern thoroughly before moving on to the next. Second, it is easy to fall into the habit of doing too much for the students and guided practice becomes the teacher completing all the work while the students watch, listen, and nod their heads. Students do not truly understand the strategy if they cannot independently demonstrate how to use it and if they are not able to reflect on their understanding of the process. Third, strategies should be practiced in a variety of texts, moving from easy to more difficult. In an effort to ensure success, teachers often limit students to independent text well below the level of their classroom materials. There is no reason why the teacher cannot use classroom textbooks allied with read-alouds, shared reading, echo reading, or rereading. Not only will the students learn the strategy, but they will also learn the content of their classroom material. If tier 2 or 3 instruction uses these materials prior to their introduction in the classroom, the students can participate in classroom activities. It is important to remember that a strategy mastered in easy material will not necessarily transfer to the mainstream classroom and if it does not, the student will not use it and the intervention will have been a wasted endeavor.

Part of RTI instruction is periodic monitoring of student progress. The best instrument for such monitoring is the work that students produce during instruction. That is, the teacher can use the graphic organizers or idea maps created in class as measures of their improvement. It is important to keep the structure separate. In accord with the recommendations of Moss (2004, 2006), instruction and assessment of progress should focus on a single structure. When students indicate an understanding of that structure, the teacher can introduce a new one.

Summary

Although teachers traditionally assess understanding by asking questions, assessing the ability to offer a complete, accurate, and coherent retelling is also important. In our everyday life, we retell more than we answer questions, and good readers use a combination of topic knowledge and text structure knowledge to construct their retellings. Some informal reading inventories include evaluation of retelling as a part of their assessment options. Generally, students experience more difficulty retelling expository text than narrative text.

There are five general principles for developing effective expository retellings:

- Focus on developing general content knowledge as a way of setting expectations for specific content.
- Focus on expository text structures.
- Provide modeling for students.
- Introduce general topic expectations and text structures in a written form, but gradually move to an oral focus.
- Encourage and support student rereading.

Instructional strategies for constructing expository retellings focus on three types of graphic organizers. The expository expectation grid helps students set general expectations for reading content. Expository idea maps are based on the expository structures of description, sequence, cause–effect, problem–solution, and compare–contrast. The main idea map is built around identification of topic and details leading to the identification or generation of a main idea statement.

Teaching expository structures to ELLs is uniformly recommended in combination with graphic organizers. Given the concept density of content text, graphic organizers can also help adolescents both to comprehend and summarize what they read. RTI teachers must realize that teaching text structure is not a quick fix and progress will not be immediately evident. Teach one structure thoroughly before moving to another and practice in a variety of text, moving from easy to more difficult. RTI teachers can also use classroom materials allied with read-alouds, shared reading, or echo reading to provide students with exposure to the content of their classroom texts.

REFERENCES AND RECOMMENDED READINGS

Expository Text Structure

Armbruster, B. B. (1986). Using frames to organize expository text. Paper presented at National Reading Conference, Austin, TX.

Armbruster, B. B., & Anderson, T. H. (1982). *Idea-mapping: The technique and its use in the classroom* (Reading Education Report No. 36). Champaign, IL: Center for the Study of Reading, University of Illinois.

Dymock, S. (2005). Teaching expository text structure awareness. *The Reading Teacher, 59,* 177–181.

Gregg, M., & Sekeres, D. C. (2006). Supporting children's reading of expository text in the geography classroom. *The Reading Teacher, 60,* 102–119.

Moss, B. (2004). Teaching expository text structure through information trade book retellings. *The Reading Teacher, 57,* 710–718.

Neufeld, P. (2006). Comprehension instruction in content area classes. *The Reading Teacher, 59,* 302–312.

Jennings, J. H., Caldwell, J. S., & Lerner, J. W. (2006). *Reading problems: Assessment and teaching strategies.* Boston: Allyn & Bacon.

English Language Learners

Bouchard, M. (2005). *Comprehension strategies for English language learners.* New York: Scholastic.

Cappellini, M. (2005). *Balancing reading and language learning: A resource for teaching English language learners, K–5.* Newark, DE: International Reading Association.

Farnum, N., Flood, J., & Lapp, D. (1994). Comprehending through reading and writing: Six research-based instructional strategies. In K. Spangenberg-Urbschat & R. Pritchard (Eds.), *Kids come in all languages: Reading instructions for ESL students* (pp. 135–157). Newark, DE: International Reading Association.

Hedrick, W. B., Harmon, J. M., & Wood, K. D. (2003). From trade books to text books: Helping bilingual students make the transition. In R. L. McCormack & J. R. Paratore (Eds.), *After early intervention, then what?* (pp. 190–207). Newark, DE: International Reading Association.

Hernandez, A. (2003). Making content instruction accessible for English language learners. In G. G. Garcia (Ed.), *English learners: Reaching the highest level of English literacy* (pp. 124–149). Newark, DE: International Reading Association.

Hill, J. D., & Flynn, K. M. (2006). *Classroom instruction that works with English language learners.* Alexandria, VA: Association for Supervision and Curriculum Development.

Moss, B. (2006). Teaching English language learners about expository text structure. In T. A. Young & N. L. Hadaway (Eds.), *Supporting the literacy development of English learners: Increasing success in all classrooms* (pp. 132–147). Newark, DE: International Reading Association.

Rea, D. M., & Mercuri, S. P. (2006). *Research-based strategies for English language learners.* Portsmouth, NH: Heinemann.

Adolescent Learners

Chandler-Olcott, K., & Hinchman, K. A. (2005). *Tutoring adolescent literacy learners: A guide for volunteers.* New York: The Guilford Press.

APPENDIX 10.1

Expository Expectation Grid

Description Idea Map

Sequence Idea Map

Cause–Effect Idea Map

Problem–Solution Idea Map

Compare–Contrast Idea Map

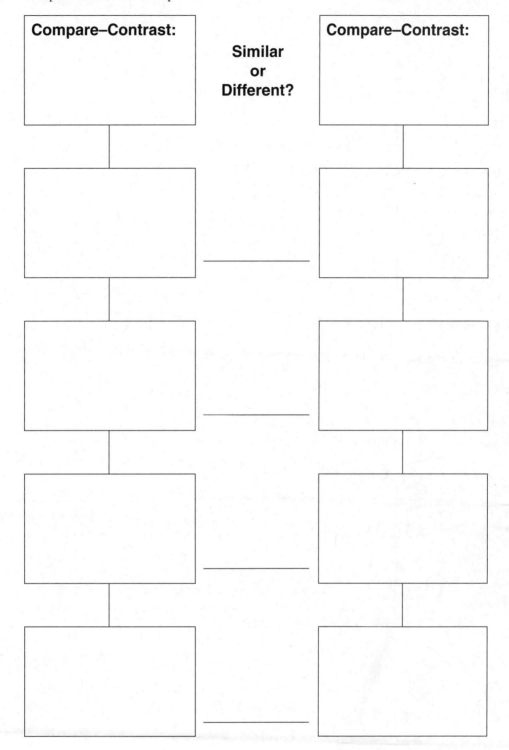

Main Idea Map

Topic:

Detail:

Detail:

Detail:

Main Idea Statement:

11

Comprehension Instruction: Answering Questions

The Complexity of Answering Questions

Asking questions is the most common way of determining if a student has understood what she or he has read. As a result, students answer many questions during the course of the school day. Some seem to have little difficulty with this; for others, especially struggling readers, providing an acceptable answer is an extremely difficult task that is often filled with anxiety. Why can't a student answer a question? We can provide no simple answer to this because many factors are involved. Of course, the primary factor is whether the student understood the text in first place, but we must also consider the type of question and the context in which it was asked.

Understanding versus Remembering

Most would agree that a student who does not understand the text will probably not be able to answer questions about it. However, we must distinguish between understanding and remembering. A student may understand the selection quite well but forget the information needed to answer a question. If we always assume lack of understanding as a reason for being unable to answer a question, we may underestimate a student's reading ability. One way to differentiate between remembering and understanding is allowing the student to look back in the text to find an answer or correct an erroneous one. If the student can do this, we can presume that she or he understood what was read. Asking students to look back can also verify understanding in very familiar text. If the topic is extremely familiar, students can sometimes draw from their background knowledge and provide acceptable answers without clearly understanding what they read. Asking them to look back to find the answer can differentiate between an answer drawn from prior knowledge and an answer drawn from understanding the text.

Question Type

There are many kinds of questions, and all are not equal. Many informal reading inventories divide questions into two main types: text explicit or factual and text implicit or inferential. Explicit questions have answers that are stated overtly in the text. Ciardiello (1998) refers to them as memory questions, and they usually begin with *who, what, where,* and *when.* Students answer memory questions by defining (What is the right of self-determination?) or identifying specific facts such as a person, time, or place (What was on the log? Where did the story take place?). Applegate, Quinn, and Applegate (2002) point out that such questions simply require recall on the reader's part.

Implicit or inferential questions require an inference by the reader, who uses a combination of text information and prior knowledge to arrive at an appropriate answer. However, there are several forms of inference questions that demand different levels of thinking. One form, called *convergent thinking* by Ciardiello, often begins with *why, how,* and *in what ways.* In order to answer the question, the reader must explain (Why did Germany attack U.S. ships?), describe relationships (Why did the mother try to distract the children from the view out of the car window?), and compare–contrast information (What is the major difference between the lytic cycle and the lysogenic cycle?).

Similar to Ciardiello's convergent thinking questions, Applegate, Quinn, and Applegate (2002) describe low-level inference questions as having answers that tend to be relatively obvious. For example, the answer may be stated in the text but in different language from that of the question. Some low-level questions ask the reader to make connections about information in the text not explicitly signaled by a grammatical marker such as *because.* Other low-level inferences require the reader to draw on personal background knowledge to answer the question without any need to refer to the text.

There are other inferential question types that students often meet in the classroom and on tests. Ciardiello (1998) refers to these as *divergent thinking* and *evaluative thinking.* Divergent thinking questions begin with such words as *imagine, predict, suppose, if . . . then, how might,* and *what might happen if.* In order to answer them, the student must move beyond the text to hypothesize, predict, or reconstruct (What might have happened if Germany had won World War I?). The student is still tied to the text, but divergent thinking questions require more constructive thought. They are not simply answered with a single sentence as implicit questions on an informal reading inventory often are. Evaluative thinking questions begin with *analyze, justify, judge, what is your opinion,* and *what do you think.* Students answer them by forming an opinion and offering a rationale for its validity (Why do you think the United Nations is or is not effective?)

Applegate, Quinn, and Applegate's high-level inference questions are similar to Ciardiello's divergent thinking questions. The reader is asked to provide an explanation or a motive for an event, provide an alternative solution to a problem, or predict a past or future action. Applegate, Quinn, and Applegate also describe response items that are similar to Ciardiello's evaluative thinking questions. These questions ask the reader to defend an idea or evaluate an action. As you can see, all inferential questions are not equal and may represent very different levels of higher thinking.

Students are not always aware of the different question types. Nor are they aware that answering these questions demands different mental activities. Younger students and second language learners may not understand the question stems and may fail to differentiate between *where, when, why,* and *how.* It is important for the teacher to explain the various question types, clarify the different stems, and teach students strategies for dealing with them.

In addition to different kinds of questions, students must also deal with a variety of question formats. Open-ended questions require the student to supply the answer. Some actually use clue words from the text, which make them somewhat easier to answer. For example, given the text "The element hydrogen makes up most of a nebula" (Leslie & Caldwell, 2006), which of the following questions is easier: What element makes up most of a nebula? or What is a nebula made of?

Multiple-choice questions provide four choices from which the student chooses the correct one. Usually, the choices are words or phrases, but sometimes test makers use sentences. Standardized tests primarily employ a multiple-choice format. Fill-in-the-blank questions provide a sentence stem and require the student to choose the correct word or words to complete the sentence. The test maker may provide a list of possible choices, but if not the student must supply the word from memory. True–false questions take the form of a statement that the student decides is true or false. Other questions ask students to arrange events in sequential order (unfortunately, if one event is misplaced all are wrong) or match two columns of terms that are related in some way.

Because of increased emphasis on standardized tests, some schools and districts are teaching test-taking skills. Although it is probably a good idea to spend some time explaining the standardized question formats and offering suggestions for dealing with them, educators must realize that questions with the same format are not necessarily equal. The effectiveness of a strategy for answering multiple-choice questions, for example, will depend on the student's understanding of the text, familiarity with the topic, and understanding of the question itself.

Question Context

To recognize the role of context, contrast a student taking a college entrance examination and hoping to attend a university that demands very high scores with a student taking a classroom test in a favorite subject on a familiar topic. Contrast a student answering oral questions in a relaxed and nonthreatening classroom environment with a student answering questions and fearing peer ridicule if unable to do so. Certainly the context of the questioning affects performance and may turn a relatively easy question into an impossible one. Fortunately, although the teacher cannot control the context of standardized test administration, she or he can control the context of the classroom.

The Importance of Self-Questioning

Good readers read with questions in mind. Our questions keep us up long past our normal bedtime as we read to find how the chapter or novel ends. Unfortunately, many struggling readers do not read with questions in mind. They believe it is the teacher's role to ask questions and theirs to answer them. In fact, many equate asking questions with being "dumb." They regard asking a question as a sign of weakness because they believe that good readers know all the answers.

Examine the key role of self-questioning in reading by considering how you read an informational article on the newest pesticides. First, you choose to read it because of questions you have: Are there more efficient pesticides? Are there dangers to pesticide use that I am not aware of? You may not overtly state them to yourself, but these questions act as motivation for reading. If you had no questions, you would probably move to another article. As you read, you continue to formulate questions: Is the author's position backed up by any research? If a specific pesticide is so dangerous, why is it still on the market? And when you finish, you probably have more questions: Should I follow the author's advice and buy the recommended pesticide? Should I check pesticides in my garage to see if they are brands that the author considers dangerous? Should I believe the author? Asking questions before, during, and after reading is natural behavior in good readers—so natural that good readers are not always aware that they are forming and answering questions as they read.

Should we teach struggling readers to self-question? Of course. As mentioned in Chapter 3, the purpose of effective intervention instruction is to turn passive, uninvolved readers into readers who actively interact with the text. Teaching students to self-question is one way to do this. In addition, we hypothesize that the ability to generate and answer one's own questions is probably related to the ability to answer someone else's. We have no proof of this, but, after all, good readers self-question and they are generally successful in answering other people's questions.

The Informal Reading Inventory as an Indicator of Ability to Answer Questions

Informal reading inventories use questions as the primary means of determining understanding. A student's score plays an important part in determining independent, instructional, and frustration levels. Is it possible that a student may have understood the text but still be unable to answer questions? We think this is a very real possibility and, for this reason, strongly encourage you to employ the strategy of looking back when you administer an informal reading inventory. Look-backs allow you to differentiate between understanding and memory. A student who understood the text but forgot the information will generally be able to look back and find the missing answer or correct the erroneous one. With younger children and those reading below a third-grade level, look-backs do not work so well. It has been our experience that students at this age and level simply reread the text instead of selectively skimming to locate the answer.

There is another issue with question answering for younger students. If they cannot answer a question, is it that they have not understood the text or that they have not understood the question? Younger students and second language learners often experience difficulty with question stems and with differentiating *what* from *why,* for example. Younger students often do not understand the demands of an implicit question and are confused because the answer is not immediately visible. How can you deal with this? If the student is at an independent or instructional level, his or her ability to answer questions at that level suggests some understanding of question formats. However, if you have a student who reaches frustration in preprimer text, you will have to probe further to determine if she or he understands question stems. The first step is to read a selection to the student and ask questions about it. If the student answers, you know two things. First, he or she comprehends what he or she hears at that level and, second, he or she understands question stems. However, if the student does not understand the selection, check knowledge of question stems by asking questions about family or favorite activities and noting if the student provides an appropriate answer to those that begin with specific stem words.

As we mentioned previously, most informal reading inventories differentiate between factual or explicit questions and inferential or implicit questions. Most provide ways to score each separately so the examiner can determine if one or both types pose difficulty for the student. Students are often confused by implicit questions that demand that they locate a text clue and match it with prior knowledge to arrive at an answer. A typical pattern that we see is the student who can answer implicit questions in familiar or narrative text but is not successful doing so in unfamiliar or expository text. Once you have determined an instructional level in narrative text, we recommend asking the student to read an expository selection at the same level. You may see a very different pattern in the student's ability to deal with implicit questions, which suggests a focus for intervention instruction.

Another pattern often emerges on an informal reading inventory, that of the student who has an acceptable score in word identification but is unable to answer questions. This student is probably more concerned with pronouncing the words than with understanding the text, and intervention should certainly focus on reading as a process of making meaning. If you have a student read silently, as we often do with older readers, and he or she is unable to answer questions, you may want to ask him or her to read a portion of the text orally in order to determine if word identification is an issue. If word identification is accurate and fluent, the student may be paying more attention to word pronunciation than to meaning.

Applegate, Quinn, and Applegate (2002) make an important point. Given the different kinds of inferential questions described earlier in this chapter, inferential questions on an informal reading inventory may vary in difficulty. It is important that you examine the individual questions that the student missed to see if a specific kind of inference question is more problematic than others.

General Principles for Helping Students to Answer Questions

Despite the prevalence of questions in our classrooms, there has been little attention paid to actually teaching students how to answer them. Educators have stressed a variety of interactive strategies for gaining meaning from text, probably under the assumption that if students understand what they are reading they will be able to answer questions. We do not disagree, but we also suggest that some struggling readers need specific instruction in how to do this.

Teach Question Types

Different question types require different thinking processes to arrive at an appropriate response. Students need to understand this so they have an idea where to find answers. Is the answer in the text? Do I have to make an inference? Do I have to form an opinion? Although we do not recommend using Ciardiello's (1998) terminology of memory, convergent, divergent, and evaluative questions with struggling readers, we do suggest that they learn the difference between question types employing user-friendly terms. Later in the chapter, we describe a strategy called Question Answer Relationships, or QARs (Raphael, 1982, 1986; Raphael, Highfield, & Au, 2006), that helps students differentiate question types according to where the answer can be found.

If a student does not understand question stems, you need to explicitly teach them. One way is to place the stem words on cards with helpful pictures. Mark *who* with a picture of a person and *where* with a place. Signal *when* with a clock or calendar. A question mark can indicate *why*. *How* can be clued by *1–2–3* to indicate that several steps are often needed to answer how something happened. *What* is a general stem that is difficult to indicate with a picture. However, we have found that if students learn the other stems, *what* does not pose a problem. Place the cards in a prominent place in the classroom or give each student a set to use during questioning. Most of us are familiar with question stems that signal literal or factual content. However, questions also ask students to make inferences or apply knowledge in some way. Figure 11.1 offers some examples of common question stems.

Emphasize Self-Questioning

Teach struggling readers to self-question before, during, and after reading and model this thinking process for them. Introduce a selection by briefly previewing it and suggest questions that the students might ask themselves: What do I think the story will be about? What do I know about the topic? As you read a selection with students, stop and help them to formulate questions. Many teachers use the strategy of prediction during reading, which is a form of question. For example, "I predict that the story will be about a little boy who washes the car" can be stated as a question: "Will this story be about a little boy who washes the car?" After reading, use self-questioning to reflect on what was read: "What did I read that made me laugh?" "What did I learn from my reading?" Make self-questioning a normal part of every lesson. It does not take extra time. It just requires that you change your focus from asking the questions to asking students to formulate their own. Praise students for asking questions, and gradually your struggling readers will realize that they can ask questions as well as you do.

In guiding students to self-question, you will often find that struggling readers just do not know what to ask. Students are relatively familiar with literal or explicit questions, and if you ask them to form a question, it will probably be a literal one. This may be because so many explicit questions are present in textbooks or asked by teachers. However, students need help in forming other kinds of questions. There are general questions that students can learn to use. These are the ones that we can ask of any narrative or expository text. For example, in narratives we can ask about the character's problem, motives, or strategies for finding a solution. We can ask if we agree with the character's actions and how we might approach the situation differently. In expository text, we can ask about the topic and what we have learned about it. We can ask how it relates to our life. Providing students with examples of possible questions fosters question generation.

Lubiner (2004) describes a sequence for teaching question generation during read-alouds. Students have questioning cue cards that remind them of the process of thinking about what the author is saying, putting ideas together to form main ideas, forming and asking questions using question words, and considering possible answers. The teacher reads aloud and models the cue card process by thinking aloud. After students demonstrate under-

FIGURE *11.1*   Question Stems

Literal Question Stems	Inferential Question Stems	Application Question Stems
who, what, where, when, define, label, list, name	why, how, in what ways, interpret, discuss, explain, describe, summarize, classify, demonstrate, show, relate, order, connect, compare, categorize, analyze	imagine, suppose, predict, how might . . . , create, what might happen if . . . , if . . . then . . . , what are some possible consequences of . . . , modify, invent, design, plan, defend, judge, justify, what do you think . . . , evaluate, what is your opinion of . . . , appraise, conclude, recommend

standing of the process, they work in groups. One student begins as the group leader, reads the text, identifies the main ideas, and generates a question. The group answers the question. Another student becomes the leader and reads and generates a question that the group answers. This continues until all students have acted as leaders or the passage is completed.

Emphasize Look-Backs

Dignify the process of looking back as one that all good readers use, and regularly ask students to look back in the text to find or verify answers. Many struggling readers seldom do this. In fact, many consider looking back to be a form of cheating. You can make the look-back procedure a regular component of teaching students to generate questions. When a student has generated an explicit question, look back to find the answer. If the student has generated an implicit question, look back to locate the text clue that will help the student infer an appropriate answer.

Tie Questioning to Text Structure

Whenever possible, use the structure of the text as a framework for asking and generating questions. This is easiest to do with narratives that have a regular and predictable structure. Ask questions that focus on identification of the characters and setting and that pertain to important components of the plot: problem, resolution, and steps to resolution. Teach students to do this as well.

As we mentioned in Chapter 10, expository text embodies several different structures: description, sequence, cause–effect, problem–solution, and compare–contrast. Use the key words in these structures to ask and generate questions. For example, given a selection on the life cycle of stars, you might phrase questions in this way:

> *Describe* a nebula.
> What *sequence* leads to the creation of a protostar?
> What *causes* a supernova?
> What *problem* do scientists have in proving the existence of black holes?
> *Compare* a red giant and a white dwarf.

Differentiate Assessment Questions and Instructional Questions

Because teachers and tests use questions as a primary form of assessment, the questioning process often produces anxiety, especially for struggling readers. It is important for the teacher to carefully distinguish questions that are part of assessment from questions that are part of instruction. Learning about different kinds of questions and how to answer them is part of instruction, as is learning how to form questions before, during, and after reading. Answering questions that will be corrected and scored in some way is part of assessment. Students need to know the difference. We also recommend that teachers tell students that looking back to locate an answer is not cheating on a standardized test.

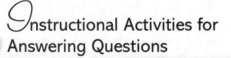 Instructional Activities for Answering Questions

Question Answer Relationships

Raphael (1982, 1986) devised a simple scheme for teaching question types, called Question Answer Relationships (QARs), that is experiencing a bit of resurgence (Raphael,

Highfield, & Au, 2006). We include it in our set of instructional activities because it provides a user-friendly and practical framework for teaching struggling readers how to answer questions. Raphael categorized questions according to where the answer could be found: In the Book or In My Head. There are two kinds of In the Book questions: Right There and Think and Search. Think and Search questions are also sometimes referred to as Putting the Parts Together (Bouchard, 2005). The answer to a Right There question can be found in the text. It is usually easy to find and generally contained in a single sentence. The sentence itself often serves as the answer, without rewording. Right There questions are also called memory questions (Ciardiello, 1998), text-explicit questions, literal questions, or factual questions; however, the term *Right There* is more understandable to struggling readers. Consider the following text from the *Qualitative Reading Inventory-4* (Leslie & Caldwell, 2006): "She looked outside the window and saw a little gray cat." An example of a Right There question would be, What did Marva see outside her window?

The second In the Book question is called Think and Search. The answer is still in the text, but the reader has to find it in different parts as opposed to a single sentence. Also, the words in the question and the words in the text are probably not the same. You are still dealing with literal or text-explicit information, but the reader has to pull together different parts of the text to arrive at an answer. An example of a Think and Search question is What series of events causes a star to go into the red giant stage? Five separate sentences in the text provide the answer to this (Leslie & Caldwell, 2006).

There are two kinds of In My Head questions: Author and Me and On My Own. Author and Me questions are text implicit or inferential. Ciardiello (1998) refers to them as convergent thinking questions. The answer is not in the text, although the text contains clues. Readers must think about what the author has said and match this to what they know. An example from the *Qualitative Reading Inventory-4* (Leslie & Caldwell, 2006) is "What kept Malcolm X motivated to continue his study of the dictionary?" In order to answer this, readers have to match what they know about motivation to Malcolm X's description of his study activities. If they understand that pride in one's accomplishments and learning can act as powerful motivators, they will focus on the clues in the text where Malcolm X discusses his pride in writing, understanding, and remembering so many new words.

The answer to an On My Own question is not in the text. In fact, sometimes it can be found without even reading the text; instead, readers use their own knowledge or experience to find it. Ciardiello (1998) might characterize On My Own questions as examples of divergent or evaluative thinking. An example is Why might copying a dictionary help someone to learn to read?

How should you teach QAR questions? We suggest using visual aids to illustrate the four question types. For example, a picture of an open book with a single line on one page written in bold can signal a Right There question. A picture of an open book with several bolded lines on each page can illustrate a Think and Search question. Author and Me can be indicated by a picture of a book and a person's head. A picture of a person's head alone can point to an On My Own question. Place these visual aids on bulletin boards or in a prominent place in the classroom so students can refer to them easily. One enterprising teacher had students make bookmarks containing the four question types. Not only was constructing the bookmark an effective instructional activity, but it resulted in a convenient tool for reminding students where to locate answers.

We suggest moving from easy to difficult. In the Book QARs are easiest, so begin with these. Success with Right There and Think and Search questions often gives students initial confidence in their ability to find answers, which in turn motivates them to grapple with more difficult questions. Beginning with In the Book questions also dignifies the idea that all readers have to refer to the book in order to find answers. Gradually move to In My Head questions, first introducing Author and Me, and finally to On My Own questions.

The following sequence may be helpful for introducing, modeling, and practicing QARs.

1. The teacher models by asking the question, giving the answer, providing the QAR label, and explaining the rationale for the label. If the question is Right There, Think and Search, or Author and Me, the teacher models locating the answer or the inference clue in the text. If the question is On My Own, the teacher models how to construct the answer.

2. The teacher asks the students the question and provides both the answer and the label. The students provide the rationale for the label by finding the answer or clue in the text or by explaining how the teacher may have arrived at an On My Own answer.

3. The teacher asks the students the question and supplies the label. The students provide the answer and the rationale for the label by locating the answer or clue in the text. If the question is an On My Own, the students explain how they crafted the answer without reference to the text.

4. The teacher gives the students the question. The students provide the answer, label, and rationale.

You can see how you can easily tie looking back with QARs. The easiest way for the students to provide the QAR rationale is by looking back in the text to point out the answer or inference clue.

In working with QARs, move from short segments of text to longer ones. Begin with two- or three-sentence passages to illustrate a specific QAR. Once all of the QARs have been introduced, use a passage of about 75 to 100 words and construct questions that exemplify all four question types. Then move to longer selections such as entire stories divided into parts. Your aim is to eventually use the QAR strategy to answer questions across an entire selection. Raphael and Au (2005) suggest that primary readers can distinguish between In the Book and In My Head questions and second graders can differentiate between Right There and Think and Search questions. In the primary classroom or the intervention setting, QAR instruction can begin with read-alouds.

You may want to begin with narrative selections because students find them somewhat easier. However, we recommend moving to expository selections as soon as possible. Students need practice with expository material, and there is no better place to do this than in a supportive intervention session.

QARs can act as a focus for discussion. You can ask students to locate answers to questions individually or in small groups. It is important that they label the question as a QAR type and indicate the page number where the answer or clue was found.

You can also ask students to construct questions using QAR guidelines. It has been our experience that students enjoy making up questions and seeing if their peers can answer them. Students can ask their questions and, if their peers are unable to answer them, provide the QAR label as a clue.

Once students understand QARs, why not label classroom test questions as question types? After all, isn't the purpose of assessment to capture the student's best performance? Labeling test questions as Right There, Think and Search, Author and Me, and On My Own supports students in demonstrating their understanding of the text. Of course, providing QAR labels only works if the student has access to the text. Some teachers are strongly against open-book tests, but they must realize that answering questions in the absence of the text is a test of memory and not necessarily one of understanding.

Raphael and Au (2005) have tied QAR categories to comprehension strategies. For example, Think and Search questions direct the readers to a variety of good reader behaviors: identifying important information, summarizing, using text organization, clarifying, and making text-to-text connections. Author and Me questions require that readers predict, visualize, make inferences, distinguish fact and opinion, and make text-to-self, text-to-theme, and text-to-world connections.

Content-Free Questions

What do we mean by *content-free* questions? Consider the following questions: At the beginning of the story, what was Rosa's problem? and What was the problem of the main character? Text content—the name of the character—is embedded in one question but is absent in the other. Consider another example: What final event caused the United States to join the Allies? and What was the next important event? Both deal with an important event, but the content elements of *United States* and *Allies* are part of one question and absent in the other.

Content-free questions are general questions that students can ask about any selection. They help students set specific expectations for reading. Why set expectations? Given any situation that you might encounter, if you anticipate what might happen you will probably have greater success in dealing with it. Content-free questions act as a kind of roadmap during reading. If students read to answer questions they have generated, there is more likelihood that they will be successful than if they read with no specific objectives in mind.

Students tend to regard questions as content specific. This is understandable given the questions they generally encounter in their classrooms. One little fellow put this quite succinctly when he rather fretfully inquired, "How can I ask a question when I haven't even read the story yet?" It is important to teach students the value of general questions and to model how such questions help them to comprehend.

Content-free questions form the basis of a strategy called Questioning the Author (Beck, McKeown, Hamilton, & Kucan, 1997). Beck and colleagues call such questions *queries,* which they say are "designed to assist students in grappling with text ideas as they construct meaning" (p. 23). Initiating queries focus on the author's purpose and can take the following forms: What is the author trying to say? What is the author talking about? What is the author's message? Follow-up queries center on integrating ideas. Examples are What does the author mean? Does the author explain this clearly? Does this connect with what we read before? How does this connect to what the author has told us? Why does the author tell us this now? Beck and colleagues (1997) provide delightful examples of students generating and reacting to queries as they attempt to make sense of what they read.

There are different content-free questions for narrative and expository text.

Narrative Content-Free Questions
- Who is the main character? Why do I think so?
- Who are other important characters? Why are they important?
- What is the character's problem?
- How is the character trying to solve his or her problem?
- How is the problem resolved?
- What are the important events?
- What words describe the setting?
- How is the setting important to the story?
- What do I predict will happen next? Why do I think so?
- Do I agree or disagree with what the character did? Why?
- Do I like or dislike this part of the story? Why?
- Is this story true to life? Why or why not?
- What is the theme of the story?
- How did the story end?
- Is there anything I don't understand?
- What surprised me about this story?
- If I were going to write to the author, what would I say?

- How is this story connected to the world?
- How is this story connected to me?

Expository Content-Free Questions
- What is the topic of this section?
- What is the author's purpose?
- What are the most important ideas?
- What is most interesting to me?
- What did I learn?
- What do I already know about this?
- What surprised me?
- What are some words that I have learned?
- What are some words that I do not know the meaning of? Does the text give me a hint?
- How is this different from what I already knew?
- How could I explain this in my own words?
- What don't I understand?
- How is this connected to me?

Place the content-free questions in a prominent place so that students can refer to them. Use them to set expectations prior to and during reading. During reading, occasionally stop and decide if the questions were answered. Make this a pleasant and positive process. Model asking content-free questions and finding answers to them. Offer feedback to students and praise their progress. Reading to answer previously identified general questions is a more effective activity than what passes for discussion in far too many classrooms: The teacher asks questions, usually literal, and the students answer them—or at least some of them do. Struggling readers go to great lengths to avoid being called on and are often quite skillful in doing so.

How much text should you read before you stop to discuss answers and generate new questions? The length of the text will depend on the age of the student and the level and structure of the selection. You can often divide narrative text into longer sections than expository material, which is generally so concept dense that it is better to focus on smaller segments.

When you begin to talk about the text, remind students to answer the content-free questions that they have generated. Students often move immediately to the answer, so make sure that they can identify the relevant question. For example, after reading a section of text a teacher asked her students to comment; one student replied, "It was about exploration and who went." The teacher asked the student to identify the question that matched his answer, which was What is the topic of the selection? It is important to emphasize to students that their responses are based on questions. You want them to be aware that they read with questions in mind. Reading with general questions in mind is not a quick fix, however. It takes a long time and a lot of practice before it becomes the effortless process engaged in by good readers.

Example of a Lesson Based on Content-Free Questions.   What follows is a brief example of how one teacher used general content-free questions as a basis for discussion.

Louis worked with a small group of fifth graders who were experiencing difficulty in comprehending expository text. His goal was to demonstrate to them the power and importance of reading with questions in mind. He chose a selection from their social studies book on the Lewis and Clark expedition, read the first heading to the students, and made certain that they understood the meaning of "expedition." Each student had his or her own list of possible general questions. Louis had laminated the lists and the students used them as bookmarks.

Louis: So the title is "President Jefferson's Expedition," and we already know what an expedition is. Good readers always read with questions in mind, so let's look at our list of questions and choose one or two. Allie, which question should we choose?

Allie: I think we should read to find out the author's purpose.

Pat: We already know it! It's to describe the president's expedition. The heading tells us this.

Allie: I still think we should read to make sure of it.

Louis: No problem there. Let's do it. Another question. Pat?

Pat: What are the most important ideas?

Latonda: What will I learn? We're supposed to learn something.

Louis: Let's stop here. We have three good questions. Let's read the first two paragraphs and see if we can find the answers.

Louis and the group read the paragraphs orally in a shared-reading format.

Louis: Any answers to our questions?

Pat: I was right. They are describing the expedition.

Allie: They're really describing all the plans for it. We haven't got to the expedition yet. That's the author's purpose, to talk about getting ready.

Louis: Good for you. You're both right. Pat recognized the author was describing something, and Allie got more detailed about it. Pat, what were those important ideas you wanted to find?

Pat: Where they got the money, like from Congress, and the guys who would lead the expedition.

Louis: And they were?

Latonda: Merrie Lewis and Clark. That a funny name for a man, Merrie.

Louis: What question did you answer?

Latonda: My question was "What will I learn?" I learned their names.

Pat: They were to go all the way to the Pacific Ocean.

Allie: And they were to describe everything they saw.

Louis wanted to keep reminding the students that they are reading to find answers to questions.

Louis: What question were you two just answering?

Allie: I think it could be what we learned or what was important. Both kind of fit.

Louis: Sometimes that happens. The same answer fits two questions.

Latonda: And they were to learn about the Indians.

Allie: And be friendly to them.

Louis: The question you're answering?

Allie: What was important?

Latonda: What will I learn?

Louis: Let's summarize. We had three questions. One was "What was the author's purpose?"

Pat: To describe the expedition.

Allie: To describe the plans for it!

Pat: Okay, the plans.

Louis: Our second question was "What were the important ideas?"

Pat: They got money from Congress, and the president told them what to do and to go all the way to the Pacific.

Latonda: Their names were Merrie Lewis and something Clark, and they were to write notes about what they saw and be friendly with the Indians.

Louis: Our third question was "What will we learn?"

Allie: We learned everything we just said!

Louis: Sounds like you guys understand this part very well. Let's move on to the next part.

Application to English Language Learners

Roit (2006) emphasizes the importance of teaching useful linguistic structures to ELLs and question stems certainly fall into this category. ELLs may easily confuse *wh* words (words that begin with *w* or *h* such as *who, what, when, where, why,* and *how*) because they have had less time to acquire them than their English-speaking peers. Pilgreen (2006) echoes this recommendation and suggests using a visual support by matching a question stem to an appropriate icon. For example, *who* would be represented by a stick figure, *when* by a clock, *why* by a question mark, and so on. The word–icon link helps the student understand the match between a question stem and an appropriate answer. Schifini (1994) and Pilgreen (2006) both recommend using *wh* words in graphic organizers for ELLs.

In a similar fashion, Newman (2001/2002) suggests using pictures to model the question generation process. A picture of an eye can signal the question What do you see in the picture? or What do you see in your mind? A cloud can suggest What are you thinking about? and a heart can signal How do you feel? Smile faces and frown faces can indicate if predictions were accurate or inaccurate. Other suggested icons to represent questions are a building to signal setting, stairs to indicate steps in a process, a lock to represent a main idea, and a key for details.

Bouchard (2005) recommends using QARs with ELLs because understanding questions and how to formulate answers can be problematic for them. QARs help ELLs to categorize and understand different kinds of questions. Bouchard suggests providing additional visual support by using QAR picture cards that describe each question type by illustrating where answers can be found. During group discussion, students can hold up or point to these cards when asked to identify a type of QAR.

Locating appropriate answers in expository text can be facilitated by question guides (Bouchard, 2005). The guide clearly states the topic of the reading (i.e., photosynthesis) and the purpose for reading (i.e., to learn the steps in the process). The teacher divides the page into two columns. In column one, the teacher indicates what pages and paragraphs the students should read. In many cases the entire text does not have to be read and the teacher can select the most important information. In column two, the teacher lists the questions to answer. Test items should be drawn from these questions. Bouchard uses this as a way of helping ELLs distinguish between essential and nonessential information.

Teacher modeling is an important factor in fostering ELLs' ability to understand and answer questions. Hill and Flynn (2006) distinguish between three question–answer patterns: In question-response-evaluation, the teacher asks a question and then evaluates the student's answer. In question-response-feedback, the teacher asks a question and, when the student answers, provides feedback in the form of paraphrasing or expanding on the student's answer. This often leads to the student rephrasing or expanding the original comment. In student-organized interaction, students ask and answer questions in small groups with the teacher acting as both a facilitator and participant. Hill and Flynn suggest that question-response-feedback and student-organized interaction are especially helpful to ELLs.

Bouchard (2005) also believes that teacher modeling is a critical factor; she recommends the ReQuest Procedure, where teacher and students read text one sentence at a time. First the students ask the teacher as many questions as they can about the sentence and the teacher answers them and models, if necessary, how the answers must match the question stems. Then the teacher takes a turn in asking questions about the same sentence, focusing attention on the topic and purpose of the selection and modeling different kinds of questions and different question stems. When the third sentence is reached, the teacher models questions that integrate information from the first two sentences. The teacher and students continue through the paragraph using the pattern of sentence reading, student questions, and teacher questions. After completing the procedure with one paragraph, the students predict what the rest of the selection will be about and read to confirm their predictions. As students become familiar with the process, the teacher shifts from a focus on a single sentence to a paragraph focus.

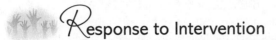

Application to Adolescent Learners

Questioning the Author (QtA) (Beck, McKeown, Hamilton and Kucan, 1997), described earlier in the section on content-free questions, is an instructional technique "designed to engage late elementary through high school students in critical reading, thinking, and discussion" (Deshler et al., 2007, p. 68). Teachers use open-ended questions, referred to as queries, to help students construct meaning. This is especially appropriate for adolescents. The purpose of queries is to foster critical thinking by asking students to consider the author's purpose and if that purpose was achieved. This is an important distinction. Authors do not always express their ideas clearly and QtA encourages students to recognize this and realize that difficulty in understanding may be as much the fault of the author as the reader. QtAs lend themselves well to whole class read-alouds and to all content areas.

McKenna (2002) suggests clustering questions for older readers, that is, asking question in a set pattern that fosters comprehension. Bottom-up question clusters begin with several literal questions followed by an inference question. The purpose of the literal questions is to elicit information that will help the students draw an appropriate inference. The top-down cluster starts with a higher-level question. If the students do not answer this question appropriately, the teacher asks one or more literal questions to provide clarifying information and then returns to the original item. An extending question cluster occurs when the students answer appropriately but the teacher attempts to elicit additional or alternative thinking on the topic. Teachers do not always have a pattern to the questions they ask, other than selecting items based on the content and sequence of the text. Question clusters provide a pattern that focuses on higher-level thinking and helps learners see a connection between the inferences they draw and the literal information provided in the text. McKenna (2002) and Chandler-Olcott and Hinchman (2005) also suggest that QARs work well with adolescent learners.

Response to Intervention

Instruction in the RTI model must be based on research as described in Chapter 1. The strategies of Questioning the Author, Question Answer Relationships, and question generation have a firm research base (Nokes & Dole, 2004; Underwood & Pearson, 2004; Stahl & Shanahan, 2004) and merit inclusion in RTI instruction.

Monitoring progress in RTI will no doubt involve using questions as assessment. It is important that the teacher carefully differentiate between literal and inferential questions. We suggest that teachers use the QAR format in designing questions for monitoring progress in comprehension. Some students can answer Right There questions but evince difficulty in dealing with Think and Search questions. Similarly, Author and Me questions may pose difficulty to a student who can answer literal questions. Some students do not know how to answer On My Own questions by tying the text to their own lives. These represent different forms of comprehension and may require different instructional emphases. Teachers should describe the comprehension abilities of their students in specific as opposed to general terms.

There is another consideration. Earlier in this chapter, we mentioned the importance of using look-backs to distinguish understanding from memory. We recommend that teachers allow students to look back in the text when using questions to assess progress in comprehension. Some teachers find the use of an "open book" assessment difficult to accept. If that is the case, we suggest that teachers report progress in two ways: comprehension without look-backs and comprehension with look-backs.

Summary

Answering questions is the most common way of determining if a student has understood what she or he has read. There are a variety of question types. Most informal reading inventories focus on explicit or literal questions and implicit or inferential ones. Several kinds of inference questions demand different thinking on the part of the reader. Students are often unaware of the different question types and how to generate appropriate answers.

There are four general principles for helping students answer questions. First, emphasize self-questioning. Good readers ask questions before, during, and after reading. We should teach struggling readers to do this. Second, teach question types. Students need to know the difference between questions that can be answered from the text and questions that require prior knowledge on the part of the reader. Third, emphasize looking back in the text to differentiate understanding from memory. Finally, differentiate for students answering questions as part of instruction and answering questions as part of formal assessment.

Two instructional activities for teaching students to answer questions are QARs and content-free questions. QARs differentiate questions according to where the answer can be found. The answers to In the Book questions can be found in the text; answers to In My Head questions require prior knowledge from the reader generally combined with text information. Content-free questions are general questions that readers can ask of any text.

Teaching question stems to ELLs is effective; it may also be helpful to add visual support by utilizing pictures to illustrate the stem as well as the question generation process. QARs are also recommended as an effective strategy for helping ELLs understand questions. Other instructional suggestions include question guides, teacher modeling, and the ReQuest procedure. Questioning the Author (QtA) is recommended as a viable strategy for adolescent learners. Questioning the Author, QARs, and question generation have a firm research base and merit inclusion in RTI. Progress monitoring should involve differentiation of literal and inferential questions. The QAR format may be useful in designing assessment questions.

REFERENCES AND RECOMMENDED READINGS

Information about Questions and Instructional Practices

Applegate, M. D., Quinn, K. B., & Applegate, A. J. (2002). Levels of thinking required by comprehension ques-

tions in informal reading inventories. *The Reading Teacher, 56,* 174–180.

Beck, I. L., McKeown, M. G., Hamilton, R. L., & Kucan, L. (1997). *Questioning the author: An approach for enhancing student engagement with text.* Newark, DE: International Reading Association.

Ciardiello, A. V. (1998). Did you ask a good question today? Alternative cognitive and metacognitive strategies. *Journal of Adolescent and Adult Literacy, 42,* 210–219.

Leslie, L., & Caldwell, J. (2006). *Qualitative reading inventory-4.* Boston: Allyn & Bacon.

Lubliner, S. (2004). Help for struggling upper-grade elementary readers. *The Reading Teacher, 57,* 430–438.

Neuman, G. (2001/2002). Comprehension strategy gloves. *The Reading Teacher, 55,* 329–332.

QARs

Bouchard, M. (2005). *Comprehension strategies for English language learners.* New York: Scholastic.

Cortest, E. E. (2003/2004). The application of Question Answer Relationship strategies to pictures. *The Reading Teacher, 57,* 374–380.

Raphael, T. E. (1982). Question-answering strategies for children. *The Reading Teacher, 36,* 186–190.

Raphael, T. E. (1986). Teaching question-answer relationships, revisited. *The Reading Teacher, 39,* 516–522.

Raphael, T. E., & Au, K. (2005). QAR: Enhancing comprehension and test taking across grades and content areas. *The Reading Teacher, 59,* 206–221.

Raphael, T. E., Highfield, K., & Au, K. (2006). *QAR now: Question answer relationships.* New York: Scholastic.

English Language Learners

Hill, J. D., & Flynn, K. M. (2006). *Classroom instruction that works with English language learners.* Alexandria, VA: Association for Supervision and Curriculum Development.

Pilgreen, J. (2006). Supporting English learners: Developing academic language in the content area classroom. In T. A. Young & N. L. Hadaway (Eds.), *Supporting the literacy development of English learners: Increasing success in all classrooms* (pp. 132–147). Newark, DE: International Reading Association.

Roit, M. L. (2006). Essential comprehension strategies for English learners. In T. A. Young & N. L. Hadaway (Eds.), *Supporting the literacy development of English learners: Increasing success in all classrooms* (pp. 80–95). Newark, DE: International Reading Association.

Schifini, A. (1994). Language, literacy and content instruction: Strategies for teachers. In K. Spangenberg-Urbschat & R. Pritchard (Eds.), *Kids come in all languages: Reading instructions for ESL students* (pp. 182–207). Newark, DE: International Reading Association.

Adolescent Learners

Chandler-Olcott, K., & Hinchman, K. A. (2005). *Tutoring adolescent literacy learners: A guide for volunteers.* New York: The Guilford Press.

Deshler, D. D., Palincsar, A. S., Biancarosa, G., & Nair, M. (2007). *Informed choices for struggling adolescent readers: A research-based guide to instructional programs and practices.* Newark, DE: International Reading Association.

McKenna, M. C. (2002). *Help for struggling readers: Strategies for grades 3–8.* New York: The Guilford Press.

Nokes, J. D., & Dole, J. A. (2004). Helping adolescent readers through explicit strategy instruction. In T. L. Jetton & J. A. Dole (Eds.), *Adolescent literacy research and practice* (pp. 162–182). New York: The Guilford Press.

Stahl, S. A., & Shanahan, C. (2004). Learning to think like a historian: Disciplinary knowledge through critical analysis of multiple documents. In T. L. Jetton & J. A. Dole (Eds.), *Adolescent literacy research and practice* (pp. 94–118). New York: The Guilford Press.

Underwood, T., & Pearson, P. D. (2004). Teaching struggling readers to comprehend what they read. In T. L. Jetton & J. A. Dole (Eds.), *Adolescent literacy research and practice* (pp. 135–162). New York: The Guilford Press.

12

Comprehension Instruction: General Interactive Strategies

- **THE INFORMAL READING INVENTORY AS AN INDICATOR OF PROBLEMS WITH COMPREHENSION**
- **FRAMEWORKS FOR INTERACTIVE TEACHING OF COMPREHENSION STRATEGIES**
  - Directed Reading–Thinking Activity
  - Visual Imagery
  - KWL
  - Reciprocal Teaching
  - Thinking Aloud
  - Discussion Cards
  - Example of a Discussion Card Lesson
- **APPLICATION TO ENGLISH LANGUAGE LEARNERS**
- **APPLICATION TO ADOLESCENT LEARNERS**
- **RESPONSE TO INTERVENTION**
- **SUMMARY**
- **REFERENCES AND RECOMMENDED READINGS**

One factor that distinguishes good readers from less successful ones is knowing what to do when reading doesn't make sense. Any strategy that fosters student engagement facilitates comprehension. Extensive data show how certain strategies facilitate comprehension, and we will discuss several of them. In the end, however, it doesn't matter which ones you choose as long as they help your students engage in deep processing of text. Students as young as second grade can be taught to actively use a variety of comprehension strategies, and long-term studies indicate positive effects (Pressley, 2000). Students with comprehension problems must not read "to be done" but rather to understand deeply what the author's message means to them. A variety of strategies can help a student construct meaning from a text, and the student should have many of them at his or her disposal. Only by knowing which strategies to use, and when, will students become the independent learners that we all want.

According to Pressley (2000), effective comprehension instruction should include

1. Direct explanation of strategies to be taught
2. Teacher modeling of strategies
3. Guided practice in strategies for reading texts in which
   a. Teacher assistance is provided on an as-needed basis
   b. Student engagement in lively interpretive discussions of text is high
   c. Application of the strategies varies depending on need

One of the most notable conclusions reached by Pressley (2000) is that this type of instruction takes semesters and even years of implementation to result in increased comprehension, likely because there are several strategies to be learned and because students must learn when, where, and how to use each one while interacting with text. The findings of the National Reading Panel (2000) are consistent with Pressley's conclusions:

- When readers are given cognitive strategy instruction, they make significant gains in reading comprehension over students trained with conventional instruction procedures.
- The specific strategies that are effective are comprehension monitoring, cooperative learning, graphic organizers, story structure, question answering, question generating, and summarization.
- Teaching a variety of comprehension strategies in natural settings and content areas is most effective.

Nokes and Dole (2004) summarize the characteristics of effective strategy instruction. They describe it as "flexible and opportunistic," based on student needs and the text they read. Such instruction focuses on multiple strategies and occurs as an ongoing process throughout the school year.

The Informal Reading Inventory as an Indicator of Problems with Comprehension

If a student can read a piece of text with at least 90 percent accuracy and a rate appropriate to his or her reading instructional level, but has sparse retelling ability and cannot answer at least 70 percent of the questions, we suspect a general problem with comprehension. However, our suspicions must be validated by having the student read other material at approximately the same level to see whether comprehension problems are found in both narrative and expository text. Thus, if a student reads narrative text with accuracy and good comprehension, we must examine his or her ability in expository text as well. If the student has difficulty retelling and answering questions in both types of text, we might conclude that a general comprehension problem exists. To be sure, it would be helpful to read a selection to the student and see how well he or she retells it and answers questions about it. If the student's listening comprehension is similar to his or her reading comprehension, and both are below grade level, then we can conclude that a general reading/language comprehension problem exists.

Frameworks for Interactive Teaching of Comprehension Strategies

In previous chapters we described how to teach word identification strategies in the context of literature. We will do likewise here. Teaching a reading comprehension strategy is not simply what to do; it also involves when to do it and why it is effective. Because different strategies help students read different types of material for different purposes, a comprehension strategy should not be taught separately from a text to which it is applied (Block, 2004). But how do we keep the theme of the story moving while teaching a new strategy? Dowhower (1999) presents a Comprehension Strategy Framework that integrates strategy instruction into an interactive guided reading of a text. This strategy is particularly useful because it applies to any comprehension instruction. For this reason, it forms the foundation on which we will present several specific comprehension strategies.

The Comprehension Strategy Framework has three phases:

1. Prereading, which includes
   a. Eliciting or activating prior knowledge
   b. Building background and relating it to prior knowledge
   c. Focusing on the strategy to be taught—what it is, why it is important, and when to use it
2. Active Reading, which consists of cycles of
   a. Students setting a purpose for reading the specific section of text
   b. Silent reading and self-monitoring, including application of the strategy being taught
   c. Shared discussion of that segment of text as it relates to overall understanding of what the story is about; discussion of how students applied the strategy and how it worked to help them understand the story or where it led to confusion
3. Postreading, which includes
   a. Recall of major points of the text
   b. Reader response to self-chosen sections of the text, such as a letter written to a character
   c. Extension of text—finding books with similar themes
   d. Strategy use and transfer—return to the discussion of the effectiveness of the new strategy but now applying it to the overall text
   e. Informal or self-assessment—add the new strategy to a list of known strategies that the student uses to self-assess when she or he uses different strategies in different books; students rate the strategies for their effectiveness or describe why they like a particular strategy more than others

Another framework involves three levels of comprehension intervention (Underwood and Pearson, 2004). Level 1 interventions teach students cognitive strategies for "creating mental representations of the content of a text" (p. 142). Students learn how to activate and draw on their prior knowledge as they read. They identify text structures, construct graphic organizers, differentiate between important and less important ideas, and learn a variety of comprehension strategies. Level 2 interventions focus on the author and teach students how to use their own comprehension to ask and answer questions; "authors are seen as fallible and intentional and readers have the right to question them" (p. 143). The goal of Level 3 interventions is to transfer learned strategies into practice both in and out of the classroom.

Within either framework you can teach anything. Let's begin by considering some tried and true strategies that classroom research has found to be effective.

Directed Reading–Thinking Activity

The Directed Reading–Thinking Activity (DRTA) (Stauffer, 1975) involves two processes that cycle throughout the text: prediction and verification. The student begins by making a prediction from some segment of text, often the title and the book cover, and then reads another segment and confirms or refutes the prediction. The student makes a second prediction, reads, and again verifies whether or not the prediction is correct. DLTA, or Directed Listening–Thinking Activity, in the case of students who are not yet reading, can be used with narrative or expository text. In the intervention program that one author directs, the children react negatively if their prediction is incorrect. Somehow they see it as a failure on their part, and no amount of teacher assurance seems to help. Unfortunately, this leads to misbehavior that can seriously disrupt a lesson. How can we prevent this? Block (2004) suggests that students read two pages or so (depending on reading level) before they make a prediction. In this way students have sufficient information to make a reasonable prediction. Also, the teacher can model enjoying the surprise that a book provides when his or her prediction does not play out in the story. If teachers model that different ideas can all be useful and reasonable, students may not feel that their predictions must be correct.

Visual Imagery

Visual imagery is the ability to develop pictures in our minds as we read. It is often thought of as automatic. As accomplished readers, we picture where we are going when someone gives us directions, and we picture the appearance of a character from an author's description. It comes as a surprise to many teachers that students do not always have pictures in their minds when they read. Yet when students are taught to generate mental images while reading, their recall increases, as does their ability to make inferences, including predicting what will come next. Hibbing and Rankin-Erickson (2003) use a television metaphor to explain to struggling middle school readers how visual imagery should work. They describe a television screen that they "watch" as they read. They remind their students that the images in their mind should match the words in the text and, if they don't, the "channel should be switched" (p. 760). In other words, they use imagery as a monitor of comprehension. We have all had the experience of reading something and having our minds wander so that we get a very different image from what the text elicits. For example, you may be reading this chapter at home when your teenage son asks, "What's for dinner?" You immediately see the piping-hot lasagna that will come out of the oven in 20 minutes. The last sentence probably gave you a visual image and may have made your mouth water. In this example, the picture is related to the text, but you also may have been thinking about the many errands that you will need to run after school tomorrow.

So, other than explaining how imagery works to help students monitor comprehension, how exactly do we teach them to make pictures? Sometimes the pictures are made for them, as in picture books. The illustrations are there precisely to enrich a reader's understanding of the story. But what about a text that describes how something is built? Again, let us return to the "Busy Beaver" text. The second paragraph is a description of how the beaver works to make a home.

> First, the beaver must build a dam. It uses sticks, leaves, and mud to block a stream. The beaver uses its two front teeth to get the sticks. The animal uses its large flat tail to pack mud into place. A pond forms behind the dam. The beaver spends most of its life near this pond.

A very helpful picture for students is one of a partially completed dam holding back a stream (and maybe widening it) and a beaver swimming toward the dam with sticks in its teeth. This provides an illustration of exactly what the text stated, and it makes the meaning of the words much more vivid. It has been documented that poor readers move from text to picture to text as they read, using the pictures as an aid to understanding (Rusted & Coltheart, 1979). Watch a struggling reader scan the pages for clues that will help him or her understand a complex text.

So, if the pictures in a book are illustrative of the concepts that students are having difficulty with, great. But what if they aren't? Teachers can often make a quick sketch to illustrate what the author is explaining. Hibbing and Rankin-Erickson (2003) provide an example that helped a student understand the making of a lean-to in the book *Earthquake Terror* (Kehret, 1996).

After stripping off as many of the lower branches as he could, he laid the root end of the alder on top of the downed maple's trunk. He did the same thing with the other two alders. Next he gathered pine and cedar boughs. . . . He laid them on top of the alders, forming a crude roof. He placed the alder branches that he had removed across the far end of the shelter, propping them up to form a back wall. The shelter was shaped like half a tent, with an opening at one end. (pp. 46–48)

The teacher drew something like this:

As the teacher was drawing she was reading the description of the process. In this way the students could see how the verbal description represented the visual illustration. And you notice how the teacher didn't need to be an artist to draw this.

Another way to use illustrations is to have students draw as they listen to a story being read. These illustrations will be everything from a simple depiction of a scene to a student's emotional response. However, they will provide some view of what the student is getting from the story. With lots of examples and practice, students will learn how to develop images and their comprehension will improve.

KWL

KWL is a comprehension strategy for use with expository text (Ogle, 1986).

    K = What do you *know* about this topic?
    W = What do you *want* to know about it?
    L = What have you *learned* from reading this?

These prompts are written on either a chalkboard or a large piece of chart paper. The teacher asks the students what they already know about the topic of the expository reading. Then he or she writes the students' responses in the K column. The teacher then asks the students what they want to know about the topic and writes that in the W column. In a small intervention group this may be done quickly. This discussion also serves to activate the students' knowledge base (see Chapter 7) prior to reading. Depending on the length of the text, the teacher may fill in the L column as the students read or after they have completed the text. When instructing students who have comprehension difficulty, teachers should stop relatively frequently to fill in the L column but not so often that it breaks up comprehension or frustrates the students.

The resulting KWL chart can be used to assist students in writing a summary about what they have learned. Each student will likely know different things prior to reading and so will learn different things from the reading. Therefore, each student's summary should be somewhat different. That is, because the students know different material to begin with, they should take different information from the L column. Be sure to keep the KWL chart handy because it will take several sessions for the students to write their summaries. You can also have them develop their own KWL chart, take it back to the classroom, and write their summary there.

Reciprocal Teaching

Reciprocal teaching was developed and used with middle school students who were failing in content area subjects (Palinscar & Brown, 1984). Its initial use was with small groups (five students) reading expository text and analyzing it paragraph by paragraph, based on the four strategies noted below. Small groups work best, because students take turns being the teacher and leading the group through the application of the strategies. The name reciprocal teaching comes from the cycle of teacher instruction followed by students leading the process. The four strategies that students learn are clarifying, predicting, summarizing, and questioning.

1. Clarifying requires the students to investigate any words they don't understand. We have found that students embrace this strategy.
2. Predicting asks the student to use information from the title and, after each paragraph, to predict what the next paragraph will be about.
3. Summarizing instructs the students to develop a summary statement that captures the major point of the paragraph and to add only the few details necessary to support the main idea.
4. Questioning requires the students to ask a question a teacher might ask that covers the main point of the paragraph. Often this is simply a question that can be answered from the summary statement.

The rate of introducing the strategies depends on whether the students have practiced predicting and clarifying. Many teachers have students predict from titles and headings, so this strategy is usually quite easy to review and have students apply.

Clarifying goes beyond giving students permission to ask about words they don't understand and requires them to do so. These two strategies can easily be taught in one day if the students have experience with one of them. Summarizing is the hardest strategy. Anyone who has attempted to teach students how to determine the main idea of a paragraph understands how difficult it is for them to state it without expanding with many details. First, the teacher must explain what summarizing is: finding the most important statement in the paragraph without all the details that explain it. Then the teacher needs to model the thinking process used to get to the main idea. Let's begin with a relatively simple paragraph and see how the summarization process works. We have crossed out redundant parts, added a few connector words, and bolded the words we added.

> House cats, lions, and tigers are part of the same family **so.** ~~When animals are part of the same family~~ they are alike in many ways. ~~House cats are like lions and tigers in many ways too.~~ When kittens are born; they drink milk from their mothers. **and so do** Lions and tigers ~~drink milk from their mothers' too.~~ When kittens are born they have claws just like big cats. **And use them to keep away from enemies.** ~~Claws are used by lions, tigers, and kittens to help them keep away enemies.~~

So, our summary states:

> House cats, lions, and tigers are part of the same family **so** they are alike in many ways. When kittens are born, they drink milk from their mothers **and so do** lions and tigers. When kittens are born they have claws just like big cats **and use them** to keep away from enemies.

This paragraph is considered relatively simple because the sentences can be combined to write main ideas that result in a satisfactory summary.

Let's take another paragraph and follow the teacher's reasoning behind generating the summary:

Computers are machines that help solve problems, but they can't do anything without directions from humans. People give computers information. Then they tell them what to do with it. Computers cannot come up with any new information, but they can save much work and time.

The teacher could go through the paragraph clause by clause underlining the ideas related to the topic and crossing out the redundant and unimportant ones. For example, the teacher might read each clause and respond:

- *Computers are machines* ("I think that's important because it states directly what computers are, so I will underline that.")
- *that help solve problems,* ("Well, this tells what computers do, so right now I think that is important so I will underline it, but when we go back through my initial summary, I may change my mind and cross it out.")
- *but they can't do anything without directions from humans.* ("This sounds important, but I have to read the rest of the paragraph to see if it explains this more. If it does, then it may be part of the main idea.")
- *People give computers information.* ("This sounds like part of the way that people give directions, so it is redundant and I'm not going to keep it.")
- *Then they tell them what to do with it.* ("This is only repeating part of what the word *directions* means. It is redundant; I don't need it.")
- *Computers cannot come up with any new information . . .* ("This sounds like another way of saying that computers depend on people for information and instructions. I don't think it is necessary.")
- *but they can save much work and time.* ("Okay, this tells me something *new,* but I have to see how important it is to the overall paragraph.")

The teacher continues, "Now let's see what we have. Then we'll go back and see if I included things that aren't so important. *Computers are machines that help solve problems, but they can't do anything without directions from humans.* I think that's okay, but I could add the word *information* just before the word *directions* to include the information from the next sentence. Now, does our first sentence include the information in the next two sentences? *People give computers information. Then they tell them what to do with it.* It sure does! *Computers cannot come up with any new information, but they can save much work and time.* Well, the first clause just restates what we have already written, but the second one tells something new. Let's see if we can add it to our summary without making it too long. So far we have *Computers are machines that help solve problems, but they can't do anything without information and directions from humans.* Where can we put that they save humans work and time? How about in the first clause? *Computers are machines that solve problems and save work and time, but they can't do anything without information and directions from humans.* I think our summary has everything that is important and still is only one sentence!"

Questioning involves the students thinking of questions that a teacher might ask. In our experience, students simply put the summary ideas into a question. For example, in the first paragraph on cats, a question could be, How are house cats like lions and tigers? and for the computer selection, How do humans and computers help each other? We haven't seen questioning result in additional skills so we have omitted it and simply ask students to use the summary to make predictions about the next paragraph.

At this point you may be thinking, I don't have time to do all that for each paragraph! And we agree. However, to teach students how to summarize and find or write a main idea sentence takes that kind of cognitive modeling. You won't have to do it forever, but this type of instruction helps students who haven't a clue how you get from the detail of each paragraph to a summary—you know, the students who write a summary by copying the entire paragraph.

Reciprocal teaching has also been used with narrative text. The teacher decides what points in the story are appropriate for stopping and discussing, and at these points the comprehension strategies are applied. For example, prior to reading the story the students make predictions from the title and perhaps the illustration on the book cover. After reading to the first stopping point, the teacher asks if anyone needs anything clarified. After clarifying, the students proceed to summarizing. The summary requires a retelling of the important elements of the story thus far. (See Chapter 9 for a complete discussion of how to improve narrative retelling.) Then predictions of what will happen next are made. After the students read the entire story, they make a summary that includes the summary statements from each segment of text. Then they review the summary statements to see if any should be combined or omitted. The summary statements can also be written on a story map (see Chapter 9).

Thinking Aloud

In several of the strategies that we have discussed, the teacher says aloud what she or he is thinking while reading. In the reciprocal teaching section of this chapter, we provided a detailed example of a teacher thinking aloud as part of summarization instruction. These examples are designed to show students how good readers think as they read. Thinking aloud (TAL) is a strategy that can effectively be taught to students who are having difficulty comprehending (Bereiter & Bird, 1985). In most research studies, students have been asked to think aloud after each sentence of text. Although this might be useful initially to demonstrate possible types of think-aloud statements, it becomes cumbersome. A system that we have found appropriate is to designate sections of text to be read by writing "STOP" at several points. When the student reaches each STOP point, she or he is to think aloud. The location of stop points chosen by the teacher will vary depending on the complexity of the text and the length of the material. For example, in the *QRI-4* we had many more sentences between STOP points in an autobiography and a history text than in a science text. Let's look at material from a fourth-grade science text and see where effective stop points would be appropriate and the reason for their location.

Animal Structures for Survival

Animals need food, water, and protection from predators and from their environment to stay alive. Like plants, animals have adaptations that help them meet their basic needs. **STOP** *We chose this location because of the main idea statements included in the first two sentences of the paragraph.* These adaptations have been inherited through many generations. Animals with features that helped them survive reproduced more successfully than animals that did not have those features. **STOP** *This stop point occurs after the text explains the process of adaptation, which is central to the specific ideas that follow.* Some adaptations help animals get food or water. Other adaptations help animals survive in very cold or very warm weather. Adaptations also help keep them from becoming some other animal's food. **STOP** *This lists general types of adaptations.* Ducks have adaptations that help them survive on rivers, ponds, and lakes. Their feathers are covered with oil, which keeps them dry and protects them from the cold. Ducks also have webbed feet that make it easier to paddle through water. **STOP** *These sentences list specific duck adaptations and the functions they serve. The next sentences change the topic to spiders.*

Many kinds of spiders make silk. The garden spider spins a web and uses it to catch insects for food. It can also use its silk as protection from predators. When a predator is near, the spider can escape by sliding down the web. **STOP** *This paragraph is about spiders, so it is a logical place to put a STOP sign. The next paragraph of this text begins a discussion about camouflage.*

Notice that STOP signs were placed every two to three sentences in this fourth-grade science material. They marked either the introduction of an important concept or the ending of a paragraph that included only one topic. In a narrative text there would be many more sentences between stops because narratives tend to include information that is descriptive and not necessary to the plot line of the story.

Now we have some idea of where students should be when they think aloud. But what do students say when asked to do that? There are many examples of thinking aloud, and the research has focused more on the type of thinking than on its content (Caldwell & Leslie, 2004). In the *Qualitative Reading Inventory-4* we present eleven types or categories of think-aloud statements; however, we have found that only a few of them are used frequently by eighth graders. Here we list the three most common types of TAL with examples provided:

1. Paraphrasing/summarizing: The student restates what she or he has just read. "Animals need food, water, and protection from predators and from their environment to stay alive. Like plants, animals have adaptations that help them meet their basic needs." **STOP** Student paraphrases: *Animals all need the same things to survive: food, water, and protection.*

2. Making new meaning: Making an inference that connects segments of the text or that connects the reader's prior knowledge to information in the text. This may also involve the reader drawing conclusions from text statements. "These adaptations have been inherited through many generations. Animals with features that helped them survive reproduced more successfully than animals that did not have those features." **STOP** Student makes an inference: *So these adaptations seem to determine who survives. And those who survive pass on their genes.*

3. Questioning: Asking questions that reflect either that students understand or do not understand what they have read. "Ducks have adaptations that help them survive on rivers, ponds, and lakes. Their feathers are covered with oil, which keeps them dry and protects them from the cold. Ducks also have webbed feet that make it easier to paddle through water." **STOP** Student asks: *I wonder what kind of adaptations fish have made?*

Less frequently used types of think-aloud statements were reporting prior knowledge ("Oh, I learned about oil in the duck's feathers from my uncle who is a hunter"), noting that they understood what was read ("I get it now"), and identifying personally with information in the text ("If I were her mother I would . . .").

Whether a student uses one or more types of think-aloud statement is less important than whether what is said reflects his or her understanding of what was read. For example, if a student is reading, comes to a think-aloud point, and doesn't understand what she or he has read, then stating the lack of understanding is important. It tells us that the student was trying to construct meaning but was unable to. At this point it would be helpful if the teacher asked the student to clarify what she or he didn't understand. Why are think-alouds helpful? Probably for the reason cited on the first page of this chapter: Thinking aloud helps students engage in deep processing of text. It forces them to think!

What do students say when they think aloud? The following selection from the *Qualitative Reading Inventory-4* includes think-alouds generated by an excellent seventh-grade reader while reading an upper middle school science text (Leslie & Caldwell, 2006). Prior to being asked to think aloud, she listened to the examiner read a social studies text and model the eleven types of thinking aloud.

Structure of Matter Part 1
Everything on the earth is made of matter. Matter is anything that takes up space and has mass. Mass, measured in kilograms, is the amount of matter making up an object. **STOP** *I'm wondering why they always measure in kilograms, not like grams or anything else that's like normal?* (Question demonstrating understanding)

If you look around, you see examples of matter everywhere. In fact, you are made of matter. Your chair, pencil, and lunch are made of matter. The trees, buildings, and stars you see outside are also made of matter. Even the air you breathe is made of matter. **STOP** *I didn't know that air was made of matter. I knew it took up space, but I didn't think of it as matter.* (Related to prior knowledge)

Properties of Matter

Because the properties of matter are different, it's easy to tell them apart. For example, rocks are usually solid, hard, and heavy. Water is a clear liquid that sometimes turns into ice or steam. Wood and coal are solids that burn easily. All of the properties of matter fall into one of two categories. They are either physical properties or chemical properties. **STOP** *It's interesting how all things fall into one of two categories.* (Summarizing)

Physical Properties

Color, shape, texture, or hardness are all examples of the physical properties of matter. Other physical properties of matter include density, ductility, buoyancy, and solubility. Density is the amount of matter in a given volume of a substance. **STOP** *I'm wondering, what is volume? How do they figure out the set amount of volume it has?* (Question indicating lack of understanding) Buoyancy, which depends on density, is the ability of a substance to float in water. Ductility is the ability of a metal or other solid to be stretched, shaped, or bent without breaking. Solubility is the amount of a substance that will dissolve in another substance. **STOP** *It's interesting how they have all the different words. It's a little hard to understand.* (Noting lack of understanding)

Chemical Properties

Every substance has an important set of properties called its chemical properties. Chemical properties describe how a certain substance reacts chemically with other substances. For example, substances such as gasoline or wood combine easily with oxygen in a reaction that produces heat and light. Substances that combine with oxygen in this way are substances that burn or combust. One chemical property of these substances is that they are combustible. Other substances, such as helium gas, aren't combustible. **STOP** *I think it's interesting that they characterize it by can it be set on fire and stuff like that.* (Paraphrase)

Atoms

What makes each kind of matter different? Each kind of matter has a unique structure. Anything with a structure is built of smaller parts that serve as building blocks. **STOP** *It's interesting how anything, not just things you build, can be structures. When I think of structures, I think of things like a house, but everything can be a structure.* (Identifying personally)

What smaller parts is matter made of? All matter is made of very tiny particles called atoms. An atom is much smaller than the smallest speck of dust you can see with your eyes. Each kind of atom has specific properties that make it different from other kinds of atoms. An atom can't be broken down into smaller pieces without losing its properties. **STOP** *It's interesting how some things are so small they can't be broken up, and I'm wondering if they're so small, then how do you see them?* (Question indicating understanding)

This student was unusual in that she generated six different types of think-alouds:

- Asking questions that indicate understanding
- Relating what she read to her prior knowledge
- Summarizing and paraphrasing
- Identifying personally
- Reporting lack of understanding
- Asking questions that indicate a lack of understanding

As indicated earlier, most students choose one or two TAL types and use them throughout their reading. This student engaged deeply and creatively in text. When asked questions about what she read, she answered 60 percent of them correctly without referring to the passage, and when allowed to look back, she raised her comprehension score to 100 percent.

During *Qualitative Reading Inventory-3* (Leslie & Caldwell, 2001) piloting of the think-aloud material at the high school level, we noticed that students having difficulty understanding the text tended to look at the passage as they thought aloud. Generally, it appeared that they were using the opportunity to reread the text in hopes of understanding it better.

Discussion Cards

Every teacher hopes for active and lively discussion following reading, with student comments indicating understanding, involvement, and appreciation of text content. Nothing is more enjoyable and personally rewarding to a teacher than student observations that are relevant and perceptive and that demonstrate higher levels of thought. Unfortunately, this seldom happens with struggling readers. For many, problems with fluent word identification ensure that what they read does not make a lot of sense. Because of negative experiences with reading, many avoid any personal involvement with it. Any comments offered at all suggest a sad passivity.

Consider the following dialogue that is unfortunately typical of so many struggling readers. The teacher and her student have read the first few pages of *Simon's Surprise* (Staunton, 1986), a delightful story about a little boy who washes the family car while his parents are asleep.

> **Teacher:** I think this is going to be a good story. Micah, what do you think?
>
> **Micah:** I think so too.
>
> **Teacher:** Why do you think so?
>
> **Micah:** I don't know. I just do.
>
> **Teacher:** Do you think what Simon is doing is a good idea?
>
> **Micah:** Yes.
>
> **Teacher:** Why?
>
> **Micah:** Well it just is.
>
> **Teacher:** Would you do what Simon is doing?
>
> **Micah:** I don't know. Maybe.

Micah's answers are typical of many struggling readers who take refuge in vague answers that do not require much of their thought or involvement. Through prompting and offering hints and suggestions, a teacher can sometimes draw forth a more appropriate reaction. However, in that case the teacher does all the work and the eventual answer is really his or hers, not the student's. Struggling readers must learn to independently generate specific and thoughtful reactions to what they read. They must take ownership for their thoughts during reading and for the reactions they share with the teacher and their peers. Using discussion cards can help struggling readers to do this.

Discussion cards provide cues to the reader as to possible comments that they might make. Each student has a set of cards labeled with possible topics such as Character, Setting, and Problem. The student holds up a card to indicate what she or he wants to talk about. If it is the Character card, she or he must comment about the character in some way. If it is the Problem card, the comment must focus on a problem of one of the characters. The students can make any comment they wish as long as they can tie it to one of the cards. If a student makes an observation that is totally unrelated to the text (and many struggling readers initially do this), the inability to attach the comment to a card clearly illustrates that it is inappropriate. The cards thus play two roles: They suggest possible topics for students' comments, and they focus the discussion on the text.

There are different cards for narrative text and for expository text. Here are some possible topics for narrative discussion cards with representative comments:

Character. The Student May
- Identify a character as the main character or as important in some other way
- Comment on the character's actions
- Suggest a motivation for the character's actions

- Predict what will happen to the character
- Note a similarity between a character in the current selection and one in another selection

Setting. The Student May
- Indicate where and when the action occurs
- Comment on the importance of the setting to the events

Problem. The Student May
- Identify a problem of the main character or other characters
- Predict a problem that might occur later in the text
- Relate the problem to his or her own life or to another selection
- Offer suggestions for solving the problem

Solution. The Student May
- Identify the solution
- Question the solution in some way
- Indicate another solution
- Comment on the steps that led to the solution

Question. The Student May
- Ask a question about something that was not understood
- Ask a question about a character's actions
- Ask why an author wrote what he or she did

My Idea. The Student May
- Relate the text to his or her life
- Make a judgment about a character's actions
- Indicate like or dislike for the entire selection or for specific parts
- Indicate how she or he might write the text differently

These are the basic cards, and the teacher can certainly add others. A Prediction card indicates the student's intention to make a prediction about text content or to comment on a previous prediction. A Vocabulary card is for comments on a new word, a new meaning for a familiar word, or an unknown word. For a Text and Me card, the student ties the content of the selection to his or her own life. For Text and Text, she or he ties the selection to a previously read text. The Text and World card indicates an intention to tie the selection to a theme, world problem, or issue. Another possible card is Author Purpose, for the students' comments on why the author wrote what he or she did. We do not recommend using all of these topics. Choose a small number, four or five at most, that parallel your goals for the discussion.

You have probably noticed that the cards are not separate; there is overlap. For example, a student could hold up a Character card to offer positive or negative comments about a character's actions or intentions. The My Idea card could signal the same intention. The key issue is that the student can justify his or her choice of card if questioned.

Example of a Discussion Card Lesson

Joy regularly employed discussion cards for a group of five third graders who were reading at a first-grade level. Her goal was to teach them how to react to text in an active and relevant way. She used discussion cards for stories that she read to them as well as those they read themselves. They enjoyed manipulating the cards and holding them up to indicate what they were going to say. Even when responding to each other's questions and comments, they tended to hold up or point to a relevant card. For the following story, Joy used Character,

Problem, Solution, Question, and My Idea cards. Consider the difference between this discussion of *Simon's Surprise* with Micah's reactions that we described earlier.

> **Joy:**　Well, we have read a few pages. Let's stop and talk about the story. Hold up your cards to let us know what you want to say.

Joy waited while the students considered their card choices. When all had indicated their readiness, she initiated the discussion.

> **Joy:**　Altonia, I see the Character card.
>
> **Altonia:**　Simon's the character, and he's a little boy and maybe he's about five like my brother.
>
> **Joy:**　Altonia has identified the main character and made a good guess as to his age. Peter, you also held up the Character card.
>
> **Peter:**　If Simon's dad doesn't want him to wash the car, he's gonna get in big trouble. 'Cause if I do something my dad doesn't like he gets mad.
>
> **Joy:**　Good for you. The Character card fits, but you could have also held up the Problem card. You gave a good reason for a problem!
>
> **Josh:**　My dad takes our car to the car wash and I stay inside while all the water squirts around. I never washed our car like Simon is going to do, but I bet I could.
>
> **Joy:**　I didn't see what card you held up, Josh. Remember, first we hold up our card and then we talk.
>
> **Josh:**　I don't know what card would fit.
>
> **Joy:**　Can anyone help Josh?
>
> **Maria:**　I think it could be My Idea or maybe Character because he was talking about Simon.
>
> **Joy:**　I think so too because Josh is saying how he might be like Simon. Rowan, you have a question?
>
> **Rowan:**　Why did his father think it was raining?
>
> **Joy:**　Can anyone help Rowan with this?
>
> **Peter:**　That's easy to answer! The hose hit the window.
>
> **Maria:**　I got another question. How can a hose hiss? Snakes hiss, not hoses. Maybe it moves kinda like a snake.
>
> **Joy:**　Good for you. You asked a question and found an answer. Peter? You want to talk about a problem?
>
> **Peter:**　The windows are getting wet and that's not good. His dad will yell at him 'cause they'll get all spotted.
>
> **Altonia:**　(*Holding up the My Idea card*) It looks like Simon is having fun, and I think his father won't be mad about the windows. Maybe they will get as clean as the car.
>
> **Rowan:**　There's another problem. There are more bubbles than at the car wash. I think he must have used too much soap.

Joy then read several more pages showing the pictures to the students as she went along. The students immediately began to choose cards.

> **Joy:**　Rowan, you are holding up the Question card.
>
> **Rowan:**　What is he doing? What is on the end of the string?

Joy: Good question. Can anyone help Rowan?

Peter: It's a square thing like a dish scrubber. I know, it's a sponge!

Joy: Maria, do you want to share an idea?

Maria: I think Simon is pretty smart to figure out how to get on top of the car.

Altonia: (*Holding up the Problem card*) Here's a problem, and it's a big one. When his father sees what he did with his fishing rod, he'll be real mad.

Joy: I see Rowan is also waving the Problem card.

Rowan: Simon could climb up on the roof but he would probably fall off. So maybe this is the only way.

Joy: You have a problem, but you also have a solution. Good for you! Josh, what card are you holding up?

Josh: My Idea. I don't think Simon is smart scrubbing a tire with a toothbrush.

Maria: But it would get into the little holes better than a big brush.

Josh: It would take too long.

Maria: (*Holding up her My Idea card*) I think Simon is doing a good job.

Rowan: I think there's a problem. He better do a good job 'cause he's making a big mess, and that's going to be a problem when his father sees the yard.

Joy: Maria, I see you're still holding a My Idea card.

Maria: I think it's not easy what he is doing. A car is big, and there's a lot to polish.

Joy: Altonia, what is your question?

Altonia: I wonder why he didn't ask his friends to help.

Peter: (*Holding up the Character card*) Maybe he doesn't have any!

Rowan: I think he wanted to do it on his own!

Joy: Can anyone talk about the solution? We are almost at the end of the book.

Maria: (*Holding up the Solution card*) He finished the car and his parents are going to be really happy.

Josh: (*Pointing to the Solution card*) I think they're going to be mad.

Maria: (*Waving the Question card*) I bet they know he wanted to surprise them. Do you think it might be their birthday, one of them?

Altonia: Nah. I bet he just wanted to have fun and get wet. I like to play in water.

Peter: (*Pointing to the Problem card*) There is still a problem. All those bubbles! How will they go away? And all the mess.

Rowan: (*Showing the Character card*) That's why his father thinks it snowed. His father's a character in the story, isn't he?

Joy: He sure is.

Maria: (*Directed at Joy*) Why don't you hold up a card?

Joy: Okay. It's My Idea. I think his parents will like what he did. Now they don't have to do it.

Joy finished reading the story. On the last page Simon asks his parents if he is big enough to paint the house. The students laughed heartily and all started waving My Idea cards.

Maria: I liked this story a lot!

Joy: Remember to tell us why you liked it.

Maria: Because Simon was so smart. Even if he was little.

Josh: It was funny, all the things he used to wash the car. I liked thinking what his mother would say when she found out he used all her things.

Altonia: Oh wow! How can he paint the house? He better not! I think that would be a real mess!

Rowan: It was an okay story, but I like stories about girls better.

Peter: I think painting the house would be worse. If he slopped all the paint around, it wouldn't go away like bubbles do.

Rowan: What things from the house would he use?

The students then began to excitedly discuss how Simon would go about painting the house.

Varieties of Discussion Cards.   Some discussion cards can be used for both narrative and expository text, such as Vocabulary, Question, Prediction, My Idea, Text and Me, Text and Text, Text and World, and Author Purpose. However, some are specific to expository text: Topic, Main or Important Idea, Details, Text Structure, I Knew, and I Learned.

Topic. The Student May
- Identify the topic
- Comment on the importance of the topic
- Comment on interest in the topic

Main or Important Idea. The Student May
- Identify the main or important idea
- Comment on the importance of the idea
- Comment on the author's intention or perspective

Detail. The Student May
- Identify explanatory details
- Question how a detail is related to the topic

Text Structure. The Student May
- Identify a structure

I Knew. The Student May
- Comment on his or her knowledge of the topic
- Indicate something that was known prior to reading

I Learned. The Student May
- Indicate what she or he learned

There is quite a lot of variety in discussion cards, and you can probably think of some that we have not mentioned. This variety allows you to choose topics that match the levels and needs of your students. Obviously, Text and World is not appropriate for first or second graders, but we have found that children at these levels respond eagerly to My Idea.

Each student should have a set of cards. You can make the cards or have the students make them. Making the cards can be an effective lesson on how readers should react during reading. If students are allowed to keep the cards in their desk, locker, or book bag, always have additional sets available. Card packets can easily become lost.

You may put pictures or icons on the cards, especially for younger readers. A stick figure is appropriate for the Character card. A picture of a house and tree indicates setting.

You can signal Problem with a frown face and Solution with a light bulb. One clever teacher took pictures of her students, and each child had his or her picture carefully pasted on their own My Idea card.

Occasionally you will have a student who holds up the same card time after time. This is probably a student who, finding success with one kind of comment, is not willing to risk possible failure with a different one. She or he needs to be gently nudged to other cards. To do this, have the students spread out their cards face up. When they have held up a specific card and offered an appropriate comment, they must place that card face down. They cannot select it again until all cards have been used.

How much text should you read before asking the students to hold up their cards? That is up to you. It will certainly vary with the type of text and the age of the students. Discussion cards work well for an individual student, a small group, or an entire class. You can also pair students to decide on the card and the comment. One interesting benefit of discussion cards is that they force teachers to wait longer before calling on a student. Teacher wait time is very small!

Application to English Language Learners

Although all of the strategies described thus far in this chapter can be used to teach English language learners, there are additional programs that have either adapted existing comprehension strategies to ELLs or developed specific strategies for them.

The Scaffolded Reading Experience (SRE) is a "set of prereading, during-reading and postreading activities specifically designed to assist a particular group of students in successfully reading, understanding, learning from and enjoying a particular selection" (Fitzgerald & Graves, 2003, p. 99). This description should remind you of the Directed Reading–Thinking Activity described earlier in this chapter. The SRE is distinguished from the DRTA because it is a flexible plan designed for a specific group of students reading a particular text in a environment with explicit goals. For example, the group of students could include English language learners who will be reading a high school text on the characteristics of viruses, with the goal of a deep understanding of how viruses replicate and how they affect cells. The goal of this reading is to be able to summarize how the cycles of the virus determine their effect on the body. The planning for an SRE using this material would require extensive knowledge of the students' understanding of viruses and the term *replication*. All students probably wouldn't know these terms at a deep level, but assume that ELL students also wouldn't know the term *cycle* to mean process of change over time. The SRE would contain the following:

● Prereading activities: The teacher would explain the term *cycle* and provide examples that were relevant to the students' lives and also explained how *cycle* relates to living things (e.g., the cycle of a flowering plant). Next, the teacher would explain the process of replication as part of the prereading activity.

● During-reading activities: Having realized that all the students will need to read the material several times to understand it and that it may take the ELLs longer than native speakers of English, the teacher nonetheless decides that he or she wants all the students to read two parts of the text at the same time in order to demonstrate what the text was describing. The teacher recognizes that a visual representation of the life cycle of a virus is crucial to students' understanding of this content, so he or she would develop (or use the text if possible) a visual graphic depicting the stages in the life cycle of a virus and whether each stage marked an active or dormant phase. The teacher would use this visual to reinforce the content explained in the text by asking all students to read one section at the same time in order to demonstrate the visual aid. For example, the text says: "When a virus enters a host cell, it may immediately begin to replicate or it may remain dormant. If it begins to replicate it is in the lytic cycle. After much replication the host cell breaks apart, releasing new viruses." The graphic illustrates the attachment of the virus to the host cell (Step 1), how the virus's DNA communicates to the host cell to make new viruses (Step 2), and how the cell eventually breaks up to release viruses that can invade other hosts (Step 3). As the students read the portion of text that describes the cycle, the teacher would point out the steps illustrated on the graphic. Because there are two cycles in the life of a virus, the teacher would have developed two graphics listing the steps that the virus goes through. As the students came to each relevant section of text the teacher would model how the graphic represented what was stated in the text.

● Postreading activities: The goal of the reading was for the students to write a summary of the life cycle of a virus. The teacher could group students to work together to write the summary using the visual aids.

In contrast to this complex plan of prereading, during-reading, and postreading activities, an SRE for a simple story would be much shorter. It might begin with the teacher reading the beginning of a story to motivate the students to read for a particular purpose. The students would then read the selection silently, and after reading they would discuss their understanding of the character's motives. Regardless of the type of reading, the SRE requires the teacher to examine the knowledge of the learner, the complexity of the text, and what type of learning is required of the reader when developing the plan.

The SRE was designed to be used with both fiction and nonfiction text. However, there is one program that stands out as the most widely researched model of how to teach academic content to ELLs. Sheltered Instruction Observation Protocol (SIOP®) (Echevarria, Vogt, & Short, 2008) is "an approach for teaching content to ELLs in strategic ways that make the subject matter concepts comprehensible while promoting the students' English language development" (p. 5). Originally an observation instrument, the SIOP is now a professional development model "best suited for content based ESL courses and sheltered content courses that are a part of a program of studies for English learners, and form mainstream content courses with English learners and struggling readers" (p. 5).

In the most effective SIOP lessons, language *and* content objects are integrated into a subject area. There are six features of lesson preparation in the SIOP model:

● Content objectives clearly defined, displayed, and reviewed with students
● Language objectives clearly defined, displayed, and reviewed with students
● Content appropriate for the age and educational background of the students
● Supplementary materials intensively used (e.g., pictures, manipulatives, visuals such as graphs and charts, demonstrations)
● Adaptation of content to all levels of student proficiency (e.g., organizational aids such as graphic organizers and outlines, rewritten text that simplifies the language but not the content, etc.)
● Meaningful activities that integrate lesson concepts with language practice opportunities

As you read the brief description of the SIOP method you might think, "But that's just good instruction," and we agree. What is different about SIOP is that the lessons take into account the linguistic needs of English language learners. Referred to in the model as "Comprehensible Input," the ELL will be learning not only the content area vocabulary but also other words of the English language. For example, a lesson on buoyancy might also contain more general words such as *predict* or *calculate*. A competent SIOP teacher recognizes those words as potentially unknown to ELLs and is sure to explain them in the lesson. Echevarria, Vogt, and Short (2008) offer an example of three teachers teaching the concept of *buoyancy* to illustrate an effective application of the Comprehensible Input feature of the SIOP model. The most effective teacher enunciated clearly, slowed his normal rate of speech, adjusted the complexity of the sentences he used to explain the main concept, and used simple vocabulary to convey the concepts being taught.

Although SIOP is designed for entire class instruction, we cite it here because it reinforces the kinds of instruction that all students need, but especially those having difficulty with comprehension. Intervention in comprehension involves the content *and* the language of the text, the essential components of SIOP.

Application to Adolescent Learners

All too often, strong elementary school readers begin to struggle when faced with the complex texts and tasks required in middle and high school. Instruction in comprehension strategies can be effective under certain conditions. It is not enough to introduce and practice a specific strategy. Adolescent learners must understand which strategy is appropriate in any given situation; that is, they must learn to think metacognitively. It is also crucial that strategy instruction be differentiated according to specific content areas. Finding a main idea or summarizing may take on different forms in science as opposed to literature or social studies (Deshler et al., 2007). When working with struggling readers, we cannot emphasize enough that teachers must use a variety of texts when teaching a specific strategy. You cannot assume that a strategy taught in social studies material will automatically or easily transfer to science.

Reading guides can "influence comprehension ability by modeling the strategic processes proficient readers use as they tackle challenging new material" (McKenna, Davis, & Franks, 2004, p. 211). Such processes include posing questions, taking notes, and recognizing key concepts. McKenna, Davis, and Franks give several suggestions for creating an effective guide:

- Decide what is important for students to understand and construct the guide with the chapter or unit test in mind.
- Make the guide interesting and interactive. Ask students to construct or fill in diagrams, complete charts, answer questions in their own words, or offer their opinions on the content. Provide a lot of blank space for the students to complete tasks.
- Keep the guide to a reasonable length. It may only cover part of a chapter.
- Include page numbers and subheadings where students can locate the answers.
- Include comprehension aids; in other words, help students to comprehend the text. These can be quick definitions or synonyms for important terms, clarifying statements, paraphrases or summaries of difficult sections, comments linking new content with previous material, and notations about which material is very important and which can be skipped.
- Carefully review the guide before distributing to students to determine if it accomplishes your instructional purposes.
- Do not assume that students will be able to complete the guide without your assistance. This is especially true of struggling readers. Initially complete the guides as a class. Make transparencies of sections of the guide and model how to complete them by thinking aloud and encouraging student input. Move to a collaborative model when small groups or partners work together.

Previously we described two interactive lesson strategies: the SRE and SIOP models. Although the SRE can be used across the curriculum, SIOP was specifically designed for middle school and high school students learning academic content. Deshler et al. (2007) describe a variety of programs directed specifically at adolescent learners.

Response to Intervention

As we have mentioned throughout this book. Response to Intervention involves two primary components: research-based instruction and frequent monitoring of student progress. The strategies described in this chapter fall under the category of research-based and would be viable additions to tier 1, 2, or 3 instruction. Monitoring student progress involves assessments that occur on a frequent and weekly basis and are technically adequate (Mellard, 2005). What is a technically adequate assessment? At a basic level, this means that the assessment should match the instruction, or in other words, the assessment measures what was taught. How can a teacher do this? There are several ways.

First, if you are teaching a strategy such as summarizing, thinking aloud, or reciprocal teaching, you can monitor strategy use on the part of the student. That is, did the student construct an acceptable summary, offer appropriate think-aloud statements, or adequately employ clarifying, predicting, summarizing, or questioning during the reciprocal teaching lesson? Strategy monitoring can take the form of a simple rubric in which the teacher evaluates the student's performance in terms of the categories shown in Figure 12.1.

A second way of monitoring progress is to assess what the student learned as a result of engaging in the strategy. For example, if the lesson involved use of a reading guide, the teacher can construct a traditional test of content to ascertain student comprehension after working through a guide. If the lesson involved use of KWL or discussion cards, what content did the student learn as a result of this? Because monitoring in RTI is weekly or biweekly, such assessments of content knowledge would be relatively short and, of course, uniform. That is, if the teacher employs literal questions in week one, he or she should maintain that format throughout the monitoring process. If the teacher suddenly inserts inferential questions, a different level of comprehension is being assessed. It is wise to maintain a uniform format as well—that is, all open-ended constructed response questions or all multiple-choice selected-response questions. A change in question format can mask progress.

FIGURE 12.1   Strategy Monitoring Rubric

Student			Strategy			
Date	Observed	Not Observed	Adequate Performance	Somewhat Adequate Performance	Inadequate Performance	Comment

Summary

This chapter described a framework in which comprehension strategies can be taught and applied. We recommended what should be done prior to reading, during active reading, and after reading to facilitate both comprehension of text and the learning and application of strategies. All of the strategies can be taught using this framework. We then provided examples of the most effective comprehension strategies: Directed Reading–Thinking Activity, visual imagery, KWL, reciprocal teaching, think-alouds, and discussion cards. It should be noted that all of the strategies require active participation by the student as well as the teacher. These strategies can also be used with English language learners as long as the teacher is aware of the language proficiency of the students and adjusts his or her language accordingly. The Scaffolded Reading Experience (SRE) and the Sheltered Instruction Observation Protocol (SIOP) are instructional structures that offer support for ELLs. All of the strategies described in this chapter are equally effective for adolescent learners and have a research base that makes them applicable for Response to Intervention instruction.

REFERENCES AND RECOMMENDED READINGS

Information on Interactive Strategies

Barton, J., & Sawyer, D. M. (2003/2004). Our students are ready for this: Comprehension instruction in the elementary school. *The Reading Teacher, 57,* 334–347.

Block, C. C. (2004). *Teaching comprehension: The Comprehension Process Approach.* Boston: Allyn & Bacon.

Clark, K. F., & Graves, M. F. (2005). Scaffolding students' comprehension of text. *The Reading Teacher, 58,* 570–579.

Diehl, H. L. (2005). Snapshots of our journey to thoughtful literacy. *The Reading Teacher, 50,* 56–69.

Dowhower, S. (1999). Supporting a strategic stance in the classroom: A comprehension framework for helping teachers help students to be strategic. *The Reading Teacher, 52,* 672–688.

Gregg, M., & Sekeres, D. C. (2006). Supporting children's reading of expository text in the geography classroom. *The Reading Teacher, 60,* 102–110.

Hashey, J. M., & Connors, D. J. (2003). Learn from our journey: Reciprocal teaching action research. *The Reading Teacher, 57,* 224–232.

Hibbing, A. N., & Rankin-Erickson, J. L. (2003). A picture is worth 1000 words: Using visual images to improve comprehension for middle school struggling readers. *The Reading Teacher, 56,* 758–768.

Leslie, L., & Caldwell, J. (2001). *Qualitative reading inventory-3.* New York: Longman.

Leslie, L., & Caldwell, J. (2006). *Qualitative reading inventory-4.* Boston: Allyn & Bacon.

Liang, L. A., & Dole, J. A. (2006). Help with teaching reading comprehension: Comprehension instructional frameworks. *The Reading Teacher, 59,* 742–751.

Marcell, B. (2007). Traffic light reading: Fostering the independent usage of comprehension strategies with informational text. *The Reading Teacher, 60,* 778–781.

McMakin, M. C., & Witherell, N. L. (2005). Different routes to the same destination: Drawing conclusions with tiered graphic organizers. *The Reading Teacher, 58,* 242–252.

Mehigan, K. R. (2005). The strategy toolbox: A ladder to strategic teaching. *The Reading Teacher, 58,* 552–566.

Moss, B. (2005). Making a case and place for effective content area literacy instruction in the elementary grades. *The Reading Teacher, 59,* 46–55.

National Reading Panel. (2000). *Report of the National Reading Panel: Teaching children to read: An evidence-based assessment of scientific-based literature on reading and its implication for reading instruction.* Washington, DC: National Institute of Child Health and Human Development.

Neufeld, P. (2005/2006). Comprehension instruction in content area classes. *The Reading Teacher, 59,* 301–312.

Nokes, J. D., & Dole, J. A. (2004). Helping adolescent readers through explicit strategy instruction. In T. L. Jetton & J. A. Dole (Eds.), *Adolescent literacy research and practice* (pp. 162–182). New York: The Guilford Press.

Ogle, D. M. (1986). K-W-L: A teaching model that develops active reading of expository text. *The Reading Teacher, 39,* 564–570.

Palinscar, A. S., & Brown, A. L. (1984). Reciprocal teaching of comprehension-fostering and comprehension-monitoring activities. *Cognition and Instruction, 1,* 117–175.

Pressley, M. (2000). What should comprehension instruction be the instruction of? In M. Kamil, P. Mosenthal, P. D. Pearson, & R. Barr (Eds.), *Handbook of Reading Research* (Vol. III, pp. 545–561). Mahwah, NJ: Erlbaum.

Rusted, J., & Coltheart, V. (1979). The effect of pictures on the retention of novel words and prose passages. *Journal of Experimental Child Psychology, 28,* 516–524.

Sampson, M. B. (2002). Confirming a K-W-L: Considering the source. *The Reading Teacher, 55,* 528–532.

Schmidt, P. R., Gillen, S., Zollo, T. C., & Stone, R. (2002). Literacy learning and scientific inquiry: Children respond. *The Reading Teacher, 55,* 534–548.

Sekeres, D. C. (2006). Supporting children's reading of expository text in the geography classroom. *The Reading Teacher, 60,* 102–110.

Stauffer, R. (1975). *Directing the reading-thinking process.* New York: Harper & Row.

Wood, K. D., & Endres, C. (2004/2005). Motivating student interest with the Imagine, Elaborate, Predict and Confirm (IEPC) strategy. *The Reading Teacher, 58,* 348–357.

Think-Alouds

Bereiter, C., & Bird, M. (1985). Use of thinking aloud in identification and teaching of reading comprehension strategies. *Cognition and Instruction, 2,* 131–156.

Block, C. C., & Israel, S. E. (2004). The ABCs of performing highly effective think-alouds. *The Reading Teacher, 58,* 154–167.

Caldwell, J., & Leslie, L. (2004). Does proficiency in middle school reading assure proficiency in high school reading? The possible role of think-alouds. *Journal of Adolescent and Adult Literacy, 47,* 324–335.

Oster, L. (2001). Using the think-aloud for reading instruction. *The Reading Teacher, 55,* 64–69.

Smith, L. A. (2006). Think-aloud mysteries: Using structured sentence-by-sentence text passages to teach comprehension strategies. *The Reading Teacher, 59,* 764–773.

Walker, B. J. (2005). Thinking aloud: Struggling readers often require more than a model. *The Reading Teacher, 58,* 688–692.

Wilhelm, J. D. (2001). *Improving comprehension with think-aloud strategies.* New York: Scholastic.

English Language Learners

Echevarria, J., Vogt, M., & Short, D. J. (2008). *Making content comprehensible for English Learners: The SIOP Model* (3rd ed.). Boston: Pearson.

Fitzgerald, J., & Graves, M. F. (2003). Scaffolding reading experiences for multilingual classrooms. In G. G. Garcia (Ed.), *English Learners: Reaching the highest level of English literacy* (pp. 96–124). Newark, DE: International Reading Association.

Adolescent Learners

Chandler-Olcott, K., & Hinchman, K. A. (2005). *Tutoring adolescent literacy learners: A guide for volunteers.* New York: The Guilford Press.

Deshler, D. D., Palincsar, A. S., Biancarosa, G., & Nair, M. (2007). *Informed choices for struggling adolescent readers: A research-based guide to instructional programs and practices.* Newark, DE: International Reading Association.

McKenna. M. C. (2002). *Help for struggling readers: Strategies for grades 3–8.* New York: The Guilford Press.

McKenna, M. C., Davis, L. W., & Franks, S. (2004). Using reading guides with struggling readers in grades 3 and above. In R. L. McCormack & J. R. Paratore (Eds.), *After early intervention, then what? Teaching struggling readers in grades 3 and beyond* (pp. 208–216). Newark, DE: International Reading Association.

Underwood, T., & Pearson, P. D. (2004). Teaching struggling adolescent readers to comprehend what they read. In T. L. Jetton & J. A. Dole (Eds.), *Adolescent literacy research and practice* (pp. 135–161). New York: Guilford.

Response to Intervention

Lose, M. K. (2007). A child's response to intervention requires a responsive teacher of reading. *The Reading Teacher, 61,* 276–279.

Mellard, D. (2005). Responsiveness to intervention: Implementation in schools. Retrieved from www.schwablearning.org/articles.aspx?r=1057.

Student Literature

Kehret, P. (1996). *Earthquake terror.* New York: Cobblehill Books/Dutton.

Staunton, T. (1986). *Simon's surprise.* Toronto: Kids Can Press.

Pulling It All Together: Designing the Intervention Structure

Now it is time to pull everything together. You have your results from the informal reading inventory, and you have identified some general patterns in your students: word identification, fluency, comprehension, or a combination of these. You probably have observed some used or misused decoding strategies. You know whether or not your students are fluent and expressive readers, and you probably have noted some strengths or weaknesses in comprehension, such as inability to retell, difficulty in locating answers to questions, and problems with unfamiliar or expository text. You have an estimate of the severity of your students' problems based on the difference between their highest instructional reading levels or their listening comprehension levels and their classroom grade placements. On the basis of an informal reading inventory and careful observation of your students' performance, you have designed objectives for your intervention sessions.

You know how much time your school or district and your schedule will allow you to work with the students. You probably have already decided if you will form small groups for intervention instruction, spend time with students in the regular classroom, or work with an individual. It is now time to design your intervention structure—the consistent framework that guides your instruction. Depending on the needs of your students, you may emphasize certain instructional components over others. However, you will maintain a balanced focus on the entire reading process—on word identification, fluency, and comprehension. It is also time to decide on the specific instructional strategies that you will employ within each component of your structure.

There are no exact and rigid guidelines for designing the intervention structure. Your professional expertise and your knowledge of your students are your most important tools. Because we have always recommended modeling as an effective learning device, we provide some models that may help you to design effective interventions. Our models are all for groups for several reasons. First, a structure for a group can easily be adapted to an individual, but the reverse is not always true. Second, we suspect that many of you will need to provide intervention instruction to groups because of budget and time constraints. Third, excellent models for individual intervention structures were presented in Chapter 3, such as Reading Recovery, Early Steps, and Book Buddies.

Primary Level

Group Pullout: Basic Consonant Sounds

In mid-December, first- and second-grade teachers approached the school's reading specialist, Francisco, concerned that several of their students did not know the sounds for all of the consonants. They asked if he could take these children to the resource room and provide instruction in consonant sound knowledge. First, Francisco analyzed the students' phonemic awareness and found that all of them could rhyme and could isolate the first phoneme in a word (e.g., *p* in *pat*). He also learned that the students had knowledge of the most common consonants, such as /r/, /s/, /t/, /n/, and /m/, although some of them confused the /m/ and /n/ sounds.

There were enough students to form two small groups and, although the skills of the first and second graders were very similar, Francisco grouped by grade level. He wanted to avoid the negative stigma that can occur when older students are put into instructional groups with younger children. Grouping by grade also made it easier for the classroom teachers to manage their daily schedules. The format for each 30-minute instructional period was as follows:

Ten Minutes: Review of Past Learning

- Reread the story or poem that was used to teach unknown consonants. This was generally a brief but engaging selection. Francisco and the students usually reread the selection in a shared reading format (Chapter 5).
- Remind the students of the previously learned sounds and isolate the words that were used to illustrate them.
- Have the students work in pairs to choose picture cards that represent the consonant sound or sounds being reviewed (see below). Have each pair isolate the first sound.
- Ask the students to write the letter that represents the sound. Then have them turn their picture over to self-check (see below).
- Reinforce the sound by an alliteration activity such as, "I see something that starts with the /s/ sound and it is . . ."

Fifteen Minutes: New Learning

- Read a new story or poem that includes the consonant sound or sounds to be learned. Sometimes Francisco read this selection to the students. At other times, he employed different oral reading techniques (Chapter 6). Francisco and the students briefly talked about the selection and their reactions to it.

- Isolate the new consonant sound.
- Present four or five pictures and model sorting them according to the first sound heard in the name of the picture. Francisco selected his pictures from a variety of sources, such as magazines, newspapers, old workbooks, and the like. His primary criterion for selection was clarity and size. A picture had to be clear enough to represent one main object or action and small enough to fit on a large index card. Francisco found many suitable pictures from advertising supplements in the Sunday papers.
- Distribute additional pictures. After modeling the process, Francisco gave the students additional pictures and asked them to sort by the first consonant sound.
- Have students choose a picture. After sorting, each student chose a picture that he or she liked to represent the consonant sound focused on during this session.
- Make picture–letter cards. The students pasted the picture on one side of a large index card and printed the letter on the other side.

Five Minutes: Sharing

- Have each student say the name of the picture that she or he chose to represent the consonant sound. Then have the student say only the first sound in the word.
- Have the students add the new card to their store of picture cards filed in a box or large envelope that is kept in the resource room for future review.

Matching Assessment to a Balanced Intervention Structure.   Observation of their students prompted first and second grade teachers to seek the help of their reading specialist, Francisco. His assessment of the first and second graders' consonant knowledge led to two groups of students being temporarily pulled out of the regular classroom for additional instruction in consonant sounds. Francisco used short, motivating selections that captured the interest of the students. He focused on the meaning of these texts before using them to illustrate letter–sound relationships. Francisco incorporated fluency in his lessons through shared reading and other oral reading techniques. He included the writing of letters to enhance understanding of letter–sound relationships as well. Francisco's goal was to return the students to the classroom within one month's time, and he met that goal.

Group Pullout: Fluency

Several third-grade teachers complained to Gloria, the school reading specialist, that some students were not involved during silent reading time. Whether they chose their own book or accepted one chosen for them by the teacher, they soon lost interest. Often this lack of interest translated into behavior problems when they attempted to involve other students in alleviating their boredom. Gloria asked the teachers to identify the worst offenders. She asked those students to orally read a grade level selection on an informal reading inventory. Although they achieved at an instructional level for word identification and comprehension, their reading rate was slow and often lacked expression. When Gloria asked them to read silently, she noted that they moved their lips as they did so and that their silent reading rate was similar to their oral rate. Gloria determined that they had not yet made a successful transition to fluent silent reading and therefore found silent reading to be both unprofitable and time consuming.

   Gloria realized that silent reading would have little attraction for these students until they became more fluent, so she arranged to come to the classroom daily at silent reading time. Gloria chose some enticing pieces of children's literature. When she arrived in the classroom, she presented one to the students in a motivating way, sharing her own excitement at what promised to be a wonderful reading experience. She then asked who would like to read it with her. Most students eagerly raised their hands. Gloria chose a small group of four or five students and made certain that several of the struggling readers were included. She did this in order to avoid singling out these children in a possibly negative way. Because Gloria was a daily visitor to the class, she was eventually able to work with all of the struggling readers. There were two students who never volunteered to join Gloria's group. However, the enthusiasm of the class, the good reports of the sessions that followed, and Gloria's own winning personality soon drew them into the process. The group then went to Gloria's office, and Gloria devised the following structure:

Fifteen Minutes
- Read the text or parts of it to the students. Gloria kept the group small so they could cluster around her and view the text. She made certain that each student had an opportunity to see the pages either during or after she read.
- Discuss the reading using a think-aloud technique (Chapter 12). Gloria directed the technique by stopping at certain times to ask for comments.

Fifteen Minutes
- Reread certain parts orally using a shared or echo format (Chapter 6). If Gloria had only a single copy of the book, she duplicated several pages, being careful to destroy them after the session in order to follow copyright guidelines. Sometimes she alternated the oral reading. She and two students read, and the others listened. Then other students took a turn.
- Briefly discuss why students might want to read this book on their own. Gloria continually stressed that good readers always reread stories and selections that they especially like.

Gloria then returned the students to their classroom but left the book for them to read on their own. She varied the selection each day. Sometimes she worked with a poem. Sometimes she read part of a book and left it for the students to finish on their own. She often used very easy but motivating pieces of children's literature. Because everyone in the group enjoyed such selections, there was no stigma attached to choosing them for silent reading. The book-reading sessions became immensely popular with the third graders, and all wanted to participate. Gloria made certain that everyone had a chance to take part, but she was careful to always include the students who most needed to develop fluency. The success of this intervention rested with her careful and creative choice of materials that were both motivating and at an appropriate reading level. It also rested with making the books available in the classroom so students could reread them, which they eagerly did. In fact, she found that she had to provide multiple copies because they were so popular.

Matching Assessment to a Balanced Intervention Structure. Gloria used a combination of oral and silent reading of informal reading inventory selections to determine that her students lacked silent reading fluency. She maintained a balanced approach by focusing on developing fluency but using the think-aloud procedure to emphasize meaning.

In Class: Phonological Awareness

During the first few weeks of the year, the first-grade teachers sought the help of Sarah, the reading specialist. They had reviewed the consonant sounds with their students and found that everyone knew them. However, before beginning to teach decoding by analogy, they asked Sarah to assess the students' rhyming skills. She found three or four students in each classroom who did not understand the concept of rhyme. When told of this, the teachers asked Sarah to come into their classrooms for 15 minutes each day to teach the auditory concept of rhyme to these children (Chapter 4). They wanted her to come into the classroom because, after the minilessons on rhyming, the children could then join the whole class in listening to poetry or engaging in rhyming activities. Sarah would stay with the group during this time to help them understand and more fully participate. With Sarah as an active participant, the teachers read poetry to different groups, listened to students repeatedly read poetry (Chapter 5), and played rhyming games. In these sessions, Sarah worked with all students but whenever possible focused on those who most needed her attention.

Fifteen Minutes

- Explain the concept of rhyme, giving examples and nonexamples.
- Model sorting pictures by rhyming sounds.
- Have the students sort pictures by rhyming sounds either in pairs or alone. Sarah distributed only five or six pictures at a time, and she included some that began with the same letter but did not rhyme.
- Say two words and ask the students if they rhyme.
- Say a word and ask each student to offer a word that rhymes with it.

Matching Assessment to a Balanced Intervention Structure.   Sarah assessed the first-grade students' knowledge of rhyme and reported the results to the classroom teachers. They asked her to come into their classrooms to support their ongoing instruction. As she taught the children, she continually assessed their understanding and ended her instruction when all students understood the concept of rhyme more completely.

In Class: Narrative Retelling

Alan, the third-grade teacher, was concerned when a group of his students could not discuss stories productively. It seemed to him that the group's discussions were "all over the place" and lacked sequence and purpose. Maria, the school reading specialist, assessed the comprehension of individual students in the group, paying particular attention to their retelling abilities. She found that each student was very good at retelling many events of the story but that his or her sequence of retelling did not coincide with the character's goal and problem. Maria believed that instruction in story structure was in order. She and Alan discussed the situation and decided that she would come into the classroom to teach the elements of a story. He thought that all of his students would benefit from her instruction, with those who already understood story structure using the review to apply their knowledge to writing stories. Maria decided she would begin with a review of the basic elements and then proceed to the explanation of how characters' conflicting goals drive the action in the story (Chapter 9). After each lesson on story elements, Maria met with the group that she had assessed to guide their application of story elements to their retelling of the stories they were reading in class. Meanwhile, Alan monitored the other groups' discussions to see how Maria's instruction affected them.

Lesson 1

Five minutes

- Explain the purpose of knowing story elements.
- Read a very simple story that students already know, such as the "Three Little Pigs" or "Three Billy Goats Gruff."

Fifteen minutes

- Explain the concepts of character, setting, and goal as explained (Chapter 9). Emphasize how to determine who the main character is so that his or her goal will be obvious. Refer back to the story for examples of these three elements. Demonstrate the use of a story map (see Chapter 9), and write in the characters, setting, and goal using the simple story that was read.
- Have each group of students read a new story at their instructional level that has a clear story structure. They should cooperatively decide the main character, the setting, and, if it is important to the story, the main character's goal.

Lesson 2

Three minutes

● Review the elements previously taught. Repeat the purpose for learning story elements.

Fifteen minutes

● Explain the problem, events, and resolution, returning to the simple story again as an example of these elements. Explain the relationship between the goal and problem and which events are important to the problem resolution. Maria was careful to model only important events that led directly from the problem to the resolution. Complete the story map began during lesson 1 by writing in the problem, important events, and resolution.

● Have the students return to the book that they read during lesson 1 and discuss the goal, problem, important events, and resolution. Write their final decisions on these elements on the story map. Maria continued to guide the students, whom she assessed through the application of the story elements to the new story.

Lesson 3

Three minutes

● Briefly review all of the elements and repeat the purpose for learning story elements.

Fifteen minutes

● Meet with the small group to apply the elements to a new story. Read the story to the point at which the main character's goal is clear. Then have the students stop and fill in their story maps. Continue reading until another appropriate stopping place, discuss what has happened, and ask the students to fill out their maps.

Matching Assessment to a Balanced Intervention Structure.   Alan and Maria worked together to see how the needs of a group of students could be met within the classroom. Maria confirmed that the students' retellings lacked organization and awareness of story structure. She came to the class and taught the elements of a simple story, using an example of a well-known children's selection. While she worked with the students who most needed the instruction, Alan monitored the application of story structure in the discussions of the other groups. He kept notes on his impressions of the cohesiveness of the discussions. Because this collaborative structure worked so well, Alan and Maria made plans to continue it. They decided to illustrate how the choice of a main character influences identification of the goal, problem, and resolution and how characters often have competing goals (Chapter 9). Alan and Maria also planned to model the application of this knowledge to writing stories.

Intermediate Level

Group Pullout: Word Identification

Elaine, the school's reading teacher, worked with five fourth-grade students. Two were reading at an instructional first-grade level for familiar narrative text, and the remaining three were at an instructional second-grade level. The students were relatively similar in that decoding was a slow, painful, and often frustrating process for them. We could describe them as primarily alphabetic readers who used partial sound cues, usually the beginnings of words, to decode unknown words. The students did have a store of automatically recognized sight words, so they were not attempting to decode everything. However, with no real strategy for unlocking the pronunciation of unfamiliar or forgotten words, their fluency was hampered by frequent pauses to deal with new ones. This in turn impaired their comprehension; their preoccupation with word identification left no cognitive room for understanding the text. As you can well imagine, they were not able to handle their classroom reading assignments, which at that level contained quite a few unfamiliar words. This frustration led to acting out by two of the students and sullen withdrawal by the others.

Elaine had four 40-minute periods a week to devote to the students. She preferred meeting with them in their regular classroom, but this was not possible as the students were from three different classes, the class schedules were quite different, and Elaine's time was limited. Therefore she prepared a pullout session in the library media center. Elaine realized that the students needed to learn strategies for pronouncing words beyond attention to initial consonants. She also understood that if she did not emphasize meaning, the students would probably become even more focused on saying words. She formed her structure and chose her activities as follows:

Five Minutes

- Orally reread sections of text from the previous day in a shared-reading format (Chapter 5). Offer the students the opportunity to read in pairs or alone.

Ten Minutes

- Work on decoding by analogy using known words with familiar spelling patterns to decode unfamiliar words (Chapter 5).

Five Minutes

- Sort words according to spelling patterns (Chapter 5).

Twenty Minutes

- Read a new selection. Sometimes Elaine read while the students followed along; sometimes they read together in a shared oral format. Using echo reading, they often reread important, exciting, or favorite parts (Chapter 6). They also silently reread.
- Set expectations for content before and during reading by asking and answering content-free questions (Chapter 11). Elaine also used discussion cards (Chapter 12) as cues for talking about the text.
- Use highly motivating but short selections that can reasonably be completed in 15 minutes. Sometimes Elaine stretched one short selection across three intervention sessions. For these students, Elaine chose selections about unusual animals or sports figures. She also chose humorous pieces of children's literature. The students all had younger siblings, and she encouraged them to take the books home to read to them. Some selections were often at a higher level than second grade because Elaine had difficulty finding material that the students did not disdain as "baby stuff." However, with Elaine reading to and with them, they were able to apply content-free questioning strategies in higher-level selections (see Chapter 11).
- End the lesson by having students talk about what they learned about reading, the strategies they employed, and the things they did well. Elaine stressed the students' improvement in dealing with long words and in making meaning.

Elaine used this structure for three of the four sessions. Because she was concerned that the students were missing so much by not being able to read the selections used in their classrooms, she read these selections to them in the fourth session. She combined the reading of important parts with judicious summaries of others and involved the students with content-free questions or discussion cards. She attempted to do this prior to or concurrent with the teacher's presentation of the material so the students could participate in classroom discussion if they chose. Unfortunately, the three classrooms did not always use the same selections, but Elaine attempted to balance readings from each. Because all three classrooms used the same social studies and science textbooks, Elaine often chose these for reading to the students.

Matching Assessment to a Balanced Intervention Structure.   Results from the informal reading inventory indicated that effective word identification was the primary problem leading to poor comprehension. Miscue analysis showed that the students used the beginning of words as their primary approach to decoding. Because of this, Elaine devoted 15 minutes to a focus on spelling patterns and decoding by analogy in order to move the students to a more effective decoding strategy. She employed various oral reading activities to maintain and increase fluency. The students spent five minutes rereading the selection from the previous lesson and orally read the new selection using a variety of formats. Elaine used content-free questions and discussion cards in order to focus on meaning. She wanted the students to learn relatively simple strategies that they could apply independently during their own reading. Finally, because the students were painfully aware of their lack of success in their regular classrooms, Elaine read selections to them so they could participate more in class activities. When she did this, she used the same comprehension strategies, such as content-free questioning, to initiate discussion and to focus on the importance of making meaning.

In Class: Word Identification and Fluency

Peter, the school reading specialist, was contacted by a fifth-grade teacher who was concerned about a small group of six students who seemed to experience difficulty with word pronunciation. Peter asked each student to orally read an informal reading inventory word list at their grade level. He noted that they did not immediately pronounce words; instead, most words were either pronounced after a lengthy delay or mispronounced. This same pattern was evident when the students read a grade level selection. Their reading rate was slow, they lacked expression, and their comprehension was poor. However, when Peter read another selection to them, their comprehension was satisfactory. Peter hypothesized that comprehension was not a major issue but that the students lacked strategies for pronouncing longer and unfamiliar words.

Peter discussed the matter with the classroom teacher, and the two set up daily 20-minute minilessons focusing on three components: working with big words, learning new word meanings, and practicing for a reader's theater performance (Chapter 6). All students in the class participated in one lesson each day. After rotating through the three lessons, they began the cycle over again. Peter taught the lesson on working with big words, the teacher handled the vocabulary lesson, and an aide worked with performance reading. Peter set up his 20-minute lesson as follows:

Two Minutes
- Review the strategy for decoding by analogy.
- Model the process of using known words to pronounce unknown ones. For example, Peter used *club, dish,* and *her* to pronounce *publisher.*

Ten Minutes
- Work with students to decode unknown words.
- Choose words from the students' textbooks.

Eight Minutes
- Work with the meaning of prefixes, suffixes, and foreign roots.
- Generate words containing a specific affix, such as those containing the foreign root *graph.*
- Place the list in a prominent place in the classroom so each group can see the work of the others.

Matching Assessment to a Balanced Intervention Structure.   Peter verified word pronunciation and fluency difficulties through an informal reading inventory using the grade level word list and two grade level selections. He focused his lesson on strategies for decoding longer words, decoding by analogy, and the use of affixes. By working with the teacher to set up minilessons and by keeping the lessons in the classroom, the six students were not singled out in any way. Because everyone in the class participated in the 20-minute lessons, the students learned from each other. All profited from a focus on big words, including students who had not demonstrated any serious problems with word identification. The use of reader's theater addressed the fluency issue. Peter worked with the aide to choose appropriate parts for the six students. He and the teacher maintained a balance in the minilessons by focusing on understanding the meanings of new words.

In Class: Expository Comprehension

Three fifth-grade teachers complained to Jon, the school reading specialist, that many students did not seem interested in social studies and received extremely poor grades on unit tests. However, they enjoyed reading trade books and participated eagerly in self-selected silent reading. Jon worked with several of these students and asked them to read two grade level informal reading inventory selections: one narrative and one expository. The students achieved at an instructional level for narrative, but did poorly on expository, complaining that it was hard and boring. They were able to retell the narrative, but their expository retellings were sparse and disjointed. Jon hypothesized that a similar pattern might well be found in the other students and that unfamiliarity with exposition could be the culprit.

Jon suggested to the teachers that the students probably did not know how to handle expository text and that the strategies they applied in narrative material did not carry over to their textbooks. He also hypothesized that the large number of unfamiliar words might be another factor. Jon presented several possible reading strategies to the teachers, and they decided that teaching expository structure using idea maps was worth a try, as well as focusing on prefixes, suffixes, and roots as guides to word meaning. Jon agreed to model the strategies for the students and to support the teachers in implementing idea maps. He agreed to come regularly to their classes during social studies instruction, and the teachers adjusted their schedules so that Jon could visit each classroom. Jon and the teachers decided that two days a week would be devoted to idea maps (Chapter 10). The teachers were concerned that a focus on idea maps might slow down their coverage of the curriculum, but Jon assured them that students would not only learn the strategy but also learn the content at the same time. The teachers selected the segments that they felt were important for Jon to emphasize.

Social studies instruction took about 45 minutes, so Jon planned the following sequence for his twice-weekly visits:

Two Minutes

- Read a short segment of the social studies text in a shared-reading format to ensure that all students have access to the text and receive modeling of good expressive reading.

Twelve Minutes

- Identify the expository structure.
- Have students fill out idea maps. Initially Jon did this on an overhead transparency with input from the students. Eventually, the students filled out their own maps in small groups, in pairs, and finally individually.

Six Minutes

- Have students identify unfamiliar words.
- If the word contains an affix, point out how this helps determine meaning.
- Generate other words with the same affix.
- Determine possible meaning from context, text aids, or a dictionary.

Jon repeated the 20-minute sequence with another segment of text. Once all of the expository patterns had been introduced, he grouped the students and asked the groups to each identify a relevant pattern on their own and justify their choice by filling out a map.

Matching Assessment to a Balanced Intervention Structure.   Jon used an informal reading inventory to determine that students were having difficulty comprehending expository material. With teacher input, he chose idea maps as his primary instructional strategy and devoted most of the instructional time to them. However, he maintained a balance by focusing on word meanings during each lesson and by modeling expressive and fluent oral reading.

Middle Level

Group Pullout: Expository Comprehension

Seven sixth-grade students from different classrooms were referred to Alycia, the school reading specialist, because of low achievement in content area subjects. The referring teachers were puzzled by this because all seven were accurate and relatively fluent oral readers. When Alycia administered an informal reading inventory, she noted that the students' instructional word identification levels were one or two levels higher than their instructional comprehension levels. For example, one student was able to effectively pronounce words at a sixth-grade level but could comprehend only at a fourth-grade level. Similar patterns were present for the other students. In addition, the students were often unable to define or explain words that they accurately pronounced. Alycia hypothesized that these students regarded reading primarily as accurate word pronunciation, and an informal interview confirmed this. When asked to define the reading process, all mentioned saying words as the principal component.

Alycia met with the students three times a week during their 50-minute scheduled study time. She realized that they needed to learn and practice comprehension strategies that they could transfer to their science and social studies reading. She formed her structure as follows:

Ten Minutes
- Silently skim the text that was read the previous day. Help students to differentiate skimming from a first reading.
- Answer questions on the text using the QARs strategy (Chapter 11).

Twenty Minutes
- Use the Expository Expectation Grid (Chapter 10) as a pre- and postreading strategy.
- Silently read a new selection in segments.
- Fill in the grid together.

Five Minutes
- Use the Expository Expectation Grid to construct a short oral summary.

Ten Minutes
- Have students select words whose meanings are unknown.
- Use affixes, context, and text aids to define the unknown words.
- Discuss the meaning of the words in relation to the students' lives.

Five Minutes
- Have students evaluate their own performance.

- Using a short checklist, rate their performance as good, okay, or needs work on each strategy: QARs, Expository Expectation Grid, and vocabulary study.

Matching Assessment to a Balanced Intervention Structure.   Alycia's use of the informal reading inventory suggested that comprehension was an issue for the students. Because of their skill in word pronunciation, they tended to focus on this and had few strategies for constructing meaning. Alycia emphasized two comprehension strategies: QARs and the Expository Expectation Grid. She also maintained a balance by having the students skim previously read text, a strategy that they had not used extensively. In addition, Alycia emphasized word study by teaching the students how to determine and remember word meanings.

In Class: Concept Development and Comprehension

Chris, a middle school teacher, was concerned that his students did not have much experience with places in the United States other than their hometown and neighborhood. The social studies curriculum for seventh grade involved the settling of the United States, and he felt that his students would have difficulty relating to the concepts of different time periods and locations and, particularly, to the concept of motivation for moving to new area. He consulted with the reading specialist, Joan, to discuss how best to meet the needs of his students. Joan engaged several of the students in informal conversation during their scheduled study and library periods. She discovered that they had few ideas about why people choose to live where they do and very sketchy notions of why immigrants came to the United States. After some discussion, Joan and Chris decided to have his 27 students interview their adult relatives to determine why they live where they do. In other words, they were to interview their parents and grandparents to find out the history behind their current homes and why they may have lived in other locations in the past. The concept that Chris hoped would emerge from the interviews was that people live where they do because of their jobs, other opportunities, and family needs.

The focus of the assigned interview was Why do we live where we do? The students interviewed their family members and wrote down their answers to the following questions:

1. When did your family move to this town?
2. Why did your family move here?
3. Why does your family continue to live here?
4. What would cause your family to move somewhere else?
5. If other members of your family live elsewhere, why do they live there?

Day One in the Classroom

Fifteen minutes

- Chris put the students into cooperative groups of three to discuss the answers to their questions one at a time. Each group had a piece of chart paper containing the interview questions. One of the students wrote down what each student's family members said in response to the questions; another looked for commonalities among the answers; and a third prepared to report these commonalities to other groups. Joan joined Chris in the classroom, and the two of them moved around facilitating group interactions.

Fifteen minutes

- After the groups completed their work, they merged into three large groups. The student reporter in each large group shared the ways in which answers to interview questions were alike. The three groups prepared a combined report to be presented to the entire class. Chris and Joan moved around facilitating the process, clarifying issues, and answering questions.

Ten minutes

● The three large groups reported their findings to the whole class. Chris facilitated the reporting process, and Joan wrote the common findings under each question. Then Chris, Joan, and the class looked for categories in which to classify the information and make a semantic map (Chapter 7). They identified the following categories: climate and land, jobs, other opportunities, and family issues.

Day Two in the Classroom

Ten minutes

● Chris took the four categories that had been generated the preceding day and made a conceptual map on chart paper. Under each category, he listed some reasons that his students' families live where they do. Then he used this information to make the bridge between his students' families and the reasons that people in the United States settled the West.

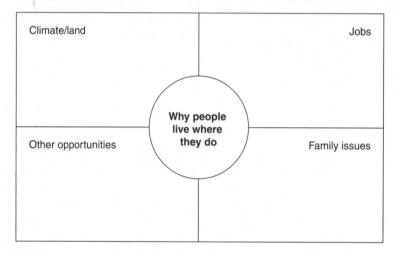

Twenty minutes

● Chris distributed copies of the semantic map to the original cooperative groups of three. As they read the new material, he asked them to determine why western pioneers left their homes and settled where they did and to record this information on their map. Chris divided the textbook reading into manageable segments. Students read to an assigned point and then stopped to discuss what they had read and to fill in the map. Throughout the process, Joan helped individual students in clarifying new words, answering questions, and assessing understanding.

Ten minutes

● Following this, the small groups merged into larger groups and compared their maps. Then, as a whole class, they discussed the beginnings of the westward movement in terms of what they had learned about their own families. As before, Chris led the discussion and Joan filled in the class semantic map that was then placed in a prominent part of the room.

Matching Assessment to a Balanced Intervention Structure. His knowledge of his students led Chris to meet with Joan, the reading specialist, who informally validated his concerns about their limited background knowledge. To remedy this, Chris and Joan set up a cooperative grouping structure in which small groups of students reported on answers to the family questionnaire and noted commonalities between them. Chris maintained a fast-paced but focused discussion activity in which small groups merged into larger groups that then reported to the entire class. Chris used the interview answers to set up categories for a semantic map, which was used to guide the students' reading.

Generic Intervention Plan

Since the publication of the first edition of this book, many individuals have contacted us and asked for an overall structure for their intervention lessons, as seen by the following typical comments and questions:

> "All the lesson plans in Chapters 3 and 13 look good but is there one that will fit most situations? I don't have time to design a separate structure for each group of kids."

> "Is there a generic template I can follow in designing my lessons?"

> "I love all the strategies but can you help me fit them into a plan? I tend to focus on a strategy and lose the flow of the entire lesson."

> "I know lesson structures should be individualized and consistent but it would really help to have a general model to work from."

Having worked with teachers and tutors and helped them construct lesson sequences and choose suitable strategies for inclusion in each section, we use these ideas to create a generic plan for literacy intervention in this second edition, shown in Figure 13.1. In addi-

FIGURE *13.1*   Intervention Lesson Plan

Student/s _____   Date/Time _____

Revisiting Previously Read Text

Text _____

Time Allotted _____

    Revisiting for Fluency

    Revisiting for Comprehension

Word Study

Time Allotted _____

    Phonological Awareness/Decoding

    Word Meaning/Vocabulary

Introduction and Reading of New Text

Text _____

Time Allotted _____

    Developing Prior Knowledge

    Reading Format

    Comprehension Strategy Instruction/Discussion

Self-Selected Reading

Time Allotted _____

tion, we use the plan as a structure for reviewing and summarizing the contents of this book in the Appendix.

The basic plan presented in Figure 13.1 can be compressed into one session or stretched out over several days. For that reason it is important to carefully allot specific time frames to each section in order to complete all components of the plan. The basic structure of the plans allows a teacher to address each of the five components of reading as identified by the National Reading Panel (2000).

In the Appendix that follows this chapter, we summarize the contents of this book. Under each heading, we place appropriate intervention strategies that we have described and the chapter each appeared in. This chart becomes a convenient planning guide to use as you select instructional activities for each component of the lesson plan. The chart indicates which strategies are appropriate for ELLs, adolescent learners, and so on. However, just because a specific strategy has not been marked as recommended for a certain purpose does not mean that you should not use it. It may work very well!

 ## Summary

This chapter provided examples of different intervention structures, both pullout and in-class. Each structure was chosen based on the needs of the students as determined by teacher observation and/or informal reading inventory verification. Each structure provided a balanced approach to intervention emphasizing all components of the reading process. This chapter also offered a generic lesson plan format for you to use as you construct your own intervention sessions.

Designing or choosing a structure for intervention and selecting appropriate instructional activities requires knowledge and expertise on your part. It also requires creativity, flexibility, and, above all, a passion for helping struggling readers enter the exciting world of literacy. We know you have that passion. We share it with you and we hope that this book has provided a valuable resource tool. Good luck and enjoy!

Summary of Intervention Strategies

Intervention Strategy	Chapter	Recommended in General—Would Include Any Student	Specifically Recommended for ELLs	Specifically Recommended for Adolescent Learners	Specifically Recommended for RTI
Revisiting Previously Read Text for Fluency					
Teacher read-alouds	6	✓	✓	✓	
Assisted reading	6	✓		✓	
Echo reading	6	✓		✓	
Paired reading	6	✓	✓	✓	
Partner reading	6	✓			
Repeated reading	6	✓	✓	✓	✓
Choral reading	6	✓	✓	✓	
Reader's theater	6	✓	✓	✓	✓
Radio reading	6	✓		✓	
Fluency development lesson	6	✓			✓
Oral recitation lesson	6	✓			✓
Supported oral reading	6	✓			
Fluency-oriented reading instruction: Rereading practice	6	✓			✓
Revisiting Previously Read Text for Comprehension					
Retelling: Story maps	9	✓	✓		✓
Retelling: Expository idea maps	10	✓	✓	✓	✓
Retelling: Main idea maps	10	✓		✓	
Answering questions: QARs	11	✓	✓		✓
Answering questions: Self-questioning	11	✓			✓
Answering questions: Content-free questions	11	✓			
Answering questions: Question types	11	✓	✓		

Intervention Strategy	Chapter	Recommended in General—Would Include Any Student	Specifically Recommended for ELLs	Specifically Recommended for Adolescent Learners	Specifically Recommended for RTI
Revisiting Previously Read Text for Comprehension *(Continued)*					
Answering questions: ReQuest	11	✓	✓		
Answering questions: QtA	11	✓		✓	✓
Answering questions: Question clusters	11	✓		✓	
KWL: Focus on L.	12	✓	✓		✓
Reciprocal teaching	12	✓	✓	✓	✓
Think-alouds	12	✓	✓		✓
Discussion cards	12	✓	✓		
Scaffolded Reading Experience (SRE)	12	✓	✓		✓
Reading guides	12	✓		✓	✓
Word Study Emphasizing Phonics and Phonological Awareness					
Teaching rhyme	4	✓	✓		✓
Connecting rhyme and spelling patterns	4	✓	✓		✓
Teaching segmenting and blending	4	✓	✓		✓
Onset-rime instruction: Alliteration, sorting, counting	4	✓	✓		✓
Adding letters to sounds	4	✓	✓		✓
Word building	4	✓	✓		✓
Teaching consonants using shared reading	5	✓	✓	✓	✓
Teaching vowel sounds: Decoding by analogy	5	✓	✓	✓	✓
Teaching high-frequency words	5	✓	✓	✓	✓
Using word cards and word sorts	5	✓	✓	✓	✓
Word Study Emphasizing Word Meaning					
Teaching the learning of word meaning through context	8	✓	✓	✓	
Focusing on morphological analysis	8	✓	✓	✓	
Using words in sentences	8	✓	✓	✓	
Personalizing word learning: Word in My Life	8	✓	✓	✓	
Clustering word learning: Semantic clusters, semantic feature analysis	8	✓	✓	✓	

Intervention Strategy	Chapter	Recommended in General—Would Include Any Student	Specifically Recommended for ELLs	Specifically Recommended for Adolescent Learners	Specifically Recommended for RTI
Building words	8	✓	✓	✓	
Comparing word meanings	8	✓	✓	✓	
Developing Prior Reading to Support Reading New Text					
Semantic map	7	✓	✓	✓	
Expectation Grid	10	✓			
KWL: Focus on K and W	12	✓			
Reading Formats to Support Reading New Text					
Teacher read-alouds	6	✓	✓	✓	
Assisted reading	6	✓		✓	
Echo reading	6	✓		✓	
Paired reading	6	✓	✓	✓	
Partner reading	6	✓			
Repeated reading	6	✓	✓	✓	✓
Silent reading	6	✓			
Comprehension Strategy Instruction for Reading New Text					
Retelling: Story maps	9	✓	✓		✓
Retelling: Expository idea maps	10	✓	✓	✓	✓
Retelling: Main idea maps	10	✓	✓	✓	
Answering questions: QARs	11	✓	✓		✓
Answering questions: Self-questioning	11	✓			✓
Answering questions: Content-free questions	11	✓			
Answering questions: Question types	11	✓	✓		
Answering questions: ReQuest	11	✓	✓		
Answering questions: QtA	11	✓		✓	✓
Answering questions: Question clusters	11	✓		✓	
KWL: Focus on L.	12	✓	✓		✓
Reciprocal teaching	12	✓	✓	✓	✓
Think-alouds	12	✓	✓		✓
Discussion cards	12	✓	✓		
Scaffolded Reading Experience (SRE)	12	✓	✓		✓
Reading guides	12	✓		✓	✓